W9-DCN-634

CONSCIENCE IN AMERICA

LILLIAN SCHLISSEL received her B.A. from Brooklyn College in 1951 and her Ph.D. in American Studies from Yale University in 1957. In 1965 she edited *The World of Randolph Bourne,* and the present book grew out of that study. Mrs. Schlissel is editing *The Peripatetic Journals of Washington Irving,* a volume in the forthcoming *Complete Works of Washington Irving* being prepared under the auspices of The Modern Language Association. Her reviews have appeared in *Sociological Abstracts* and in *The American Quarterly.* Mrs. Schlissel has been Visiting Professor of English at the University of Santa Clara; she is now Assistant Professor of English at Brooklyn College of the City University of New York.

Conscience in America

A Documentary History of Conscientious
Objection in America, 1757–1967

Edited by
LILLIAN SCHLISSEL

*A Dutton
Paperback*

New York   E. P. DUTTON & CO., INC.

First published 1968 by E. P. Dutton & Co., Inc. / Copyright ©
1968 by Lillian Schlissel / All rights reserved. Printed in the
U.S.A. / No part of this book may be reproduced in any form
whatsoever without permission in writing from the publishers,
except by a reviewer who wishes to quote brief passages in connection with a review written for inclusion in a magazine, newspaper or broadcast. / Library of Congress catalog card number:
67–11369 / Published simultaneously in Canada by Clarke, Irwin
& Company Limited, Toronto and Vancouver /

SBN 0-525-47210-X

Grateful acknowledgment is made to the following for permission
to quote from copyright material:

Albert S. Bigelow: from *The Voyage of the Golden Rule.* Excerpts reprinted by permission of Doubleday & Company, Inc.
Copyright © 1959 by Albert S. Bigelow.

E. E. Cummings: "i sing of Olaf glad and big." Reprinted from
Poems 1923–1954 by E. E. Cummings by permission of Harcourt,
Brace & World, Inc., Copyright, 1931, renewed 1959, by E. E.
Cummings.

James Farmer, "I Will Keep My Soul." Reprinted from *The
Progressive,* Vol. XXV, No. 11, November, 1961, by permission
of the editor.

J. William Fulbright: from "The Higher Patriotism" and from
"The Arrogance of Power." Excerpts reprinted by permission of
the author.

Martin Luther King, Jr.: "Declaration of Independence from
the War in Vietnam." Reprinted by permission of Joan Daves.
Copyright © 1967 by Martin Luther King, Jr.

A. J. Muste: from "Of Holy Disobedience." Excerpts reprinted
from Pendle Hill Pamphlet No. 64 by permission of the director.
Copyright, 1952, by Pendle Hill.

Linus Pauling: "A Proposal: Research for Peace" and "Scien-
tists' Petition to the United Nations." Reprinted from *No More
War!* by Linus Pauling by permission of Dodd, Mead & Company,
Inc. Copyright © 1958, 1962 by Linus Pauling.

Jules Rabin: from "How We Went." Excerpts reprinted from
Liberation, Vol. VI, No. 9, November, 1961, by permission of
the author and editor.

Earle Reynolds: from *Forbidden Voyage.* Excerpts reprinted by
permission of David McKay Company, Inc. Copyright © 1961
by Earle Reynolds.

Bertrand Russell and Albert Einstein: "An Appeal for the
Abolition of War." Chapter 56 of *The Atomic Age,* ed. Morton
Grodzins and Eugene Rabinowitch. Copyright © 1963 by Basic
Books, Inc., and reprinted with their permission.

Leo Szilard: from "Are We on the Road to War?" Excerpts reprinted from *The Bulletin of the Atomic Scientists,* Vol. XVIII, April, 1962, by permission of the editor.

Leo Szilard: "A Petition to the President of the United States." Chapter 4 of *The Atomic Age,* ed. Morton Grodzins and Eugene Rabinowitch. Copyright © 1963 by Basic Books, Inc. and reprinted with their permission.

to my husband,
to my father

CONTENTS

"If all mankind minus one, were of one opinion, and only one person were of the contrary opinion, mankind would be no more justified in silencing that one person, than he, if he had the power, would be justified in silencing mankind. . . . If the opinion is right, they are deprived of the opportunity of exchanging error for truth; if wrong, they lose, what is almost as great a benefit, the clearer perception and livelier impression of truth, produced by its collision with error."

—John Stuart Mill, *On Liberty* (1859)

INTRODUCTION

This book is an attempt to follow the course of conscientious objection as it has developed in the United States from colonial times to the present. It is a record of the collision of convictions—the individual's belief that he must not violate the voice of his conscience or the word of his God, and the state's assertion that it must preserve its own viability, by force of arms when need be, and that this heavy burden is for all citizens to share.

The documents that have been selected are not treatises or essays or tracts. They are for the most part the responses of men who undertook conscientious objection in times of crisis, who listened to an inner voice when all the nation heard the drums of war. The selections contradict the idea that conscientious objection is a phenomenon of the twentieth century; they show that some Americans protested compulsion to military service in the earliest days of our national history. The nation's laws on conscientious objection change, but the pacifist's plea that he not be constrained to war against his conscience remains constant.

The conscientious objector is one who opposes war and refuses to take up arms. Conscientious objection has never been a constitutional right: if a conscientious objector is exempted from military service it is a privilege extended to him by legislative grace. And even exemption from military service does not free the conscientious objector of his responsibility to the state; it merely makes him eligible for one of the several forms of noncombatant military service or civilian service that Congress has provided to accommodate his scruples.* To be eligible for alternate service today the objector must satisfy two tests: 1) his objection to war must grow out of "religious training and belief," which Congress specifically defines as

---

* Noncombatant military service usually means service with the Medical Corps, the Quartermaster Corps, or the Engineers. Civilian service means reclamation work on government lands or it may mean work in a mental hospital.

"belief in a relation to a Supreme Being. . . ." 2) his objection must be to "war in any form."* The legislative stipulations are not intended to admit all who claim to be conscientious objectors. The law tacitly requires the objector to recognize the right of the state to conscript, for only by permitting himself to be registered, and then petitioning for exemption, can the objector gain the status he desires. An "absolutist" is a conscientious objector who refuses registration and alternate service because he finds all cooperation with the military to be a compromise of his opposition to war.** For his stringent principles, the absolutist may be prosecuted and imprisoned. The language of Congress specifically excludes the conscientious objector who does not believe in a Supreme Being. Thus, the atheist and the agnostic have no legal basis upon which to claim status as conscientious objectors. Finally, the present law specifically excludes selective objection, i.e., objection to one particular war, holding that such objection is political, not moral. Many who oppose the Vietnam War can not, under present law, claim to be conscientious objectors. In the broadest sense, the legislative policy of this country holds to the traditional view that conscientious objection is defined by religious pacifism and social quietism. Many individual objectors, however, are offering more unconventional definitions: increasingly they are secular in their beliefs and politically activist in their commitments.

The sense of inner conviction that brings some men to protest against military service brings others to protest broader social ills, like segregation and the arms race. A determined minority in the past decade has taken upon itself the rigorous course of conscientious protest in the cause of peace and civil rights. Their sit-ins, ride-ins,*** teach-ins, and prayer vigils are also forms of conscientious protest.

In the natural rhythm of our history, peace and civil rights have often proved to be related movements. The Quakers who

* The present Selective Service law was approved by Congress on June 19, 1951, as an amendment to and extension of the Selective Service Act of 1948. In 1963 the Act was extended for four years, ending July 1, 1967.

** See A. J. Muste, "Of Holy Disobedience," Document 37 in this book.

*** Sit-ins and ride-ins in the cause of civil rights are actually not new forms of protest, but were used as early as the 1870's. See Alan F. Westin, "Ride-In!" *American Heritage,* August, 1962, 130.

opposed the French and Indian War in 1756 opposed slavery as well. Similarly, the Abolition movement of the 1830's had its roots in religious revivalism and nonviolence. Even trade unionism, which sought economic rather than civil rights, was influenced in some degree by theories of nonviolence: the sit-down strike and the general strike were among the first tools of union leaders.* The American Civil Liberties Union came into being in 1916—transformed from its parent organization, the American Union Against Militarism.

It should come as no surprise today, then, that the peace and civil rights movements overlap. The men and women who protested atomic testing also joined freedom rides; the youths who volunteered for voter registration drives took part in peace vigils outside army germ warfare research centers. Interrelationships between such groups as the Committee for Nonviolent Action and the War Resisters League, the Congress of Racial Equality (CORE) and the Student Nonviolent Coordinating Committee (SNCC) remain for future historians to explore. What concerns us here is the fact of conscientious objection itself; the act of a single individual who seeks to right a social injustice; who seeks, by his own protest or nay-saying, to turn the state from war. The term conscientious objector is used here, then, in the same sense that Henry Thoreau wrote of a "majority of one," and thought of civil disobedience as a higher form of citizenship.

The first conscientious objectors in America were members of religious sects whose principles forbade them the use of arms in warfare. The Quakers arrived here in 1656; the Mennonites (including the Amish and the Hutterites) came in

---

* Staughton Lynd carries this observation down to the present, pointing out that "The nonviolent movement since World War II is in many ways the direct descendant of the labor movement of the 1930's. Many leaders, such as A. J. Muste and James Peck, were labor-union organizers during the Depression. The theme song of Negro sit-inners, 'We Shall Overcome,' was previously sung by striking Appalachian textile workers. And the sit-in technique was unquestionably influenced by the sit-down strikes of the previous generation." Introduction, *Nonviolence in America,* ed. Staughton Lynd (New York: Bobbs-Merrill Co., 1966), p. xxxvii. Lynd's Introduction contains seminal ideas for American historians.

1683; the Brethren (sometimes called Dunkards, Tunkers, Dunkers) in 1719. Smaller pacifist sects—the Shakers, Christadelphians, Rogerenes—joined them soon after. But America was no haven for pacifists. Quakers on their arrival were persecuted throughout the colonies from Massachusetts to Virginia. They were considered heretics and blasphemers, freethinkers who would be subversive of law and order. In spite of whippings and executions, the Quakers maintained the ways of their church, and they refused the injunctions to "lerne or practice" war. Quakers and Mennonites stood aside when their neighbors fought off the Indians and repaired the breastworks of their forts. Quakers did not drill or carry arms. However small the burdens of militia duty may have been in the 1700's, pacifists were scrupulous in withdrawing from military enterprise.

Their steadfastness—or stubbornness—won them grudging recognition from colonial legislatures, which generally permitted them exemption from militia duty. On occasion, as in the French and Indian War, during Indian uprisings, in the American Revolution, pacifists would be required to pay a tax or to provide substitutes, but they were rarely coerced to do either. The men of "tender conscience" may have tried the patience of their fellow citizens, but communities were generally content to let them stand aside. And Quakers, on their part, adhered strictly to a doctrine of social quietism. They were God-fearing, law-abiding men and women, hard workers, well-thought-of by their neighbors. Their views on war were known in the community and they claimed indulgence on no other point. They fulfilled all civic obligations—save one.

As long as militia service remained a local duty, the pacifist remained within the borders of his native state, often within the precincts of his home community. If some mishap befell him and he were taken for militia duty, his church elders and his family were quick to petition local officials and state legislators in his behalf. But when the Civil War burst across the lives of Americans and brought with it the first national conscription act, the conscientious objector often found himself taken to an army camp in another state where he knew no one and no one knew him, and where his past diligence as a good citizen availed him nothing. It took weeks for his letters of distress to reach his family and his minister, and by the time his news reached them, he was more than likely to have been transferred to a new camp in another state. When family or church sought to aid him, they found they had to go to Washington, where long lines of petitioners preceded them before every Senator's door, and it was an even more discouraging task to reach the President.

Meanwhile, the objector was in the hands of military officers who themselves had been conscripted and who had little or no sympathy for his scruples. On the contrary, corporals and sergeants were often hostile, and for the first time, there are records of pacifists tortured. To be hung by the thumbs, to be pierced by bayonets were not infrequently the fate of those few men who refused to carry a musket.

Just before the Civil War began, a radical document on the theme of conscientious objection was being written in Concord, Massachusetts, by Henry David Thoreau. The "Essay on Civil Disobedience" was Thoreau's declaration of ethical and political objection. Thoreau wrote that a conscientious objector, the man he called a "majority of one," might be a secular man moved by social injustice. Thoreau's conscientious objection, unlike religious pacifism, which taught that a man must *refrain* from certain actions, urged that each citizen had an *obligation to disobey* any law that sought to bring him to violate his own conscience. Thoreau's essay was so radical, so much a departure from Quaker quietism that it would take Americans a century to rediscover its meaning.

By 1917 conscientious objectors had become a diverse group. The historic peace churches of the eighteenth century had been swelled by pacifist sects from the newer waves of immigrants, such as the Molokans and the Dukhobors, who had come from Russia after 1903 to escape service in the Czar's army. The problems of dealing with objectors were complicated by the Jehovah's Witnesses, who claimed exemption not as conscientious objectors but as ministers; by the "absolutists," who refused to register; by political objectors such as the Socialists and the members of the I.W.W.; and by the few idealists, without church or politics, who simply did not believe in war. As in the Civil War, there was alternate service for religious objectors. But those who refused to place themselves under military jurisdiction were marched off to Leavenworth and Alcatraz. They were manacled to the bars of their cells, hosed with cold water, and thrown into solitary confinement in places called "the hole." Next to its traitors, America meted out its most stringent punishment to its "uncooperative" pacifists.

The nation's attitude after World War I underwent considerable change, and by the time World War II began, there was a genuine desire to extend to conscientious objectors a more generous accommodation. Congress, using the Civilian Conservation Corps as its model, created a series of Civilian Public Service Camps, where objectors worked under the supervision of church-appointed administrators rather than under military authority. But even this proved an imperfect solution. The objector received no pay. On the contrary, he had to be supported by his church or by his family, and his family was without a provider. Many an objector who labored earnestly was bitter at what he felt to be merely a new form of penalty placed upon him for his convictions. The nation had moved a step forward in an attempt to extend liberty of conscience to conscientious objectors in wartime; but at the same time it revealed its deep-lying suspicion that, unless penalties were applied, conscience might prove a convenient disguise for cowardice. Sincere objectors were not slow to feel the stigma that attached to their principles.

Since the end of the Korean conflict in 1953, two new forms of conscientious objection have appeared with greater prominence, each one indicating a major turning point in traditional patterns. There has been an increasing number of secular, or nonreligious objectors, and an increasing number of political, or what is now being called "selective" objectors. Nonreligious objection signals a parting of pacifism from its historic roots in religion. Selective objection is an even more radical departure, because it involves a turning away from pacifism itself, toward a qualified acceptance of violence.

The nonreligious objector bases his opposition to war upon personal and ethical principles. He thereby places himself outside the refuge of institutional religious affiliation. The courts have been sympathetic to nonreligious objectors. The Supreme Court so adroitly manipulated the language of the Selective Service Act that the mantle of "religion" can now be extended to cover the most nebulous admission of a "force for good" in the universe (see the Seeger case, Part VII in this book). But Congress still insists upon the *pro forma* acknowledgment of a "Supreme Being," almost as if it would *legislate* the image of America as a nation of believers. The issue is far from resolved. Does conscientious objection to war become less sincere when it grows out of personal or ethical principle? Can a man be a conscientious objector and an atheist? Or an agnostic? These questions will surely measure our sophistication as a nation.

The issues raised by the political or selective conscientious objector are more complex. This man does not claim to be a pacifist. The nation may engage in a just war, in which case, presumably, the selective objector would voluntarily bear arms. But he claims the right to judge the morality of any war. The case of David Mitchell (see Part VII in this book) is a clear statement of selective objection. According to Mitchell, the citizen's primary obligation is to resist the unjust orders of his state, and he cites American judges at the Nuremberg War Crimes Trials to support his argument. He asserts that the United States is violating its own international treaties and agreements and the United Nations Charter by fighting in Vietnam. The burden rests upon each individual citizen, says Mitchell, to decide for himself whether to lend his life to his country's enterprise, especially when that enterprise is war.

The idea of a *just* war is as old as Saint Augustine, but it has come today, in this democracy, to mean something different from what Augustine envisioned: it has come to mean—to Mitchell and to others who share his beliefs—the necessity for *each* man to determine for himself and by himself whether Caesar's war is just. Whether the state can tolerate the potential anarchy of such ideas is a matter each of *us*, not merely legislators alone, must answer.

The American Civil Liberties Union has recently agreed to undertake the defense of Benjamin Sherman, who is petitioning for status as a selective conscientious objector (see Part VIII in this book). The ACLU will argue, if Sherman's case comes before the courts, that objection does not cease to be conscientious and sincere when it is confined to one particular war. The President's Advisory Panel on Selective Service, on the other hand, in reconsidering the draft laws before their revision in July, 1967, specifically refused to recommend liberalizing the conditions of conscientious objection.

The departure of the newer forms of conscientious objection from traditional moorings—pacifism and religion—affords one of the most profound insights into the younger generation. Secular and selective objectors, although few in number, reflect deep changes in American society. More and more, youth is abandoning religious institutional attachments. More and more, *even as conscientious objectors*, they are abandoning pacifism for a reluctant acceptance of the occasional necessity for violence. Or perhaps it is more accurate to say they refuse to commit themselves to any absolute principle, any absolute method of meeting the contingencies and urgencies of life. They are clinging tenaciously to their *right to judge* each situation, each war. No one can claim that these few young men are typical, either of youth in America or of conscientious objectors. Yet for each nonreligious objector who risks jail because he declares himself an atheist, for each selective objector who may be imprisoned because he will not fight in Vietnam—one is free to speculate on how many share similar beliefs. It is possible that secular and selective conscientious objectors articulate some of the uneasy doubts and the half-formed thoughts of thousands of American youths, and not a few of the brushed-aside ideals of middle age.

Conscientious protest against American participation in the Vietnam War is not limited to conscientious objectors who are directly confronted with an obligation to military service. Disaffection with the government's Vietnam policy is widespread: ranking members of both major political parties, leading figures in the intellectual community, student groups across the nation have all expressed opposition to this war. Whether the criticism is in the form of congressional debate, or in letters and petitions, or in advertisements in *The New York Times*, there is no question about the unpopularity of the war, or the disagreement on the fundamental conditions of our involvement.

Student protests are the most flamboyant forms of criticism, the most easily observed. On and off college campuses peace activists proclaim their horror of napalm and gas warfare, their fears of nuclear holocaust. In small bands they may march before nuclear submarine installations. Their placards bear references to the Nuremberg decisions. Why, they ask, when the United States judges condemned German and Japanese officers for obeying immoral military commands, shall we be compelled to what seem to us similar immoralities? Their analogies are glib and their protests are emotional, but their questions are not altogether easily answered. With banners and buttons that proclaim "Make love, not war," they insist upon reminding us that there *are* alternatives to violence.

There is no question that the Vietnam War serves as a focal point for youthful dissatisfactions and frustrations. But protests, whether discreet or unruly, reflect a crisis of faith in political leadership. They represent a complaint against a government that is felt to be unresponsive. It is just possible that American participation in the Vietnam War may have by-products we have not counted on: it is possible that this war may foster a generation disaffected from both major political parties, skeptical of its own ability to influence public policy, and disillusioned with the functioning of democratic processes.

At the moment, neither conscientious objectors nor peace activists wield inflluence or political power. Their number and their impact upon the nation as a whole is negligible. Attempts have been made to bring splinter groups into closer working relations, and to bring into the peace movement sympathetic factions from the civil rights movements.* But the chance that these groups will come together to influence policy in one of the major political parties is the most doubtful of contingencies; splinter groups are notoriously unharmonious and resistant to efforts at amalgamation.** If no coalition occurs, then the momentum behind the peace movement will most probably be dissipated. Indignation, as Eric Bentley has pointed out, has a rhythm of its own; it boils up and over and is gone.*** The peace movement of the 1960's may well be lost in the great consensus of voices that, in American history, has always supported the government in time of war.

Philosophically and psychologically, conscientious objection constitutes a special form of dissent, for the conscientious objector, more than other dissenters, is open to suspicion of

* The national director of the Spring (1967) Mobilization Committee to End the War in Vietnam, for example, is the Rev. James Bevel, on special leave from the Rev. Martin Luther King Jr.'s Southern Christian Leadership Conference.

** Even a partial listing of groups in the peace movement suggests the difficulties inherent in any attempt to weld them together: The National Committee for a Sane Nuclear Policy, the War Resisters League, the Committee for Nonviolent Action, the Catholic Peace Fellowship, the Fellowship for Reconciliation, the Teachers Committee to End the War in Vietnam, Youth Against War and Fascism. Whether these groups can effectively cooperate with an equally diverse cross section from the civil rights movement is the doubtful issue.

*** "Conscience Versus Conformity," *Playboy*, **XIV** (January, 1967), 150.

treason and disloyalty. The reasons are not hard to find. The objector sets himself apart from his neighbors when the nation is in danger; he dissents from public policy when a common threat binds all other men together. Liberty and freedom of conscience may be rallying cries when the nation is at peace, but let the country be threatened and the call is for a closing of the ranks. At such times, "the American way" comes to mean doing what other Americans are doing, and to be "un-American" is to be different.

Because he refuses to stand with his fellow citizens when crisis is upon them, the conscientious objector often finds himself outside the pale of society. The community feels him to be a coward or even worse, a turncoat. Because his defection comes in time of common danger, his neighbors tend to forget that the conscientious objector, unlike the traitor, seeks to make his life *within* the nation and that he accepts the punishment or the penalties placed upon him, hoping, by his fortitude, to win the respect of his fellow citizens. He does not seek to destroy the nation. He desires to keep his place within it and to live as he can, according to his own lights.

Social resentment of the conscientious objector does not stem from any real threat that objectors pose. For example, there have always been fewer conscientious objectors than there have been draft dodgers; yet the nation has tended to treat the draft dodger as a delinquent and a nuisance, while it has often felt that the conscientious objector is a threat to its very existence. The draft dodger wishes only to avoid the draft, not to change it. The conscientious objector, on the other hand, however docile he may be, represents the principle that the draft and the war are wrong. He is a tacit argument against human pugnacity, and he is, perhaps, resented in proportion as we have succeeded in convincing ourselves of the necessity of aggression, in proportion as we may welcome aggression as a release from personal frustrations.

There are, of course, differences in society's responses to the different forms of conscientious objection. Where the conscientious objector is a church member and a thoroughgoing pacifist, society respects his principles, which may be only a way of saying it does not fear him. He is understood to be a dreamer and an idealist. This man looks to the millennium; he is not of this world. And because he is not of this world, he may be commended and tolerated. Even when the conscientious objector has no religious affiliation, society generally will attempt to aid him. He is socially and politically a quietist, and that is the crucial issue.

But when the conscientious objector claims the privilege of *selective* objection, when he says, I, too, am willing to fight, but I will not fight this war because it is an *unjust* war, or an *unwise* war, then society closes its ranks against him.

Protest is all things to all people. It is the self-indulgence of a letter to the editor complaining of a change in parking regulations; it is the concern expressed by a telegram to a Senator about his vote on a pending bill; it is the collection of names on a petition to protest busing the children to school. For the majority of us, this is the extent of protest. We are too comfortable or too busy to be more angry or more involved. Our jobs, our family, friends, comfortable existence itself—all are hostage to conformity. The more radical forms of protest seem not an extension of our own actions, but a different sort of thing, performed by people who are the "lunatic fringe" of our predictable worlds.

It may take some effort to remember that protest—even civil disobedience—is not an odious concept. Civil disobedience may be even more difficult to accept as an adjunct of the democratic process in a constitutional system. Yet, on occasion, there may be no other way to obtain authoritative review of a questionable law except by the test of an actual case, that is, by the violation of the law and the imposition of a penalty. Further, it has become part of the grain of the American experience that the merits of conflicting interests are not likely to be represented fully *save in an actual controversy* the outcome of which will affect some freedom or vital interest. The very genius of the American democracy is just this ability to accommodate change within a context of law—a context of law that is not shattered by contest or undone by the strains of dissent.

American history has had its share of insurrections and rebellions. The Boston Tea Party in 1773, when a group of respectable merchants disguised themselves as Indians and dumped the cargoes of three British ships into Boston harbor was a flagrant act of civil disobedience; Shays' Rebellion 1786, when mobs of farmers forcibly prevented county courts from sitting in order to stop judgments for debt was civil disobedience; the Underground Railroad in the 1840's and 1850's, when good churchgoers hid runaway slaves in attics and haystacks and smuggled them onto ships, was organized civil disobedience; the suffragette marchers and pickets committed civil violations; Coxey's Army, that ragged band of unemployed men who marched on Washington in 1894 in search of jobs, was arrested for trespassing and civil disobedience. These incidents have lost some of their color, but they were full of passion in their own brief moment of "now."

As citizens, all of us are committed to dual roles; we desire to see order maintained, but we also desire progress and change. We make decisions—or we fail to make decisions—and the sum of these acts and omissions becomes fixed into what we like to call "public policy." In the imperfect context, then, of public policy, conscientious objectors and demonstrators serve to remind us that laws are made by men, and that there is sometimes no other way save by protest demonstrations and nay-saying to awaken the conscience of the majority to the demands for justice of a too easily ignored minority.

Civil disobedience and conscientious objection, at least philosophically, represent the citizen's right to judicial review. Judge Learned Hand once wrote, "Liberty lies in the hearts of men and women; when it dies there, no constitution, no law court can save it."* The Weimar Republic had a written constitution that proved to be only a vehicle for the rise of Nazism. There are Communist nations which conduct elections, and the Union of South Africa has written guarantees against arbitrary police practices. But constitutions and guarantees cannot secure justice. The law is necessary, but the temper of a people to permit dissenters to be heard, that is essential. The voice of dissent in any nation is often the measure of its social health and stamina.**

Conscientious objection to war and to discrimination remind us that there are and there must be alternatives to violence and to injustice. And in a world where violence and injustice often appear to be pervasive and ineluctable, we should suffer conscientious objectors gladly and with dignity, for in the last analysis, no one of us can be sure from whose lips the word of God will come.

* *The Spirit of Liberty: Papers and Addresses of Learned Hand,* collected by Irving Dilliard (New York: Alfred A. Knopf, 2nd ed. enl., 1953), p. 190.
** See Norman Dorson, "Civil Liberties Under a Constitutional Document," *Arts and Sciences,* New York University Bulletin, LXVI (Spring, 1966), 22.

PREFACE

Among the adventurers and debtors who arrived in America in the first years of settlement there were also the pacifists —the Quakers, Brethren (first called Tunkers, Dunkers, and Dunkards), Mennonites, Rogerenes, Schweckenfelders. These came to live in a new land in peace, but they were to find that life in the New World was not tranquil. The process of settlement was bloody. Indian wars were savage and unremitting. The Puritans were stalwart fighters who considered their wars against the Indians to be the work of "the Lord's Revenge." "At least one [Indian] captive was tortured by the Puritans, and others were sold into slavery. . . . Roger Williams . . . protested when he had to forward to Boston the hands from slain Pequots."*

The Puritan persecution of Quakers in Massachusetts between 1635 and 1660 was part of a pattern of persecutions of separatist sects whose doctrines the Puritans considered heretical. The Familists, Seekers, Generalists, Anabaptists, Antinomians, the Quakers, and their sister pacifist churches —these did not easily win liberty of conscience in the New World.

As time passed, however, some measure of accommodation was reached, and on the fundamental issue of service in the colonial militia, Quakers and other men of "tender conscience" did win recognition. Massachusetts in 1661, Rhode Island in 1673, and Pennsylvania in 1757 all relieved men of conscientious scruples from the necessity of bearing arms. Rhode Islanders, who were particularly sympathetic to dissidents, provided in 1673 that since "the inhabitants of this colony have a conscience against requiring taking an oath; how much ought such men [to] forbear to compel their equal

* Merle Curti, *Peace or War: The American Struggle 1636–1936* (New York: Canner, 1936), p. 16. See also Nathaniel Hawthorne's short story "The Gentle Boy" (in *Twice-Told Tales*), in which Quakers are stoned and executed in the "bloody town" of Boston.

Part I

neighbors against their consciences to trayne to fight and to kill."*

In 1701, William Penn made it clear that Pennsylvania would grant religious liberty to men of all persuasions. The Charter of Privileges stipulated that "No person or persons . . . who shall confess and acknowledge one Almighty God . . . and profess him or themselves obliged to live quietly under the civil government, shall be in any case molested or prejudiced in his or their person or estate because of his or their conscientious persuasion or practice."**

Yet legislation proved to be uncertain protection in days of crisis, and outbreaks of Indian war signaled the imposition of fines and punishments on those who would neither "trayne nor fight."

In New York, Friends who were penalized for "not learning war" protested to the Governor in 1672:

> Whereas it was desired of the country that all who would willingly contribute towards repairing the fort of New York would give in their names and sums, and we whose names are underwritten not being found on the list, it was since desired by the High Sheriff that we would give our reasons unto the Governor, how willing and ready we have been to pay our customs, as country rates and needful town charges, and how we have behaved ourselves peaceable and quietly amongst our neighbours and are ready to be serviceable in anything which doth not infringe upon our tender consciences, but being in a measure redeemed of wars and stripes we cannot for conscience' sake be concerned in upholding things of that nature as you yourselves well know. It hath not been our practice in old England since we were a people; and this in meekness we declare. In behalf of ourselves and our friends, love and good will unto thee and all men.***

Virginia legislators, finding that "divers refractory persons" refused to attend the militia exercises in 1666, inflicted a fine of a hundred pounds of tobacco for each offense. In

---

* Rufus M. Jones, *The Quakers in the American Colonies* (New York: Russell and Russell, 1962), p. 179.

** Isaac Sharpless, *A Quaker Experiment in Government* (Vol. I of *A History of Quaker Government in America*) (Philadelphia: T. S. Leach & Co., 1898), p. 123.

*** Jones, *op. cit.*, pp. 249–50.

1711, Quakers wrote home to England that some of their number had been "imprest to make fortifications," and were imprisoned for their refusal.

As events led the colonists toward the French and Indian War, members of the several peace sects were usually required to hire militia substitutes; and when they refused to pay for substitutes, as they generally did, their property was taken to cover the amount in question. Virginia passed militia laws in 1756 whereby every twentieth man was sent to fight under "colonel Washington." Seven Quakers were carried to the frontier, but when they would not fight, they were sent home. Washington did not forget the stubborn Quakers when he met them again some twenty years later in the Revolution.

In 1776, Quakers and other pacifist groups found themselves in difficult straits. They did not support the principle of revolution, and their countrymen bitterly accused them of being Loyalists and traitors. Moreover, Quakers sometimes let it be known that they were in sympathy with neither side. The Friends of Pennsylvania were sharp-spoken in their opinions:

> We did not approve the proceedings of the British Ministry, which irritated the Americans; we thought them ill-advised and . . . wicked; we would have joined with our fellow-citizens in peaceful legal resistance to them and have suffered . . . for the principles of liberty and justice. But we do not believe in revolutions, and we do not believe in war. . . . We are out of the whole business and will give aid and comfort to neither party.*

"A pox on both your houses," said the pernickety Quakers! —It was not to be a popular stand.

As the Revolution wore on and the difficulty of financing military campaigns strained the tempers of the colonists, protests began to mount against the leniency shown to those with conscientious scruples against fighting. The Officers of the Military Association for the City and Liberties of Philadelphia, feeling the real—and sometimes imagined—inequities of the situation, petitioned their representatives:

* Isaac Sharpless, *Quakers in the Revolution* (Vol. II of *A History of Quaker Government in America*) (Philadelphia: T. S. Leach & Co., 1899), pp. 130–31.

Fatal Mischiefs will arise from the Lenity shown towards Persons professing to be conscientiously scrupulous against bearing Arms;—that People sincerely and religiously scrupulous are but few in Comparison to those who upon this Occasion, as well as others, make Conscience Convenience; —that a very considerable Share of the Property of this Province is in the Hands of People professing to be a tender Conscience in military Matters;—that the Associators think it extremely hard that they should risk their Lives and injure their Fortunes in the Defense of those who will not be of the least Assistance in this great Struggle;—that the Memorialists therefore humbly conceive that some decisive Plan should be fallen upon to oblige every Inhabitant of the Province either with his Person or Property to contribute toward the general Cause, and that it should not be left, as it is at present, to the Inclinations of those professing tender Conscience, but that the Proportion they shall contribute, may be certainly fixed and determined.*

After deliberation, the legislature found itself in agreement with the petitioners, and thereafter the "contribution" for conscientious objectors in Philadelphia was fixed at two pounds and 10 shillings annually, and this modest sum was raised from time to time.

The Continental Congress admonished conscientious objectors on the same point:

As there are some people who from Religious Principles cannot bear Arms in any case, this Congress intends no Violence to their Consciences, but earnestly recommends it to them to CONTRIBUTE LIBERALLY, in this time of universal calamity, to the relief of their distressed Brethren in the several Colonies, and to do all other services to their oppressed country, which they can consistently with their Religious Principles.**

Nonresisters were expected to contribute goods and supplies to the troops, and since many felt they could not sell to the army, they sometimes gave produce away and sometimes had it taken. Quaker barns were the objects of foraging parties

* United States Selective Service Special Monograph No. 11, Part I: *Conscientious Objection* (Washington, D.C., 1950), p. 34.
** *Ibid.,* pp. 33–34.

of both the British and the American troops. "From John Feree four Horse creatures, thirteen cattle, seven and a half bushels of wheat, twenty of clean rye, one stack of do., forty bushels of corn, two stacks of oats, and one of hay. . . ."*

In a few cases, pacifists were taken away bodily by the Revolutionary Army as it grew more hard-pressed for men. In 1777, fourteen Friends were taken from their homes and brought to Washington's camp at Valley Forge. Muskets were tied on their backs, but they refused to betray their "testimony" or their scruples. When Washington heard of the arrival of the conscripts, he ordered them sent home.

Through the rough and tumble of the first years of settlement in America, Quakers and other pacifists won legal recognition in colonial America. Exemption from militia service was usually granted until military emergency placed the community under stress, and then pacifists were usually required to hire a substitute or contribute a sum of money toward the common enterprise. Occasionally, they were pressed in a more forceful fashion.

Indian wars and revolution meant that Quakers and men of similar belief walked a tightrope of allegiances. Subject to the sanctions of the secular government if they did not take up arms, they were subject to the sanctions of their own church and conscience if they did. As objectors to war they were always suspected by the community of cowardice and disloyalty. And they, in turn, tended to demand their "rights" precisely at the time when society was most aroused. The pacifist asked for tender treatment when the nation was sore with conflict.

The documents in this section, quaint in their language and apparent distance from our own day, nevertheless raise issues that are as current as our daily newspapers. Document 1 is a reasoned defense of the citizen's refusal to pay taxes for the waging of war; Documents 2 and 5 explain the conscientious objector's reasons for refusing to bear arms; Document 3 challenges the government's right to require that a citizen swear an oath of loyalty before he be permitted to practice his profession (cf. the Supreme Court decision, 1945, *in re* Summers, Part VIII in this book); Document 4 shows James Madison including the right of conscientious objection when he proposed to the Congress that it adopt a Bill of

* Sharpless, *Quakers in the Revolution,* p. 178.

Rights; Document 5 explains the pacifists' refusal to pay
either fine or fee for the privilege of exemption from military service. For all their odd spelling and outdated speech,
these documents provide an introduction to contemporary constitutional law.

1. John Woolman, from *The Journal*: "Considerations on the Payment of a Tax laid for Carrying on the War against the Indians; The Drafting of the Militia in New Jersey, 1757, 1758."*

John Woolman (1720–1772) was a Quaker tailor and itinerant minister. As early as 1754 he wrote of slavery that it was a "dark gloominess hanging over the land." He preached against slavery in the North and in the South, and was instrumental in bringing Quaker communities to renounce the institution of slavery and to free any slaves they held. A pacifist, he saw the root of war in property and self-aggrandizement. By refusing to pay taxes that were to be used for carrying on the French and Indian War, Woolman initiated this form of protest against government policy.

A few years past, money being made current in our province for carrying on wars, and to be called in again by taxes laid on the inhabitants, my mind was often affected with the thoughts of paying such taxes; and I believe it right for me to preserve a memorandum concerning it. I was told that Friends in England frequently paid taxes, when the money was applied to such purposes. I had conversation with several noted Friends on the subject, who all favored the payment of such taxes; some of them I preferred before myself, and this made me easier for a time; yet there was in the depth of my mind a scruple which I never could get over; and at certain times I was greatly distressed on that account.

I believed that there were some upright-hearted men who paid such taxes, yet could not see that their example was a sufficient reason for me to do so, while I believe that the spirit of truth required of me, as an individual, to suffer patiently the distress of goods, rather than pay actively.

To refuse the active payment of a tax which our Society generally paid was exceedingly disagreeable; but to do a thing contrary to my conscience appeared yet more dreadful. When this exercise came upon me, I knew of none under

* *The Journal of John Woolman and a Plea for the Poor*, Introd. by F. B. Tolles (New York; Corinth Books, 1961), pp. 74–83.

the like difficulty; and in my distress I besought the Lord to enable me to give up all, that so I might follow him wheresoever he was pleased to lead me. Under this exercise I went to our Yearly Meeting at Philadelphia in the year 1755; at which a committee was appointed of some from each Quarterly Meeting, to correspond with the meeting for sufferings in London; and another to visit our Monthly and Quarterly Meetings. After their appointment, before the last adjournment of the meeting, it was agreed that these two committees should meet together in Friends' school-house in the city, to consider some things in which the cause of truth was concerned. They accordingly had a weighty conference in the fear of the Lord; at which time I perceived there were many Friends under a scruple like that before mentioned.

As scrupling to pay a tax on account of the application hath seldom been heard of heretofore, even amongst men of integrity, who have steadily borne their testimony against outward wars in their time, I may therefore note some things which have occurred to my mind, as I have been inwardly exercised on that account. From the steady opposition which faithful Friends in early times made to wrong things then approved, they were hated and persecuted by men living in the spirit of this world, and, suffering with firmness, they were made a blessing to the church, and the work prospered. It equally concerns men in every age to take heed to their own spirits; and in comparing their situation with ours, to me it appears that there was less danger of their being infected with the spirit of this world, in paying such taxes, than is the case with us now. They had little or no share in civil government, and many of them declared that they were, through the power of God, separated from the spirit in which wars were, and being afflicted by the rulers on account of their testimony, there was less likelihood of their uniting in spirit with them in things inconsistent with the purity of truth. We, from the first settlement of this land, have known little or no troubles of that sort. The profession of our predecessors was for a time accounted reproachful, but at length their uprightness being understood by the rulers, and their innocent sufferings moving them, our way of worship was tolerated, and many of our members in these colonies became active in civil government. Being thus tried with favor and prosperity, this world appeared inviting; our minds have been turned to the improvement of our country, to merchandise and the sciences, amongst which are many things useful, if followed in pure wisdom; but in our present condition I believe it will not be denied that a carnal mind is gaining upon us. Some of our members, who are officers in civil government, are, in one case or other, called upon in their respective stations to assist in things relative to the wars; but being in doubt whether to act or to crave to be excused from their office, if they see their brethren united in the payment of a tax to carry on the said wars, may think their case not much different, and so might quench the tender movings of the Holy Spirit in their minds. Thus, by small degrees, we might approach so near to fighting that the distinction would be little else than the name of a peaceable people.

It requires great self-denial and resignation of ourselves to God, to attain that state wherein we can freely cease from fighting. . . .

The calamities of war were now increasing; the frontier inhabitants of Pennsylvania were frequently surprised; some were slain, and many taken captive by the Indians; while these committees sat, the corpse of one so slain was brought in a wagon, and taken through the streets of the city in his bloody garments, to alarm the people and arouse them to war.

Friends thus met were not all of one mind in relation to the tax, which, to those who scrupled it, made the way more difficult. To refuse an active payment at such a time might be construed into an act of disloyalty, and appeared likely to displease the rulers, not only here but in England; still there was a scruple so fixed on the minds of many Friends that nothing moved it. It was a conference the most weighty that ever I was at, and the hearts of many were bowed in reverence before the Most High. Some Friends of the said committees who appeared easy to pay the tax, after several adjournments, withdrew; others of them continued till the last. At length an epistle of tender love and caution to Friends in Pennsylvania was drawn up, and being read several times and corrected, was signed by such as were free to sign it, and afterward sent to the Monthly and Quarterly Meetings.

Ninth of eighth month, 1757.—Orders came at night to the military officers in our county (Burlington), directing them to draft the militia, and prepare a number of men to go off as soldiers, to the relief of the English at Fort William Henry, in New York government; a few days after which, there was a general review of the militia at Mount Holly, and a number of men were chosen and sent off under some officers. Shortly after, there came orders to draft three times as many, who were to hold themselves in readiness to march when fresh orders came. On the 17th there was a meeting of the military officers at Mount Holly, who agreed on draft; orders were sent to the men so chosen to meet their respective captains at set times and places, those in our township to meet at Mount Holly, amongst whom were a considerable number of our Society. My mind being affected herewith, I had fresh opportunity to see and consider the advantage of living in the real substance of religion, where practice doth harmonize with principle. Amongst the officers are men of understanding, who have some regard to sincerity where they see it; and when such in the execution of their office have men to deal with whom they believe to be upright-hearted, it is a painful task to put them to trouble on account of scruples of conscience, and they will be likely to avoid it as much as easily may be. But where men profess to be so meek and heavenly-minded, and to have their trust so firmly settled in God that they cannot join in wars, and yet by their spirit and conduct in common life manifest a contrary disposition, their difficulties are great at such a time.

When officers who are anxiously endeavoring to get troops to answer the demands of their superiors see men who are insincere pretend scruple of conscience in hopes of being excused from a dangerous employment, it is likely they will be roughly handled. In this time of commotion some of our young men left these parts and tarried abroad till it was over; some came, and proposed to go as soldiers; others appeared to have a real tender scruple in their minds against joining in wars, and were much humbled under the apprehension of a trial so near. I had conversation with several of them to my satisfaction. When the captain came to town, some of the last-mentioned went and told him in substance as follows: That they could not bear arms for conscience' sake; nor could they hire any to go in their places, being resigned as to the event. At length the captain acquainted them all that they might return home for the present, but he required them to provide themselves as soldiers, and be in readiness to march when called upon. This was such a time as I had not seen before; and yet I may say, with thankfulness to the Lord, that I believed the trial was intended for our good; and I was favored with resignation to him. The French army having taken the fort they were besieging, destroyed it and went away; the company of men who were first drafted, after some days' march, had orders to return home, and those on the second draft were no more called upon on that occasion.

Fourth of fourth month, 1758.—Orders came to some officers in Mount Holly to prepare quarters for a short time for about one hundred soldiers. An officer and two other men, all inhabitants of our town, came to my house. The officer told me that he came to desire me to provide lodging and entertainment for two soldiers, and that six shillings a week per man would be allowed as pay for it. The case being new and unexpected I made no answer suddenly, but sat a time silent, my mind being inward. I was fully convinced that the proceedings in wars are inconsistent with the purity of the Christian religion; and to be hired to entertain men, who were then under pay as soldiers, was a difficulty with me. I expected they had legal authority for what they did; and after a short time I said to the officer, if the men are sent here for entertainment I believe I shall not refuse to admit them into my house, but the nature of the case is such that I expect I cannot keep them on hire; one of the men intimated that he thought I might do it consistently with my religious principles. To which I made no reply, believing silence at that time best for me. Though they spake of two, there came only one, who tarried at my house about two weeks, and behaved himself civilly. When the officer came to pay me, I told him I could not take pay, having admitted him into my house in a passive obedience to authority. I was on horseback when he spake to me, and as I turned from him, he said he was obliged to me; to which I said nothing; but, thinking on the expression, I grew uneasy; and afterwards, being near where he lived, I went and told him on what grounds I refused taking pay for keeping the soldier.

2. "A Candid Declaration of Some So-called Schwenkfelders Concerning Present Militia Affairs, May 1, 1777."*

The Schwenkfelders were followers of Casper Schwenkfeld, sixteenth-century German reformer. In 1734 they migrated in a group from Saxony to Pennsylvania. One of their leaders, Christopher Schultz, wrote that:

> In the year 1755 Indians made frequent attacks, people were killed and houses were laid desolate. It became necessary to place a heavy guard along the exposed frontier, and residents were at times called upon to come to the rescue in resisting the enemy. Our people willingly helped to bear their respective shares of the burdens that fell to the various townships without personally taking up arms against the enemy, a substitute being placed by them as their term of service came.**

The Society continued its conscientious objection to military service and, during the American Revolution, issued the following declarations:

We who are known by the name Schwenkfelders hereby confess and declare that for conscience' sake it is impossible for us to take up arms and kill our fellowmen; we also believe that so far as knowledge of us goes this fact is well known concerning us.

We have hitherto been allowed by our lawmakers to enjoy this liberty of conscience.

We have felt assured of the same freedom of conscience for the future by virtue of the public resolution of Congress and our Assembly.

We will with our fellow citizens gladly and willingly bear

* See H. W. Kriebel, *The Schwenkfelders in Pennsylvania, a Historical Sketch*, Pennsylvania-German Society Publications, Vol. XIII, Part XII (Lancaster, Pa., 1904), pp. 152–53. Also E. N. Wright, *Conscientious Objectors in the Civil War* (Cranbury, N.J.: A. S. Barnes & Co., 1961), pp. 29–31.

** Kriebel, *op. cit.*, p. 141; see also Wright, *op. cit.*, p. 29.

our due share of the common civil taxes and burdens excepting the bearing of arms and weapons.

We can not in consequence of this take part in the existing militia arrangements, though we would not withdraw ourselves from any other demands of the government.

Whereas, at present through contempt of the manifested divine goodness and through other sins, heavy burdens, extensive disturbances by war and divers military regulations are brought forth and continued,

Whereas, we on the first of this month made a candid declaration concerning present military arrangements to the effect that we can not on account of conscience take part in said military affairs and

Whereas, it seems indeed probable that military service will be exacted from many of our people and that on refusal to render such service heavy fines will be imposed;

Therefore, the undersigned who adhere to the apostolic doctrines of the sainted Casper Schwenkfeld and who seek to maintain the same by public services and by instruction of the young have mutually agreed, and herewith united themselves to this end that they will mutually with each other bear such fines as may be imposed on account of refusal for conscience' sake to render military service in case deadly weapons are carried and used. Those on whom such burdens may fall will render a strict account to the managers of the Charity Fund in order that steps may be taken to a proper adjustment.

3. Quaker Memorial (against oath taking) to the General Assembly of Pennsylvania, 1779.*

As the American Revolution went on, the communities often demanded oaths of loyalty from groups they suspected of not being in sympathy with the cause of the Revolution. The legislature of Pennsylvania, for example, passed a law requiring that all school teachers swear an oath of allegiance under penalty of heavy fine. Quakers, whose faith forbade oath taking, had some of their schools closed and some of their teachers jailed. Under these conditions they petitioned the Assembly on November 3, 1779.

Eleventh month 3d, 1779:

To the General Assembly of Pennsylvania: The memorial and address of the religious Society called Quakers respectfully sheweth:

That divers laws have been lately enacted which are very injurious in their nature, oppressive in the manner of execution, and greatly affect us in our religious and civil liberties and privileges, particularly a law passed by the last Assembly entitled "A further supplement to the test laws of this State," in the operation whereof the present and succeeding generations are materially interested. We therefore apprehend it a duty owing to ourselves and our posterity to lay before you the grievances to which we are subjected by these laws.

Our predecessors on their early settlement in this part of America, being piously concerned for the prosperity of the colony and the real wellfare of their posterity, among other salutary institutions promoted at their own expence the establishment of schools for the instruction of their Youth in useful and necessary learning and their education in piety and virtue, the practice of which forms the most sure basis for perpetuating the enjoyment of Christian liberty and essential happiness.

* Isaac Sharpless, *A History of Quaker Government in Pennsylvania* (Philadelphia: T. Leach & Co., 1899), II, 184–87.

By the voluntary contributions by the members of our religious Society, Schools were set up in which not only their children were taught but their liberality hath been extended to poor children of other religious denominations generally, great numbers of whom have partaken thereof; and these schools have been in like manner continued and maintained for a long course of years.

Duty to Almighty God made known in the consciences of men and confirmed by the holy Scriptures is an invariable rule which should govern their judgment and actions. He is the only Lord and Sovereign of Conscience, and to him we are accountable for our conduct, as by him all men are to be finally judged. By conscience we mean the apprehension and persuasion a man has of his duty to God and the liberty of conscience we plead for is a free open profession and unmolested exercise of that duty, such a conscience as under the influence of divine grace keeps within the bounds of morality in all the affairs of human life and teacheth to live soberly righteously and godly in the world.

As a religious Society, we have ever held forth [that] the Gospel dispensation was introduced for completing the happiness of mankind by taking away the occasion of strife, contention, and bloodshed, and therefore we all conscientiously restrained from promoting or joining in wars and fightings: and when laws have been made to enforce our compliance contrary to the conviction of our consciences, we have thought it our duty patiently to suffer though we have often been grievously oppressed. Principle we hold in this respect requires us to be a peaceable people and through the various changes and revolutions which have occurred since our religious Society has existed, we have never been concerned in promoting or abetting any combinations insurrections or parties to endanger the public peace or by violence to oppose the authority of government apprehending it our duty quietly to submit and peaceably to demean ourselves under every government which Divine Providence in his unerring wisdom may permit to be placed over us; so that no government can have just occasion for entertaining fears or jealousies of disturbance or danger from us. But if any professing with us deviate from this peaceful principle into a contrary conduct and foment discords, feuds or animosities, giving just occasion of uneasiness and disquiet, we think it our duty, to declare against their proceeding.

By the same divine principle, we are restrained from complying with the injunctions and requisitions made on us of tests and declarations of fidelity to either party who are engaged in actual war lest we contradict by our conduct the profession of our faith.

It is obvious that in these days of depravity, as in former times, because of oaths the land mourns and the multiplying the use of them and such solemn engagements renders them familiar, debases the mind of the people and adds to the number of those gross evils already lamentably prevalent which have drawn down the chastisement of heaven on our guilty country.

We are not actuated by political or party motives; we are real friends to our country, who wish its prosperity and think a solicitude for the enjoyments of our equitable rights, and that invaluable priviledge, Liberty of Conscience, free from coercion, cannot be justly deemed unreasonable. Many of us and other industrious inhabitants being exposed to heavy penalties and sufferings, which are abundantly encreased by the rigour of mistaken and unreasonable men under the sanction of law, whereby many are allready reduced to great straits and threatened with total ruin, the effects of whose imprisonment must at length be very sensibly felt by the community at large through the decline of cultivation and the necessary employments.

We have been much abused and vilified by many anonymous publications and our conduct greatly perverted and misrepresented by groundless reports and the errors of individuals charged upon us as a body in order to render us odious to the people and prepossess the minds of persons in power against us; being conscious of our innocence and "submitting our cause to the Lord who judgeth righteously" we have preferred patience in bearing the reproach to public contest, not doubting that as the minds of the people became more settled and composed, our peaceable demeanour would manifest the injustice we suffered, and being persuaded that on a cool dispassionate hearing we should be able to invalidate or remove the mistaken suggestions and reports prevailing to our prejudice.

The matters we have now freely laid before you are serious and important, which we wish you to consider wisely as men and religiously as Christians manifesting yourselves friends to true liberty and enemies to persecution, by repealing the several penal laws affecting tender consciences and restoring to us our equitable rights that the means of education and instruction of our youth which we conceive to be our reasonable and religious duty, may not be obstructed and that the oppressed may be relieved. In your consideration whereof, we sincerely desire that you may seek for and be directed by that supreme "wisdom which is pure, peaceable, gentle and easy to be entreated, full of mercy and good fruits" and are your real friends.

Signed on behalf of a meeting of the Representatives of the said people held in Philadelphia the 4th Day of the 11 mo 1779.

JOHN DRINKER, Clerk.

4. James Madison, Proposals to the Congress for a Bill of Rights, 1789.*

When the Federalists were pressing hard for the adoption of the Constitution, James Madison proposed a Bill of Rights to reassure those who still hesitated to support the new Federal government. Among the principles he enumerated was the permanent exemption of conscientious objectors from military service. Although a Bill of Rights was adopted, the exemption of objectors did not carry the vote of the Congress.

Mr. Madison (speaking to the House of Representatives):

It cannot be a secret to the gentlemen in this House, that, notwithstanding the ratification of this system of Government by eleven of the thirteen United States, in some cases unanimously, in others by large majorities;** yet still there is a great number of our constituents who are dissatisfied with it; among whom are many respectable for their talents and patriotism, and respectable for the jealousy they have for their liberty, which, though mistaken in its object, is laudable in its motive. There is a great body of the people falling under this description, who at present feel much inclined to join their support to the cause of Federalism, if they were satisfied on this one point. We ought not to disregard their inclination, but, on principles of amity and moderation, conform to their wishes, and expressly declare the great rights of mankind secured under this Constitution. The acquiescence which our fellow-citizens show under the Government, calls upon us for a like return of moderation. But perhaps there is a stronger

* *Annals of Congress: The Debates and Proceedings in the Congress of the United States,* Vol. I, First Congress, First Session, June, 1789 (Washington, D.C.: Gales and Seaton, 1834), pp. 431–42.

** Madison did not mention the states in which the margins had been dangerously slim, as in Massachusetts, where ratification had been won by nineteen votes, or in Virginia, where the margin was ten votes, and New York, where there had been only a three-vote majority. (Editor's note)

motive than this for our going into a consideration of the subject. It is to provide those securities for liberty which are required by a part of the community; I allude in a particular manner to those two States [North Carolina and Rhode Island] that have not thought fit to throw themselves into the bosom of the Confederacy. It is a desirable thing, on our part as well as theirs, that a reunion should take place as soon as possible. I have no doubt, if we proceed to take those steps which would be prudent and requisite at this juncture, that in a short time we should see that disposition prevailing in those States which have not come in, that we have seen prevailing in those States which have embraced the Constitution.

. . . There have been objections of various kinds made against the Constitution. Some were levelled against its structure because the President was without a council; because the Senate, which is a legislative body, had judicial powers in trials on impeachments; and because the powers of that body were compounded in other respects, in a manner that did not correspond with a particular theory; because it grants more power than is supposed to be necessary for every good purpose, and controls the ordinary powers of the State Governments. I know some respectable characters who opposed this Government on these grounds; but I believe that the great mass of the people who opposed it, disliked it because it did not contain effectual provisions against the encroachments on particular rights, and those safeguards which they have been long accustomed to have interposed between them and the magistrate who exercises the sovereign power; nor ought we to consider them safe, while a great number of our fellow-citizens think these securities necessary.

It is a fortunate thing that the objection to the Government has been made on the ground I stated; because it will be practicable, on that ground, to obviate the objection, so far as to satisfy the public mind that their liberties will be perpetual, and this without endangering any part of the Constitution, which is considered as essential to the existence of the Government by those who promoted its adoption.

The amendments which have occurred to me, proper to be recommended by Congress to the State Legislatures, are these:

That there be prefixed to the Constitution a declaration, that all power is originally vested in, and consequently derived from, the people.

The Government is instituted and ought to be exercised for the benefit of the people; which consists in the enjoyment of life and liberty, with the right of acquiring and using property, and generally of pursuing and obtaining happiness and safety.

That the people have an indubitable, unalienable, and indefeasible right to reform or change their Government, whenever it be found adverse or inadequate to the purposes of its institution. . . .

That in article 1st, section 9, between clauses 3 and 4, be inserted these clauses, to wit: The civil rights of none shall be abridged on account of religious belief or worship, nor shall any national religion be established, nor shall the full and equal rights of conscience be in any manner, or on any pretext, infringed. . . .

The people shall not be restrained from peaceably assembling and consulting for their common good; nor from applying to the Legislature by petitions, or remonstrances, for redress of their grievances.

The right of the people to keep and bear arms shall not be infringed; a well armed and well regulated militia being the best security of a free country: *but no person religiously scrupulous of bearing arms shall be compelled to render military service in person.* [Editor's italics]

No soldier shall in time of peace be quartered in any house without the consent of the owner; nor at any time, but in a manner warranted by law.

No person shall be subject, except in cases of impeachment, to more than one punishment or one trial for the same offence; nor shall be compelled to be a witness against himself; nor be deprived of life, liberty, or property, without due process of law; nor be obliged to relinquish his property, where it may be necessary for public use, without a just compensation.

Excessive bail shall not be required, nor excessive fines imposed, nor cruel and unusual punishments inflicted.

The rights of the people to be secured in their persons, their houses, their papers, and their other property, from all unreasonable searches and seizures, shall not be violated by warrants issued without probable cause, supported by oath or affirmation, or not particularly describing the places to be searched, or the persons or things to be seized.

In all criminal prosecutions, the accused shall enjoy the

right to a speedy and public trial, to be informed of the cause and nature of the accusation, to be confronted with his accusers, and the witnesses against him; to have a compulsory process for obtaining witnesses in his favor; and to have the assistance of counsel for his defense. . . .

No state shall violate the equal rights of conscience, or the freedom of the press, or the trial by jury in criminal cases. . . .

The powers not delegated by this Constitution, nor prohibited by it to the States, are reserved to the States respectively. . . .

These are the points on which I wish to see a revision of the Constitution take place. How far they will accord with the sense of this body, I cannot take upon me absolutely to determine; but I believe every gentleman will readily admit that nothing is in contemplation, so far as I have mentioned, that can endanger the beauty of the Government in any one important feature, even in the eyes of its most sanguine admirers. I have proposed nothing that does not appear to me as proper in itself, or eligible as patronized by a respectable number of our fellow-citizens; and if we can make the Constitution better in the opinion of those who are opposed to it, without weakening its frame, or abridging its usefulness in the judgment of those who are attached to it, we act the part of wise and liberal men to make such alterations as shall produce that effect.

5. A Letter from One of the Society of Friends relative to the Conscientious Scrupulousness of its Members to Bear Arms, 1795.*

On the occasion of the presentation of a new militia bill in the Pennsylvania legislature (1795), a Quaker spokesman set forth the following explanation and defense of the Quaker refusal to serve in the militia and to pay fines.

Esteemed Friend

The desire thou intimatedst to me, to see something written by one of the society of friends, in favor of the exemption from military service, which we, from religious motives, feel it our duty to adhere to, and upon principles of natural right, to expect will not be denied us, in the United States of America; and the satisfaction I derive from conferring with thee on subjects of serious import, prompt me to address thee at this time.

To do justice to the subject, is what I do not pretend; nor shall I enter into a consideration of the soundness or fallacy of the reasons, which dictate to us, the observance of this conduct—Theological controversy, or an attempt to confute the religious tenets of any sect, is, in my opinion, improper. Let every one have free access to every source of human information in religious concerns, of which mankind is possessed; and practice without control, those precepts, which he believes it is his duty to observe. If this be conceded, it necessarily follows, that it would be equally improper for me, to insist upon the orthodoxy of a practice, which thy sense of religious obligation does not enjoin thee to, in order to convince thee of the expedience of leaving me to the exercise of it.

It is not, therefore, upon the ground of our scrupulousness, in this respect, being well founded, that we require to be exempted, (though it be the real one for our refusing

* From the Special Collections, Columbia University Libraries.

49

to do military service) but, upon the ground of unrestrained FREEDOM OF OPINIONS, which is the BIRTH-RIGHT— the CONSTITUTIONAL RIGHT of EVERY CITIZEN OF THESE STATES, whether in religious or other concerns: to enjoy which, was the leading object of the grant for the territory of Pennsylvania being obtained from Charles the Second, by William Penn, under whose auspices, our ancestors migrated thither, and first began to feel the blessings which their inoffensiveness, and moral and religious habits were suited to afford them, under the benign influence of religious liberty—blessings, in the enjoyment of which we were (though a British colony) up to the late revolution in America. —And will the citizens of this new born nation, place us in a worse situation than we were before, and debar us from continuing to enjoy them? Would it be consistent with the spirit which actuated them to undertake, and in accomplishing that revolution? Every one who has learnt the political creed of 1774, knows that it would not. —The constitution of the union, which is intended to secure to the citizens, as well quakers, as others, those blessings, which they acquired by the revolution, declares that it is not: "Congress shall make no law respecting an establishment of religion, or PROHIBITING THE FREE EXERCISE THEREOF."

I am aware, that it has been tauntingly observed by some, that it is from the impulse of fear and cowardice, and not from a sense of religious duty, that we desert the scenes of human bloodshed, and renounce the laurels which adorn the hero. This observation, however, I am persuaded, obtains belief with few, if any, who have had an opportunity of associating with many of the society of friends; and those who have never had such an opportunity, are incompetent judges of the truth of the observation: —The ardor of youth, ambition, and other powerful springs, which exist in the human breast, it may be reasonably supposed, are common to the members of our, as well as to those of every other, society; but it is the early and assiduous care, which is bestowed upon the formation of our minds, and the direction of our ideas, which first initiates us into the habit of restraining our ambition, and other passions; and finally deters us from engaging in the field of battle: and permit me to add, that true bravery as assuredly exists, where fortitude and humanity reside, as that, the man who can restrain the force of his passions, is possessed of no small share of those qualities. . . .

The scruples of friends are several, and it may serve to evince the materiality in which we hold an observance of them, to enquire whether we relaxed or grew less tenacious in adhering to them, either from the sufferings to which they subjected us, or from the progressive elapse of time.

One of them respects the conforming to the taking an oath. Friends hold the truth obligatory on them always, and that the true intention of a corporal or external ceremony, preparatory to speaking it on occasions of moment, is to make the person, by solemnly undertaking to adhere to it, in any particular, liable to incur the legal penalties, which await a violation of it, in that particular: but we refuse to impart solemnity to a ceremony of that kind, as frequently practiced, by making an appeal to, and use of the name of the Deity: from a conviction, that to do so, is profane. . . .

It is to be hoped, and reasonably to be expected, that we shall not be compelled to suffer so much in America, before we attain to the enjoyment of the same share of discretion in carrying arms, as we suffered in England on account of our scrupulousness to swear, and to contribute to the maintenance of the ministers of other religious societies; that arbitrary acts of congress will not be passed in imitation of the statute of Charles II, to take away the freedom of the mind in religious concerns, whilst the liberty of political opinions, which are more apt to affect the harmony of social compacts, be preserved inviolate and unlimited.

That the infliction of fines, or other punishments, would be as ineffectual in reconciling quakers in America, to carry arms, as they proved in prevailing upon them in England to make oath, there is no reason to doubt.

It is therefore, with much uneasiness, that I learn from the 17th clause of the militia bill, which is postponed until the next session of congress, that such citizens as are conscientiously scrupulous of bearing arms, are to be exempted from doing so, upon paying a fine—to pay a fine, in lieu of bearing arms, would be as repugnant to the principles of friends, as the performance of the service, from which it were to exempt them; and for reasons synonymous to those, which deter them from contributing to the support and maintenance of hireling ministers—to collect these fines, therefore, the subordinate magistracy of the country must interpose their authority, which will put it in their power (and their inclination to exercise it in general cannot be denied) to impose upon and distress the unfortunate victims of their rapacity, to a degree far beyond every benefit, which the country could derive from such a source of revenue. . . . It is a maxim, that the law ought not to require impossibilities; and it is the language of reason, and religion, that a man should not be forced to wrong his own conscience: and a quaker must either do the latter, or be incapable of complying with the requisites of this clause of the bill—it would be tantamount to the taxing the opinions of one class of the citizens, in exclusion of every other. To tax a man for not doing a particular service, which his *conscience* forbids *him* to do, in order to make up for that omission, is as unreasonable, as it would be to extra-tax the members of a community, who possess one kind of property, to make their contribution equivalent to that, which the public coffers receive from those who possess another kind of property.

Why then should friends be prohibited the exemption from military service which they claim? Let us proceed to enquire into some of the reasons which are assigned against it.

One of them, and which is said to display the absurdity of the claim, is, that if such a scruple were to prevail in the breasts of a large majority of a nation, self-defence must be dispensed with, and the nation submit to the injustice and will of their invaders. . . .

Let me first take the objection, upon the largest possible scale; and suppose the principle of friends in this respect, to be observed by every nation in the world—in this point of view, the objection vanishes. The energy of the principle itself, becomes the bulwark of self-defence—no violence would be offered to the rights of each other, to require opposition; but this mode of reasoning, however just, were mankind as they ought to be, regardful of the rights of one another, is objectionable on account of the inapplicability of it, to the actual state in which mankind are—then, the question results to this: viewing the states of human societies, as they really exist, might the invasions, of the rights of nations or states, which take place, be prevented or adjusted without having recourse to arms? . . .

Experience teaches, that man can effect more by the powers of his mind, than he can by those of his body. The latter, form the first and chief dependence of man, in a state of nature, as well to support, as to protect and defend himself. But, they barely enable the savage to obtain a scanty nourishment for his body, whilst the citizen, by the former, is put into the full enjoyment, of not only the necessaries, but all the elegancies and luxuries of life. However, to protect and defend ourselves, in the enjoyment of these advantages, we seem to remain in a natural state, resorting to violence and oppression against the invader; adhering to the same system, which man, in a barbarous and rude state, is impelled to observe, for the purposes of abstract self-preservation. Little doubt exists with me, but that an alternative may always be found out, if as much ingenuity were expended for the purpose, as there usually is to excel in arts of cruelty; and which might be as superior to the use of arms, as the civilized pursuits of agriculture, commerce, and navigation, are to the robust toils of the chase, for the acquirement of the necessaries and comforts of life.

It is inconsistent with christianity to resort to arms—one crime will not justify another. The *lex talionis* is not a part of the christian religion; and the using of arms, to resist an attack, is returning violence for violence, and opposing force with force; involving ourselves in the like criminality; and making ourselves as deserving of chastisement as they are on whom we inflict it, for imitating the evil example which incurs our displeasure. . . .

That country was inhabited by, and in the possession of the aborigines, at the time that William Penn landed there. They regarded the soil as their own. They were in a savage state, disposed to be inimical to whoever attempted to settle upon their lands, and to oppose the encroachments of European emigrants. But the measures of William Penn were not those of force, not the use of arms, not the exertion of power, he sought not to entwine his temples with the trophies of conquest, or to render himself terrible—he shaded his brow with the olive, and distributed its branches among the belligerent tribes—his measures were at once adequate to the attainment of every object that he had in view, and were calculated to establish and preserve harmony with, to acquire the friendship of, and to do justice to those, who were the prior occupants of the soil. No bloodshed, no stratagem, or outrage took place, but the security of the colony, rested upon the confidence of the Indians, and was preserved by a due adherence to justice and humanity.

Contrast the progress and occurrences on this occasion,

with those of the colonization of New-Spain, and say, what benefit was there which was derived by the Spanish settlers, which was not enjoyed by the companions of William Penn? And yet, the former conquered by massacre, whilst the latter subdued the savage, by contributing to the alleviation of his necessities. The former triumphed by the arts of war, the latter, by those of peace. . . .

Another objection, which is made to the exemption of friends from military service, is the unfairness and unreasonableness of a part only of the citizens, being compellable to perform it. But, if this be a natural, a constitutional right, reserved to the citizens of that description, with which however all dispense, who come not within the already cited clause of the constitution, no unfairness, or unreasonableness exists, because it is the free and voluntary act of those, who do not claim the exemption, which imposes upon them the performance of such service: or, if this were not the case, ought not the degree in which friends contribute to the preservation of tranquillity and order, in a state, and rarity of its laws, being violated by members of the society, to entitle them to some indulgence of their conscientious scrupulousness to enter into military service?

That such an exemption would not afford an opportunity to others, who might be desirous of eluding military service; to avoid the performance of it, will appear manifest to every one, who makes enquiry into the rigid discipline of the society, in identifying those, who are entitled to membership in it, and of particularly disclaiming the pretensions of such as are not. But as thou art, though not one of the society, sufficiently informed on this point, it is unnecessary for me, to enter into a detail of the regulations and rules of the society, to display the impossibility of such an evasion becoming practicable.

I therefore dismiss the subject here, nor shall I detain thy attention longer, with assurance of personal regard, persuaded as I am, that it is unnecessary for me to express, with how much esteem and sincerity,

> I continue thy friend,
> and well-wisher,
> ——— ———,

FIFTH MONTH,
    12, 1795.

Part II

PREFACE

The close of the American Revolution brought the country respite from war, but not peace. The frontier was a kind of "military training school." Frontiersmen slept on their arms. Indian wars and border skirmishes persisted. Pacifists were bothersome irritants to troubled communities (see Document 6 in this book).

Kentuckians and Tennesseans came into political power in the congressional elections of 1810-1811. To the "war hawks" and border settlers, the booty to be won from England lay in the lands of Upper Canada. When a vote was taken in Congress in 1812, the representatives of Ohio, Kentucky, and Tennessee voted for war, while the men of the maritime states of New England, which directly suffered the impressment of seamen, voted against it. To such complex dynamics of national and international politics and policies, the destinies of pacifists, like those of other men, were committed.

The War of 1812 made the necessity of raising an adequate army acute. The British sacked Washington, and the Thirteenth Congress met in a somber mood. James Monroe, Secretary of War, pressed for a national conscription bill to supplement the state militias. Daniel Webster rose in opposition, arguing that the Constitution no more intended to give Congress the power to conscript a man than it meant to give it the power to tax him! (See Document 8 in this book.) Webster's arguments against conscription were not pacifist-inspired; they were the arguments of the middle class, which saw each man an entrepreneur, his person as sacred as his property, his time as important as his money. Webster's opposition to conscription was not so much founded on antiwar sentiment, as on middle-class interest in public credit and stable currency.

The peace churches, although they were a small enough constituency, maintained a constant opposition to all forms of military activity, and they also maintained a close discipline over their members. The minutes of Quaker meetings show clearly the predicaments in which conscientious objectors found themselves, for they were punished by the state if they did not attend militia drill, and by their church if they did!

> Isaac Lamborn was disowned for "attending a mustary [mustering] parade" and several other offenses. (Minutes of Center Monthly Meeting, Center County, Pennsylvania, 3rd month 4, 1807)
>
> . . . three of our young men have suffered imprisonment for different periods rather than submit to military requisitions. . . . Jim Peck Dukehart, having violated our testimony against war, by joining a Military Company . . . we hereby disown him, from membership with us. (Minutes of Baltimore Monthly Meeting for Western District, 3rd. month 4, 1807)
>
> . . . one Friend has had property taken from him to the value of $30.25 in a military demand amounting to $8.00; that four others had property taken from them to the amount of $40.50, for a later demand of $16.00, and one Friend was imprisoned part of a day on a similar account. (Minutes of New York [Hicksite] Monthly Meeting, 4th month 1, 1846)*

Largely because the churches maintained their "testimony" so persistently, they continued to win recognition from the new states entering the Union. The constitutions of Illinois (1818), Alabama (1819), Iowa (1846), Kentucky (1850), Indiana (1851), Kansas Territory (1855), and Texas (1859) all granted exemptions to conscientious objectors with provisions for the payment of a fee for exemption or for the hiring of substitutes. In 1838, Pennsylvania provided that "The freemen of this Commonwealth shall be armed, organized and disciplined for its defense. . . . [but] Those who conscientiously scruple to bear arms, shall not be compelled to do so, but shall pay an equivalent for personal service." The constitutional pattern that was evolving revealed a general recognition of the scruples of conscientious objectors, but it also revealed a growing belief that such recognition— or indulgence—should be paid for.

In the 1830's, peace became a popular concern with secular

* Found in Wright, *op. cit.*, p. 12.

societies. The American Peace Society and the New England Non-Resistance Society, combining a spirit of religious revival with social reform, agitated against the Mexican War (1846). The legislature of Massachusetts called the Mexican War a war of conquest, a war to strengthen the "slave power," a war against the free states, unconstitutional, insupportable by honest men, to be concluded without delay. But as the War was fought largely by volunteers from the Mississippi valley and Texas (which sent 49,000 men as compared with only 13,000 from the eastern states), it was quickly forgotten by all save a few men of conscience.

War and slavery turned Henry David Thoreau, the naturalist who spent most of his lifetime observing and recording with meticulous accuracy the cycles of plant growth, who would squat, patient and immobile for hours, to watch a woodchuck, into Thoreau the social revolutionary.

Convinced that he must not contribute toward the government's participation in the Mexican War, or to its tolerance of and acquiescence in slavery, Thoreau refused to pay his taxes. Thoreau put his case laconically: "I meet this American government, or its representative, the state government, directly, and face to face, once a year—no more—in the person of its tax-gatherer; this is the only mode in which a man situated as I am necessarily meets it; and it then says distinctly, Recognize me; and the simplest, most effectual, and . . . indispensablest mode of treating with it . . . is to deny it then."* Whereas the Quaker John Woolman refused to pay taxes out of a desire to keep Quakers *separate* from the worldly and warlike affairs of government, Thoreau, on the contrary, saw his refusal to pay taxes as the beginning of a discourse with his government. He affirmed, by his action, the efficacy of saying "No."

Out of a simple act, and a single night in a Concord jailhouse, Thoreau evolved a new morality in which a citizen, moved by ethical compulsion, acts to turn his society from its given course. Quaker pacifism had been inward and socially quietist, and the nonresistance of the peace societies had been largely hortatory, but Thoreau wrote of a conscientious objection committed to social change. Confronted with slavery and with war, a man of conscientious principle must do more than stand aside.

* Henry David Thoreau, "Essay on Civil Disobedience," in *Walden and Other Essays,* ed. Brooks Atkinson (New York: Random House, Modern Library Edition, 1950), p. 645.

Thoreau meant to affect his society, and he was willing to break its laws and go to prison. "Under a government which imprisons any unjustly, the true place for a just man is also a prison."* Conscience and revolution were inseparable principles. "Must the citizen ever for a moment, or in the least degree resign his conscience to the legislator? . . . It is not desirable to cultivate a respect for the law, so much as for the right."** After the Constitution, Thoreau's "Essay on Civil Disobedience" is the most uniquely radical document in American history.

That Thoreau's life, at the end, should have been intertwined with John Brown's is one of history's paradoxes. Thoreau, sometime recluse and solitary, saw in Brown the man who had turned transcendental principle into historic action. John Brown had gambled all—his sons, his fortunes, his life—to topple slavery. The Jacobinism implicit in Thoreau's "Essay" ("But even suppose blood should flow. Is there not a sort of blood shed when the conscience is wounded?"***) flowed forth in his impassioned defense of Brown (see Document 11 in this book):

> I shall not be forward to think him mistaken in his method who quickest succeeds to liberate the slave. I speak for the slave when I say that I prefer the philanthropy of Captain Brown to that philanthropy which neither shoots me nor liberates me. . . . I do not wish to kill nor to be killed, but I can forsee circumstances in which both these things would be by me unavoidable. . . . I think that for once the Sharps rifles and the revolvers were employed in a righteous cause.

Thoreau at the end accepted the principle of violence. Before the nightmare of four million slaves, and what he believed to be the piracy of the government's policy in the Mexican War, there seemed no other recourse. After Thoreau, conscientious objection in America would have a new course to follow. It would no longer be essentially quietist and separatist in impulse and social import. Rather, the conscientious objector might be a man of ethical principle and political awareness who steps forward of his own accord to stop the machinery of government when he feels its workings are intolerable.

* *Ibid.*, p. 646.
** *Ibid.*, pp. 636–37.
*** *Ibid.*, p. 647.

6. Alexander Rogers, "Petition to My Fellow Countrymen," 1810.*

A small sect, the Rogerenes, settled in the Connecticut towns of New London, Groton, and Ledyard. Followers of John Rogers (1648–1721), these men and women shared with Quakers a belief in nonresistance. Because they were few in number and little known, it was difficult for them to maintain their ways; yet, the following petition leaves no doubt that they were zealous in holding to their beliefs and their adherence to their testimony. The document is dated 1810, and indicates that matters of militia service and the payment of military fines troubled pacifists in times of peace as well as times of war.

Whereas I am once more called to suffer for conscience's sake, in defense of the gospel of Christ; on the account of my son, who is under age, in that it is against my conscience to send him into the train-band. For which cause, I have sustained the loss of my only cow that gave milk for my family; through the hands of William Stewart, who came and took her from me and the same day sold her at the post. Which circumstance, together with the infirmity of old age, has prevented my making my usual defence at such occasion. I have therefore thought proper and now do (for myself and in behalf of all my brethren that shall stand manfully with me in defense of the gospel of Christ) publish the following as a petition to my countrymen for my rights and privileges; and especially to those that have or shall have any hand in causing me to suffer.

Fellow Countrymen:

You esteem it a great blessing of heaven that you live in a country of light, where your rights and privileges are not

* J. R. Bolles and A. B. Williams, *The Rogerenes* (Boston: Stanhope Press, 1904), pp. 386–87.

invaded by a tyrannical Government. And for this great blessing of heaven do you not feel yourselves under obligation of obedience to heaven's laws; to do unto all men as you would that men should do unto you? Or which of you on whom our Lord hath bestowed ten thousand talents should find his fellow servant that owed him fifty pence and take him by the throat, saying, "Pay that thou owest me," and, on refusal, command his wife and children to be sold and payment to be made?

Fellow Countrymen, this case between you and me I shall now lay open before your eyes, seeing it is pending before the judgment seat of the same Lord. Our Lord and Master hath commanded us not to hate our enemies, like them of old times under the law of Moses. But hath, under the clear gospel dispensation, commanded us, saying: "I say unto you love your enemies, do good to them that hate you and pray for them that despitefully use you and persecute you, and if any man shall sue you at the law and take away your coat, forbid him not to take your cloak also." "If thine enemy hunger, feed him, if he thirst, give him drink." And again: "I say unto you that ye resist not evil."

For these, and many other like commands of our Saviour, Christ, I have refused to bear arms against any man in defense of my rights and privileges of this world. For which cause, you have now taken me by the throat, saying: "Go break the laws of your Lord and Master." And because I have refused to obey man rather than God, you have taken away the principal part of the support of my family and commanded it to be sold at the post.

And thus you, my fellow-servants (under equal obligation of obedience to the same laws of our Master) have invaded my rights and privileges and robbed me of my living, for no other reason but because I will not bear the sword to defend it. And if a servant shall be thought worthy of punishment for transgressing his master's laws, of how much punishment shall he be thought worthy that shall smite his fellow servant, because he will not partake with him in his transgression? But I wist that through ignorance you have done it, as have also your rulers; and for this cause do I hold the case before you, that you may not stand in your own light, to stretch out against me the sword of persecution; but agree with your adversary whilst you are in the way with him. But if you shall refuse to hear this my righteous cause and shall pursue your fellow servant that owes you nothing, and who wishes you no evil, neither would hurt one hair of your head, and although you take away his goods, yet he asks them not again, but commits his cause to Him that shall judge righteously; I say if you shall follow hard after him, as the Egyptians did after Israel, God shall trouble your host and take off your chariot wheels, so that you shall drive them heavily. For I know, by experience, that no device shall stand against the counsel of God; for I am not a stranger in this warfare, neither is it only the loss of goods that I have suffered heretofore; but extreme torments of body, while my life lay at stake under the threat of my persecutors, and yet God, through his mighty power, has never suffered me to flee before my enemies, but has brought me to the 83d year of my age, though all my persecutors have been dead these many years.

ALEXANDER ROGERS.

January 7th, 1810. Waterford, New London County.

7. Memorial of the Religious society of Friends to the Legislature of Virginia on the Militia Laws, 1813.*

At the Yearly Meeting of Friends in Virginia, in 1813, a memorial was prepared for presentation to the Legislature of that state concerning Quaker views—and anxieties— about possible changes in the militia laws as the War of 1812 went on.

In this enlightened age and country, and before this Legislature, your Memorialists conceive it unnecessary to urge the unalienable rights of conscience, or to adduce any arguments to shew that the relations between man and his Creator, neither can, nor ought to be prescribed or controlled by any human authority. It is unnecessary, because the proposition is self evident, and especially because it is one of the fundamental principles upon which the civil and political institutions of this country are established. . . . [The] *state itself,* by its convention which ratified the federal constitution, expressly declared, that the "liberty of conscience cannot be cancelled, abridged, restrained, or modified by any authority of the United States. . . ." They therefore respectfully petition, that the laws imposing military requisitions and penalties for non-compliance, may be considered as they respect your petitioners, and such relief afforded as to the wisdom of the legislature shall seem just and necessary.

* *Niles' Weekly Register,* XI, No. 14, 211–12. Also Wright, *op. cit.,* p. 14.

8. Daniel Webster, Speech Against the Conscription Bill, House of Representatives, December 9, 1814.*

When James Monroe, then Secretary of War, proposed to the Congress that a national military conscription bill was needed if the country were to fight off the British and win the War of 1812, Webster rose in eloquent opposition. The framers of the Constitution, he argued, no more intended to permit Congress to raise an army than they intended to give Congress the power to tax!

Mr. Chairman,

After the best reflection which I have been able to bestow on the subject of the bill before you, I am of opinion that its principles are not warranted by any provision of the constitution.

This bill . . . is an attempt to exercise the power of forcing the free men of this country into the ranks of an army, for the general purposes of war, under color of a military service. To this end it commences with a *classification*, which is no way connected with the general organization of the Militia, nor, to my apprehension, included within any of the powers which Congress possesses over them. All the authority which this Government has over the Militia, until actually called into its service, is to enact laws for their organization & discipline. This power it has exercised. It now possesses the further power of calling into its service any portion of the Militia of the States, in the particular exigencies for which the Constitution provides, & of governing them during the continuance of such service. Here its authority ceases. The classification of the whole body of the Militia, according to the provisions of this bill, is not a measure which respects either their general organization or their discipline. It is a distinct system, introduced for new purposes, & not connected with any power, which the Constitution has conferred on Congress.

* *The Letters of Daniel Webster,* ed. C. H. Van Tyne (New York: McClure, Phillips & Co., 1902), pp. 56–68.

But, Sir, there is another consideration. The services of the men to be raised under this act are not limited to those cases in which alone this Government is entitled to the aid of the militia of the States. These cases are particularly stated in the Constitution—"to repel invasion, suppress insurrection, or execute the laws." But this bill has no limitation in this respect. The usual mode of legislating on the subject is abandoned. The only section which would have confined the service of the Militia, proposed to be raised, within the United States has been stricken out; & if the President should not march them into the Provinces of England at the North, or of Spain at the South, it will not be because he is prohibited by any provision in this act.

This, then, Sir, is a bill for calling out the Militia, not according to its existing organization, but by draft from new created classes;—not merely for the purpose of "repelling invasion, suppressing insurrection, or executing the laws," but for the general objects of war—for defending ourselves, or invading others, as may be thought expedient;—not for a sudden emergency, or for a short time, but for long stated periods; for two years, if the proposition of the Senate should finally prevail; for one year, if the amendment of the House should be adopted. What is this, Sir, but raising a standing army out of the Militia by draft, & to be recruited by draft, in like manner, as often as occasion may require. . .?

The question is nothing less, than whether the most essential rights of personal liberty shall be surrendered, & despotism embraced in its worst form.

I had hoped, Sir, at an early period of the session, to find gentlemen in another temper. I trusted that the existing state of things would have impressed on the minds of those, who decide national measures, the necessity of some reform in the administration of affairs. . . . Although they had, last year, given no credit to those who predicted the failure of the campaign against Canada, yet they had seen that failure. Although they then treated as idle all doubts of the success of the loan, they had seen the failure of that loan. Although they then held in derision all fears for the public credit, & the national faith, they had yet seen the public credit destroyed, & the national faith violated & disgraced. They had seen much more than was predicted; for no man had foretold, that our means of defence would be so far exhausted in foreign invasion, as to leave the place of our own deliberations insecure, & that we should, this day, be legislating in view of the crumbling monuments of our national disgrace. No one had anticipated, that this City would have fallen before a handful of troops, & that British Generals & British Admirals would have taken their airings along the Pennsylvania Avenue, while the Government was in full flight, just awaked perhaps from one of its profound meditations on the plan of a Conscription for the conquest of Canada. . . .*

It is time for Congress to examine & decide for itself. It has taken things on trust long enough. It has followed Executive recommendation, till there remains no hope of finding safety in that path. What is there, Sir, that makes it the duty of this people now to grant new confidence to the administration, & to surrender their most important rights to its discretion? On what merits of its own does it rest this extraordinary claim? . . . That every town on the coast is not now in possession of the enemy, or in ashes, is owing to the vigilence & exertions of the States themselves, & to no protection granted to them by those on whom the whole duty of their protection rested.

Or shall we look to the acquisition of the professed objects of the war, & there find grounds for approbation & confidence. The professed objects of the war are abandoned in all due form. The contest for sailors' rights is turned into a negotiation about boundaries & military roads, & the highest hope entertained by any man of the issue, is that we may be able to get out of the war without a cession of territory.

Look, Sir, to the finances of the country. What a picture do they exhibit of the wisdom & prudence & foresight of Government. "The revenue of a State," says a profound writer, "is the state." If we are to judge of the condition of the country by the condition of its revenue, what is the result? . . . What, Sir, is our present supply, & what our provision for future resource? I forbear to speak of the present condition of the Treasury; & as to public credit. . . . I say it does not exist. This is a state of things calling for the soberest counsels, & yet it seems to meet only the wildest speculations. Nothing is talked of but Banks, & a circulating paper medium, & Exchequer Notes, & the thousand other contrivances, which ingenuity, vexed & goaded by the direst

* The British burned public buildings in Washington, D.C., in retaliation for the American sacking of Toronto, Canada. [Editor's note]

necessity, can devise, with the vain hope of giving value to mere paper. All these things are not revenue, nor do they produce it. They are the effect of a productive commerce, & a well ordered system of finance, & in their operation may be favorable to both, but are not the cause of either. In other times these facilities existed. Bank paper & Government paper circulated, because both rested on substantial capital or solid credit. Without these they will not circulate, nor is there a device more shallow or more mischievous, than to pour forth new floods of paper without credit as a remedy for the evils which paper without credit has already created. . . .

Let us examine the nature & extent of the power, which is assumed by the various military measures before us. In the present want of men & money, the Secretary of War has proposed to Congress a Military Conscription. For the conquest of Canada, the people will not enlist; & if they would, the Treasury is exhausted, & they could not be paid. Conscription is chosen as the most promising instrument, both of overcoming reluctance to the Service, & of subduing the difficulties which arise from the deficiences of the Exchequer. The administration asserts the right to fill the ranks of the regular army by compulsion. It contends that it may now take one out of every twenty-five men, & any part or the whole of the rest, whenever its occasions require. Persons thus taken by force, & put into an army, may be compelled to serve there, during the war, or for life. They may be put on any service, at home or abroad, for defence or for invasion, according to the will & pleasure of Government. This power does not grow out of any invasion of the country, or even out of a state of war. It belongs to Government at all times, in peace as well as in war, & is to be exercised under all circumstances, according to its mere discretion. This, Sir, is the amount of the principle contended for by the Secretary of War.

Is this, Sir, consistent with the character of a free Government? Is this civil liberty? Is this the real character of our Constitution? No, Sir, indeed it is not. The Constitution is libelled, foully libelled. The people of this country have not established for themselves such a fabric of despotism. They have not purchased at a vast expense of their own treasure & their own blood a Magna Charta to be slaves. Where is it written in the Constitution, in what article or section is it contained, that you may take children from the parents, &

parents from their children, & compel them to fight the battles of any war, in which the folly or the wickedness of Government may engage it? Under what concealment has this
power lain hidden, which now for the first time comes forth,
with a tremendous & baleful aspect, to trample down & destroy the dearest rights of personal liberty? Who will show
me any constitutional injunction, which makes it the duty
of the American people to surrender every thing valuable
in life, & even life itself, not when the safety of their
country & its liberties may demand the sacrifice, but whenever
the purposes of an ambitious & mischievous Government
may require it? Sir, I almost disdain to go to quotations &
references to prove that such an abominable doctrine has no
foundation in the Constitution of the country. It is enough to
know that that instrument was intended as the basis of a
free Government, & that the power contended for is incompatible with any notion of personal liberty. . . .

The Secretary of War has favored us with an argument
on the constitutionality of this power. . . . Congress having,
by the Constitution a power to raise armies, the Secretary
contends that no restraint is to be imposed on the exercise
of this power, except such as is expressly stated in the written
letter of the instrument. In other words, that Congress may
execute its powers, by any means it chooses, unless such
means are particularly prohibited. . . . But it is said, that it
might happen that an army would not be raised by voluntary
enlistment, in which case the power to raise armies would
be granted in vain, unless they might be raised by compulsion.
If this reasoning could prove any thing, it would equally show,
that whenever the legitimate powers of the Constitution should
be so badly administered as to cease to answer the great
ends intended by them, such new powers may be assumed
or usurped, as any existing administration may deem expedient. This is a result of his own reasoning, to which the
Secretary does not profess to go. But it is a true result.
For if it is to be assumed, that all powers were granted,
which might by possibility become necessary, & that Government itself is the judge of this possible necessity, then
the powers of Government are precisely what it chooses
they should be. Apply the same reasoning to any other
power granted to Congress, & test its accuracy by the
result. Congress has power to borrow money. How to exercise
this power? Is it confined to voluntary loans? There is no ex-

press limitation to that effect, &, in the language of the Secretary, it might happen, indeed, it has happened, that persons could not be found willing to lend. Money might be borrowed then in any other mode. In other words, Congress might resort to a *forced* loan. It might take the money of any man, by force, & give him in exchange Exchequer notes or Certificate of Stock. Would this be quite constitutional, Sir? It is entirely within the reasoning of the Secretary, & it is a result of his argument, outraging the rights of individuals in a far less degree, than the practical consequences which he himself draws from it. A compulsory loan is not to be compared, in point of enormity, with a compulsory military service.

If the Secretary of War has proved the right of Congress to enact a law enforcing a draft of men out of the Militia into the regular army, he will at any time be able to prove, quite as clearly, that Congress has power to create a Dictator. . . .

Sir, I invite the supporters of the measures before you to look to their actual operation. . . . It must come to the draft at last. If the Government cannot hire men voluntarily to fight its battles, neither can individuals. If the war should continue, there will be no escape & every man's fate, & every man's life will come to depend on the issue of the military draught. Who shall describe to you the horror which your orders of Conscription shall create in the once happy villages of this country? Who shall describe the distress & anguish which they will spread over those hills & valleys, where men have heretofore been accustomed to labor, & to rest in security & happiness. Anticipate the scene, Sir, when the class shall assemble to stand its draft, & to throw the dice for blood. What a group of wives & mothers, & sisters, of helpless age & helpless infancy, shall gather round the theatre of this horrible lottery, as if the stroke of death were to fall from heaven before their eyes, on a father, a brother, a son or an husband. And in a majority of cases, Sir, it will be the stroke of death. Under present prospects of the continuance of the war, not one half of them on whom your conscription shall fall, will ever return to tell the tale of their sufferings. They will perish of disease & pestilence, or they will leave their bones to whiten in fields beyond the frontier. Does the lot fall on the father of a family? His children, already orphans, shall see his face no more. When they be-

hold him for the last time, they shall see him lashed &
fettered, & dragged away from his own threshold, like a
felon & an outlaw. Does it fall on a son, the hope &
the staff of aged parents. That hope shall fail them. On that
staff they shall lean no longer. They shall not enjoy the
happiness of dying before their children. They shall totter
to their grave, bereft of their offspring, & unwept by any
who inherit their blood. Does it fall on a husband? The
eyes which watch his parting steps may swim in tears forever. She is a wife no longer. There is no relation so tender
or so sacred, that, by these accursed measures, you do not
propose to violate it. There is no happiness so perfect, that
you do not propose to destroy it. Into the paradise of domestic life you enter, not indeed by temptations & sorceries,
but by open force & violence. . . .

I would ask, Sir, whether the supporters of these measures
have well weighed the difficulties of their undertaking. Have
they considered whether it will be found easy to execute
laws, which bear such marks of despotism on their front, &
which will be so productive of every sort & degree of misery
in their execution? For one, Sir, I hesitate not to say, that
they can not be executed. No law professedly passed for the
purpose of compelling a service in the regular army, nor any
law, which under color of military draft, shall compel men
to serve in the army, not for the emergencies mentioned in
the Constitution, but for long periods, & for the general objects of war, can be carried into effect. In my opinion, it
ought not to be carried into effect. The operation of measures
thus unconstitutional & illegal ought to be prevented, by a
resort to other measures which are both constitutional & legal.
It will be the solemn duty of the State Governments to protect their own authority over their own Militia, & to interpose between their citizens & arbitrary power. These are
among the objects for which the State Governments exist;
& their highest obligations bind them to the preservation of
their own rights & the liberties of their people. . . .

In my opinion, Sir, the sentiments of the free population
of this country are greatly mistaken here. The nation is not
yet in a temper to submit to conscription. The people have
too fresh & strong a feeling of the blessings of civil liberty
to be willing thus to surrender it. You may talk to them as
much as you please, of the victory & glory to be obtained
in the Enemy's Provinces; they will hold those objects in

light estimation, if the means be a forced military service. You may sing to them the song of Canada Conquests in all its variety, but they will not be charmed out of the remembrance of their substantial interests, & true happiness. Similar pretences, they know, are the graves in which the liberties of other nations have been buried, & they will take warning.

Laws, Sir, of this nature can create nothing but opposition. If you scatter them abroad, like the fabled serpents' teeth, they will spring up into armed men. A military force cannot be raised, in this manner, but by the means of a military force. If administration has found that it can not form an army without conscription, it will find, if it venture on these experiments, that it can not enforce conscription without an army. The Government was not constituted for such purposes. Framed in the spirit of liberty, & in the love of peace, it has no powers which render it able to enforce such laws. The attempt, if we rashly make it, will fail; & having already thrown away our peace, we thereby throw away our Government.

Allusions have been made, Sir, to the state of things in New England, &, as usual, she has been charged with an intention to dissolve the Union.* The charge is unfounded. She is much too wise to entertain such purposes. She has had too much experience, & has too strong a recollection of the blessings which the Union is capable of producing under a just administration of Government. It is her greatest fear, that the course at present pursued will destroy it, by destroying every principle, every interest, every sentiment, & every feeling, which have hitherto contributed to uphold it. Those who cry out that the Union is in danger are themselves the authors of that danger. They put its existence to hazard by measures of violence, which it is not capable of enduring. They talk of dangerous designs against Government, when they are overthrowing the fabric from its foundations. They alone, Sir, are friends to the union of the States, who endeavor to maintain the principles of civil liberty in the country, & to preserve the spirit in which the Union was framed.

* New England opposition to the War of 1812 culminated in the Hartford Convention (December, 1814–January, 1815). Although there was talk of secession, no action was taken, and news of peace ended the meeting. [Editor's note]

9. Resolution of the Annual Conference of Brethren, 1815.*

The 1815 Conference of Brethren (Dunkers) was held during the excitement of the British invasion of Maryland. Brethren, who were opposed not only to war, but also to oath-taking and to the paying of fines, stood firm as the pressures of war mounted against those who held pacifist principles.

It has been discussed by us concerning the war matter, and it is agreed by all the brethren that if a brother or brother's sons who consider themselves according to the teaching of the brethren "defenceless" and prove themselves to be such and wish to obey the teaching of the Brethren—when these shall be hard oppressed with the payment of fines they shall be assisted by the brethren according to the teaching of the apostle—let one bear the burden of another, thus you will fulfill the law of Jesus Christ.

* Wright, *op. cit.*, p. 24.

10. A Memorial of the Society of People commonly called Shakers, containing a brief statement of the principles and reasons on which their objections and conscientious aversion to bearing arms, hiring substitutes, or paying an equivalent in lieu thereof, are founded, 1818.*

The problems of raising and maintaining militia were present within the several states—particularly the border states—even when the country was at peace. This document, written by the small sect called Shakers and addressed to the Legislature of New Hampshire, sets forth clearly the relations of such religious groups to their civil government. It explains their scruples against war and begs the state's indulgence against the hiring of substitutes, and the paying of fines; it declares again the Shakers' obedience to their government in all of its other demands.

To the respectable Legislature of the State of New-Hampshire.

It will be remembered, that, at the June session of the Legislature 1816, a committee was appointed to report a bill for regulating the militia, &c. also at the November session the same year, the committee made report, and the House amended it by adding a clause subjecting each and every able-bodied Quaker or Shaker between 18 and 45 years of age, to the payment of the annual sum of two dollars. On the same day this amendment was made, the bill was by the House postponed to June session 1817, and as this postponement has continued to the present session, June 1818:

Therefore, on our part, in consequence of the above, we have sufficient cause, and deem it necessary to object to the contemplated amendment of the militia bill, by pleading our claim and consciencious right of exemption from military requisitions, by our natural, inherent, and constitutional rights of conscience; and by stating reasons on which our

* From the Special Collections, Columbia University Libraries.

scruples and consciencious aversion to bearing arms, hiring substitutes, or paying equivalents in lieu thereof, are founded.

We the members of a religious Society associated upon the principles of duty to God, and peace and goodwill to man, considering the duty of conscience a matter of special concern between a man and his Maker, respectfully submit to the consideration of the Legislature of this State a few sentiments on this important subject.

In all free governments it is acknowledged as a self-evident truth, that the liberty of conscience is an unalienable right; consequently no human authority has a right to claim any jurisdiction over the conscience, either to control or interfere with its sacred requirements in any manner or under any pretence whatever.

And it is well known that compulsion in matters of conscience is entirely contrary to those liberal principles laid down by those venerable patriots of freedom who formed and established the fundamental laws of our State and nation.

According to these well known and generally acknowledged principles of liberty, we are persuaded that nothing more can be required, than a *full proof of sincerity*, to entitle any individual or society of people to the full enjoyment of any principle of conscience which in its nature can do no moral injury to others.

We therefore with a confidant reliance upon the liberal sentiments of this respectable body, do exhibit our consciencious scruples and objections to bearing arms, hiring substitutes, paying fines or rendering any equivalent whatever in lieu thereof, since all contribute to support the same cause; and plead for a continued exemption from those acts which would virtually operate against the free exercise and enjoyment of our religious rights.

The conscience is formed according to the different conceptions of the human mind, and the different degrees of light planted in the soul; and we believe it to be the indispensable duty of man strictly to obey the light of his own conscience, how much soever this light may lead him to differ from general opinion or practice.

Hence agreeable to the measure of divine light revealed to us, we do, in many important things, make a sacrifice of that which is most agreeable to our natural inclinations, for conscience' sake; therefore those who have not received that light may be justified where we cannot.

Until the appearance of Jesus Christ upon earth, we have no account that the lawfulness of war was ever called in question; but when Christ came, he taught both by precept and example, to love our enemies, to render good for evil, and to do to others as we would that others should do to us. He also commanded saying, put up again thy sword into his place, for all they that take the sword shall perish with the sword. . . .

It may be asked, cannot a man be a christian and yet bear arms in defence of his country? To which we answer. Christ has expressly said, "No man can serve two masters."

This refusal on our part to intermeddle with political affairs, is by some made an objection to our claim to the right of exemption from military services, upon the ground, that, if peace be our object, we ought to aid its cause by voting for such public officers as will be disposed to promote that object. But should we do this, we should unquestionably have no more claim to the right of exemption than any other people; since we should thereby involve ourselves in the political affairs of the world, and consequently obligate ourselves equally with them, to support the measures of government, which might tend to war as well as to peace. But it ought to be remembered, that Christ has said, "My Kingdom is not of this world." And we cannot, as we have already shown, intermeddle with the affairs of both. The candid will therefore readily acknowledge that this refusal is a clear evidence of our sincere and entire devotion to the service of God; since it must appear obvious to every one, that otherwise, we should naturally be as ambitious of honor and distinction in the political world as the rest of our fellow men. In this respect, as well as in many others, we stand entirely distinct from every other religious denomination.

It may however, be objected by some, that our exemption from military requisitions, would form a precedent for others to claim the same privilege. . . .

It is not for us, however, to decide in regard to the conscience of others; nor the justice of their compliance with military requisitions. All we claim is liberty of conscience for ourselves; and we are willing that all others should enjoy the same.

It may be said by some, that our object in claiming an exemption from military services and from paying an equivalent, proceeds from a parsimonious design of screening ourselves from public expenses. But no person who is fully acquainted with our society, can reasonably draw this conclusion; because such must know that we have given sufficient proof to the contrary. . . .

We . . . support the poor of our own denomination; and in addition to this, we pay our equal proportion of the poor rate.

As public donations for the relief of the suffering inhabitants of different places who had been distressed by fires, &c we have sent from time to time in money, provisions, &c, to the amount of more than two thousand dollars. . . .

The money expended and labor performed in making and repairing the public roads and bridges, in and near the towns to which we belong, over and above our legal taxation, will amount to nearly three thousand dollars.

Those whom we send out as missionaries, instead of taking contributions from others or being chargeable to those among whom they are sent, their expenses are defrayed by the society. In this way we have expended many thousands of dollars.

All that we gain by honest industry more than for our own support, and for the support of gospel labors, we bestow to charitable uses agreeable to our covenant.

We grant that civil government is necessary in the present state of the world, and it is to the providential work of God we owe the establishment of those benign institutions by which our civil and religious rights are protected; we have a right therefore to avail ourselves of these; and for the civil protection which they afford us, we willingly render tribute to whom tribute is due. . . .

The only benefit we claim of the government is, protection against the abuses of those lawless members of society, who violate its internal regulations. For this we pay liberally, and what more can justly be required of us? We are the friends of our country and its government, but we are also the friends of man and the principles of true christianity inculcate universal benevolence and good will to all the human family; therefore we cannot, by a partial connection with one community, assist in the destruction of another. . . .

Since therefore we have devoted ourselves and all that we possess for the sole purpose of doing good, can it be just or constitutional to require any thing of us as a penalty for refusing to violate our consciences?

We consider it unjust for us to bear the imputation of crime, which is necessarily attached to fines and imprisonments to which we must be exposed; (should the contemplated law exist,) nor can we consider a tax as an equivalent, in any other light, than as muster fines in disguise—a price to be paid for the liberty of conscience to which we have a natural and constitutional right.

The constitution of the United States declares that Congress shall make no law respecting an establishment of religion, or prohibiting the free exercise thereof. The Constitution of this State as well as the Declaration of Independence, declares the rights of conscience to be unalienable; because no equivalent can be *given* or *received* for them.

Any thing then of a coercive nature, under whatever name, practised against conscience, must be a pointed violation of these rights. Fines, taxes, or imprisonments, imposed upon conscience, can be nothing less than an abridgement of these rights; then where is liberty and the pursuit of happiness, if they must be obtained by violating the conscience? can they be anything more than an empty name?

And should we consent to pay a tax as an equivalent this would be a virtual acknowledgement that the liberty of conscience is not our natural right; but may be purchased of government at a stated price. [Editor's italics]

Such a concession involves in it, a principle derogatory to the Almighty; because it requires us to purchase of government, liberty to serve God with our persons, at the expense of sinning against him with our property. This we cannot do. Hence it is as decidedly against our consciences to procure a substitute or pay an equivalent as to render our personal services, since they equally promote the same cause.

Therefore viewing the liberty of conscience more dear to us than life itself, we feel ourselves impelled by the most sacred obligations of duty, to decline rendering our personal services, hiring substitutes, paying an equivalent, or doing any thing whatever to aid, or abet the cause of war, let the consequences be what they may.

If any should argue that our noncompliance with military requisitions, is manifesting a spirit of opposition to the government, we answer: Nothing is more foreign from our intentions. Surely such a charge would be an aspersion unwarranted by our conduct; nor can it be justly applied to us on any other ground, than it could have been to all the sufferers in the cause of conscience in all ages. Nay we sincerely respect the government, and the liberal Constitutions of this State and nation; nor have any of our society ever violated or disobeyed any law of the land; for the government hitherto, has never imposed any law upon us, which stands in competition with our duty to God; for which we owe our grateful acknowledgements; nor do we make this application for the redress of any existing grievance from the government whatever; but solely for the purpose of conveying correct information to those respectable members who may be unacquainted with our peculiar tenets of faith; and to plead for a continued exemption from those requisitions, which would materially involve those natural and sacred rights given us of God; and which we conceive to be guaranteed to us by our state and national constitutions.

As we consider the conscience to be the throne of God in man, and the only medium through which the light, mind, or will of God, can be revealed; hence should we consent, either directly or indirectly, to any cause diametrically contrary to the light or voice of God in our own consciences, we conceive that no human law or authority whatever, can palliate the crime or atone for the sin; therefore, we must decline, let the subsequent effect be what it may.

The number of individuals in our society, who, by the militia laws, are considered liable to military service, is very small in proportion to the whole society; consequently, the sum to be obtained by equivalents, must be trifling on the one side, while on the other, it must be obtained at the expence of wounding and violating the consciencious feelings of a whole society; as well as have a direct tendency to discourage acts of benevolence. But we cannot entertain such an opinion of the enlightened rulers of this State; and therefore confidently hope, that they wish to encourage the exercises of benevolent principles.

We are not ungrateful to God for the privileges and freedom we enjoy, nor do we forget the patriotic Legislature of 1808, who considered our consciencious scruples, and sacred rights in the fifth section of the militia bill; and concurred with the constitution and rights of man, that we should, and of right ought to be exempt from military duty, and from all equivalents on that account.*

* Prior to which, the state of Massachusetts had done the same; and since that time the Legislature of New York, Connecticut, and Kentucky have followed the example; and wisely considered the natural and constitutional rights of our brethren in those states; and have exonerated them from all military duty, and from rendering any equivalent whatever for the same.

Although we maintain our claim by a tenacious adherence to the natural and unalienable rights of man, sanctioned by the Constitutions of our state and nation, yet, it has been far from our intention, to advance any thing to wound, or give offence to the feelings of any; our only motive has been to carry conviction to the mind, and give circumstantial proofs of the sincerity and justice of our claim; and we hope our observations on this subject may be heard with candour.

And should any of our statements be distrusted, or our consciencious integrity called in question, we *shrink not* from investigation by any competent authority where due satisfaction may be obtained. However, while we practically support the testimony of Jesus Christ, both by precept and example, we do not expect to avoid those censorious reproaches which he promised in consequence, viz. "Blessed are ye when men shall revile you and persecute you and shall say all manner of evil against you falsely for my sake."*

Therefore to conclude in short. We gratefully acknowledge the overruling hand of Divine Providence in regard to those benign and liberal institutions which have so long secured and protected our civil and religious rights; with due respect to that civil authority which has contributed to administer and support the same.

Therefore we confidently trust, that the enlightened Legislature of this State will not hesitate to recognize a right which constitutes the very first principle of liberty; and that they will continue our exemption from those requisitions so contrary to all our views of religious liberty; to whose consideration and candour, our consciencious sentiments and observations on this subject are respectfully submitted.

Signed by order and in behalf of the Society.

FRANCIS WINKLEY,
NATHANIEL DRAPER,
ISRAEL SANBORN,
TRUWORTHY HEATH,
JOHN WHITCHER,
EZRA WIGGIN,
TIMOTHY JONES,
JOHN LYON,
JOHN BARKER.

* Matt. v. 11.

11. Henry David Thoreau, "A Plea for Captain John Brown," 1859.*

Thoreau met John Brown in 1857 and heard him talk eloquently about slavery in Kansas. Two years later the world heard the astonishing news of Brown's raid on Harper's Ferry. For three days Thoreau wrote into his Journal *his impassioned thoughts on what Brown had done. On October 30, 1859, he summoned the people of Concord to the town hall to hear what he had to say about Brown's action. He had chosen to defend a man even the abolitionists were calling mad.*

Thoreau repeated his speech on November 1 in Boston and two days later in Worcester. His cause was unpopular; few newspapers reported on it. The speech was a piece of closet drama; unheard by Thoreau's contemporaries, it can be read today by students and scholars.

I trust that you will pardon me for being here. I do not wish to force my thoughts upon you, but I feel forced myself. Little as I know of Captain Brown, I would fain do my part to correct the tone and the statements of the newspapers, and of my countrymen generally, respecting his character and actions. It costs us nothing to be just. We can at least express our sympathy with, and admiration of, him and his companions, and that is what I now propose to do.

First, as to his history. . . . Though he was tempted by the offer of some petty office in the army, when he was about eighteen, he not only declined that, but he also refused to train when warned, and was fined for it. He then resolved that he would never have anything to do with any war, unless it were a war for liberty.

When the troubles in Kansas began, he sent several of his sons thither to strengthen the party of the Free State men,

* See *Thoreau: People, Principles and Politics,* ed. Milton Meltzer (New York: Hill & Wang, Inc., 1963), pp. 170–91; also *Henry David Thoreau: Anti-Slavery and Reform Papers* (Montreal, Canada: Harvest House, 1963), pp. 42–65.

fitting them out with such weapons as he had; telling them that if the troubles should increase, and there should be need of him, he would follow, to assist them with his hand and counsel. This, as you all know, he soon after did; and it was through his agency, far more than any other's, that Kansas was made free.

I should say that he was an old-fashioned man in his respect for the Constitution, and his faith in the permanence of this Union. Slavery he deemed to be wholly opposed to these, and he was its determined foe. . . .

He was one of that class of whom we hear a great deal, but, for the most part, see nothing at all,—the Puritans. It would be in vain to kill him. He died lately in the time of Cromwell, but he reappeared here. . . .

"In his camp," as one has recently written, as I have myself heard him state, "he permitted no profanity; no man of loose morals was suffered to remain there, unless, indeed, as a prisoner of war. 'I would rather,' said he, 'have the small-pox, yellow fever, and cholera, all together in my camp, than a man without principle.' ". . .

He was a man of Spartan habits, and at sixty was scrupulous about his diet at your table, excusing himself by saying that he must eat sparingly and fare hard, as became a soldier, or one who was fitting himself for difficult enterprises, a life of exposure.

A man of rare common sense and directness of speech, as of action; a transcendentalist above all, a man of ideas and principles,—that was what distinguished him. Not yielding to a whim or transient impulse, but carrying out the purpose of a life. I noticed that he did not overstate anything, but spoke within bounds. . . .

The newspapers seem to ignore, or perhaps are really ignorant, of the fact that there are at least as many as two or three individuals to a town throughout the North who think much as the present speaker does about him and his enterprise. I do not hesitate to say that they are an important and growing party. We aspire to be something more than stupid and timid chattels, pretending to read history and our Bibles, but desecrating every house and every day we breathe in. Perhaps anxious politicians may prove that only seventeen white men and five negroes were concerned in the late enterprise; but their very anxiety to prove this might suggest to themselves that all is not told. Why do they still dodge the truth? They are so anxious because of a dim consciousness of the fact, which they do not distinctly face, that at least a million of the free inhabitants of the United States would have rejoiced if it had succeeded. They at most only criticise the tactics. Though we wear no crape, the thought of that man's position and probable fate is spoiling many a man's day here at the North for other thinking. If any one who has seen him here can pursue successfully any other train of thought, I do not know what he is made of. If there is any such who gets his usual allowance of sleep, I will warrant him to fatten easily under any circumstances which do not touch his body or purse. I put a piece of paper and a pencil under my pillow, and when I could not sleep I wrote in the dark.

On the whole, my respect for my fellow-men, except as one may outweigh a million, is not being increased these days. . . . when we heard at first that [John Brown] was dead, one of my townsmen observed that "he died as the fool dieth;" which, pardon me, for an instant suggested a likeness in him dying to my neighbor living. Others, craven-hearted, said disparagingly, that "he threw his life away," because he resisted the government. Which way have they thrown *their* lives, pray?—such as would praise a man for attacking singly an ordinary band of thieves or murderers. I hear another ask Yankee-like, "What will he gain by it?" as if he expected to fill his pockets by this enterprise. . . .

Such do not know that like the seed is the fruit, and that, in the moral world, when good seed is planted, good fruit is inevitable, and does not depend on our watering and cultivating; that when you plant, or bury, a hero in his field, a crop of heroes is sure to spring up. This is a seed of such force and vitality, that it does not ask our leave to germinate. . . .

"Served him right,"—"A dangerous man,"—"He is undoubtedly insane." So they proceed to live their sane, and wise, and altogether admirable lives. . . .

Our foes are in our midst and all about us. There is hardly a house but is divided against itself, for our foe is the all but universal woodenness of both head and heart, the want of vitality in man, which is the effect of our vice; and hence are begotten fear, superstition, bigotry, persecution, and slavery of all kinds. We are mere figure-heads upon a hulk, with livers in the place of hearts. . . .

A church that can never have done with excommunicating Christ while it exists! Away with your broad and flat churches, and your narrow and tall churches! Take a step forward, and invent a new style of out-houses. Invent a salt that will save you, and defend our nostrils. . . . The evil is not merely a stagnation of blood, but a stagnation of spirit. Many, no doubt, are well disposed, but sluggish by constitution and by habit, and they cannot conceive of a man who is actuated by higher motives than they are. Accordingly they pronounce this man insane, for they know that *they* could never act as he does, as long as they are themselves. . . .

I read all the newspapers I could get within a week after this event, and I do not remember in them a single expression of sympathy for these men. . . . Even the *Liberator* called it "a misguided, wild, and apparently insane —effort. . . ."

A man does a brave and humane deed, and at once, on all sides, we hear people and parties declaring, "I didn't do it, nor countenance *him* to do it, in any conceivable way. It can't be fairly inferred from my past career." I, for one, am not interested to hear you define your position. I don't know that I ever was or ever shall be. I think it is mere egotism, or impertinent at this time. Ye needn't take so much pains to wash your skirts of him. No intelligent man will ever be convinced that he was any creature of yours. He went and came, as he himself informs us, "under the auspices of John Brown and nobody else. . . ." "It was always conceded to him," *says one who calls him crazy*, "that he was a conscientious man, very modest in his demeanor, apparently inoffensive, until the subject of Slavery was introduced, when he would exhibit a feeling of indignation unparalleled."

The slave-ship is on her way, crowded with its dying victims; new cargoes are being added in mid-ocean; a small crew of slaveholders, countenanced by a large body of passengers, is smothering four millions under the hatches, and yet the politician asserts that the only proper way by which deliverance is to be obtained is by "the quiet diffusion of the sentiments of humanity," without any "outbreak." As if the sentiments of humanity were ever found unaccompanied by its deeds, and you could disperse them, all finished to order, the pure article, as easily as water with a watering-pot, and so lay the dust. What is that that I hear cast overboard?

The bodies of the dead that have found deliverance. That is the way we are "diffusing" humanity, and its sentiments with it. . . .

I wish I could say that Brown was the representative of the North. He was a superior man. He did not value his bodily life in comparison with ideal things. He did not recognize unjust human laws, but resisted them as he was bid. For once we are lifted out of the trivialness and dust of politics into the region of truth and manhood. No man in America has ever stood up so persistently and effectively for the dignity of human nature, knowing himself for a man, and the equal of any and all governments. In that sense he was the most American of us all. . . . When a man stands up serenely against the condemnation and vengeance of mankind, rising above them literally *by a whole body*. . . . we become criminal in comparison. Do yourselves the honor to recognize him. He needs none of your respect. . . .

Insane! A father and six sons, and one son-in-law, and several more men besides,—as many at least as twelve disciples,—all struck with insanity at once; while the same tyrant holds with a firmer gripe than ever his four millions of slaves, and a thousand sane editors, his abettors, are saving their country and their bacon! . . .

"All is quiet at Harper's Ferry," say the journals. What is the character of that calm which follows when the law and the slaveholder prevail? I regard this event as a touchstone designed to bring out, with glaring distinctness, the character of this government. We needed to be thus assisted to see it by the light of history. It needed to see itself. When a government puts forth its strength on the side of injustice, as ours to maintain slavery and kill the liberators of the slave, it reveals itself a merely brute force, or worse, a demoniacal force. It is the head of the Plug-Uglies. It is more manifest than ever that tyranny rules. . . .

The only government that I recognize—and it matters not how few are at the head of it, or how small its army—is that power that establishes justice in the land, never that which establishes injustice. What shall we think of a government to which all the truly brave and just men in the land are enemies, standing between it and those whom it oppresses? . . .

The United States have a coffle of four millions of slaves. They are determined to keep them in this condition; and

Massachusetts is one of the confederated overseers to prevent their escape. Such are not all the inhabitants of Massachusetts, but such are they who rule and are obeyed here.
It was Massachusetts, as well as Virginia, that put down his
insurrection at Harper's Ferry. She sent the marines there,
and she will have *to pay the penalty of her sin.* . . .

[S]uch is the character of our Northern States generally
[that] each has its Vigilant Committee. And, to a certain
extent, these crazy governments recognize and accept this
relation. They say, virtually, "We'll be glad to work for you
on these terms, only don't make a noise about it." And
thus the government, its salary being insured, withdraws into
the back shop, taking the Constitution with it, and bestows
most of its labor on repairing that. . . .

I hear many condemn these men because they were so
few. When were the good and the brave ever in a majority?
Would you have had him wait till that time came?—till you
and I came over to him? . . .

When I think of him, and his six sons, and his son-in-law,
not to enumerate the others, enlisted for this fight, proceeding coolly, reverently, humanely to work, for months if
not years, sleeping and waking upon it, summering and win-
tering the thought, without expecting any reward but a good
conscience, while almost all America stood ranked on the
other side,—I say again that it affects me as a sublime spec-
tacle. . . .

*It was his peculiar doctrine that a man has a perfect
right to interfere by force with the slaveholder, in order to
rescue the slave. I agree with him.* [Editor's italics] They
who are continually shocked by slavery have some right
to be shocked by the violent death of the slaveholder, but
no others. Such will be more shocked by his life than by
his death. *I shall not be forward to think him mistaken in
his method who quickest succeeds to liberate the slave. I
speak for the slave when I say that I prefer the philanthropy*
of *Captain Brown to that philanthropy which neither shoots
me nor liberates me. . . . I do not wish to kill nor to be killed,
but I can foresee circumstances in which both these things
would be by me unavoidable.* [Editor's italics] We preserve the
so-called peace of our community by deeds of petty violence
every day. Look at the policeman's billy and handcuffs! Look
at the jail! Look at the gallows! Look at the chaplain of the
regiment! We are hoping only to live safely on the outskirts

of *this* provisional army. So we defend ourselves and our hen-roosts, and maintain slavery. I know that the mass of my countrymen think that the only righteous use that can be made of Sharps rifles and revolvers is to fight duels with them, when we are insulted by other nations, or to hunt Indians, or shoot fugitive slaves with them, or the like. I think that for once the Sharps rifles and the revolvers were employed in a righteous cause. The tools were in the hands of one who could use them.

Who is it whose safety requires that Captain Brown be hung? Is it indispensable to any Northern man? . . . If you do not wish it, say so distinctly. . . . When a government takes the life of a man without the consent of his conscience, it is an audacious government, and is taking a step towards its own dissolution. Is it not possible that an individual may be right and a government wrong? Are laws to be enforced simply because they were made? or declared by any number of men to be good, if they are *not* good? Is there any necessity for a man's being a tool to perform a deed of which his better nature disapproves? . . .

I am here to plead his cause with you. I plead not for his life, but for his character,—his immortal life; and so it becomes your cause wholly, and is not his in the least. . . .

"Misguided!" "Garrulous!" "Insane!" "Vindictive!" So ye write in your easy-chairs, and thus he wounded responds from the floor of the Armory, clear as a cloudless sky, true as the voice of nature is: "No man sent me here; it was my own prompting and that of my Maker. I acknowledge no master in human form. . . .

"I pity the poor in bondage that have none to help them; that is why I am here; not to gratify any personal animosity, revenge, or vindictive spirit. It is my sympathy with the oppressed and the wronged, that are as good as you, and as precious in the sight of God.

"I wish to say, furthermore, that you had better, all you people at the South, prepare yourselves for a settlement of that question, that must come up for settlement sooner than you are prepared for it. The sooner you are prepared the better. You may dispose of me very easily. I am nearly disposed of now; *but this question is still to be settled,—this negro question, I mean; the end of that is not yet."* [Editor's italics]

Part III

PREFACE

The Civil War brought conscription for the first time to the States, both North and South. For the North, Lincoln signed the Enrollment Act on March 3, 1863, whereby "All able-bodied male citizens—between the ages of 20 and 45—constitute the national forces, and shall be liable to perform military duty in the service of the United States when called out by the President." A provost marshal, a commissioner of enrollment, and a surgeon were to make house-to-house checks to register eligible men, and they often found that they proceeded in peril of their lives. In Illinois it was reported that "One County . . . was obliged to be enrolled in the presence and by the aid of a company of cavalry, and a bitter and dangerous spirit was for a time manifested. . . . A military force had also to be sent into Fayette, Clarke . . . and some other counties, and a few men were killed and wounded on both sides before the disturbances were quelled."*

The poor saw conscription as a "rich man's act" because the law allowed for the payment of $300 in lieu of service. In New York City there were three days of rioting and the Governor declared that city in a state of insurrection. Two thousand policemen and five army regiments were needed to put down the mobs. And after the riots were over, 10,000 infantrymen and three batteries of artillery remained in the city to keep order.**

The conscription law as it was first passed in the North provided for the payment of commutation monies, but there was no provision for exemption on the grounds of religious

* Selective Service Special Monographs, No. 14 (Washington, D.C., 1951) *Enforcement of the Selective Service Law*, p. 8.

** The anti-draft riots were considered the equivalent of Confederate victory, for "Meade's army was so weakened by detachments for guard duty in Northern cities that he was unable to take the offensive against Lee after Gettysburg." S. E. Morison and H. S. Commager, *The Growth of the American Republic* (New York: Oxford University Press, 1951, 2nd ed.), Vol. I, p. 706.

scruples against war. Some pacifists were willing to pay $300; others, knowing that the money would be used to pay a substitute to go to war, refused. The Society of Friends, the largest and best organized of the peace churches, was assiduous in urging civil and military authorities to exempt members of their church not only from service, but from fines as well.

Lincoln was openly sympathetic to the plight of conscientious objectors (see Document 16 in this book), and there were men around him who shared his views. Thaddeus Stevens in the Senate and William Stanton, the Secretary of War, were often personally instrumental in mitigating the lot of pacifists (see Document 14 in this book).

In February, 1864, Congress acknowledged the scruples of conscientious objectors and provided that they could perform alternate service in hospitals or by caring for freedmen. This was the first national legislation of its kind. But even this effort did not accommodate all conscientious objectors, for some "absolutists" believed that any cooperation with the army was a betrayal of their testimony, and these refused to serve in hospitals (see Document 15 in this book). When authorities in the North found that neither alternate service nor payment for a substitute was acceptable to a *bona fide* pacifist, they "paroled" him for the duration of the war.

> The Provost-Marshal-General directs that . . . persons who establish the fact before boards of enrollment that they are conscientiously opposed to bearing arms and to paying the commutation money for the exemption from the draft, and that they belong to a religious society whose creed forbids them to serve in the Army or to pay commutation money, shall when drafted be put on parole by the provost-marshal of the district in which they were drafted, to report when called for.*

The lot of pacifists in the South was considerably more difficult than that of their northern brothers. All of the peace sects were antislavery in sentiment and in teaching; southern pacifists not only refused to fight in the common cause, but they were known to be in sympathy with the North!

The Confederacy passed its first conscription bill in April, 1862, and in it exempted long lists of occupations—newspa-

---

* Quoted in Wright, *op. cit.,* pp. 75–76.

permen, lawyers, school teachers, druggists, mail carriers, ferrymen, pilots and railroad employees, tanners, shoemakers, wagonmakers, millers, shipbuilders, saltmakers, and so on. Fraud was rampant: schools were established without pupils, newspapers without readers, and drug stores sprang up everywhere. None of the persons so exempted were required to pay commutation fees, but in October of that same year an act specifically exempting Friends, Nazarenes, Mennonites, and Dunkards provided that—whatever their occupations— they must furnish substitutes or pay a tax of $500. At that, the Confederacy was more liberal than individual states had been. Only months earlier, Virginia had ordered noncombatants of military age to pay a tax of $500 *plus* 2 percent of all their property.

Jefferson Davis tolerated religious objectors, but, unlike Abraham Lincoln, he was not sympathetic to their views (see Document 18 in this book). As the war dragged on and the need for manpower increased, the Confederacy drastically cut the number of exemptions and those based on religious grounds were entirely eliminated.

Occasionally, conscientious objectors, North and South, fell into the hands of the military—because they would not pay their commutation fees; because they would not provide substitutes; or because they had been kidnapped by desperate armies. Conditions in military camps and prisons were bleak on both sides, but beyond this, objectors were the special butt of camp brutality. The Civil War provides the first records of cruel punishment and deaths among conscientious objectors. They were put to forced marches and drills; they were starved and hung by the thumbs (see Documents 15, 19, and 20 in this book).

When higher authorities could be prevailed upon to act in their behalf, conscientious objectors were released. But where they came into contact with officers of lower rank, objectors often met with harassment and cruelty. What relation existed between the advent of conscription and these instances of sadistic treatment? Were officers of lower rank—themselves conscripted for duty—especially prone to acts of hostility against conscientious objectors who refused to be conscripted? Some day social psychologists will consider the evidence.

What was the number of conscientious objectors during the Civil War? It is necessary to extrapolate from random statistics.

In the North, it was reported to Secretary of War Stanton in November, 1864, that $121,800 had been paid by noncombatants in the preceding eight-month period, and that the sum represented payment by 406 persons.* The Society of Friends in Philadelphia reported in 1866 that more than 150 of its members had been called by the draft throughout the course of the Civil War. These figures, of course, do not include men who refused to pay the commutation fee, nor do they give any idea of how many pacifists were called from other areas than Philadelphia.

The number exempted by the Confederacy during the war appears in Confederate records as 515. But, again, that number does not include men who refused to pay for the privilege.

The total of the figures available is 1,071, with 406 of that number representing noncombatants recorded in one eight-month period. Speculation would put the total number of religious objectors in the Civil War at somewhere between 1,200 and 1,500 men—a small enough percentage of the more than two million men that the North and the South committed to battle. But that small percentage of conscientious objectors was sufficient to maintain the principle that no man be compelled by the state to do the thing his conscience forbids him.

* In the North, monies received from noncombatants were deposited in a special fund "for the benefit of sick and wounded soldiers."

12. Claim for Exemption from Militia Duty in the State of Pennsylvania, 1862.*

Treatment of conscientious objectors differed in the several states at the outbreak of the Civil War. Some states, like Pennsylvania, did make provision for the exemption of those whose religious principles forbade them to bear arms.

Under the Enrollment and Draft of Militia ordered by the President of the United States, on the Fourth Day of August, 1862.

Philadelphia, Sept. _____ 1862.

I, _____ aged _____ years, by occupation a _____ residing at No. _____ _____ Street, in the _____ Precinct of the _____ Ward of the City of Philadelphia, in the State of Pennsylvania, do claim exemption from military duty under the enrollment and draft aforesaid, by reason of my conscientious scruples against bearing arms, either in self-defense, the defense of my country, or otherwise howsoever

Signed _____

STATE OF PENNSYLVANIA, ⎫
City and County of Philadelphia. ⎰ ss.

Before me, Commissioner to superintend drafting for said City and County, personally appeared _____. The claimant above named, who being duly affirmed, did depose and say, that he conscientiously scruples to bear arms, believes it unlawful to do so, whether in self-defense or in defense of his country, or otherwise howsoever: that the scruples and belief above stated have not been formed lightly, but carefully, deliberately and conscientiously, and are now declared and professed, not for the purpose of evading the military service of his country in the present exigency, but because he

* Wright, *op. cit.,* pp. 59–60.

solemnly and religiously holds and maintains them, and in his conscience believes that it is his bounden duty to act in accordance with them on all occasions and under all circumstances.

Affirmed and subscribed before me, this, _____ day of September, 1862.

_____

Commissioner.

By reason of Conscientious Scruples against bearing Arms, of _____
_____ Ward
_____ Precinct

Philadelphia, Sept. _____ 1862.

To _____
You are hereby notified that, having been exempted from military duty because of conscientious scruples against bearing arms, in accordance with Section 2, Article VI., of the Constitution of Pennsylvania, you will be held liable to pay to the Commonwealth such sum (as "an equivalent for personal service") as the Legislature may direct, by a law enacted for that purpose.

_____

Commissioner.

I accept service of this notice on the date above stated.

_____

13. "The Quakers and the War"*

Harper's Weekly, *ordinarily belligerent in all respects on the subject of fighting the Confederacy, printed in 1862 a rather tolerant editorial on the subject of Quaker pacifism.*

The Legislature of Rhode Island lately debated a proposition not to exempt Quakers from military duty. The ground of those who wished that they should serve like other citizens was that the Quakers enjoyed all the benefits of the Government, sued in the courts, and shared a protection which rested at last upon the bayonet; and that consequently to release them from the duty of supporting that Government, in the last resort, was to be guilty of class legislation.

The reply to this was, that non-resistance was a tenet of the sect, and that to compel them to fight was to interfere with that religious liberty and equal respect of sects which the fundamental law guarantees.

The proposition was lost by a heavy majority.

Yet the ground of the defense seems to be unsound. To excuse the Quakers, as a religious sect, from duties which are imposed upon all other sects, is evidently a very unequal respect for sects. The only true ground of excuse should be not that the man is a Quaker, but that he is a non-resistant. For by what just law can a non-resistant Quaker be excused from military service, and a non-resistant Baptist or Methodist compelled to serve? Suppose that a new sect should appear with a new tenet of non-resistance, to the effect that governments should be supported by voluntary contributions, should the members of the sect be excused from taxation? And if the members of the sect, then why not all citizens who hold similar opinions?

Unless, therefore, all persons who conscientiously object to fighting are to be released from military duty, there is no good reason why any of them should be.

The law in regard to the exemption of Quakers is of no great importance in itself, because they are not a large class,

* *Harper's Weekly,* VI (1862), 579.

and because many of them practically disregard it, and are as gallant soldiers as any in the field. But the principle of the law is very important. It favors one sect. It discriminates between equal citizens. It is really a law of privilege, and ought to be repealed. Then if it shall be thought wise to excuse all citizens who have true conscientious scruples against fighting, let a law be made to secure their release.

14. a. Report of a Quaker Meeting with Secretary of War Stanton, 1863.*

Members of the Society of Friends from Baltimore called on the Secretary of War to plead for two conscripted Quakers. Stanton used the opportunity to put before them a proposal for a special fund to be created with the monies received from pacifists claiming exemption from the draft.

The Secretary set forth with much feeling and stress the embarrassment which our position caused the Government, and our own Society, as well as himself personally in his efforts to grant us exemption unconditionally, for which he had no law. He spoke of a large draft which will soon be enforced and the necessity of some definite settled course for him to pursue.

He wished Friends to have a general Conference of their Committees to consider a proposition from him, "which he believed would satisfy them and relieve him, and the Government." And he expects to hear from them in relation to it. He proposes to create a Special Fund for the benefit of the Freedmen, and to exempt Friends from Military Service upon the payment of $300. into this fund. Such payment not to be as in other cases to the District Provost Marshal, but to his fiscal Agent at Washington to be credited on his books to the Freedmen, and that Friends can have the disbursement of it through their own agents, and laborers. He expressed deep interest in organized, and individual efforts of Friends to elevate the moral, and physical condition of the manumitted Slaves, and was "willing to accept this medium as a relief for our members from the draft—the only legal mode in his power."

* Wright, *op. cit.,* pp. 72–73.

14. b. Plea to Secretary of War Stanton on Behalf of a Conscripted Quaker, 1863.*

Because the Secretary of War was known to be sympathetic to Quaker principles, many applications were directed to him on behalf of conscientious objectors who had been drafted. One such application addressed to Stanton by four citizens of Massachusetts read as follows. It is of special interest because of the privations it describes.

The following facts in relation to the young man we have from such authority as leaves us no doubt of their substantial correctness. He has from boyhood been a non-resistant, and regarded all wars as criminal, and has entirely abstained from voting as a religious duty. Since then he has done everything in his power to aid the Government against the assaults of the slaveholders. Drafted in October last, the authorities of the camp on Long Island appreciated his religious scruples against bearing arms, and treated him with kindness and respect. But in Virginia, the officer in charge, a Major Cook of Gloucester, Massachusetts, has endeavored to force him to yield his conscientious convictions. He has been tied up in the woods with mules, suspended by his hands after the manner of slaves, until he could hardly stand alone, deprived of shelter, food, and finally put in the guardhouse, where he has been for six or seven weeks. All this the soldier has borne with great courage and patience. His health is seriously impaired by such exposure and severity.

You have already generously discharged several Quakers who have been drafted into the Army. This leads us to hope that you will not hesitate to discharge from military service this young man who is suffering from his adherence to the same principles as theirs.

* *Congressional Globe,* XLIV, Part I, p. 255. Also in Wright, *op. cit.,* p. 127.

14. c. Legislation Providing Noncombatant Service for Conscientious Objectors, 1864.*

When the first conscription bill was passed on March 3, 1863, there had been no provision for exemption on religious grounds. Largely due to the energetic petitions of the peace churches, the act as it was revised on February 24, 1864, made provisions for conscientious objectors as follows:

That members of religious denominations, who shall by oath or affirmation declare that they are conscientiously opposed to the bearing of arms, and who are prohibited from doing so by the rules and articles of faith and practice of said religious denominations, shall when drafted into the military service, be considered non-combatants, and *shall be assigned by the Secretary of War to duty in the hospitals, or to the care of freedmen, or shall pay the sum of three hundred dollars* to such person as the Secretary of War shall designate to receive it, *to be applied to the benefit of the sick and wounded soldiers: Provided*; that no person shall be entitled to the provisions of this section unless his declaration of conscientious scruples against bearing arms shall be supported by satisfactory evidence that his deportment has been uniformly consistent with such declaration. [Editor's italics]

* *U.S. Statutes at Large,* 38th Congress, 1st Session, XIII, p. 9.

14. d. Quaker Opposition to Noncombatant Service, 1864. *

Some Friends felt that not only military service but all substitutes for it were morally wrong. These men refused to work in hospitals or among the newly freed slaves. An editorial in The Friend *expressed the views of these absolutists.*

While, therefore, we fully appreciate the good motives which, we doubt not, prompted the adoption of the section above quoted, and hail it as a cheering indication of the advance of correct views upon this important subject, we do not see how it can relieve our members, or they consistently avail themselves of any of its provisions; inasmuch as to be sent into the hospitals or serve as nurses, etc., or to be assigned to the care of freedmen, is just as much a penalty imposed for obeying the requisitions of our religion in not performing military service, as is the fine of three hundred dollars. It matters not whether the commutation for military service is money or personal service in some other department; in either case it is an assumption on the part of the government of a right to oblige the subject to violate his conscience, or to exact a penalty if he elects to obey God rather than man.

* *The Friend*, **XXXVII**, No. 27, p. 215. Also in Wright, *op. cit.*, pp. 83–84.

14. e. Report of a Quaker Meeting with Secretary of State Seward, 1865.*

A Quaker named Ethan Foster visited Washington, D.C., on behalf of several New England Friends who had been conscripted. His record of the visit shows that not all of Lincoln's Cabinet possessed the President's sympathetic patience with pacifists.

Soon after we entered the War Office, the Secretary of State (William H. Seward) came in and took a seat. He remained silent until our conference with Secretary Stanton was concluded; when Charles Perry (who had an impression that Seward, when Governor of New York, had recommended the passage of a law to exempt from military service those who were conscientiously opposed to war) turned to him expecting a word of sympathy and encouragement, and remarked that he would perceive why we were there; upon which he suddenly and with much vehemence of manner asked, "Why don't the Quakers fight?" Charles replied, "Because they believe it wrong, and cannot do it with a clear conscience " He reprimanded us severely because we refused to fight. After a little pause I said, "Well, if this world were all, perhaps we might take thy advice," to which he responded, "The way to get along in the next world is to do your duty in this." I replied, "That is what we are trying to do; and now I want to ask thee one question, and I want thee to answer it; whose prerogative is it to decide what my duty is, thine or mine?" He did not answer the question, became more angry and excited; asked, "Why, then, don't you pay the commutation." We told him we could see no difference between the responsibility of doing an act ourselves and that of hiring another to do it for us. On this he sprang from his seat and strided around in a circle of some eight or ten feet across, exclaiming, *"Then I'll pay it for you,"* and thrusting his hand into his coat pocket, added, *"I'll give you my check."*

---

* Ethan Foster, *The Conscript Quakers*, being a narrative of the distress and relief of four young men from the draft for the year 1863 (Cambridge, Mass.: Riverside Press, 1883), pp. 14–16.

Immediately after this exhibition, we took our leave in much sadness at treatment so opposite to that we had expected from Secretary Seward.

15. From Cyrus Pringle, "The Record of a Quaker Conscience," 1863.*

On July 13, 1863, Cyrus Pringle, with two fellow Quakers of Charlotte, Vermont, was drafted into the Union Army. Pringle was an "absolutist" who refused to bear arms and to perform any kind of alternate service. The punishments exacted upon him were severe. His diary is one of the fullest accounts that remains to us of conscientious objection in the Civil War.

At Burlington, Vt., on the 13th [day] of the seventh month, 1863, I was drafted.

Brattleboro, Vt., 26*th* [day], 8*th* month, 1863.

Frederick Holbrook,

Governor of Vermont:—

We, the undersigned members of the Society of Friends, beg leave to represent to thee, that we were lately drafted in the 3d Dist. of Vermont, have been forced into the army and reached the camp near this town yesterday.

That in the language of the elders of our New York Yearly Meeting, "We love our country and acknowledge with gratitude to our Heavenly Father the many blessings we have been favored with under the government; and can feel no sympathy with any who seek its overthrow."

But that, true to well-known principles of our society, we cannot violate our religious convictions either by complying with military requisitions or by the equivalents of this compliance,—the furnishing of a substitute or payment of commutation money. That, therefore, we are brought into suffering and exposed to insult and contempt from those who have us in charge, as well as to the penalties of insubordination, though liberty of conscience is *denied* us by the Constitution of Vermont as well as that of the United States.

* Cyrus Guernsey Pringle, "The United States *Versus* Pringle," *The Atlantic Monthly,* III (February, 1913), 145–62. See also Cyrus Guernsey Pringle, *The Record of a Quaker Conscience* (New York: The Macmillan Company, 1918).

Therefore, we beg of thee as Governor of our State any assistance thou may be able to render, should it be no more than the influence of thy position interceding in our behalf.

Truly Thy Friend,

CYRUS G. PRINGLE.

P.S.—We are informed we are to be sent to the vicinity of Boston tomorrow.

27th.—On board train to Boston. The long afternoon of yesterday passed slowly away. This morning passed by,—the time of our stay in Brattleboro, and we neither saw nor heard anything of our Governor. We suppose he could not or would not help us. So as we go down to our trial we have no arm to lean upon among all men. . . .

28th.—Over the hard and stony counties of northern Massachusetts, through its suburbs and under the shadow of Bunker Hill Monument we come into the City of Boston, "the Hub of the Universe." Out through street after street we were marched double guarded to the wharves, where we took a small steamer for the island some six miles out in the harbor. A circumstance connected with this march is worth mentioning for its singularity: at the head of this company, like convicts (and feeling very much like such), through the City of Boston walked, with heavy hearts and down-cast eyes, two Quakers.

Here are many troops gathering daily from all the New England States except Connecticut and Rhode Island. Their white tents are dotting the green slopes and hill-tops of the island and spreading wider and wider. This is the flow of military tide here just now. The ebb went out to sea in the shape of a great shipload just as we came in, and another load will be sent before many days. All is war here. We are surrounded by the pomp and circumstance of war, and enveloped in the cloud thereof. . . . Yesterday L. M. M. and I appeared before the Captain commanding this camp with a statement of our cases. He listened to us respectfully and promised to refer us to the General commanding here, General Devens; and in the mean time released us from duty. In a short time afterward he passed us in our tent, asking our names. We have not heard from him, but do not drill or stand guard; so, we suppose, his release was confirmed. At that interview a young lieutenant sneeringly told us he thought we had better throw away our scruples and fight in the service of the country; and as we told the Captain we could neither accept pay, he laughed mockingly. . . .

Prison Experiences For Conscience' Sake—Our Prison

31*st.*, 8*th* month, 1863. IN GUARD HOUSE.—Yesterday morning L. M. M. and I were called upon to do fatigue duty. The day before we were asked to do some cleaning about camp and to bring water. We wished to be obliging, to appear willing to bear a hand toward that which would promote our own and our fellows' health and convenience; but as we worked we did not feel easy. Suspecting we had been assigned to such work, the more we discussed in our minds the subject, the more clearly the right way seemed opened to us; and we separately came to the judgment that we must not conform to this requirement. . . . [The Major] inquired concerning the complaint he had heard of us. Upon our statement of our position, he apparently undertook to argue our whimsies . . . but he soon turned to bullying us. . . . Our terms were, submission or the guard-house. We replied we could not obey.

The subjects of all misdemeanors, grave and small, are here confined. Those who have deserted or attempted it; those who have insulted officers and those guilty of theft, fighting, drunkenness, etc. In *most*, as in the camps, there are traces yet of manhood and of the Divine Spark, but some are abandoned, dissolute. There are many here among the substitutes who were actors in the late New York riots. They show unmistakably the characteristics and sentiments of those rioters, and, especially, hatred to the blacks drafted and . . . exhibit this in foul and profane jeers heaped upon these unoffending men at every opportunity. In justice to the blacks I must say they are superior to the whites in all their behavior.

31*st.*, 8*th.* month, p.m.—Here we are in prison in our own land for no crimes, no offense to God nor man; nay, more: we are here for obeying the commands of the Son of God and the influences of his Holy Spirit. I must look for patience in this dark day. I am troubled too much and excited and perplexed.

3d., 9th. month.—Yesterday a little service was required of our dear L. M. M., but he insisted he could not comply. A sergeant and two privates were engaged. They coaxed and threatened him by turns, and with a determination not to be baffled took him out to perform it. Though guns were loaded he still stood firm and was soon brought back. We are happy here in guard-house,—too happy, too much at ease. We should see more of the Comforter,—feel more strength,—if the trial were fiercer; but this is well. This is a trial of strength of patience.

AT THE HOSPITAL, *7th., 9th* month.—Yesterday morning came to us Major Gould again, informing us that he had come to take us out of that dirty place, as he could not see such respectable men lying there, and was going to take us up to the hospital. We assured him we could not serve there, and asked him if he would not bring us back when we had there declared our purpose. He would not reply directly; but brought us here and left us. When the surgeon knew our determination, he was for haling us back at once; what he wanted, he said, was willing men. We sat on the sward without the hospital tents till nearly noon, for some one to take us back. . . . Later in the day L. M. M. and P. D. were sitting without, when he passed them and, laughing heartily, declared they were the strangest prisoners of war he ever saw. . . .

13th.—Last night we received a letter from Henry Dickinson, stating that the President, though sympathizing with those in our situation, felt bound by the Conscription Act, and felt liberty, in view of his oath to execute the laws, to do no more than detail us from active service to hospital duty, or to the charge of the colored refugees. For more than a week have we lain here, refusing to engage in hospital service; shall we retrace the steps of the past week? Or shall we go South as overseers of the blacks on the confiscated estates of the rebels, to act under military commanders and to report to such? What would become of our testimony and our determination to preserve ourselves clear of the guilt of this war?

P.S. We have written back to Henry Dickinson that we cannot purchase life at cost of peace of soul.

16th.—Yesterday a son-in-law of N. B. of Lynn came to see us. He was going to get passes for one or two of the

Lynn Friends, that they might come over to see us to-day.
He informed us that the sentiment of the Friends hereabouts
was that we might enter the hospital without compromising
our principles; and he produced a letter from W. W. to S. B.
to the same effect. W. W. expressed his opinion that we
might do so without doing it in lieu of other service. How
can we evade a fact? Does not the government both demand
and accept it as in lieu of other service. Oh, the cruelest
blow of all comes from our friends. . . .

CAMP NEAR CULPEPER. 25th.—My distress is too great for
words; but I must overcome my disinclination to write, or
this record will remain unfinished. So, with aching head and
heart, I proceed.

Yesterday morning we were roused early for breakfast
and for preparation for starting. After marching out of the
barracks, we were first taken to the armory, where each man
received a gun and its equipments and a piece of tent. We
stood in line, waiting for our turn with apprehensions of coming trouble. . . . [W]e felt decided we must decline receiving
the guns. . . .

A council was soon holden [among the junior officers]
to decide what to do with us. One proposed to place us under arrest . . . but another, in some spite and impatience,
insisted, as it was their duty to supply a gun to every man
and forward him, that the guns should be put upon us, and
we be made to carry them. Accordingly the equipment was
buckled about us, and the straps of the guns being loosened,
they were thrust over our heads and hung upon our shoul-
ders. In this way we were urged forward through the streets
of Alexandria; and, having been put upon a long train of dirt
cars, were started for Culpeper. We came over a long stretch
of desolated and deserted country, through battlefields of previous summers, and through many camps now lively with
the work of this present campaign. Seeing, for the first time,
a country made dreary by the war-blight, a country once
adorned with graves and green pastures and meadows and
fields of waving grain, and happy with a thousand homes,
now laid with the ground, one realizes as he can in no other
way something of the ruin that lies in the trail of a war. But
upon these fields of Virginia, once so fair, there rests a two-
fold blight, first that of slavery, now that of war.

Through the heat of this long ride, we felt our total lack
of water and the meagreness of our supply of food. Our

thirst became so oppressive as we were marched here from Culpeper, some four miles with scarcely a halt to rest, under our heavy loads, and through the heat and deep dust of the road, that we drank water and dipped in the brooks we passed, though it was discolored with the soap the soldiers had used in washing. . . . We were taken to the 4th Vermont regiment and . . . we were required immediately after to be present at inspection of arms. We declined, but an attempt was made to force us to obedience . . . [and] we were ordered by the colonel to be tied, and, if we made outcry, to be gagged also, and to be kept so till he gave orders for our release. After two or three hours we were relieved and left under guard; lying down on the ground in the open air, and covering ourselves with our blankets, we soon fell asleep from exhaustion, and the fatigue of the day.

This morning the officers told us we must yield. We must obey and serve. We were threatened great severities and even death. We seem perfectly at the mercy of the military power, and, more, in the hands of the inferior officers, who, from their being far removed from Washington, feel less restraint from those Regulations of the Army, which are for the protection of privates from personal abuse.

REGIMENTAL HOSPITAL, 4th Vermont. 29*th*., 9*th* month.— On the evening of the 26th the Colonel came to us. . . .

He urged us to go into the hospital, stating that this course was advised by Friends about New York. We were too well aware of such a fact to make any denial, though it was a subject of surprise to us that he should be informed of it. He gave us till the next morning to consider the question and report our decision. In our discussion of the subject among ourselves, we were very much perplexed. If all his statements concerning the ground taken by our Society were true, we seemed to be liable, if we persisted in the course which alone seemed to us to be in accordance with Truth, to be exposed to the charge of over-zeal and fanaticism even among our own brethren. Regarding the work to be done in hospital as one of mercy and benevolence, we asked if we had any right to refuse its performance; and questioned whether we could do more good by endeavoring to bear to the end a clear testimony against war, than by laboring by word and deed among the needy in the hospitals and camps. . . .

At first a great load seemed rolled away from us; we rejoiced in the prospect of life again. But soon there prevailed a feeling of condemnation, as though we had sold our Master. And that first day was one of the bitterest I ever experienced. . . . No Friend, who is really such, desiring to keep himself clear of complicity with this system of war and to bear a perfect testimony against it, can lawfully perform service in the hospitals of the Army in lieu of bearing arms.

3*d*., 10*th*. month.—To-day dawned fair and our Camp is dry again. I was asked to clear the gun I brought, and declining, was tied some two hours upon the ground.

6*th*. AT WASHINGTON.—At first, after being informed of our declining to serve in his hospital, Colonel Foster did not appear altered in his kind regard for us. But his spleen soon became evident. . . . When we marched next day I was compelled to bear a gun and equipments. . . .

The next morning the men were busy in burnishing their arms. When I looked toward the one I had borne, yellow with rust, I trembled in the weakness of the flesh at the trial I felt impending over me. Before the Colonel was up I knocked at his tent, but was told he was asleep, though, through the opening, I saw him lying gazing at me. Although I felt I should gain no relief from him, I applied again soon after. He admitted me and, lying on his bed, inquired with cold heartlessness what I wanted. I stated to him, that I could never consent to serve, and . . . he replied that he had shown us all the favor he should; that he had, now, turned us over to the military power and was going to let that take its course; that is, henceforth we were to be at the mercy of the inferior officers, without appeal to law, justice, or mercy. . . . He declared, furthermore, his belief, that a man who would not fight for his country did not deserve to live. I was glad to withdraw from his presence as soon as I could.

I went back to my tent and laid down. . . . The lieutenant called me out, and pointing to the gun that lay near by, asked if I was going to clean it. I replied to him, that I could not comply with military requisitions, and felt resigned to the consequences. 'I do not ask about your feelings; I want to know if you are going to clean that gun.' 'I cannot do it,' was my answer. He went away, saying, 'Very well,' and I crawled into the tent again. Two sergeants soon called for me, and taking me a little aside, bid me lie down on my back and stretching my limbs apart tied cords to my wrists and ankles and these to four stakes driven in the ground somewhat in the form of an X.

I was very quiet in my mind as I lay there on the ground [soaked] with the rain of the previous day, exposed to the heat of the sun, and suffering keenly from the cords binding my wrists and straining my muscles. . . . I wept, not so much from my own suffering as from sorrow that such things should be in our own country, where Justice and Freedom and Liberty of Conscience have been the annual boast of Fourth-of-July orators so many years. . . .

After something like an hour had passed, the lieutenant came with his orderly to ask me if I was ready to clean the gun. I replied . . . that it could but give me pain to be asked or required to do anything I believed wrong. . . . About the end of another hour [the] orderly came and released me.

I arose and sat on the ground. I did not rise to go away. I had not where to go, nothing to do. . . . Some of the men came about me, advising me to yield, and among them one of those who had tied me down, telling me what I had already suffered was nothing to what I must yet suffer unless I yielded. . . .

I had not yet eaten the mean and scanty breakfast I had prepared, when I was ordered to pack up my things and report myself at the lieutenant's tent. I was accustomed to such orders and complied, little moved.

The lieutenant received me politely with, "Good-morning, Mr. Pringle," and desiring me to be seated, proceeded with the writing with which he was engaged. I sat down in some wonderment and sought to be quiet and prepared for any event.

"You are ordered to report to Washington," said he. . . . As the slave many times before us, leaving his yoke behind him, turned from the plantations of Virginia and set his face toward the far North, so we from out a grasp as close and as abundant in suffering and severity, and from without the line of bayonets that had so many weeks surrounded us, turned our backs upon the camp of the 4th Vermont and took our way over the turnpike that ran through the tented fields of Culpeper.

We understand it is through the influence of Isaac Newton

that Friends have been able to approach the heads of Government in our behalf and to prevail with them to so great an extent. He explained to us the circumstance in which we are placed. That the Secretary of War and President sympathized with Friends in their present suffering, and would grant them full release, but that they felt themselves bound by their oaths that they would execute the laws, to carry out to its full extent the Conscription Act. That there appeared but one door of relief open,—that was to parole us and allow us to go home, but subject to their call again ostensibly, though this they neither wished nor proposed to do. That the fact of Friends in the Army and refusing service had attracted public attention so that it was not expedient to parole us at present. That, therefore, we were to be sent to one of the hospitals for a short time, where it was hoped and expressly requested that we would consent to remain quiet and acquiesce, if possible, in whatever might be required of us. That our work there would be quite free from objection, being for the direct relief of the sick; and that there he would release none for active service in the field, as the nurses were hired civilians.

These requirements being so much less objectionable than we had feared, we felt relief, and consented to them. I. N. went with us himself to the Surgeon General's office, where he procured peculiar favors for us: that we should be sent to a hospital in the city, where he could see us often; and that orders should be given that nothing should interfere with our comfort, or our enjoyment of our consciences.

Thence we were sent to Medical Purveyor Abbot, who assigned us to the best hospital in the city, the Douglas Hospital.

9th.—. . . During the day we called upon our friend I. N. in the Patent Office. When he came to see us on the 7th, he stated he had called upon the President that afternoon to request him to release us and let us go home to our friends. The President promised to consider it over-night. Accordingly yesterday morning, as I. N. told us, he waited upon him again. He found there a woman in the greatest distress. Her son, only a boy of fifteen years and four months, having been enticed into the Army, had deserted and been sentenced to be shot the next day. As the clerks were telling her, the President was in the War Office and could not be seen, nor did they think he could attend to her case that day. I. N. found her almost wild with grief. "Do not despair, my good woman," said he, "I guess the President can be seen after a bit." He soon presented her case to the President, who exclaimed at once, "That must not be, I must look into that case, before they shoot that boy"; and telegraphed at once to have the order suspended.

I. N. judged it was not a fit time to urge our case. We feel we can afford to wait, that a life may be saved. But we long for release. We do not feel easy to remain here.

11th., *6th.* month.—Last evening E. W. H. saw I. N. particularly on my behalf, I suppose. He left at once for the President. This morning he called to inform us of his interview at the White House. The President was moved to sympathy in my behalf, when I. N. gave him a letter from one of our Friends in New York. After its perusal he exclaimed to our friend, "I want you to go and tell Stanton, that it is my wish all those young men be sent home at once." He was on his way to the Secretary this morning as he called.

Later. I. N. has just called again informing us in joy that we are free. At the War Office he was urging the Secretary to consent to our paroles, when the President entered. "It is my urgent wish," said he. The Secretary yielded; the order was given, and we were released. What we had waited for so many weeks was accomplished in a few moments by a Providential ordering of circumstances.

7th.—I. N. came again last evening bringing our paroles. The preliminary arrangements are being made, and we are to start this afternoon for New York.

Note. Rising from my sick-bed to undertake this journey, which lasted through the night, its fatigues overcame me, and upon my arrival in New York I was seized with delirium from which I only recovered after many weeks, through the mercy and favor of Him, who in all this trial had been our guide and strength and comfort.

16. Two Lincoln Letters, 1862, 1864.*

As President of a nation seized by Civil War, Lincoln had problems besetting him at every turn. Nevertheless, he found the time to see many of those who came to him with petitions on behalf of conscientious objectors. He sympathized with the pacifist's scruples, and on numerous occasions he pardoned or paroled men whose cases came to his attention. The two letters that follow illustrate Lincoln's attitudes and feelings, as well as the complexities of his position.

Reply to the Memorial of the New England Quakers:

> Execuive Mansion
> Washington
> March 19, 1862

Engaged, as I am, in a great war, I fear it will be difficult for the world to understand how fully I appreciate the principles of peace, inculcated in this letter, and everywhere, by the Society of Friends.

Grateful to the good people you represent, for their prayers in behalf of our common country, I look forward hopefully to an early end of war, and return of peace.

> Your obliged friend,

> A. Lincoln

* John C. Nicolay and John Hay, *Abraham Lincoln—A History* (New York: The Century Co., 1890), VI, pp. 328–29.

To Mrs. Eliza Paul Gurney:

September 4, 1864

My Esteemed Friend:

I have not forgotten—probably never shall forget—the very impressive occasion when yourself and friends visited me on a Sabbath forenoon, two years ago; nor has your kind letter, written nearly a year later, ever been forgotten. In all, it has been your purpose to strengthen my reliance on God. I am much indebted to the good Christian people of the country for their constant prayers and consolations, and to no one of them more than to yourself. The purposes of the Almighty are perfect, and must prevail, though we erring mortals may fail to accurately perceive them in advance. We hoped for a happy termination of this terrible war long before this; but God knows best, and has ruled otherwise. We shall yet acknowledge his wisdom, and our own error therein. Meanwhile we must work earnestly in the best lights he gives us, trusting that so working still conduces to the great ends he ordains. Surely he intends some good to follow this mighty convulsion, which no mortal could make, and no mortal could stay. Your people—the Friends—have had, and are having, a very great trial. On principle and faith, opposed to both war and oppression, they can only practically oppose oppression by war. In this hard dilemma, some have chosen one horn and some the other. For those appealing to me on conscientious grounds, I have done, and shall do, the best I could and can, in my own conscience, under my oath to the law. That you believe this I doubt not; and believing it, I shall still receive, for our country and myself, your earnest prayers to our Father in Heaven.

Your sincere friend,

A. Lincoln

17. Statement of Quaker Principles Against Bearing Arms and Paying Fines, 1865.*

The following is a section from the Minutes of the Meeting for Sufferings of the Philadelphia (Orthodox) Yearly Meeting of Friends, 1865. It includes accounts of those Friends of the congregation who were conscripted, and also restates the principles underlying conscientious objection and the difficulties of maintaining those principles in times of war.

To the Meeting for Sufferings.

The Committee to advise and assist such of our members as might be drafted for service in the army of the United States: Report;

That numerous applications have been made to them, all of which have been attended to; and such counsel and aid given to the parties as their respective cases appeared to require.

Three Friends were taken from their homes, in the interior of Pennsylvania, and sent to Camp Curtin at Harrisburg; from whence they wrote to the Committee, informing of their trying situation. Application was promptly made to the proper Officers in Philadelphia, and a letter procured from one of them to the Military Commander at the Camp, recommending the cases to his favorable attention. Two of the Committee went with this to Harrisburg; and had an interview with the officer in charge, who treated them kindly, and granted permission to the three young men to return to their homes until called for; since which they have not been disturbed. —

In two other cases military passes have been granted to drafted Friends; releasing them from the rendezvous, and permitting their return home; and these have been renewed on the application of the Committee; evincing a Friendly feeling toward those who are conscientiously engaged, under a sense of religious duty to uphold the christian testimony to peace.

* Quoted in Wright, *op. cit.*, pp. 215–17.

One young man, when before the Provost Marshall, in his anxiety to escape being sent to the field, inadvertently expressed his willingness to serve in the Army Hospitals. He was soon sent to Camp, where he was expected to drill, and to do other acts which were trying to his feelings; and the more so, because he felt that he had compromised the testimony of Truth by choosing Hospital duty; and thus had deprived himself of the inward strength and support which are the accompaniments of faithfulness.

When assigned to a Hospital, he found the associations and examples extremely repugnant to his moral and religious feelings, and in several letters, deplored the mistake he had made, and the sad situation into which he had introduced himself. Being taken sick, his feelings were more fully awakened, and in another letter, he entreated Friends to intercede for his release, that he might not end his days amid scenes of such wickedness. He was favored to recover, was discharged, and restored to his Father's family, deeply impressed with his error, and more than ever attached to the principles of Friends. His experience, we think, furnishes evidence of the great importance of steadily and unflinchingly adhering to religious principles, without compromise.

The 17th Section of the "Amandatory enrolment Act" approved the 24th of 2nd month 1864 provides "that members of religious denominations, who shall by oath or affirmation declare that they are conscientiously opposed to the bearing of arms, and who are prohibited from doing so by the rules and articles of faith and practice of said religious denominations, shall when drafted into the military service, be considered non-combatants, and shall be assigned by the Secretary of War to duty in the hospitals, or to the care of freedmen, or shall pay the sum of three hundred dollars to such person as the Secretary of War shall designate to receive it, to be applied to the benefit of the sick and wounded soldiers: Provided, That no person shall be entitled to the provisions of this section unless his declaration of conscientious scruples against bearing arms shall be supported by satisfactory evidence that his deportment has been uniformly consistent with such declaration."

This, we believe, is the first recognition in the Statutes of the United States, of a religious scruple against war, and, coming in the midst of so mighty and desperate a struggle as that then pending, it may well be considered as a most important movement in favor of the Christian principle of "Peace on earth and good-will toward men."

There can be no doubt that it had its origin in feelings of kind consideration for the members of our Religious Society, and of any other which may hold the same views of the peaceful nature of the gospel: and it demands our grateful acknowledgment to the government. It should also be an incentive to Friends, to maintain with integrity their religious testimony; for if those who preceded us had balked or betrayed it, there is no probability that this advance would have been obtained.

That it is a relief to be placed on the list of non-combatants is obvious; inasmuch as it releases from liability to be sent into the battle-field; but the law does not afford a mode of escape from military duty which our discipline acknowledges as consistent with the religious principles of Friends.

Believing that liberty of conscience is the gift of the Creator to man, Friends have ever refused to purchase the free exercise of it, by the payment of any pecuniary or other commutation, to any human authority.

From no other class of citizens, is the payment of $300, the service in hospitals, or among the Freedmen, required; and it is obviously in consequence of their conscientious scruple against war that these are demanded of Friends; and the payment of the money, or the performance of the service, would be an acknowledgment that human authority may abridge and control the Christian's liberty of conscience, which our Society has ever denied.

The money, moreover, is only applicable to military purposes; and therefore paying it, is violating our Christian testimony. The long established Discipline of Friends prohibits such payment; declaring it to be "the judgment of the Yearly Meeting that," if any of its members do, either openly or by connivance, pay any fine, penalty or tax in lieu of personal service for carrying on war "and are not brought to an acknowledgment of their error, Monthly Meetings should proceed to testify against them." This rule was confirmed and explained, a few years afterwards by another, which says: "It is the sense and judgment of this meeting that it is inconsistent with our religious testimony and principles for any Friends to pay a fine or tax levied on them on account of their refusal to serve in the militia, although such fine or imposition may be applied toward defraying the expenses of *civil* government;" and it directs the same course to be pursued by monthly meetings, as in the former case, toward such as violate it.

The Committee have been weightily impressed with the seriousness of making a solemn affirmation of conscientious scruple against bearing arms or being concerned in war, as the law we have quoted calls for; and have much desired that it may not be lightly done by any of our members; but that such as are required to do it, in order to be placed on the list of non-combatants, may be encouraged closely to examine themselves, and be satisfied that they do it from sincere conviction, and not merely from a desire to escape suffering, or to make their way easier.

In endeavoring to discharge the duties of their appointment; while the committee have been much aided and cheered by the kind consideration shown by the officers of the government; they have been pained to find that some of our members have compromised our peace principles by paying the penalty imposed; thus lowering our profession of religious scruple in the estimation of those in authority, and greatly adding to the embarrassment and difficulty of such members as could not, for conscience sake comply with the demand.

Another source of trial and discouragement to us has been that some members have subscribed to funds raised for the payment of bounties to Soldiers, and others have paid taxes levied and applied expressly for the same object; both which are clearly violations of our Christian testimony and discipline, and have tended to discourage and weaken the hands of faithful Friends, as well as to lessen the weight and influence of the Society when appealing to government for the relief of our drafted members.

If those who thus aid in hiring men to fight were transported to the field of battle, and could witness the angry passion engendered, see the soldier who was tempted to enlist, and hired for his work, in part by their money, dealing destruction around him, wounding, maiming, and killing men who are strangers to him; hear the piercing cries and groans of the poor sufferers, and perhaps behold the man himself sent from the murderous employ to his final reckoning; and witness the grief of the bereaved widows and the destitute orphans, in their desolate homes; surely they could not but lament that they had incurred the responsibility of helping forward the dreadful business, with its awful consequences. Distance from the scene of action does not lessen their accountability.

The Committee impressed with a lively sense of the great value and importance of the testimony to universal peace, as an integral part of the Gospel dispensation: and, convinced that we can only hope to see it spread in the world, by individual faithfulness, and consistency; affectionately desire that these views may claim the serious attention of Friends, and that under the influence of Divine love, we may, as brethren of the same household of Faith, feel for, and with, each other; and endeavor as well by example as precept to strengthen, encourage, and help one another, in the upright support of our religious profession.

Signed on behalf and by direction of the Committee.

THOMAS EVANS
MORRIS COPE
AARON SHARPLESS
DAVID ROBERTS
JOHN E. SHEPPARD

Philada 4th mo. 13, 1865

18. The Case of Seth Laughlin of Virginia, 1863.*

The case of Seth W. Laughlin is one of the few instances where a conscientious objector died after harsh treatment by the military. Laughlin was a new member of the Society of Friends when he was arrested and taken to a military camp near Petersburg, Virginia.

First they kept him without sleep for thirty-six hours, a soldier standing by with a bayonet to pierce him, should he fall asleep. Finding that this did not overcome his scruples, they proceeded for three hours each day to buck him down. He was then suspended by his thumbs for an hour and a half. This terrible ordeal was passed through with each day for a week. Then, thinking him conquered, they offered him a gun; but he was unwilling to use the weapon. Threats, abuse and persecution were alike unavailing, and in desperate anger the Colonel ordered him court-martialed. After being tried for insubordination he was ordered shot. Preparations were accordingly made for the execution of this terrible sentence. The army was summoned to witness the scene, and soldiers were detailed. Guns, six loaded with bullets and six without, were handed to twelve chosen men. Seth Laughlin, as calm as any man of the immense number surrounding him, asked time for prayer, which, of course, could not be denied him. The supposition was natural that he wished to pray for himself. But he was ready to meet his Lord; and so he prayed not for himself but for them: "Father, forgive them, for they know not what they do."

Strange was the effect of this familiar prayer upon men used to taking human life and under strict military orders. Each man, however, lowered his gun, and they resolutely declared that they would not shoot such a man, thereby braving the result of disobeying military orders. But the chosen twelve were not the only ones whose hearts were touched. The officers themselves revoked the sentence.

* Fernando G. Cartland, *Southern Heroes; or the Friends in War Time* (Cambridge, Mass.: Riverside Press, 1895), pp. 211–13; quoted also in Wright, *op. cit.*, pp. 176–77.

He was led away to prison, where for weeks he suffered uncomplainingly from his severe punishments. He was finally sent to Windsor Hospital at Richmond, Virginia, where he was taken very sick, and after a long, severe illness . . . he passed quietly away, leaving a wife and seven children.

19. From the Diary of Himelius M. Hockett, 1863.*

Hockett's diary is a vivid account of the torments inflicted upon one pacifist in the Confederate Army. It also conveys the pride and the wry humor of a Quaker sorely beset.

We were notified of our conscription and ordered to camp, but we did not choose to go, and remained quietly about our own affairs. Soon, however, the militia colonel appeared and took us from our work in the fields to the camp at Raleigh. We stated our reasons for not answering the summons, and told the officers we went as prisoners and not as soldiers.

Arriving in Raleigh April 4th, 1863, we, with a neighbor named Reynolds, were ordered to go at once to get wood for the use of the camp. This we declined to do, for we considered that by so doing we would commit ourselves to further military requirements. The officers then ordered soldiers to drive us into the service with bayonets, swearing that they would make examples of such men before they would have their orders disobeyed. We told them we meant no disrespect to them as men or officers, but that it was in obedience to a higher authority that we felt that we must refuse to obey orders that conflicted with the laws of God.

We were left in camp over night, and the next morning were ordered to similar work, but declining, were told that they would soon bring us out of our religious notions. The enrolling officer of the company told us that over $20,000 had been paid to him for Quaker taxes by Orthodox Quakers, and they would subdue us before they had done with us.

I then told my brother that they were in no condition to hear truth, and it would be like casting pearls before swine to reply to them. We meekly let them go on with their tirades of abuse until they pretty well exhausted themselves. Noticing our composure, one said: "I reckon you think you are persecuted for righteousness' sake, don't you?" Every man was then ordered into line to march to the adjutant-general's

* Cartland, *op. cit.,* pp. 256–73.

office to be assigned to his place in the army. We declined to march in line, and for this the soldiers were ordered to run us through with their bayonets. They ran the glittering steel through our clothing without inflicting the least damage to our persons, in a way that seemed strange to us. We told them we would go to the office as prisoners, but not in military drill. This we were allowed to do, and we did it with such coolness that one of the officers was heard to remark: "That fellow is no coward and might make a splendid field officer if he only had the right disposition in him."

We were assigned with Wenlock Reynolds and another Friend to a battery of artillery. Military clothing was given us but we declined it. We were sent at once to Kinston and placed in a battery of horse-artillery. Next day we were all three ordered to drill with the rest, but refusing to take arms, we were told by the lieutenant to consider ourselves under arrest for disobeying orders. Much curiosity was aroused among the men, many of whom could not seem to realize that religion had anything in it to justify exemption from military duty. . . .

General Ransom had been informed of our position, and meeting us at the gate of his office said that he was a man of decision and would have "no equivocations nor prevarications" from us; as to our religion, we should not bring that up, for he knew as much about that as he cared to know. His decision was already made. We could go on duty under arms, pay the tax settled upon, or go to the salt-works, and he would give us as much time as we wanted to make our decision, but under the following circumstances: to be shut up in prison under guard, without one morsel of anything to eat or drink, or any communication with any one until we complied with his orders. . . .

The captain of the guard seemed at first harsh and rough in his manner, but a little incident, small though it may seem, took hold of his feelings. After committing us to the room and charging the guard in our presence to keep us with all diligence, he told them not to allow any communication between us and any one else, nor to allow us to have a morsel of anything to eat or drink, as the general had ordered. We were impressed that it would be right to make a full surrender and to trust wholly to a kind Providence, so we told him we had some cakes and cheese in our valises, that had been furnished us by our wives at home. We then opened the valises and showed him before the guards what we had, and told him if it was right to execute such a sentence, he could take them. "O!" he said, "I guess you might keep that," and he seemed very tender, but looking at the guards who were looking at him, there seemed no way for him to evade the command he had received and given, and so they took the food away. . . .

The night before our release, Colonel Eaton came to our prison with half a pint of water and one spoonful of sugar in it, saying: "I have come to relieve you from this punishment. I have a little water and sugar which I am happy to furnish you." . . .

The next morning, fully five days after our confinement, a small amount of food was given us. . . .

On the eleventh of Sixth month, 1863, I was summoned to appear for trial by court-martial. I appeared on the thirteenth. The charges read were: "Positive disobedience to orders when required to take arms and drill."

The judge-advocate asked me if I wished a lawyer to plead my case. I told him I did not wish it. He said my case was a grave one, and I had better have a lawyer. One could be had for $100. I told him if allowed to speak for myself that was all the defense I asked. He said I could have that privilege. I then asked if that was the only charge there was against me. They said it was. I then asked if I gave no reason for refusing to drill. The lieutenant had been called to prove that I refused to drill. He was now called again to answer my question, and he said that I did; that it was on account of religious scruples. I then told them that was no more than I had a constitutional right to do. They replied that the military code made no such provision. I said that was very likely, but the constitution was potent over all laws of government, and no law could be rightfully enacted inconsistent therewith. The constitution as it then was secured to every man the right to liberty of conscience. I then asked if it was not known that I came into camp as a prisoner on account of religious scruples; if ever there was a charge against me for not answering at roll-call except when reported on the sick list, or if I had ever attempted in any way to escape the custody of the authorities that held me. To this he replied: "I never knew of any cause of complaint outside of the charges preferred against you." . . .

On the 3d of Eighth month I was called out on dress-parade to receive with others the sentence of the court-martial. For desertion some were to have the letter D branded indelibly on their bodies, three inches broad. This was done in my presence with a hot iron, accompanied by the screams of the unhappy victims. There were similar punishments for other offenses. At last my turn came. I was sentenced to six months' hard labor in one of the military forts, bound with heavy ball and chain. Some of the soldiers who had a high regard for and deep sympathy with me said they believed the sentence of the court-martial was in my case grossly perverted. They had overheard a conversation of the officers, from which they gathered that no sentence had been passed on me, and that clemency had been recommended. I was informed that all the officers accorded with this until it reached Jefferson Davis, who refused to sign the decision and recommended that examples be made of all offenders, by adequate punishment.*

On the 6th of Eighth month a new guard was appointed, and on the 7th we were ordered to assist in unloading ordnance cars for the government, and the officers ordered that we should be pierced four inches deep with bayonets if we refused. On declining to do this service my brother was pierced cruelly with bayonets, while I was hung up by the thumbs almost clear of the ground. After I had remained in this suffering position for some time, the corporal was told that he had no orders to tie up either of us, but to pierce us with bayonets, and that he had better obey orders. So I was untied and pierced with a bayonet, though slightly, perhaps on account of having already suffered unauthorized punishment. . . .

* Jefferson Davis was far less sympathetic to pacifists than was Lincoln. [Editor's note.]

20. Quaker Memorial to Jefferson Davis Concerning Draft Laws, 1864.*

As the Civil War went on, the Confederate Government passed increasingly stringent versions of its draft laws. On May 16, 1864, a committee of Friends, fearful of losing the exemption their congregation had been afforded in the past, petitioned President Davis and the House of Representatives, urging that exemption on payment of a tax of $500 be continued in the pending draft bill.

To Jefferson Davis, President of the Confederate States.

The undersigned were appointed by the Meeting for Sufferings representing the North Carolina Yearly Meeting of Friends to wait on the proper authorities on behalf of those of our members who by the late law are liable to be brought into suffering on account of their Religious principles.

Those between the ages of 18 and 45 have heretofore been exempt from military service upon the payment of a tax of $500 and from information received from some members of Congress being induced to believe that it was the intention of the late law to leave the subject of our further exemption discretionary with the President, we are desirous of knowing whether the law will be so construed as to allow those between the ages of 17 and 18 and 45 and 50 the same privilege, and if not whether they will be exempt under that part of the law which allows the Secretary of War under the direction of the President, to exempt such persons as he may be satisfied ought to be exempt on account of public necessity.

While Friends cannot consistently enter into a contract to perform anything in lieu of personal service in the army, we can confidently state our belief that they will be of more real service to the country if allowed to pursue their usual occupations of farming, etc., than if forced into the army, when according to one of their primary principles they could not in any event bear arms.

* Quoted in Wright, *op. cit.,* pp. 113–14.

We trust that the Confederate Government in Christian Charity will not be behind the Federal Government which we have good authority for saying does not attempt to force Friends to bear arms; but exempts them on their affirmation that they are members of our Society.

The Confederate Government may well be liberal towards Friends when according to the best of our information and belief there are at least eight men at the North to one at the South, who are restrained by our Religious principles from taking any part in this war. It may be worthwhile to consider too what the Confederacy would really gain by disregarding our religious scruples when we state that the whole number of our members rendered liable by the late law probably does not amount to 125 persons.

NEREUS MENDENHALL, ISHAM COX, JONATHAN HARISS

Part IV

PREFACE

After 1865, the nation turned its energies to settling the western territories and to building its industries. But economic growth, like war, took its own toll of life and limb. Labor unrest after 1880 brought more than 38,000 strikes and lockouts, and involved nine and one-half million workers. The Spanish-American War in 1898, with an American loss of 289 men, was a skirmish by comparison.

The cause of peace was not forgotten but was taken up, increasingly, by secular thinkers and writers. In 1910, the psychologist and philosopher William James advised his fellow Americans to channel their bellicose energies into avenues of domestic reform.* And in 1916, the political writer Randolph Bourne proposed, in effect, the creation of a domestic Peace Corps.** There was no lack of reasoned arguments for peace, but Norman Thomas was probably right when he adjudged that the pacifist impulse in America was superficial: "Pacifism . . . seldom interfered with the march of . . . empire. We ruthlessly disposed of the Indians and took what we desired from Mexico; we continuously lynched Negroes, and carried on labor struggles with more bloodshed than England, France, and Germany combined. This is not the record of a pacific people."***

The recklessness with which popular sentiment turned from peace to war between 1916 and 1917 was a case in point. Woodrow Wilson, reelected in 1916 on the slogan, "He kept us out of war," led the country into war only one year later. Americans went to war in a state of giddy hysteria. Men

* See William James, "A Moral Equivalent of War," in *Essays on Faith and Morals* (Cleveland, Ohio: The World Publishing Co., Meridian Books, 1962), pp. 311–28.

** See Randolph Bourne, "A Moral Equivalent for Universal Military Service," in *The New Republic*, VII (July 1, 1916), 217–19.

*** Norman M. Thomas, *The Conscientious Objector in America* (New York: B. W. Huebsch, Inc., 1923), p. 65.

and women long restrained by Puritanism tended to find, through war, a release of emotions, a near sexual excitement.

Conscription in World War I was universal and absolute. No allowance was made for substitutes or commutation fees. Nevertheless 9,585,508 men were registered without any reported disorders. On the contrary, the public showed itself so zealous that "slacker raids" carried out by the Department of Justice were abetted by the local police, by members of the self-styled American Protective League, and by private citizens. In one such raid, all persons entering New York City by ferry were challenged to prove their draft status. In such an atmosphere, any man claiming still to hear the voice of his conscience was hardly safe walking the streets in civilian clothes. When Eugene V. Debs urged his fellow-Socialists, "Let us swear by all that is dear to us and all that is sacred to the cause never to become soldiers and never to go to war," the multitude of Americans were convinced that pacifism and social radicalism were one and the same. The pacifists were "slackers," "yellowbacks," "atheists," or "pro-Germans." Above all, they were aliens and foreigners. Popular feelings were never more virulent against those who hewed to the line of conscience (see Document 27 in this book).

The Selective Service Act of 1917 provided exemptions for religious objectors, but stipulated that "no persons so exempted shall be exempted from service in any capacity that the President shall declare to be noncombatant. . . ." The effect of this stipulation was to put all conscientious objectors into some form of noncombatant service under the authority of the President or the Secretary of War.

Some peace churches recommended that their members of military age register and accept noncombatant service, but many objectors balked at a policy that placed them under military jurisdiction. On March 16, 1918, Congress provided that the Secretary of War might grant "furloughs" without pay to enlisted men for work on farms or in Red Cross units, but military directives were not issued until June and July, and the war was over in November.

The men who claimed exemption as conscientious objectors during the First World War were a varied group. The ranks of the Quakers and Mennonites had been swelled by new waves of immigration that brought Molokans, Dukhobors, Seventh Day Adventists, Jehovah's Witnesses, Russellites, and Christadelphians, and the Hutterian, Plymouth, and River

Brethren to the United States. The Molokans, in fact, had come all the way from Russia for the express purpose of avoiding army service.

In addition to the variety of pacifist sects, there were new groups whose objection to war was nonreligious. Atheists, humanists, socialists, and radicals opposed the war on ethical and on political grounds. A directive from the Adjutant General of the Army, dated December, 1917, stated that "until further instructions on the subject are issued 'personal scruples against war' should be considered as constituting 'conscientious objection' and such persons should be treated in the same manner as other 'conscientious objectors.' . . ." But the real decisions were left to a presidential Board of Inquiry,* whose job it was to determine which conscientious objector was "sincere" and which was "insincere." Traveling from camp to camp, the Board of Inquiry had only a few minutes to hear each man, and often such cursory examinations were the bases for determining whether an objector was to be granted a civilian furlough or held for a military court-martial.

The public engaged in its own harassment of dissident elements in society. Those who refused to buy Liberty bonds were threatened with tarring and feathering. Socialists, anarchists, and members of the I.W.W. were seized, assaulted, and horsewhipped. Senator Robert La Follette of Wisconsin, an open critic of conscription, was publicly insulted. Max Eastman, the publisher, and Victor Berger, the socialist leader, both opponents of the war, were indicted for treason under the Sedition Act. Eugene Debs was sentenced to ten years in federal prison for inciting resistance to the war in a speech. In the end, it was not only the pacifists and conscientious objectors who were persecuted, but the wide spectrum of individuals who expressed political opinions at variance with the consensus of American society.

Conscientious objectors themselves were a small enough proportion of the general population, considering that there were an estimated 171,000 draft "evaders," and 2,810,296 men who were actually inducted into the armed forces. Army records show that between May, 1917, and November, 1918, 64,693 claims were filed by men claiming conscientious ob-

* Composed of Major Walter G. Kellogg, U.S. Circuit Court Judge Julian W. Mack, and Dean Harlan F. Stone of the Columbia University Law School.

jector classification. Of these, 20,973 were inducted, and 3,989 refused at first to accept noncombatant status from the Army. About 1,300 from this latter group, under pressure, accepted assignment to the Medical or Engineering or Quartermaster Corps; some 1,200 were given farm furloughs; and about 100 were assigned to Quaker war relief work in France. Five hundred men remained intransigent and were court-martialed. The military courts were severe with "absolutists" who refused all cooperation with the army (see Documents 23 and 24 in this book). There were seventeen death sentences, 142 life terms, and 345 sentences where the average term was sixteen and one-half years. None of the death penalties was carried out, and 185 of the sentences were eventually reduced, but it was not until 1933 that the last full pardon was issued by President Roosevelt and the last conscientious objector of World War I was released from prison.*

The treatment of objectors who had chosen the absolutist position differed from camp to camp, but there were no-torious instances, as at Camp Funston and Camp Riley, where cruelty was known to be commonplace. Conditions at Camp Funston were so flagrant that a congressional investi-gation was held in 1919.** During the hearings, one of the officers of the Camp admitted that guards had been "too drastic" in giving c.o.'s cold showers, striking them, com-pelling them to exercise, feeding them on bread and water, placing them in solitary confinement, manacling them to the bars of their cells, and hanging them by their thumbs. One young objector who refused to wear a uniform while alive,*** died in prison, whereupon his body was dressed in the hated army uniform and sent home to his parents.

It was in these confrontations, remote from public atten-tion and social restraint, that personal frustration and igno-rance were rooted. Without the benefit of an enlightened legis-lative policy, military prisons too often became the scenes of punitive excess (see Documents 25 and 26 in this book).

* See Secretary of War, *Statement Concerning the Treatment of Conscientious Objectors in the Army* (Washington, D.C., 1919), p. 16; and Milford Sibley and Philip E. Jacob, *Conscription of Conscience* (Ithaca, N.Y.: Cornell University Press, 1952), p. 14.

** See *Congressional Record,* 65th Congress, 3rd Session (Washington, D.C., 1919), p. 3240.

*** The Amish Mennonites are forbidden by their religion to wear clothes with buttons.

Congressional hearings and newspaper accounts brought the cause of conscientious objectors before the intellectual community, where it won a sympathetic response from such eloquent spokesmen as Roger Baldwin, Roderick Seidenberg, and Norman Thomas (see Documents 23 and 24 in this book). Liberal organizations such as the National Civil Liberties Bureau, founded in 1917, and its successor the American Civil Liberties Union, established in 1920, undertook the defense of conscientious objectors and often succeeded in bringing their cases to the Supreme Court.

The objectors whose cases came before the courts after 1918 were not primarily the religious objectors, for the majority of them were able to come to terms with the activities of the nation at war by accepting alternate service. The objectors whose beliefs brought them to the courts were the aliens and the absolutists, and the nonreligious and political objectors. Conscientious objection in America was becoming a problem in political and social tolerance for dissidents—for those who were conscientiously contentious. The issues they raised confounded honest men and infuriated bigots.

21. a. Selective Service Regulations, 1917.

Classification Rules and Principles, section 79, rule XIV.— Any registrant who is found by a local board to be a member of any well-recognized religious sect or organization organized and existing May 18, 1917, and whose then existing creed or principles forbid its members to participate in war in any form, and whose religious convictions are against war or participation therein in accordance with the creed or principles of said religious organizations, shall be furnished by such local board with a certificate (Form 1008, sec. 280, p. 225) to that effect and to the further effect that, by the terms of section 4 of the Selective Service law, he can only be required to serve in a capacity declared by the President to be noncombatant. He shall be classified, however, as is any other registrant; but he shall be designated upon all classifications, forms, records, certificates, and other writings of local and district boards in which his name appears by the insertion of a cipher (0) after his name.

21. b. Selective Service Questionnaire (Form 1001), 1917.

Series IX. Religious Conviction Against War

Instructions.—Every registrant must answer the first question. If he answers "no," he need not answer the other questions nor sign his name. If he answers "yes," he must answer ALL the questions and sign his name.

Q. 1. Are you a member of a well-recognized religious sect or organization organized and existing May 18, 1917, whose then existing creed or principles forbid its members to participate in war in any form? If so, state the name of the sect or organization and location of its governing body or head. A. 1. _____. If your answer is "no," do not answer any other questions and do not sign your name.

Q. 2. By reason of your membership in such sect or organization, do you claim exemption from military service, except in some capacity declared by the President to be noncombatant? A. 2. _____
            (Yes or no)

Q. 3. State number of adherents of such religious sect or organization in the United States. A. 3. _____

Q. 4. When did said religious sect or organization adopt opposition to war as a part of its creed or principles? A. 4. _____

Q. 5. When, where, and how did you become a member of such religious sect or organization? A. 5. _____

Q. 6. Are your religious convictions against war or participation therein in accordance with the creed or principles of such religious sect or organization? A. 6. _____

Q. 7. Give the name, location, and date of organization of the particular local church or congregation of which you are a member. A. 7. _____

_____
(Signature of registrant)

[Registrants claiming exemption from combatant service in accordance with the above were not to be placed in a deferred class on this claim alone. In other words, men who declared themselves to be conscientious objectors were to be classified as any other registrant. However, no matter how they were classified, they were to be issued a Certificate of Exemption from Combatant Service (PMGO Form 1008) if found to qualify. This Certificate read as follows:]

Certificate of Exemption from Combatant Service

Local board for _____

Date _____

This is to certify that _____ Order No. _____ Serial No. _____, has been found to be exempt from combatant service and is eligible only to such military service as may be declared noncombatant by the President of the United States.

Member of Local Board.

22. Carl Haessler, Statement of a Political Objector, 1918.*

Carl Haessler, Rhodes Scholar and professor of philosophy, thus stated his inability to fight in what he saw as a capitalistic and nationalistic war.

I, Carl Haessler, Recruit, Machine Gun Company, 46th Infantry, respectfully submit the following statement in extenuation in connection with my proposed plea of guilty to the charge of violation of the 64th Article of War, the offense having been committed June 22, 1918, in Camp Sheridan, Ala.

The offense was not committed from private, secret, personal, impulsive, religious, pacifist or pro-German grounds. An admixture of quasi-personal motives is admitted, but they were in no sense the guiding or controlling factors. I have evidence for each of these assertions, should it be required.

The willful disobedience of my Captain's and of my Lieutenant-Colonel's orders to report in military uniform arose from a conviction which I hesitate to express before my country's military officers but which I nevertheless am at present unable to shake off, namely, that America's participation in the World War was unnecessary, of doubtful benefit (if any) to the country and to humanity, and accomplished largely, though not exclusively, through the pressure of the Allied and American commercial imperialists.

Holding this conviction, I conceived my part as a citizen to be opposition to the war before it was declared, active efforts for a peace without victory after the declaration, and a determination so far as possible to do nothing in aid of the war while its character seemed to remain what I thought it was. I hoped in this way to help bring the war to an earlier close and to help make similar future wars less probable in this country.

I further believe that I shall be rendering the country a service by helping to set an example for other citizens to follow in the matter of fearlessly acting on unpopular convic-

* Quoted in Thomas, *op. cit.,* pp. 23–24.

tions instead of forgetting them in time of stress. The crumbling of American radicalism under pressure in 1917 has only been equalled by that of the majority of German socialist leaders in August, 1914.

Looking at my case from the point of view of the administration and of this court, I readily admit the necessity of exemplary punishment. I regret that I have been forced to make myself a nuisance and I grant that this war could not be carried on if objections like mine were recognized by those conducting the war. My respect for the administration has been greatly increased by the courteous and forbearing treatment accorded me since having been drafted, but my view of international politics and diplomacy, acquired during my three years of graduate study in England, has not altered since June, 1917, when I formally declared that I could not accept service if drafted. Although officers have on three occasions offered me noncombatant service if I would put on the uniform, I have regretfully refused each time on the ground that "bomb-proof" service on my part would give the lie to my sincerity (which was freely granted by Judge Julian Mack when he and his colleagues examined me at Camp Gordon). If I am to render any war services, I shall not ask for special privileges.

I wish to conclude this long statement by reiterating that I am not a pacifist or pro-German, not a religious or private objector, but regard myself as a patriotic political objector, acting largely from public and social grounds.

I regret that, while my present view of this war continues, I cannot freely render any service in aid of the war. I shall not complain about the punishment that this court may see fit to mete out to me.

23. Roderick Seidenberg, "I Refuse to Serve," 1918.*

When World War I began, Seidenberg, an architect and writer, registered as a conscientious objector. In May, 1918, he was drafted. Two days after the armistice was declared, Seidenberg was tried at Fort Riley, Kansas, on the charge of having refused to clean up the parade grounds. He was sentenced to life imprisonment at hard labor, but he was discharged after one-and-one-half years.

The Disciplinary Barracks of the Army are at Fort Leavenworth—not more than a stone's throw from the monument which marks the exact geographic center of the United States. Nothing, in those days of war, could have seemed to me more appropriate than a military prison at the very heart of America. I was a war resister, serving a life sentence at hard labor. . . .

I refused to work. Thus I quickly learned that prison has its prison; on the second day of my term I found myself in solitary confinement. The heretic was at least alone. Not alone, however, in what he had done. Thirty-five of us had refused to do anything whatsoever. We were absolutists.

To steal, rape or murder, to slap an officer's face and call him a son of a bitch—these are the standard peace-time entrance requirements to the Disciplinary Barracks. But in time of war too firm a belief in the words of Christ, too ardent a faith in the brotherhood of man, is even more acceptable. . . .

The first to arrive at Leavenworth who refused to work were six stalwart Molokans, true Christians if ever there were any. They went cheerfully into the "hole," each one in a pitch-dark cell on bread and water, manacled standing to the bars of their cells for nine hours every day—to sleep, exhausted on the bare cement floor. Others followed. Evan Thomas, who had at first accepted work, hearing their fate, joined them in heroic protest. That is like him—a fiery spirit beneath his unflinching calm.

* The American Mercury, XXV (1932), 91–99.

Two weeks and a new trial! . . . This time we were to have food, then another trial and two more weeks without food. But manacled we must be, nine hours every day. It was the end of December, 1919; the war had been over since the eleventh of November. The Molokans, refusing, because of their strange religious scruples, everything but a little milk, even when permitted food on the alternate fortnights, had stood the treatment for fifty-five days without a sign of weakening.

I was in the middle of my third term when word came from the Secretary of War that henceforth prisoners of the Army were no longer to be manacled. . . .*

We were placed in a stockade outside the prison walls— all but the two Hofer brothers, who had died.

In the stockade beyond the prison wall we played, we read books, we received and wrote letters once more, and we ate, with relish, the indescribable food of Leavenworth. Half our number were religious objectors: Hutterites, Dunkards, Seventh Day Adventists, an orthodox Jew, and the six Molokans. The rest of us were so-called political objectors: Socialists, humanitarians, individualists. . . .

We had refused to participate in organized slaughter; we were considered insensitive and unfeeling toward the higher causes of humanity. We had thought to stand aloof from the madness of war; we were antisocial and doctrinaire. We had taken what appeared to us the one direct and positive and unarguable position for peace; we were negative obstructionists. We had refrained from any propaganda, we believed in freedom of conscience; we were ego-centric heretics. We thought ourselves tolerably sane; we were psychopathic.

By the end of January things had come to such a pass that one day the first gang suddenly refused to work. That night the quartermaster's warehouse burned to the ground. The following morning, after having been called to work, the men were sent back to their cells. At noon they were all assembled once more in the prison yard, and called to their gangs. "First gang, second gang, third gang. . . ." No one moved. It must have been a terrifying moment. . . .

Now the men acted with quiet deliberation. Was it the work of the conscientious objectors, who were scattered throughout the prison on the work gangs and in the offices,

---

* See Document 26 in this book.

and housed in all the seven wings? At the beginning of the
strike they had organized themselves. Under the leadership
of H. Austin Simons, the son of a judge, Carl Haes[s]ler
a Rhodes scholar from Oxford and instructor in philosophy
at the University of Wisconsin, and others, the entire prison
had been mobilized to stand firm with arms folded. There
must be no violence! . . .

Colonel Rice was equally brave. He acknowledged that
the prisoners had grievances, and wisely he consented to
arbitrate. It was a momentous decision and a triumph for
the prisoners. Colonel Rice listened to their demands: that
men in solitary for complicity in the disturbance be immediately restored to regular status, that a telegram be sent to the
Secretary of War petitioning for amnesty, that the commandant
recognize a permanent grievance committee. Colonel Rice proposed to go to Washington himself to present the resolutions. . . .

A general reduction of sentences followed the colonel's return; men were released, and a grievance committee became
an established institution. But not for long. . . . Six months
later the conscientious objectors who still remained were suddenly transferred to Fort Douglas in Utah, and six days
later a second strike broke out.

It was crushed with bullets, and Leavenworth returned
once more to the peaceful days of iron discipline. . . .

New men were constantly added to our group, men who
had stopped working. Our cells were badly overcrowded and
once more we were shifted back to the Disciplinary Barracks.
The first tier of cells in the sixth wing was to be our home,
we were informed, until released. When would that be—in
ten, in twenty years? Many of us still had life sentences. We
did not take them seriously.

In time they were all reduced, now one, then another.
They were reduced to three years, to five years or perhaps
to one year. I received a sentence of a year and a half.
The days moved slowly, to be checked off, one at a time,
on a little calendar. The days turned into weeks and the
weeks into months. . . .

We now numbered close to a hundred men. We enjoyed
such freedom as the cell-block permitted, but it was a dreary
freedom at best. We were never permitted outside, even for

* See Document 22 in this book.

exercise, and the months passed without our ever seeing the sunshine except through the barred windows. . . .

I began to lose something of my New York provincialism and to learn of this America. Here were men from all quarters and from all walks of life: religious farmers from the Middle West who alone seemed capable of community living; I.W.W.'s from the Far West; Socialists from the East Side of New York; men from Chicago, from the South; men who had been sailors, carpenters, college students, tailors. One was a statistician, one a prize-fighter from Philadelphia, one a music teacher. . . . I missed a few of the older friends who were no longer with us—Evan Thomas, with whom I could talk of philosophy and a *Weltanschauung*; Maurice Hess, a Dunkard, now a college professor, a man of exceptional erudition and amazing courage behind the mildest exterior.

But most of all, in a way, I missed my friend Sam Solnitski. His racy, ironic humor helped many an hour along. In the guardhouse at Fort Riley, while we awaited trial, he would pace up and down with me, telling of his life in Poland, of his escape to America to avoid military service, of his days in this country as a skilled worker on the uppers of women's shoes—the very finest—for prostitutes! Best of all, however, he had read, it seemed to me, all of literature—in Yiddish. Now he told the grand stories of Maupassant, of Balzac, of Anatole France, in a mixture, half-English, half-Yiddish, which made these tales of elegant ladies and Parisian life more real than ever. Solnitski had distinguished himself at his court-martial. In his own way he had attempted to explain to the twelve precise majors of the court the reasons for his opposition to military service—but in vain. He broke off in despair, "Ow, shucks, what's the use!"

24. The Case of Roger N. Baldwin.*

In 1917, Roger N. Baldwin was Director of the American Union Against Militarism and, when that organization became the National Civil Liberties Bureau, he served as its Executive Officer. On October 9, 1918, Baldwin notified his draft board that he would refuse induction. On October 30, 1918, he was sentenced to one year in a federal penitentiary, a sentence he served in spite of the fact that the armistice was signed only twelve days later on November 11th. After the war, in 1920, Baldwin, with John Dewey and others, went on to form the American Civil Liberties Union. Baldwin served that organization as its director until 1950.

24. a. Baldwin's Statement to the Court, October 30, 1918.

Your Honor, I presume that myself, and not the National Civil Liberties Bureau, is on trial before this court this morning. I do not object to the reading into this record of the letters which the Government's attorney has read. Some of them I did not write. They represent one side of a work which I have been conducting as the Executive Officer of that organization during the past year. Our work is backed up and supported both by those who call themselves Pro-War Liberals, who are supporters of the war, and by those who are so-called Pacifists.

I have not engaged in personal propaganda. I have not made public addresses, except upon the subject matter of this Bureau. I have not written articles, except upon the subject matter of the Bureau, and I have felt throughout that it was a work which could be supported genuinely and honestly by those who opposed the war in principle, and by those who were supporting the war. I believe that the examination of the records of the Bureau now being made by the Department of Justice will conclusively demonstrate that the

* *The Individual and the State, The Problem as Presented by the Sentencing of Roger N. Baldwin* (New York, 1918).

work has been undertaken with that sole purpose in view, and that it has been in the interest of the solution of certain democratic problems that this country has to face during war time.

I will say, in that connection for instance, that although the Post Office censorship throughout the war has been intolerant, narrow and stupid, but one little pamphlet which we have issued—and we have issued a great many of them—has been excluded from the mails, and that in this Court within the last two weeks an injunction was issued, requiring the Post-Master of New York to accept for mailing all the pamphlets of this Bureau. I think that demonstrates pretty clearly that where the law is narrowly interpreted, rigidly interpreted, arbitrarily interpreted, as it is in the Post-Office Department at Washington, no exception has been taken to the general matter which has been sent out by this organization.

I know that the Government's Attorney is merely attempting to put before this Court my state of mind in taking the position I have about this act—in coming here as its deliberate violator.

I want to read to the Court, if I may, for purposes of record, and for purposes of brevity too, a statement which I have prepared, and which I hope will get across a point of view which the United States Attorney does not consider logical, but which I trust, at least, with the premises I hold, is consistent.

I am before you as a deliberate violator of the draft act. On October 9, when ordered to take the physical examination, I notified my local board that I declined to do so, and instead presented myself to the United States Attorney for prosecution. I submit herewith for the record the letter of explanation which I addressed to him at the time.

I refused to take bail, believing that I was not morally justified in procuring it, and being further opposed to the institution of bail on principle. . . .

The compelling motive for refusing to comply with the draft act is my uncompromising opposition to the principle of conscription of life by the State for any purpose whatever, in time of war or peace. I not only refuse to obey the the present conscription law, but I would in future refuse to obey any similar statute which attempts to direct my choice of service and ideals. I regard the principle of conscription of life as a flat contradiction of all our cherished ideals of individual freedom, democratic liberty and Christian teaching.

I am the more opposed to the present act, because it is for the purpose of conducting war. I am opposed to this and all other wars. I do not believe in the use of physical force as a method of achieving any end, however good.

The District Attorney calls your attention your Honor, to the inconsistency in my statement to him that I would, under extreme emergencies, as a matter of protecting the life of any person, use physical force. I don't think that is an argument that can be used in support of the wholesale organization of men to achieve political purposes in nationalistic or domestic wars. I see no relationship at all between the two.

My opposition is not only to direct military service but to any service whatever designed to help prosecute the war. I could accept no service, therefore, under the present act, regardless of its character.

Holding such profound convictions, I determined, while the new act was pending, that it would be more honest to make my stand clear at the start and therefore concluded not even to register, but to present myself for prosecution. I therefore resigned my position as director of the National Civil Liberties Bureau so as to be free to follow that personal course of action. But on the day my resignation took effect (August 31) agents of the Department of Justice began an examination of the affairs of that organization, and I was constrained to withdraw my resignation and to register in order to stand by the work at a critical moment. With that obligation discharged, I resigned, and took the next occasion, the physical examination, to make my stand clear.

I realize that to some this refusal may seem a piece of willful defiance. It might well be argued that any man holding my views might have avoided the issue by obeying the law, either on the chance of being rejected on physical grounds, or on the chance of the war stopping before a call to service. I answer that I am not seeking to evade the draft; that I scorn evasion, compromise and gambling with moral issues. It may further be argued that the War Department's liberal provision for agricultural service on furlough for conscientious objectors would be open to me if I obey the law and go to camp, and that there can be no moral objection to farming, even in time of war. I answer first, that I am opposed to any service under conscription, regardless of whether that service is in itself morally objectionable; and second, that, even if that were not the case, and I were opposed only to war, I can make no moral distinction between the various services which assist in prosecuting the war —whether rendered in the trenches, in the purchase of bonds or thrift stamps at home, or in raising farm products under the lash of the draft act. All serve the same end—war. Of course all of us render involuntary assistance to the war in the processes of our daily living. I refer only to those direct services undertaken by choice.

I am fully aware that my position is extreme, that it is shared by comparatively few, and that in the present temper it is regarded either as unwarranted egotism or as a species of feeble-mindedness. I cannot, therefore, let this occasion pass without attempting to explain the foundations on which so extreme a view rests.

I have had an essentially American upbringing and background. Born in a suburban town of Boston, Massachusetts, of the stock of the first settlers, I was reared in the public schools and at Harvard College. Early my mind was caught by the age-old struggle for freedom; America meant to me a vital new experiment in free political institutions; personal freedom to choose one's way of life and service seemed the essence of the liberties brought by those who fled the mediæval and modern tyrannies of the old world. But I rebelled at our whole automatic industrial system—with its wreckage of poverty, disease and crime, and childhood robbed of its right to free growth. So I took up social work upon leaving college, going to St. Louis as director of a settlement and instructor in sociology at Washington University. For ten years I have been professionally engaged in social work and political reform, local and national. That program of studied, directed social progress, step by step, by public agitation and legislation, seemed to me the practical way of effective service to gradually freeing the mass of folks from industrial and political bondage. At the same time I was attracted to the solutions of our social problems put forth by the radicals. I studied the programs of socialism, the I. W. W., European syndicalism and anarchism. I attended their meetings, knew their leaders. Some of them became my close personal friends. Sympathizing with their general ideals of a free society, with much of their program, I yet could see no effective way of practical daily service. Some six years ago, however, I was so discouraged with social work and reform, so challenged by the sacrifices and idealism of some of my I. W. W. friends, that I was on the point of getting out altogether, throwing respectability overboard and joining the I. W. W. as a manual worker.

I thought better of it. My traditions were against it. It was more an emotional reaction than a practical form of service. But ever since, I have felt myself heart and soul with the world-wide radical movements for industrial and political freedom,—wherever and however expressed—and more and more impatient with reform. . . .

When the war came to America, it was an immediate challenge to me to help protect those ideals of liberty which seemed to me not only the basis of the radical economic view, but of the radical political view of the founders of this Republic, and of the whole mediæval struggle for religious freedom. Before the war was declared I severed all my connections in St. Louis and offered my services to the American Union Against Militarism to help fight conscription. Later, that work developed into the National Civil Liberties Bureau, organized to help maintain the rights of free speech and free press, and the Anglo-Saxon tradition of liberty of conscience, through liberal provisions for conscientious objectors. This work has been backed both by pro-war liberals and so-called pacifists. It is not anti-war in any sense. It seemed to me the one avenue of service open to me, consistent with my views, with the country's best interest, and with the preservation of the radical minority for the struggle after the war. Even if I were not a believer in radical theories and movements, I would justify the work I have done on the ground of American ideals and traditions alone—as do many of those who have been associated with me. They have stood for those enduring principles which the revolutionary demands of war have temporarily set aside. We have stood against hysteria, mob-violence, unwarranted prosecution, the sinister use of patriotism to cover attacks on radical and labor movements, and for the unabridged right of a fair trial under war statutes. We have tried to keep open those channels of expression which stand for the kind of world order for which the President is battling today against the tories and militarists.

Now comes the Government to take me from that service and to demand of me a service I cannot in conscience undertake. I refuse it simply for my own peace of mind and spirit, for the satisfaction of that inner demand more compelling than any consideration of punishment or the sacrifice of friendships and reputation. I seek no martyrdom, no publicity. I merely meet as squarely as I can the moral issue before me, regardless of consequences.

I realize that your Honor may virtually commit me at once to the military authorities, and that I may have merely taken a quicker and more inconvenient method of arriving at a military camp. I am prepared for that—for the inevitable pressure to take an easy way out by non-combatant service —with guard-house confinement—perhaps brutalities, which hundreds of other objectors have already suffered and are suffering today in camps. I am prepared for court martial and sentence to military prison, to follow the 200–300 objectors already sentenced to terms of 10–30 years for their loyalty to their ideals. I know that the way is easy for those who accept what to me is compromise, hard for those who refuse, as I must, any service whatever. And I know further, in military prison I shall refuse to conform to the rules for military salutes and the like, and will suffer solitary confinement on bread and water, shackled to the bars of a cell eight hours a day—as are men of like convictions at this moment.

I am not complaining for myself or others. I am merely advising the court that I understand full well the penalty of my heresy, and am prepared to pay it. The conflict with conscription is irreconcilable. Even the liberalism of the President and Secretary of War in dealing with objectors leads those of us who are "absolutists" to a punishment longer and severer than that of desperate criminals.

But I believe most of us are prepared even to die for our faith, just as our brothers in France are dying for theirs. To them we are comrades in spirit—we understand one another's motives, though our methods are wide apart. We both share deeply the common experience of living up to the truth as we see it, whatever the price. . . .

I hope your Honor will not think that I have taken this occasion to make a speech for the sake of making a speech. I have read you what I have written in order that the future record for myself and for my friends may be perfectly clear, and in order to clear up some of the matters to which the District Attorney called your attention. I know that it is pretty nigh hopeless in times of war and hysteria to get across to any substantial body of people, the view of an out and

out heretic like myself. I know that as far as my principles
are concerned, they seem to be utterly impractical—mere
moon-shine. They are not the views that work in the world
today. I fully realize that. But I fully believe that they are
the views which are going to guide in the future.

Having arrived at the state of mind in which those views
mean the dearest things in life to me, I cannot consistently,
with self-respect, do other than I have, namely deliberately
to violate an act which seems to me to be a denial of everything which ideally and in practice I hold sacred.

24. b. Judge Mayer's Remarks in Imposing Sentence, 1918.

In all that you have said, I think that you have lost sight of
one very fundamental and essential thing for the preservation of that American Liberty of which by tradition you feel
that you are a genuine upholder. A Republic can last only
so long as its laws are obeyed. The freest discussion is permitted, and should be invited in the processes that lead up
to the enactment of a statute. There should be the freest opportunity of discussion as to the methods of the administration of the statutes. But the Republic must cease to exist
if disobedience to any law enacted by the orderly process
laid down by the constitution is in the slightest degree permitted. That is, from my point of view, fundamental. That
is the sense, not only from an ideal standpoint, but from a
practical standpoint. We should not be able, as I think most
Americans believe, to maintain what we regard as a Government of free people, if some individual, whether from good
or bad motives, were able successfully to violate a statute,
duly and constitutionally and properly passed, because his
own view of the same might differ from that entertained by
the law makers who have enacted the law, and from that of
the Executive who has given it his approval.

Now that is my point of view, based upon a system whose
perpetuity rests upon obedience of the law.

It may often be that a man or woman has greater foresight than the masses of the people. And it may be that in
the history of things, he, who seems to be wrong today, may

be right tomorrow. But with those possible idealistic and academic speculations a Court has nothing to do. . . .

You have made my task this morning an entirely easy one. I have no difficulty in concluding how your case will be treated, because at the moment you represent one extreme of thought, and in my capacity at the moment, I represent another. I cannot emphasize too strongly that in my view, not only could this war not have been successfully and in a self-respecting way carried on by the United States Government if such an attitude as yours had prevailed, but I think such an attitude would have led inevitably to disorder and finally to the destruction of a Government, which with all of the imperfections that may attach to human government, has proved itself, as I view it, to be a real people's Government, as evidenced by the millions upon millions of men who voluntarily obey the laws—and some of them requiring great sacrifice—which, as enacted by the legislature, embody the judgment of the people at large.

Now in such circumstances, you representing the utterly contrary view, you representing—although possibly not meaningly—a position which in my judgment if carried out would mean the subversion of all the principles dear to the American people, and the ultimate destruction of the Republic, there is nothing left for me to do except to impose the full penalty of the statute. It would be obviously most unwise to permit you to go into the army now, and there become a disturbing element and cause the military authorities only an increase to the many great and difficult problems with which they are now dealing. The case is one, from the standpoint of the penalty to be imposed, no different from that which has been imposed in many similar cases. The maximum penalty, as I understand it, is one year in the penitentiary. You have already spent twenty days in imprisonment. You ask for no compromise. You will get no compromise. You are sentenced to the penitentiary for eleven months and ten days.

25. From *Political Prisoners in Federal Military Prisons, 1918.* *

Part of the work of the National Civil Liberties Bureau during World War I was to publish the reports it received of prison brutalities against conscientious objectors. By this method, the organization hoped to bring pressure to bear on the War Department and on the prison administrations to ameliorate conditions.

The National Civil Liberties Bureau has come into possession of information regarding conditions in the military prisons of the United States which it believes it would not be justified in withholding from the public. These prisons, called Disciplinary Barracks, are located at Fort Jay, Governors Island, New York; Fort Leavenworth, Kansas; and Alcatraz Island, San Francisco Bay. Concerning the last named prison we have at present no information. The other two are fairly well run as prisons go, with the exception of the form of punishment for recalcitrant prisoners which consists of solitary confinement in dark cells, manacling and a diet of bread and water. The conditions are described in the following documents. Primarily this protest has nothing to do with the offence for which the prisoners were sentenced. The first point is that torture inflicted upon any prisoner for any reason is as stupid as it is wicked and abhorrent to the American spirit. The second point is the justice of a distinction between political and criminal offenders.

I. Statement of conditions at Fort Jay, on August 20, as reported by Dr. Judah L. Magnes and Mr. John S. Codman.

August 27, 1918.

Mr. John S. Codman of Boston and I went to Governors Island on the 3:15 boat and returned on the 6:30 boat.

Major Ward received us very courteously, and gave us every opportunity to interview the three conscientious objectors, and to examine the conditions under which they are now imprisoned.

* (New York: National Civil Liberties Bureau, 1918.)

He took us to the cells where Sterenstein and Eichel are in solitary confinement. . . . The door of Sterenstein's cell was opened first. We found him with his wrists shackled to the iron bars of the small opening in the door. He was in his underwear and in bare feet. There was no pail in his cell. The only thing in the cell was a blanket. When Eichel's cell was opened, we found him shackled in the same way to the bars of the grating in the door. He was in his underclothes and had on one stocking. There was a pail in his cell.

Major Wood explained to us that they were sentenced to solitary confinement for refusing to work, and to obey prison instructions.* They were shackled to the bars of the grating from 7:30 A.M. to 11:30 A.M. and then from 12:30 to 4:30 P.M.—The theory being that this is equivalent to an eight-hour working day. They are given two slices of bread three times a day and a pitcher of water three times a day. They are given no water with which to wash. If they wish to wash, they must use some of their drinking water. They are not permitted a tooth brush. They are taken on Saturday night and given a shower-bath.

After 14 days of such confinement, the prisoners are released into the prison yard for 14 days. They are given raw food, an ax for chopping wood, cooking utensils, and

---

* Such refusal to work will be found throughout these documents to be one of the chief sources of difficulty between the conscientious objector and the military. To the average reader it may seem difficult to understand and quite indefensible. The objectors' position may be clarified by the following explanation:

(a) In certain cases, the objectors felt that the work assigned to them amounted to the non-combatant service which they had refused in the first place because it relieved other men to do the very work in the army to which they were conscientiously opposed. Other objectors considered that the mere acceptance of work under military orders was a recognition of the whole principle of conscription which they are convinced must be everywhere condemned before the world can ever become safe for real democracy.

(b) At Fort Leavenworth all but a few of the objectors had consented to work, but a number finally ceased working, not so much because they were opposed to the work itself, but because such a stand was the only effective way by which to register their protest against the brutal treatment of fellow prisoners in solitary confinement. Rather than acquiesce in such wrong they would share their suffering.

shelter at night. Otherwise they are regarded as men on a desert island, bound to shift for themselves. If, after these 14 days of desert island life, they are still unwilling to yield their conscientious convictions, they are placed in solitary confinement again for another 14 days. This can go on indefinitely for the term of 20 or 30 years, to which these men have been sentenced, or until they are broken, either physically or mentally. . . .

[Sterenstein] came into the room blinking because of the light, after the darkness of his cell. He had been permitted to put on his prison garb. We were very grateful that because of our visit both he and Eichel were given a few minutes' respite from their shackles. Sterenstein had quite a heavy growth of beard. (The prisoners in solitary confinement not being permitted, of course, to shave.) He seemed to be physically the weakest of the three. He informed us that he had been sentenced to 30 years for refusing inoculation and refusing to work. Neither he nor Eichel had been adjudged as insincere by Judge Mack's Board [of Inquiry]. It was his opinion that he and Eichel were being kept at Fort Jay because it was necessary for the authorities to subject a few men to severe punishment as an example to others. Other men who held precisely the same views, and who had refused to obey certain orders, had been transferred to Fort Leavenworth. He said that as a Socialist and humanitarian it was not possible for him to do anything to further the war; that he realized his life did not belong to him at a time when thousands of men were losing their lives, and that he was ready to be shot if only in that way he might give testimony to the faith that was in him. When he and Eichel came to Fort Jay they were undecided to as whether or not they would work on the stone pile. They worked on the stone pile for one day, and then came to the conclusion that it was wrong to do this because they would then be relieving some other men for military work. They thereupon refused to do other prison work, and were placed in solitary confinement for this. Major Ward later cited their one day's work as conclusive evidence of their insincerity. Sterenstein complained of the petty annoyances to which the objectors were being treated by some of the guards. He was ready to serve his complete sentence without flinching but did not think that they should be subjected to severer treatment than their sentence called for. He said

that guards had beaten up at least two men to his knowledge, one of them in a cell, and that Major Ward himself
had declared that one man would have to be beaten up,
inasmuch as that was the only way to deal with him. Major Ward declared afterwards that as far as he knew, no
man had been beaten up at the prison for a whole year.
Sterenstein said that at certain times of the day some
rays of light came into his cell, so that it was possible for
him to read surreptitiously. He pulled out a tattered copy
of the New Testament from his stocking, saying that he
had been able to conceal this. He complained of the trouble the vermin gave at night. He thought also that if he
might be permitted, when shackled, to stand in his shoes,
it would be easier for him because he had flat feet. He had
a handkerchief during the 14 days, inasmuch as there was
one in his clothes. No handkerchief had been offered him
by the authorities. When asked if he objected to our re-
peating some of his remarks, he said that he was entirely
willing to suffer any reprisal that might be meted out, if
only the cause of the conscientious objector might thus be
helped.

Eichel appeared to be stronger physically than Sterenstein, and just as steadfast in his determination to hold out
as long as he could. His attitude was practically the same
as that of Sterenstein. There was no discrepancy between
the statements of any of the three prisoners. Eichel was
particularly anxious to have his family know that he was
still at Fort Jay. They had not been permitted to hear from
their families.

As a result of our complaint to the War Department, based
upon this and other reports, the conscientious objectors in
question were transferred to Fort Leavenworth, where the
cells are said to be more sanitary, but the use of these cells
at Fort Jay for the punishment of recalcitrant prisoners still
continues to this day.

II. Statements as to conditions at the Disciplinary Barracks,
Fort Leavenworth, Kansas.

This is the chief military prison in the United States. At this
time it contains approximately 3,000 prisoners, of whom
about 300 are conscientious objectors. Most of these latter

are under sentences ranging from 10 to 30 years. Whatever the particular charges on which they were courtmartialed, they are imprisoned for one reason only and that is their steadfast refusal on religious or other conscientious grounds to accept any form of conscript service under military authority.

The documents which follow come from prisoners whose names we cannot publicly disclose but who are known to us to be trustworthy:

1. Bulletin on conditions within the prison as they were about Nov. 6.

Evan W. Thomas finally refused to continue work . . . and the following day he was put in solitary confinement. His final statement was that, in going to the "hole," he was protesting against the entire prison system as well as the fact that conscientious objectors are not distinguished from ordinary criminals and against the mistreatment of individual conscientious objectors.

He believes that officials here are acting according to instructions from authorities in Washington.

He plans to remain in "solitary" until he collapses physically, if conditions are not changed.

Nine conscientious objectors, serving long sentences at the U.S. Disciplinary Barracks for refusal to submit to military conscription, are in solitary confinement in the institution because they have declined to engage in prison labor. . . .

Five of these men have been brutally beaten and manhandled since they arrived.

These nine men are handcuffed and chained by their wrists to the bars of the door, for nine hours a day in darkened cells. The solitary cells here are in the sub-basement of the prison. Prisoners in such confinement are rationed on bread and water. Most of these executive sentences are for fourteen days, but some of the objectors have been in solitary thirty, forty, or even, in one case, fifty days. . . .

Following is a list of the nine conscientious objectors enduring solitary punishment:

Thomas Reed (colored), religious, arrived from Fort Jay, N.Y., on Sept. 13th, in solitary since Sept. 15th.

Hyman Bloch, religious, from Camp Funston, Sept. 20th, in solitary since Nov. 4th.

Jacob Wurtzman, socialist, from Fort Riley, Nov. 4th.

Henry Monsky, socialist, from Camp Funston, Nov. 4th.

Abraham Gelerter, orthodox Jew, from Fort Jay, Sept. 13th.

Jake Conovaloff, religious, Camp Funston, Oct. 20th.

Fred Uren, religious, Camp Funston, Oct. 20th.

Morris Shuben, religious, Camp Funston, Nov. 2nd.

Andre Shuben, religious, Camp Funston, Oct. 28th.

Prisoners, including at least two conscientious objectors, witnessed the brutal treatment given Dan Yoder and S. Herschberger, both from Camp Sherman, Ohio, Nov. 1st, and their accounts are substantially as follows:

These men are members of the Amish Mennonite sect, one of the religious rules of which forbids the wearing of clothes fastened by buttons. Upon their arrival, they refused to don the uniform of military offenders. They were taken to the clothing storeroom, and undressed forcibly by sentries and were put into prison clothes.

Sergeant Morris, foreman of the clothing storeroom, then took the two prisoners to the bathroom. There they again refused to co-operate. Again they were disrobed roughly. They were led under the cold showers and held there for between ten and fifteen minutes.

Herschberger took the coarse "laundry" soap that was forced upon him, and washed himself. Yoder was led, or almost dragged, by the hair, shivering and crying noisily. Sgt. Morris, who was holding him, still by the hair, then ordered all the warm water to be turned off. Yoder refused to wash himself. The sergeant took a large cake of soap and a heavy fibre brush and began to scrub him, rubbed the soap up and down over his face and roughly applied the scrubbing brush to his body.

They refused to put on the uniform. Herschberger dried himself and was dressed by other prisoners and sentries. Yoder, in the hands of the sergeant, was knocked down onto the cold cement floor. Without being dried, he was forced into the uniform. During this process his head was held between the knees of Sgt. Morris. When his underclothes were on, the sergeant lifted him up by the ears. This treatment has caused these two men to submit to prison labor, against their beliefs.

Instances can be multiplied. Gelerter, when he refused to drill, was beaten by sentries before he was put into solitary.

Even there he was deprived of his phylactery, a religious article, indispensable to him. Uren and A. Shuben were beaten in the Executive Office. Corporal Harry Hunter inflicted the bodily punishment in these last cases. His actions were unauthorized and, in consequence, he has been suspended as yard corporal. . . .

[Evan W.] Thomas has stated briefly how most of the political conscientious objectors regard this situation. When he submitted his letter to Colonel Sedgewick Rice, the commandant, he was read an order from Washington, stating that C.O.'s who have been sentenced shall be treated as the ordinary criminal soldier.

2. Extract from letter written Nov. 7th.

You will wonder at my sanity if I tell you that I am trying to pick a vegetarian existence out of the limited rations in the mess hall. There are several of us now. . . .

The Russians from Riley came out of confinement yesterday wan and staggering. They have gone to work. Both are religious objectors. Some of the Russians now in confinement have gone through the worst experiences in jail which the worst of the Tzars had to offer. They say that there they were permitted to cook their own food and were let alone. They swear that their life there was easy in comparison to this.

Fellows who came from Camp Sherman last week declined to don the prison garb.* Two of them persisted. They were beaten into submission and the clothes were forced on them. For a time one of them wore his bundle around his neck, refusing to touch it, but he, too, was forcibly dressed. It is said that a Captain witnessed the original beating and that he turned his back and walked off without interceding. The sentries to whom he left the job dragged the boys to the bathroom and treated them to Gelerter's experience, scrubbing the flesh of one with the ubiquitous galvanic soap and a coarse scrubbing brush. The water was so cold that the rest of us spent scarcely three minutes under it and retreated. Yet these C.O.'s were held under it for nearly fifteen minutes. Corporal _____ is being tried for beating up two Russians—Holy Jumpers from

* From other sources, we learn that this was because of religious scruples against wearing buttons.

Texas—for their refusal to salute and work. He administered one of his pummelings in the office of the Executive Officer who himself had to stop the struggle. But he is being tried because his specific act was not authorized. The "hole" treatment is known by everyone in all its details and is accepted by the authorities. . . .

3. Letters of Nov. 14 and 15 on the situation to date.

Box 60, Fort Leavenworth,

Nov. 14.

My dear ———

. . . .

Several Russians—Holy Jumpers from Arizona—have been hunger striking in the hole. Two of them were beaten so bestially that even the authorities were shocked and the sentry is to be courtmartialed. The sentry is being tried, however, only because he exceeded his authority. The other beatings and tortures are matters of general knowledge and are accepted by the authorities as justifiable. These Russians were so weak at the end of six days that two of them had to be sent to the hospital—veritable ghosts. . . . They are ready to die in this dungeon. Their courage, so firm and beautiful, shames the others of us. . . .

Evan Thomas, Howard Moore, Rose of Philadelphia, Hennessy and about 20 others are now in the pit. They are protesting against the brutalities and tortures, compulsory work, compulsory chapel on Sunday and against the imprisonment itself. The local officers are relentless in punishing this breach of discipline and promise one man a courtmartial, I am told, as a lesson to the rest of us. . . . But from Washington we hope that some recognition of the condition may be drawn. . . .

"Very truly yours,

"(Signed) ———

4. Documents illustrating the reason why some of the men quit work in protest against the punishment of certain of their comrades.

    (a) Letter of Prisoner No. 14822 to the Adjutant General, Washington, D.C.

U.S. Disciplinary Barracks,
Fort Leavenworth,
Nov. 5th, 1918.

From:
General Prisoner Evan W. Thomas,
Serial Number 14822, U.S. Disciplinary Barracks,
Ft. Leavenworth, Kansas.
To:
The Adjutant General, Washington, D.C.
Subject:
Treatment of Conscientious Objectors.
Sir:
In a letter written by you dated August 18th, 1918, to
David E. Eichel at Fort Riley, Kansas, you declared that
it is not the policy of the government to coerce the con-
science of individual objectors, but that, on the other
hand, great and liberal concessions have been made to
conscientious objectors. I know that the same impression
has been given by the government to many other individuals through letters as well as through the public statements of officials.

Yet the fact remains that in accordance with the regulations a number of the many conscientious objectors, now
confined in the Disciplinary Barracks here, are in solitary
confinement, chained to the bars of their cells nine hours
a day for conscience sake. I have been witness of the mental
anguish through which some of the men have gone because they could not work in this institution, no matter
what the consequences might be. I myself have on repeated occasions before coming here declared to army
officers that I would not work in the Disciplinary Barracks
if the consciences of others were coerced or if the work
was the same as non-combatant service in the army.

Nevertheless since my arrival here on Oct. 20th, I have
been working. It is not my desire, even if it were possible,
to interfere with the discipline of this institution, nor do
I believe that that is the intention of the objectors now in
solitary confinement. But the fact remains that in spite of
the many liberal statements made by the government, the
conscientious objector is being treated exactly as the recalcitrant or criminal soldier.

In view of the explicit promises made by the government,

cannot some provision be made to relieve the situation here?

Respectfully yours,
(Signed)   EVAN W. THOMAS.

The facts which we have cited raise two issues:

(1) The use of torture in military prisons to enforce obedience. This is as unnecessary as it is barbarous. Conscientious objectors may be rendering a real social service in calling attention to the use of solitary confinement, such as we have described, to which ordinary military offenders have been subjected for years.

(2) Political prisoners, of whom conscientious objectors are one group, should be distinguished from ordinary offenders against the criminal law. Such is the almost universal practice in Europe. In Great Britain, the so-called "absolutists" objectors were never confined in military prisons and no sentences exceeded two years. This policy was carried out in the heat of the war. Our own government has repeatedly declared its intention not to coerce the conscience of any recognized objector, yet by confining these men in military prisons, it raises the question of coercion in an acute form. From the standpoint of the well-being of the State, as truly as of the ancient American liberties of conscience and free speech, what possible good end is served by the indefinite confinement of political prisoners who are eager to render useful service outside prison walls? The situation is urgent. This torture can have but one end—the utter breaking of the men in body, mind or spirit.

No solution of this problem short of complete pardon will satisfy the generosity or sense of fair play of the American people. But, in the meantime, it is our particular purpose to urge (a) the immediate release of men now chained in solitary confinement and the permanent abolition of this and similar obsolete forms of discipline in military prisons; (b) the recognition of the status of conscientious objectors as political prisoners.

26. Statement by the Secretary of War, 1918.*

Evidence that the work of the National Civil Liberties Bureau was, at least in some measure, successful is this communiqué issued at the end of 1918 by the War Department.

From the War Department News Bureau

No. 9

Immediate release   December 6, 1918

The Secretary of War authorizes the following statement:

Disciplinary regulations in force in military prisons have been modified by the War Department Order. Fastening of prisoners to the bars of cells will no more be used as a mode of punishment. This and milder devices have been effective in the past in breaking the willful or stubborn opposition of prisoners of the usual military type, who would not submit to the work requirements of disciplinary barracks. Instead of being allowed to lie in bunks while others worked, they have been compelled to choose between working or standing in discomfort during working hours. Practically, under usual conditions, this has been more a threat than an actuality, and as such it has been effective. But during recent months, with the influx of political prisoners to disciplinary barracks, particularly Fort Leavenworth [Kansas], extremity of attitude on the part of this new type of prisoner has at times led to extremity of discipline, as provided by military regulations. These clearly were not formulated with the political type of prisoner in mind, and their effectiveness as deterrents has been questionable. Men have returned for repeated experiences of the severest forms of discipline. The most extreme of these is now discarded and the order is comprehensive. It applies not merely to political prisoners, but to those of every type.

* Quoted in Thomas, *op. cit.,* pp. 195–96.

27. From *The Congressional Record*: On Conscientious Objectors, 1919.*

Sympathy for pacifists was by no means typical of the nation at large. The following excerpt from The Congressional Record *reveals the animus felt by one congressman and his constituency against "German sympathizers and craven cowards." Army personnel, similarly, had little sympathy for pacifists and were openly hostile to political objectors and atheists. The statement of Major Frank S. White, Jr., of Camp Funston, which was read into the record, helps to explain why conditions at that particular camp had become so exacerbated that a Congressional Inquiry had been instituted.*

The SPEAKER. The Chair recognizes the gentleman from Minnesota [Mr. Newton] for 20 minutes.

Mr. NEWTON of Minnesota. Mr. Speaker, immediately following the adjournment of Congress I spent several weeks in France, Belgium, and Germany going over the war-swept areas of France and Belgium. It was my privilege to visit the battle fields, including the area around Chateau-Thierry, including a little wood near there known as Belleau Wood, made forever famous by the valiant fighting of the Fifth and Sixth Marine Regiments. I followed the pathway of the glorious Rainbow Division, representing, as it did, 26 of the States of our Union, including a Minnesota regiment—the One hundred and fifty-first Field Artillery. I saw where it pounded its way through the German lines into the St. Mihiel salient. Then I traveled through the scene of the great Meuse-Argonne conflict, the greatest of American battles, where over 26,000 American soldiers paid the last supreme measure of devotion and countless other thousands added new luster to American arms.

Among these valiant men in these various conflicts were many young men from my own city—the city of Minneapolis. Early in the spring of 1917 the high schools and the State University in my city furnished 600 of their young men, eager

* 66th Congress, 1st Session (Washington, 1919), pp. 3063–66.

to be the "first to fight." They joined the Marine Corps. Others joined our efficient National Guard regiments or went into the Regular Army, while still more, accepting their country's call, went in to swell the ranks of the great National Army. Here and there I visited the battle-field cemeteries where rested the fallen.

On my return, in speaking before the Marine Fathers' Association of Minneapolis, telling them somewhat of my experiences, at the close of my talk I was asked, as a Member of Congress, to use my best efforts to find out who was responsible for the consideration, sympathy, and undue favor shown to so-called conscientious objectors. The one making the request had a son in the service. He voiced the sentiments of not only every father and mother there present but of every parent whose son had willingly responded to the call of country. He also voiced the sentiments of numerous men in the service who could not understand the policy of the Government toward the man who would not fight.

From the fall of 1917 until the present time everyone has known that numerous conscienceless objectors, consisting of pro-Germans, I. W. W., political Socialists, and cowardly slackers, were being exempted from all military service; that they were being shown special consideration in the camps, and were not being held to obey military law or to submit to military discipline. These were not mere idle rumors, for practically everyone with friends in the various camps knew these conditions to be true. There was in the minds of many a pressing inquiry as to who was responsible. Was it Congress? No; it was not Congress. The selective-service law, passed on May 18, 1917, contained this provision:

(i) Any person who is found by such local board to be a member of any well-recognized religious sect or organization organized and existing May 18, 1917, and whose then existing creed or principles forbid its members to participate in war in any form, and whose religious convictions are against war or participation therein in accordance with the creed or principles of said religious organization. —Any such person upon presentation to such local board at any time within 10 days after the filing of a claim for discharge by or in respect of such person, of an affidavit made by such person stating that he is a member in good faith and in good standing of a well-recognized religious sect or organization (giving the name thereof) organized and existing May 18, 1917, and whose then existing creed or principles forbid its members to participate in war in any form, and that his religious convictions are against war or participation therein in accordance with the creed or principles of said religious organization. And upon the presentation to such local board of an affidavit made by the clerk or minister of the well-recognized religious sect or organization to which such person claiming exemption is a member, stating that said person is a member of said religious sect or organization, which was well recognized and was organized and existing May 18, 1917, and that the then existing creed or principles of said religious sect or organization forbid its members to participate in war in any form; and upon presentation by affidavits of such other evidence as may be required in the opinion of the local board to substantiate the claim of any such person.

Said act of Congress provides, section 3:

But no person so exempted shall be exempted from service in any capacity that the President shall declare to be noncombatant.

In case any such person substantiates, in the opinion of the local board, his claim, such local board shall issue a certificate stating that such person shall not be required or compelled to serve in any capacity except in some capacity declared by the President to be noncombatant.

Note, to be exempt from combatant service he must personally have religious convictions against war. Those convictions must be in accordance with the then existing creed of a religious organization and of which he must have been a member. Failing in any one of these particulars, exemption could not be given. The individual with mere conscientious scruples against war was not exempt. The individual with conscientious religious scruples against war must serve. The only exemption was to a member of a religious organization with an existing creed against war which he believed in and subscribed to, and even in that event persons were exempt from combatant service only. Congress in that way tried to prevent the law from exempting only those who by long religious training and association had conscientious convictions against war.

This remained the law throughout the war. The exemption proviso framed by Congress did not include the pro-German, the I. W. W., the political Socialist, or cowardly slacker. This was the expression of Congress upon the subject.

Congress, then, was not responsible. Was it the draft boards? No.

The selective-service regulations further safeguarded the law by providing for the filing of affidavits with the draft board and the issuance by the board of a certificate exempting the person certified thereon from combatant service only. The draftee had to report at the camp and await his assignment by military authorities to noncombatant service. On the whole, the draft boards conscientiously carried out the law and the regulations to the very letter. In my district and, as I am advised, throughout the country they were made up of patriotic, high-grade men, who performed their duties well.

My investigation disclosed that the responsibility was not with Congress nor with the draft boards, but rested entirely upon the War Department. I propose now to demonstrate this by documentary evidence of the department itself.

First. The Secretary of War issued his order setting aside the selective-draft act relating to conscientious objectors and enlarging the exemption clause, thereby permitting the I. W. W., the pro-German, the political Socialist, and cowardly slacker to evade military service both combatant and noncombatant.

Second. The War Department, through the Secretary, supplied information to and cooperated with an organization formed to enable men to evade the draft.

Third. It issued orders to the various cantonment commanders kindly, considerately, and specially to treat and deal with the so-called conscientious objectors, going so far as to engage sympathetic men to travel about the country at the expense of the Government to see to it that such treatment was in fact accorded.

Fourth. These orders were issued covertly, accompanied by instructions enjoining secrecy.

As to the first proposition: On December 10, 1917, the Secretary issued his order directing "that personal scruples against war" should be considered as constituting "conscientious objections."

Note carefully the language of the order given:

[Confidential.]

December 10, 1917

From: The Adjutant General of the Army.

To: The commanding generals of all National Army and National Guard camps except Camp Grant.

Subject: Conscientious objectors.

1. The Secretary of War directs that until further instructions on the subject are issued "personal scruples against war" should be considered as constituting "conscientious objections" and such persons should be treated in the same manner as other "conscientious objectors" under the instructions contained in confidential letter from this office dated October 10, 1917.

2. Under no circumstances should these instructions be communicated to the newspapers.

H. G. Learnard,
Adjutant General.

Here was a deliberate change and enlargement of the exemption proviso in palpable violation of law and by the exercise of authority which the Secretary did not possess. What right had the Secretary of War to legislate? What power did he possess to amend an act of Congress? Under the term "personal scruples" the I. W. W., pro-German, political Socialist, and cowardly slacker sought and obtained exemption. The I. W. W. could qualify thereunder, for he had scruples against war and certainly they were personal. The pro-German could qualify, for personally he loved Germany better than America, and he had scruples against waging war against Germany. His reasons were personal. The same would apply to certain political Socialists and slackers seeking exemption. Their reasons also were "personal" and they "scrupled" against making war on behalf of any country, many of them despising the institutions of their own country. This change was made advisedly. I call attention to the memorandum of the Secretary of War to the General Staff bearing date December 8, 1918:

The so-called conscientious objectors present a novel problem in military administration. To some extent the novelty and difficulty of this problem was recognized by the Congress, which made express provision for a part of the general class. However, when the law came to be administered it was found that only certain varieties of religious experience had been adequately provided for, and that other varieties of religious obligation and the whole class of conscientious objection based upon ethical considerations and not directly associated with formal religious beliefs was unprovided for. The President, as Commander in Chief of the Army, thereupon laid down a definite policy for the administration of the law, and the discipline of those called to the service who were affected by any of these forms of conscientious objection not specifically included within the limits of the statute.

This order constitutes a perversion of the Federal statute. Congress did not make provision for a part only of a general class, but in accurate and certain terms defined the class of persons to be considered conscientious objectors. And by careful reservations and restrictions eliminated the very persons included in the Secretary's order. In other words, the Secretary of War, as the administrative officer, did not confine himself to an application of the act of Congress, but treated the act as an elastic thing to be stretched by him to cover such persons as in his judgment should have been included by the Congress.

One variety of conscientious objector was not enough for the Secretary of War. He would add thereto; he would change and amend the act of Congress so as to include Heinz's 57 varieties of conscientious objectors. . . .

I quote from the following order of the Secretary of War commanding that kindly and special consideration be given these men:

[Confidential.]
Exhibit 6.

October 10, 1917

From: The Adjutant General of the Army.
To: The commanding generals of all National Army and National Guard division camps.
Subject: Conscientious objectors.
1. The Secretary of War directs that you be instructed to segregate the conscientious objectors in their divisions and to place them under supervision of instructors who shall be specially selected with a view of insuring that these men will be handled with tact and consideration and that their questions will be answered fully and frankly.

2. With reference to their attitude of objecting to military service these men are not to be treated as violating military laws, thereby subjecting themselves to the penalties of the Articles of War, but their attitude in this respect will be quietly ignored and they will be treated with kindly consideration. Attention in this connection is invited to a case where a number of conscientious objectors in one of our divisions, when treated in this manner, renounced their original objections to military service and voluntarily offered to give their best efforts to the service of the United States as soldiers.

3. It is desired that after the procedure above indicated shall have been followed for a sufficient length of time to afford opportunity to judge of the results derived from it, a report of the action taken and the results obtained under these instructions be submitted to the War Department by each division commander. As a result of the consideration of all these reports further instructions will be issued by the Secretary of War as to the policy to be observed in future in the case of conscientious objectors.

4. Under no circumstances are the instructions contained in the foregoing to be given to the newspapers.

> H. G. Learnard,
> Adjutant General.

This order needs no comment.

I quote further from the letter of the Secretary of War bearing date of June 1, 1918:

If, however, any drafted man, upon his arrival at camp, either through the presentation of a certificate from his local board or by written statement addressed by himself to the commanding officer, shall record himself as a conscientious objector, he shall not, against his will, be required to wear a uniform or to bear arms; nor if, pending the final decision as to his status, he shall decline to perform, under military direction, duties which he states to be contrary to the dictates of his conscience, shall he receive punitive treatment for such conduct.

Is it not extending undue consideration, is it not disgusting coddling, to permit a soldier to fix his status in the Army by an unsworn statement that "I object"?

Even this was insufficient for this zealous and sympathetic friend of the so-called conscientious objector. Following the issuance of these orders a special board* consisting of a military officer and two civilians, was appointed to visit the camps and to see that this special consideration was being uniformly given these men. Moreover, in violation of the letter and spirit of the law, men who refused noncombatant service were furloughed to work on the farm; and for fear that the farmer would mistreat this citizen, additional help was employed for the purpose of protecting this governmental favorite against the farmer's exploitation. I quote from a letter of the Third Assistant Secretary of War to the Secretary of War, bearing date June 13, 1919:

> In placing men that enjoy the cooperation of the Department of Agriculture we engage a special commissioner to look after the details of their assignment and to see, on the one hand, that they perform their duty efficiently, and, on the other hand, that they are not exploited.

Would that the department had shown one part of the consideration for the fighting men who unwittingly transgressed military laws and regulations that they did for the so-called conscientious objector! [Applause.] . . .

What was the result of this course of catering and coddling? Maj. Frank S. White, Jr., camp judge advocate at Camp Funston, a resident of Birmingham, Ala., in a public interview, said:

> Camp Funston was selected as a dumping ground for the segregation of a large number of these so-called conscientious objectors. The military authorities had no trouble whatever in dealing with those having religious scruples against engaging in combatant service. They all readily accepted such noncombatant service as was assigned to them. There was, however, a large number of alleged conscientious objectors, who, when selected under the draft act, made no claim that they had religious scruples against fighting, but pretended to have conscientious objections based upon the view of the obligations which they owed to the country.

MOSTLY FOREIGN RADICALS.

They were composed in the main of German, Austrian, and Russian Socialists, and I. W. W., who openly denied the

---

* The special board referred to is described in Document 22 in this book. [Editor's note.]

right of the United States to induct them into the military service, some of whom had endeavored to get commissions in the Army and after having failed to do so, when drafted, conveniently found themselves opposed to engaging in military service, and then, when ordered to perform noncombatant duty, openly declared that they owed this country no duty, refused to obey any order from a military source, thereby defying the military arm of the Government.

These men had conspired together and refused to obey the lawful commands of a superior officer to wear the uniform of the United States Army or to take a rake and rake up hay and load it on a wagon; or to police up around their own quarters. Charges had been preferred against them for violation of the sixty-fourth article of war, and they were in confinement in the provost guardhouse awaiting trial or result of trial by general court-martial.

DID NOT BELIEVE IN DEITY.

The selective-service law exempted from combatant service all persons who because of religious belief claimed exemption from military service, but no person so exempted from combatant service was exempted from noncombatant service. These men did not come within the purview of the act affording exemption from military service to sincere, religious objectors. They were admittedly Socialists and proven to be pro-Germans, who did not believe in Deity, and whose aim was to spread insidious and treasonable propaganda throughout this country, and were actually caught in disseminating it in this military camp, which was subversive of all discipline and destructive of the morale of our Army.

The act referred to was never intended, as the War Department interpreted it, to extend exemption to men such as those, who were nothing less than slackers and cowards or pro-Germans. If men of this character were not dealt with promptly and vigorously the whole principle of universal service would fall to the ground. These simulated objectors were confined with a large number of general prisoners and with these other prisoners, under military custom, were required to police their quarters and around their premises. This they openly and defiantly refused to do, throwing their share of the work upon the other prisoners, dissatisfying them, and setting before these other prisoners this example of disobedience and defiance of authority.

ENCOURAGED FROM OUTSIDE.

They would even refuse to march in orderly formation to and from their mess, but would straggle along as they saw fit, and when being ordered out to mess or exercise they would stand in the doorway and block it so that the guards or other persons could not pass, defying the guards and officers to move them; they refused to take exercise, baths, and keep their bodies and belongings clean and in a sanitary condition; they refused to be vaccinated or inoculated in order to safeguard themselves as well as their fellow soldiers from sickness and disease. In fact, they refused to obey and apparently took pleasure in letting it be known that they would take no part under the Military Establishment nor obey any military command whatever. In their attitude they repeatedly let it be known that they were receiving encouragement from outside sources and claiming they would be protected in their attitude by the War Department.

To illustrate their recalcitrant attitude, if the meals which were provided for them and other prisoners did not suit them they would engage in throwing the dishes, camp stools, and their mess kits around the mess hall, acting in the most mutinous and disorderly manner. When ordered to stand at attention by officers engaged in inspection duty, they would refuse to assume a proper position; in order to provoke these officers they would defiantly put their feet as far apart as possible and make grimaces at them, asking them what they were going to to about it.

In brief, Maj. White claims that as a result of the law as amended by the Secretary of War the camps were infested with I. W. W., German sympathizers, and even craven cowards —men who would not fight nor even obey mere police and health regulations of the camp.

The above attitude and the acts connected therewith were the acts of the Secretary of War; but, in addition to that, by reason of the position he occupied and the fact that his attitude in this matter was known to the President, they were also the acts of the President of the United States. For in a letter to the President bearing date July 2, 1918, the Secretary of War informed the Commander in Chief that—

We are now doing all that public opinion will stand in the interest of conscientious objectors and others whose views do not happen to coincide with those of the vast majority of their fellow countrymen.

Yes, indeed; they were doing far more than public opinion would have stood for.

Is it any wonder that the camp officers were warned not to disclose the situation to the newspapers?

Further . . . I now quote from an Executive order of the President issued on March 23, 1918:

2. Persons ordered to report for military service under the above act who have (a) been certified by their local boards to be members of a religious sect or organization as defined in section 4 of said act; or (b) who object to participating in war because of conscientious scruples but have failed to receive certificates as members of a religious sect or organization from their local board, will be assigned to noncombatant military service as defined in paragraph 1 to the extent that such persons are able to accept service as aforesaid without violation of the religious or other conscientious scruples by them in good faith entertained. Upon the promulgation of this order it shall be the duty of each division, camp, or post commander, through a tactful and considerate officer, to present to all such persons the provisions hereof with adequate explanation of the character of noncombatant service herein defined, and upon such explanations to secure acceptances of assignment to the several kinds of noncombatant service above enumerated; and whenever any person is assigned to noncombatant service by reason of his religious or other conscientious scruples, he shall be given a certificate stating the assignment and reason therefor, and such certificate shall thereafter be respected as preventing the transfer of such person from such noncombatant to combatant service by any division, camp, post, or other commander under whom said person may thereafter be called to serve but such certificate shall not prevent the assignment of such person to some other form of noncombatant service with his own consent. So far as may be found feasible by each division, camp, or post commander, future assignments of such persons to noncombatant

military service will be restricted to the several detachments and units of the medical department in the absence of a request for assignment to some other branch of noncombatant service as defined in paragraph 1 hereof. . . .

It will be noted that the President after the congressional definition of conscientious objector inserts the following:

Or who objects to participating in war because of conscientious scruples.

And later on uses the expression "religious or other conscientious scruples."

The only change from the words of his Secretary is that the President uses the term "conscientious scruples" whereas the Secretary uses the term "personal scruples." Both refer to other than religious conscientious objectors. By this Executive order an act of Congress was deliberately amended and enlarged, not in furtherance of the legislative will but in direct conflict therewith. Under the proviso as changed by the Secretary of War and by the President anyone religious or atheistic, believer in a creed or disbeliever, organizationist or individual, a person with convictions against war in existence when war broke out or a person who had conceived these convictions while on his way to the draft board, were brought within this peculiar exemption.

Under the Constitution it is the duty of Congress to raise armies. In raising the Army to wage war against Germany they laid down the principle that in a country where there was equality of opportunity there was a corresponding duty upon our citizens to serve that country and to defend it against enemies, both foreign and domestic, but recognizing that there were a few individuals belonging to certain religious organizations who had subscribed to certain creeds in good faith and had conscientious convictions against shooting their fellow men even in time of war. In deference to such individuals they were exempted from service as combatants, but were expressly directed that notwithstanding these convictions they must serve in a noncombatant capacity.

Congress had determined what constituted a conscientious objector and by implication what did not. Yet the Secretary of War and the President assumed the authority to make addition of the terms "personal scruples" and "conscientious scruples" and to apply perhaps the rule of self-determination and to permit the individual to decide for himself whether or not he would serve his country. In that connection I quote from the letter of the Third Assistant Secretary of War, bearing date September 28, 1918:

To the Committee on Public Information:

It has been the liberal American policy of according a measure of self-determination to the few who in all sincerity have not been able to adjust their minds to the needs of this sudden and desperate emergency.

There can be but one answer to the oft-repeated question as to responsibility for the policy pursued in reference to the conscientious objector. That responsibility rests upon the Secretary of War and the President of the United States. [Applause.]

28. E. E. Cummings, "i sing of Olaf glad and big."*

Edward Estlin Cummings, poet, Harvard graduate, and Harvard M.A., enlisted in the Norton Harjes Ambulance Corps and was sent to France for active duty a full year in advance of America's entry into World War I. His experiences in a French detention camp, and later in the American army gave him an intimate knowledge of war. Yet, like so many other intellectuals and artists, he was opposed to his government's treatment of conscientious objectors. His sense of outrage and injustice explodes in this poem.

> i sing of Olaf glad and big
> whose warmest heart recoiled at war:
> a conscientious object-or
>
> his wellbelovéd colonel(trig
> westpointer most succinctly bred)
> took erring Olaf soon in hand;
> but—though an host of overjoyed
> noncoms(first knocking on the head
> him)do through icy waters roll
> that helplessness which others stroke
> with brushes recently employed
> anent this muddy toiletbowl,
> while kindred intellects evoke
> allegiance per blunt instruments—
> Olaf(being to all intents
> a corpse and wanting any rag
> upon what God unto him gave)
> responds,without getting annoyed
> "I will not kiss your f.ing flag"
>
> straightway the silver bird looked grave
> (departing hurriedly to shave)

* From *Poems, 1923–1954* (New York: Harcourt, Brace & World, Inc., 1954).

but—though all kinds of officers
(a yearning nation's blueeyed pride)
their passive prey did kick and curse
until for wear their clarion
voices and boots were much the worse,
and egged the firstclassprivates on
his rectum wickedly to tease
by means of skilfully applied
bayonets roasted hot with heat—
Olaf(upon what were once knees)
does almost ceaselessly repeat
"there is some s. I will not eat"

our president,being of which
assertions duly notified
threw the yellowsonofabitch
into a dungeon,where he died

Christ(of His mercy infinite)
i pray to see;and Olaf,too

preponderatingly because
unless statistics lie he was
more brave than me:more blond than you.

Part V

PREFACE

In September, 1917, a political radical named Louis Fraina addressed a meeting in New York and challenged the government's right to recognize only religious objectors. "Since when must a man necessarily belong to a church . . . before he can have a conscience?" (See Document 29 in this book.) Fraina went on, pointing out that the government need have nothing to fear from religious objectors, but "it has everything to fear from the non-religious because [he] is not interested in his conscience alone, but . . . is trying to overthrow a system of things that produces war and produces other evils." (See Document 29 in this book.) Fraina's analysis was accurate, but it was not one calculated to win the sympathy of the courts. Predictably, his conviction was upheld; the court found no violation of his rights under the First Amendment.

In *Arver* v. *United States* (1918), the defendant challenged Congress' right to pass Selective Service legislation, contending that conscription was a form of involuntary servitude prohibited under the Thirteenth Amendment. With Wilsonian rhetoric and rectitude, the Supreme Court declared itself "unable to conceive upon what theory the exaction by government from the citizen of the performance of his supreme and noble duty of contribution to the defense of the rights and honor of the nation as the result of a war declared by the great representative body of the people can be said to be the imposition of involuntary servitude of the 13th amendment. . . ."*

The cases of Eugene V. Debs (1919)** and Roger Baldwin*** gave further evidence that the Supreme Court would countenance little dissension from political activists while the nation was at war.

* *Arver* v. *United States,* 245 U.S. 388 (1918).
** *Debs* v. *United States,* 249 U.S. 211 (1919).
*** See Part IV in this book, Document 24.

By the end of the war, the public image of the conscientious objector had undergone a basic transformation. No longer was he recognized as a Quaker or Mennonite, pacifist in demeanor and in doctrine. The term *conscientious objector* had become synonymous with political radical, communist, anarchist, atheist, slacker, "yellowback." So many foreign-born people had swelled the ranks of conscientious objectors that the pacifist disciples of William Penn, as indigenous to America as the Pilgrims, were forgotten. The nation felt itself threatened by the alien and the unorthodox who claimed —and occasionally demanded—not merely tolerance, but, as it seemed, special privilege.

The case of the *United States* v. *Schwimmer* became a *cause célèbre* in its day. In 1928, Mme. Roszika Schwimmer, a Hungarian pacifist who had been one of the leaders of Henry Ford's Peace Ship mission to end World War I, applied for American citizenship, but refused to swear to bear arms in defense of her adopted country. The American Civil Liberties Union carried her appeal to the Supreme Court, but the Court, choosing to ignore the fact that the defendant was a woman of 50 years, held that her refusal to bear arms made her ineligible for citizenship. Justice Sutherland, speaking for the Court, declared "Naturalization is a privilege, to be given, qualified, or withheld as Congress may determine. . . . The conscientious objector is relieved from the obligation to bear arms in obedience to no constitutional provision, express or implied; but because, and only because it has accorded with the policy of Congress thus to relieve him."* (See Document 30 in this book.)

In 1930, the ACLU brought the issue again to the Supreme Court, and again it lost. The plaintiff this time was Professor Douglas C. Macintosh of the Yale Divinity School, a Canadian who declared he would bear arms but only in a war he considered morally justifiable—a line of conscientious objection Americans would hear more often during the years of the Vietnam war. Justices Holmes, Brandeis, Stone, and Hughes dissented, but the majority of the Court upheld the principle established in the Schwimmer case: Citizenship was a privilege bestowed or withheld at the discretion of Congress.**

* Justices Holmes and Brandeis dissented from this opinion.
** In both the Schwimmer and the Macintosh cases, the Supreme Court reversed lower court decisions to grant naturalization.

The right to claim citizenship as an alien and a pacifist was not won until 1946, in the case of *Girouard* v. *United States*. This time, the Supreme Court reversed its position, and held that Girouard, a Canadian Seventh-Day Adventist who declared himself willing to perform noncombatant service, was eligible for citizenship.* The decision gave no hint, however, of whether the Court would reverse itself for an alien who refused noncombatant service, or who, like Macintosh, reserved the right to decide whether the war were just.

Jehovah's Witnesses constituted a special case among conscientious objectors during the Second World War. Their religion required them to fight at Armageddon, so they could not claim to be opposed to all wars; and their church considered each individual member to be a minister of the gospel. Jehovah's Witnesses, therefore, claimed exemption as ministers rather than as conscientious objectors, and they were refused. In July of 1943 there were 1,600 objectors in military prisons, most of them Jehovah's Witnesses. One year later, the total number of conscientious objectors in military prisons rose to 3,000, a large proportion of them Witnesses.

Conscientious objectors often encountered legal difficulties in civilian life too. In 1944, a Methodist pacifist was denied admission to the Illinois bar, which considered him "morally unfit" because his objection to war prohibited him from taking an oath to support the State Constitution, if necessary, by force of arms. The case divided the Supreme Court five to four, but the majority held that Illinois had not violated the Fourteenth Amendment, since a State might determine its own standards of fitness. Justice Black, for the dissenting Justices, declared "I cannot agree that a State can lawfully bar from a semi-public position, a well-qualified man of good caracter solely because he entertains a religious belief which might prompt him at some time in the future to violate a law which has not yet been and may never be enacted." (See Document 33 in this book.)

A new group of conscientious objectors, the so-called nonreligious objectors, brought suits before the courts, petitioning that personal ethical or moral beliefs also constituted

* Seventh-Day Adventists encourage their young men of draft age to accept noncombatant service and even run summer camps where draft age youths can prepare for alternate service with the Medical Corps.

proper bases for c.o. classification. These men were nonreligious only in the sense that they maintained no affiliations with recognized churches. Their objections to war were born out of their own strong ethical precepts. Throughout the 1940's and 1950's, lower court decisions in this area were contradictory. The Supreme Court did not agree to review the question until 1965.*

In sharp contrast to the court's uncertainty as to what constituted proper religious basis for exemption, all courts were in agreement on the matter of the conscientious objector who stated that his opposition to war was social or political rather than religious. Every court denied the appeal of the political objector.

* See Part VII in this book, the Seeger case, Document 38.

29. *Fraina et al.* v. *United States*, 1918.*

In September, 1917, a group of political radicals held a conscientious objectors' meeting in New York City. Louis C. Fraina was among the leaders. In his address, Fraina asked, "Since when must a man necessarily belong to a church, belong to a creed, a recognized creed, before he can have a conscience?" Fraina then distributed pamphlets in which conscientious objectors were urged to refuse all forms of service. It was not difficult to predict the verdict of the courts in his case.

Louis C. Fraina and Edward Ralph Cheyney were convicted of conspiring to commit an offense against the United States by aiding and abetting, etc., unknown persons unlawfully to evade the requirements of the Selective Service Act, and they bring error. Affirmed. . . .

The overt acts enumerated in respect of both counts all consisted of sundry alleged doings of one or both of the plaintiffs in error at what is described as "a mass meeting of so-called conscientious objectors held" within the Southern district of New York. Said overt acts may be summarized thus: Cheyney was chairman of said mass meeting; both plaintiffs in error and other persons, whose names are unknown, distributed certain pamphlets entitled "Conscientious Objectors" at the said meeting. Fraina being the author of said pamphlet, the same purporting to be issued by the "League of Conscientious Objectors," and that Fraina at the said meeting and in a speech there delivered uttered certain words set forth at length.

The applicable language of section 37 is that, "if two or more persons conspire either to commit any offence against the United States, . . . and one or more of such parties do any act to effect the object of the conspiracy, each of the parties" shall be fined or imprisoned.

Section 332 provides: "Whoever . . . aids, abets, counsels, commands, induces or procures" the commission of

* 255 Fed. 28 (2nd Cir. 1918).

"any act constituting an offence in any law of the United States" is a principal.

Section 6 of the Selective Service Act contains these material words: "Any person who . . . evades or aids another to evade the requirements of this act, . . . or who, in any manner, shall fail or neglect fully to perform any duty required of him in the execution of this act," shall be guilty of a misdemeanor.

Plaintiffs in error were acquitted upon the first count and convicted on the second, and, sentence having been passed upon them, they took this writ. . . .

Before ROGERS, HOUGH, and MANTON, Circuit Judges (Second Circuit Court of Appeals)

HOUGH, Circuit Judge (after stating the facts as above). . . .

The facts shown at trial were few, and substantially uncontradicted: Outside a building was a poster announcing a meeting within; inside a large audience and a platform, on which sat defendant Cheyney who presided, defendant Fraina, and one Sonnenschein. Of those present very many were obviously of the age rendering them liable to conscription. Men moved through the audience, distributing gratis a printed speech by Fraina, obtaining the same from the platform on which defendants sat.

Cheyney opened the proceedings with a speech. Most of the sentences began with "I object," and his objections extended to the war with Germany and every step taken to make it effective, also to all war, because "you cannot achieve anything by force." He also denied "the right of any individual to compel me to do anything against my will," and exhorted his hearers "not [to] go across the seas in order to fight a foreign fight" but to fight autocracy "through industrial and economic means." . . .

Fraina then spoke at greater length, though not differing in universal objection from Cheyney. He said inter alia:

We find they are going to conscript the conscientious objector. The conscientious objector refuses to be conscripted. It is against his principle, it is against his conscience to serve in the army, and to perform military service. . . . The government in this conscription law recognizes only those conscientious objectors that are affiliated with some recognized religious association, cult, or creed, such as the Quakers, for instance. Now, the other conscientious objectors are not recognized by the conscription law. . . . But since when must a man necessarily belong to a church, belong to a creed, a recognized creed, before he can have a conscience? . . . The government in making conscientious objection to war a part of religion or creed, is placing a premium upon religion. It is placing a premium upon the superstitions of religion. It is placing a premium upon the passive attitude of the religion of the Quakers. . . .

Now, the nonreligious conscientious objector is a distinctly different type. The nonreligious conscientious objector is one of the people, a social being, and as such has an objection to war. I do not object to war because my father was a Quaker and I inherited his religion. I object to war because I have acquired my conscientious convictions, I have acquired the objection by experience, by thinking, action, and I have felt it flow into my conscience and my life.

The government is perfectly content in placing a premium upon religious conscientious objection, and penalizing the nonreligious ones, because the system of things that this government represents, the infamous system of capitalism, has nothing to fear from the religious conscientious objector; . . . but it has everything to fear from the nonreligious, from the social, conscientious objector, because the nonreligious conscientious objector is not interested in his conscience alone, but interested in his social principle that his conscience represents, and is trying to overthrow a system of things that produces war and produces other evils. . . .

The Fraina pamphlet, distributed as above shown, declares:

. . . The conscientious objector refuses *any* participation in this war, and his refusal is based, not alone upon the objections of his individual conscience, but upon the general social necessity of striking at war and at the reactionary purposes that war promotes. Alternative service is as necessary a factor in war as actual military service at the front. They are inseparable. They are equally objectionable. . . .

This closed for the prosecution. Defendants showed that Sonnenschein organized the meeting, was the "organizer" of what he called "the League of Conscientious Objectors," and on behalf of and in the name of the League had telegraphically demanded of the Secretary of War as follows:

"Representatives of 3,500 conscientious objectors in New York whose idealism compels them to decline all forms of military service, we ask: What of the conscientious objector?"

What the count under consideration seeks to charge is plain enough, viz. it is an offense against the United States to evade the requirements of the Selective Service Act, therefore it is another offense under section 37 to conspire so to evade; but every one who evades being a criminal, every one who counsels evasion is also a criminal, under section 332, and those who unite for the purposes of so counseling are conspirators, and as such liable to the pains and penalties of section 37. . . .

If, as per advertisement, an audience is gathered before a platform containing intending speakers, and is called to order by a chairman, who announces the object of the gathering, again, as per advertisement, it is impossible not to infer a combination. . . .

The matter at bottom is political, not legal. Men can be punished for words, if the Legislature so decrees, within constitutional limits. Men commit crimes when they counsel or procure others to sin against the statute law, and they also commit crimes when they confederate to effect that object, and yet it is difficult to imagine any more suitable or usual method of procuring or counseling than by speech. In this inaccurate sense men have very often been punished for words by statutory enactment.

The free speech secured federally by the First Amendment means complete immunity for the publication by speech or print of whatever is not harmful in character, when tested by such standards as the law affords. For these standards we must look to the common-law rules in force when the constitutional guaranties were established and in reference to which they were adopted. By legislative action the boundaries of unpunishable speech have doubtless and often been much enlarged; but the constitutional limit remains unchanged, and what the Legislature has done it can undo. Legal talk-liberty never has meant, however, "the unrestricted right to say what one pleases at all times and under all circumstances.". . .

The regulations promulgated under the Service Act . . .

[are] reserved for noncombatant service members of any "well-recognized religious sect or organization," and no others, and after that the court as such was concerned only with the law as it stood, not as some persons thought it should be. . . .

30.   *United States* v. *Schwimmer,* 1929.*

Mme. Roszika Schwimmer was a Hungarian pacifist and feminist. In 1915 she was a delegate from Hungary to the International Conference of Women at The Hague and in the same year she was one of the organizers of the Henry Ford Peace Ship Mission. She was appointed Hungarian Minister to Switzerland in 1918, one of the first women to hold a diplomatic post. In 1921 she moved to the United States, and she applied for citizenship in 1926. Because she refused to swear that she would bear arms in defense of this country, her petition was denied by the Supreme Court, with Justices Holmes and Brandeis dissenting.

30.   a.   Majority Opinion.

Mr. Justice Butler delivered the opinion of the Court.

Respondent filed a petition for naturalization in the District Court for the Northern District of Illinois. The court found her unable, without mental reservation, to take the prescribed oath of allegiance and not attached to the principles of the Constitution of the United States and not well disposed to the good order and happiness of the same; and it denied her application. The Circuit Court of Appeals reversed the decree and directed the District Court to grant respondent's petition.

The Naturalization Act of June 29, 1906 requires:

"He [the applicant for naturalization] shall, before he is admitted to citizenship, declare on oath in open court. . . . that he will support and defend the Constitution and laws of the United States against all enemies, foreign and domestic, and bear true faith and allegiance to the same."

"It shall be made to appear to the satisfaction of the court . . . that during that time [at least 5 years preceding the application] he has behaved as a man of good moral character, attached to the principles of the Constitution of

* 279 U.S. 644 (1929).

the United States, and well disposed to the good order and happiness of the same. . . ."

Respondent was born in Hungary in 1877 and is a citizen of that country. She came to the United States in August, 1921, to visit and lecture, has resided in Illinois since the latter part of that month, declared her intention to become a citizen the following November, and filed petition for naturalization in September, 1926. On a preliminary form, she stated that she understood the principles of and fully believed in our form of government and that she had read, and in becoming a citizen was willing to take, the oath of allegiance. Question 22 was this: "If necessary, are you willing to take up arms in defense of this country?" She answered: "I would not take up arms personally."

She testified that she did not want to remain subject to Hungary, found the United States nearest her ideals of a democratic republic, and that she could whole-heartedly take the oath of allegiance. She said: "I cannot see that a woman's refusal to take up arms is a contradiction to the oath of allegiance." . . .

She also testified: "If . . . the United States can compel its women citizens to take up arms in the defense of the country—something that no other civilized government has ever attempted—I would not be able to comply with this requirement of American citizenship. In this case I would recognize the right of the Government to deal with me as it is dealing with its male citizens who for conscientious reasons refuse to take up arms."

The district director of naturalization by letter called her attention to a statement made by her in private correspondence: "I am an uncompromising pacifist. . . . I have no sense of nationalism, only a cosmic consciousness of belonging to the human family." She answered that the statement in her petition demonstrated that she was an uncompromising pacifist. "Highly as I prize the privilege of American citizenship I could not compromise my way into it by giving an untrue answer to question 22, though for all practical purposes I might have done so, as even men of my age—I was 49 years old last September—are not called to take up arms. . . ."

And at the hearing she reiterated her ability and willingness to take the oath of allegiance without reservation and added: "I am willing to do everything that an American citizen has to do except fighting. If American women would be compelled to do that, I would not do that. I am an uncompromising pacifist. . . . I do not care how many other women fight, because I consider it a question of conscience. I am not willing to bear arms. In every other single way I am ready to follow the law and do everything that the law compels American citizens to do." . . .

Except for eligibility to the Presidency, naturalized citizens stand on the same footing as do native born citizens. All alike owe allegiance to the Government, and the Government owes to them the duty of protection. These are reciprocal obligations and each is a consideration for the other. But aliens can acquire such equality only by naturalization according to the uniform rules prescribed by the Congress. They have no natural right to become citizens, but only that which is by statute conferred upon them. . . . And, in order to safeguard against admission of those who are unworthy or who for any reason fail to measure up to required standards, the law puts the burden upon every applicant to show by satisfactory evidence that he has the specified qualifications.

That it is the duty of citizens by force of arms to defend our government against all enemies whenever necessity arises is a fundamental principle of the Constitution.

The common defense was one of the purposes for which the people ordained and established the Constitution. It empowers Congress to provide for such defense, to declare war, to raise and support armies, to maintain a navy, to make rules for the government and regulation of the land and naval forces, to provide for organizing, arming and disciplining the militia, and for calling it forth to execute the laws of the Union, suppress insurrections and repel invasions; it makes the President commander in chief of the army and navy and of the militia of the several States when called into the service of the United States; it declares that a well regulated militia, being necessary to the security of a free State, the right of the people to keep and bear arms, shall not be infringed. We need not refer to the numerous statutes that contemplate defense of the United States, its Constitution and laws by armed citizens. This Court, in the *Selective Draft Law Cases*, 245 U. S. 366, speaking through Chief Justice White, said (p. 378) that "the very conception of a just government and its duty to the citizen includes the reciprocal obligation of the citizen to render military service in case of need." . . .

The influence of conscientious objectors against the use of military force in defense of the principles of our Government is apt to be more detrimental than their mere refusal to bear arms. The fact that, by reason of sex, age or other cause, they may be unfit to serve does not lessen their purpose or power to influence others. . . . And her testimony clearly suggests that she is disposed to exert her power to influence others to such opposition. . . .

It is shown by official records and everywhere well known that during the recent war there were found among those who described themselves as pacifists and conscientious objectors many citizens—though happily a minute part of all—who were unwilling to bear arms in that crisis and who refused to obey the laws of the United States and the lawful commands of its officers and encouraged such disobedience in others. Local boards found it necessary to issue a great number of noncombatant certificates, and several thousand who were called to camp made claim because of conscience for exemption from any form of military service. Several hundred were convicted and sentenced to imprisonment for offenses involving disobedience, desertion, propaganda and sedition. It is obvious that the acts of such offenders evidence a want of that attachment to the principles of the Constitution of which the applicant is required to give affirmative evidence by the Naturalization Act.

The language used by respondent to describe her attitude in respect of the principles of the Constitution was vague and ambiguous; the burden was upon her to show what she meant and that her pacifism and lack of nationalistic sense did not oppose the principle that it is a duty of citizenship by force of arms when necessary to defend the country against all enemies, and that her opinions and beliefs would not prevent or impair the true faith and allegiance required by the Act. She failed to do so. The District Court was bound by the law to deny her application.

The decree of the Circuit Court of Appeals is reversed. The decree of the District Court is affirmed.

30. b. Mr. Justice Holmes, Dissenting.

The applicant seems to be a woman of superior character and intelligence, obviously more than ordinarily desirable as a citizen of the United States. It is agreed that she is qualified for citizenship except so far as the views set forth in a statement of facts "may show that the applicant is not attached to the principles of the Constitution of the United States and well disposed to the good order and happiness of the same, and except in so far as the same may show that she cannot take the oath of allegiance without a mental reservation." The views referred to are an extreme opinion in favor of pacifism and a statement that she would not bear arms to defend the Constitution. So far as the adequacy of her oath is concerned I hardly can see how that is affected by the statement, inasmuch as she is a woman over fifty years of age, and would not be allowed to bear arms if she wanted to. And as to the opinion, the whole examination of the applicant shows that she holds none of the now-dreaded creeds, but thoroughly believes in organized government and prefers that of the United States to any other in the world. Surely it cannot show lack of attachment to the principles of the Constitution that she thinks that it can be improved. I suppose that most intelligent people think that it might be. Her particular improvement looking to the abolition of war seems to me not materially different in its bearing on this case from a wish to establish cabinet government as in England, or a single house, or one term of seven years for the President. To touch a more burning question, only a judge mad with partisanship would exclude because the applicant thought that the 18th Amendment should be repealed. . . .

She is an optimist and states in strong and, I do not doubt, sincere words, her belief that war will disappear and that the impending destiny of mankind is to unite in peaceful leagues. I do not share that optimism nor do I think that a philosophic view of the world would regard war as absurd. But most people . . . even if not yet ready for cosmopolitan efforts, would welcome any practicable combinations that would increase the power on the side of peace. The notion that the applicant's optimistic anticipations would make her a worse citizen is sufficiently answered by her examination, which seems to me a better argument for her admission than any that I may offer. Some of her answers might excite popular prejudice, but if there is any principle of the Constitution that more imperatively calls for attachment than any other it is the principle of free thought—not free thought for those who agree with us but freedom for the thought that we hate. I think that we should adhere to that principle with regard to admission into, as well as to life within this country. And recurring to the opinion that bars this applicant's way, I would suggest that the Quakers have done their share to make the country what it is, that many citizens agree with the applicant's belief and that I had not supposed hitherto that we regretted our inability to expel them because they believe more than some of us do in the teachings of the Sermon on the Mount.

Mr. Justice Brandeis concurs in the opinion.

31. *United States* v. *Macintosh,* 1931.*

Douglas Clyde Macintosh was a native of Canada. He was a Baptist minister, a member of the Yale University Divinity School, Chaplain of the Graduate School, and Dwight Professor of Theology when he applied for American citizenship in 1925. He had served as a Chaplain with the Canadian Army during World War I, but he stated in his application for American citizenship that he "would have to believe that the war was morally justified" before he would commit himself to defending the country by force of arms. On the basis of this crucial reservation, the Supreme Court, in a five to four decision, denied his petition, Justices Hughes, Holmes, Brandeis and Stone dissenting.

31. a. Majority Opinion.

Mr. Justice Sutherland delivered the opinion of the Court.

The respondent was born in the Dominion of Canada. He came to the United States in 1916, and in 1925 declared his intention to become a citizen. His petition for naturalization was presented to the federal district court for Connecticut, and that court, after hearing and consideration, denied the application upon the ground that, since petitioner would not promise in advance to bear arms in defense of the United States unless he believed the war to be morally justified, he was not attached to the principles of the Constitution. The Circuit Court of Appeals reversed the decree and directed the district court to admit respondent to citizenship.

The Naturalization Act provides that an alien may be admitted to citizenship in the manner therein provided and not otherwise. By Section 3 of the same act, jurisdiction to naturalize aliens is conferred upon the district courts of the United States and other enumerated courts of record. The applicant is required to make and file a preliminary declaration in writing setting forth, among other things, his intention to become a citizen of the United States and to renounce all allegiance to any foreign prince, etc.

* 283 U.S. 605 (1931).

"He shall, before he is admitted to citizenship, declare on oath in open court that he will support the Constitution of the United States, and that he absolutely and entirely renounces and abjures all allegiance and fidelity to any foreign prince, potentate, state, or sovereignty, and particularly by name to the prince, potentate, state, or sovereignty of which he was before a citizen or subject; that he will support and defend the Constitution and laws of the United States against all enemies foreign and domestic, and bear true faith and allegiance to the same." . . .

Naturalization is a privilege, to be given, qualified or withheld as Congress may determine, and which the alien may claim as a right only upon compliance with the terms which Congress imposes. That Congress regarded the admission to citizenship as a serious matter is apparent from the conditions and precautions with which it carefully surrounded the subject. Thus, among other provisions, it is required that the applicant not only shall reside continuously within the United States for a period of at least five years immediately preceding his application, but shall make a preliminary declaration of his intention to become a citizen at least two years prior to his admission. He must produce the testimony of witnesses as to the facts of residence, moral character and attachment to the principles of the Constitution, and in open court take an oath renouncing his former allegiance and pledging future allegiance to the United States. At the final hearing in open court, he and his witnesses must be examined under oath, and the government may appear for the purpose of cross-examining in respect of "any matter touching or in any way affecting his right to admission," introduce countervailing evidence, and be heard in opposition. . . .

. . . we come [now] to a consideration of the case now before us. The applicant had complied with all the formal requirements of the law, and his personal character and conduct were shown to be good in all respects. His right to naturalization turns altogether upon the effect to be given to certain answers and qualifying statements made in response to interrogatories propounded to him.

Upon the preliminary form for petition for naturalization, the following questions, among others, appear: "20. Have you read the following oath of allegiance? [which is then quoted]. Are you willing to take this oath in becoming a citizen?" "22. If necessary, are you willing to take up arms in defense of this country?" In response to the questions designated 20, he answered "Yes." In response to the question designated 22, he answered, "Yes; but I should want to be free to judge of the necessity." By a written memorandum subsequently filed, he amplified these answers as follows:

> 20 and 22. I am willing to do what I judge to be in the best interests of my country, but only in so far as I can believe that this is not going to be against the best interests of humanity in the long run. I do not undertake to support "my country, right or wrong" in any dispute which may arise, and I am not willing to promise beforehand, and without knowing the cause for which my country may go to war, either that I will or that I will not "take up arms in defense of this country," however "necessary" the war may seem to be to the Government of the day.
>
> It is only in a sense consistent with these statements that I am willing to promise to "support and defend" the Government of the United States "against all enemies, foreign and domestic." But, just because I am not certain that the language of questions 20 and 22 will bear the construction I should have to put upon them in order to be able to answer them in the affirmative, I have to say that I do not know that I can say "Yes" in answer to these two questions.

Upon the hearing before the district court on the petition, he explained his position more in detail. He said that he was not a pacifist; that if allowed to interpret the oath for himself he would interpret it as not inconsistent with his position and would take it. He then proceeded to say that he would answer question 22 in the affirmative only on the understanding that he would have to believe that the war was morally justified before he would take up arms in it or give it his moral support. He was ready to give to the United States all the allegiance he ever had given or ever could give to any country, but he could not put allegiance to the government of any country before allegiance to the will of God. He did not anticipate engaging in any propaganda against the prosecution of a war which the government had already declared and which it considered to be justified; but he preferred not to make any absolute promise at the time of the hearing, because of his ignorance of all the circumstances which might affect his judgment with reference to such a war.

He did not question that the government under certain conditions could regulate and restrain the conduct of the individual citizen, even to the extent of imprisonment. He recognized the principle of the submission of the individual citizen to the opinion of the majority in a democratic country; but he did not believe in having his own moral problems solved for him by the majority. The position thus taken was the only one he could take consistently with his moral principles and with what he understood to be the moral principles of Christianity. He recognized, in short, the right of the government to restrain the freedom of the individual for the good of the social whole; but was convinced, on the other hand, that the individual citizen should have the right respectfully to withhold from the government military services (involving, as they probably would, the taking of human life), when his best moral judgment would compel him to do so. He was willing to support his country, even to the extent of bearing arms, if asked to do so by the government, in any war which he could regard as morally justified.

There is more to the same effect, but the foregoing is sufficient to make plain his position.

These statements of the applicant fairly disclose that he is unwilling to take the oath of allegiance, except with these important qualifications: That he will do what he judges to be in the best interests of the country only in so far as he believes it will not be against the best interests of humanity in the long run; that he will not assist in the defense of the country by force of arms or give any war his moral support unless he believes it to be morally justified, however necessary the war might seem to the government of the day; that he will hold himself free to judge of the morality and necessity of the war, and, while he does not anticipate engaging in propaganda against the prosecution of a war declared and considered justified by the government, he prefers to make no promise even as to that; and that he is convinced that the individual citizen should have the right to withhold his military services when his best moral judgment impels him to do so.

Thus stated, the case is ruled in principle by *United States* v. *Schwimmer, supra*. In that case the applicant, a woman, testified that she would not take up arms in defense of the country. She was willing to be treated on the basis of a conscientious objector who refused to take up arms in the recent war, and seemed to regard herself as belonging in that class. She was an uncompromising pacifist, with no sense of nationalism, and only a cosmic sense of belonging to the human family. Her objection to military service, we concluded, rested upon reasons other than her inability to bear arms because of sex or age; and we held that her application for naturalization should be denied upon the ground, primarily, that she failed to sustain the burden of showing that she did not oppose the principle making it a duty of citizens, by force of arms when necessary, to defend their country against its enemies. We said:

> That it is the duty of citizens by force of arms to defend our government against all enemies whenever necessity arises is a fundamental principle of the Constitution.
>
> The common defense was one of the purposes for which the people ordained and established the Constitution. . . . We need not refer to the numerous statutes that contemplate defense of the United States, its Constitution and laws by armed citizens. This Court, in the *Selective Draft Law Cases*, speaking through Chief Justice White, said that "the very conception of a just government and its duty to the citizen includes the reciprocal obligation of the citizen to render military service in case of need. . . ."
>
> Whatever tends to lessen the willingness of citizens to discharge their duty to bear arms in the country's defense detracts from the strength and safety of the Government. And their opinions and beliefs as well as their behavior indicating a disposition to hinder in the performance of that duty are subjects of inquiry under the statutory provisions governing naturalization and are of vital importance, for if all or a large number of citizens oppose such defense the "good order and happiness" of the United States can not long endure. And it is evident that the views of applicants for naturalization in respect of such matters may not be disregarded. The influence of conscientious objectors against the use of military force in defense of the principles of our Government is apt to be more detrimental than their mere refusal to bear arms. The fact that, by reason of sex, age or other cause, they may be unfit to serve does not lessen their purpose or power to influence others. It is clear from her own statements that the declared opinions of respondent as to armed defense by citizens against enemies of the country were directly pertinent to the investigation of her application.

There are few finer or more exalted sentiments than that which finds expression in opposition to war. Peace is a sweet and holy thing, and war is a hateful and an abominable thing to be avoided by any sacrifice or concession that a free people can make. But thus far mankind has been unable to devise any method of indefinitely prolonging the one or of entirely abolishing the other; and, unfortunately, there is nothing which seems to afford positive ground for thinking that the near future will witness the beginning of the reign of perpetual peace for which good men and women everywhere never cease to pray. The Constitution, therefore, wisely contemplating the ever-present possibility of war, declares that one of its purposes is to "provide for the common defense." In express terms Congress is empowered "to declare war," which necessarily connotes the plenary power to wage war with all the force necessary to make it effective; and "to raise . . . armies," which necessarily connotes the like power to say who shall serve in them and in what way.

From its very nature, the war power, when necessity calls for its exercise, tolerates no qualifications or limitations, unless found in the Constitution or in applicable principles of international law. In the words of John Quincy Adams,—"This power is tremendous; . . . ."

These are but illustrations of the breadth of the power; and it necessarily results from their consideration that whether any citizen shall be exempt from serving in the armed forces of the Nation in time of war is dependent upon the will of Congress and not upon the scruples of the individual, except as Congress provides. . . .

The conscientious objector is relieved from the obligation to bear arms in obedience to no constitutional provision, express or implied; but because, and only because, it has accorded with the policy of Congress thus to relieve him. The alien, when he becomes a naturalized citizen, acquires, with one exception, every right possessed under the Constitution by those citizens who are native born; but he acquires no more. The privilege of the native-born conscientious objector to avoid bearing arms comes not from the Constitution, but from the acts of Congress. That body may grant or withhold the exemption as in its wisdom it sees fit; and if it be withheld, the native-born conscientious objector cannot successfully assert the privilege. No other conclusion is compatible with the well-nigh limitless extent of the war powers as above illustrated, which include, by necessary implication, the power, in the last extremity, to compel the armed service of any citizen in the land, without regard to his objections or his views in respect of the justice or morality of the particular war or of war in general. . . .

The applicant for naturalization here is unwilling to become a citizen with this understanding. He is unwilling to leave the question of his future military service to the wisdom of Congress where it belongs, and where every nativeborn or admitted citizen is obliged to leave it. In effect, he offers to take the oath of allegiance only with the qualification that the question whether the war is necessary or morally justified must, so far as his support is concerned, be conclusively determined by reference to his opinion. . . .

It is not within the province of the courts to make bargains with those who seek naturalization. They must accept the grant and take the oath in accordance with the terms fixed by the law, or forego the privilege of citizenship. There is no middle choice.

The burden was upon the applicant to show that his views were not opposed to "the principle that it is a duty of citizenship, by force of arms when necessary, to defend the country against all enemies, and that [his] opinions and beliefs would not prevent or impair the true faith and allegiance required by the Act." We are of opinion that he did not meet this requirement.

The decree of the court of appeals is reversed and that of the district court is affirmed.

31. b. Mr. Chief Justice Hughes, Dissenting.

I am unable to agree with the judgment in this case. It is important to note the precise question to be determined. It is solely one of law, as there is no controversy as to the facts. The question is not whether naturalization is a privilege to be granted or withheld. That it is such a privilege is undisputed. Nor, whether the Congress has the power to fix the conditions upon which the privilege is granted. That power is assumed. Nor, whether the Congress may in its discretion compel service in the army in time of war or punish the refusal to serve. That power is not here in dispute. Nor is the question one of the authority of Congress to exact a promise to bear arms as a condition of its grant of naturalization. That authority, for the present purpose, may also be assumed.

The question before the Court is the narrower one whether the Congress has exacted such a promise. That the Congress has not made such an express requirement is apparent. The question is whether that exaction is to be implied from certain general words which do not, as it seems to me, either literally or historically, demand the implication. I think that the requirement should not be implied. . . .

In examining the requirements for naturalization, we find that the Congress has expressly laid down certain rules which concern the opinions and conduct of the applicant. Thus it is provided that no person shall be naturalized "who disbelieves in or who is opposed to organized government, or who is a member of or affiliated with any organization entertaining and teaching such disbelief in or opposition to organized government, or who advocates or teaches the duty, necessity, or propriety of the unlawful assaulting or killing of any officer or officers, either of specific individuals or of officers generally, of the government of the United States, or of any other organized government, because of his or their official character, or who is a polygamist." Act of June 29, 1906. The respondent, Douglas Clyde Macintosh, entertained none of these disqualifying opinions and had none of the associations or relations disapproved. Among the specific requirements as to beliefs, we find none to the effect that one shall not be naturalized if by reason of his religious convictions he is opposed to war or is unwilling to promise to bear arms. . . .

Putting aside these specific requirements as fully satisfied, we come to the general conditions imposed by the statute. We find one as to good behavior during the specified period of residence preceding application. No applicant could appear to be more exemplary than Macintosh. A Canadian by birth, he first came to the United States as a graduate student at the University of Chicago, and in 1907 he was ordained as a Baptist minister. In 1909 he began to teach in Yale University and is now a member of the faculty of the Divinity School, Chaplain of the Yale Graduate School, and Dwight Professor of Theology. After the outbreak of the Great War, he voluntarily sought appointment as a chaplain with the Canadian Army and as such saw service at the front. Returning to this country, he made public addresses in 1917 in support of the Allies. In 1918, he went again to France where he had charge of an American Y.M.C.A. hut at the front until the armistice, when he resumed his duties at Yale University. It seems to me that the applicant has shown himself in his behavior and character to be highly desirable as a citizen and, if such a man is to be excluded from naturalization, I think the disqualification should be found in unambiguous terms and not in an implication which shuts him out and gives admission to a host far less worthy.

The principal ground for exclusion appears to relate to the terms of the oath which the applicant must take. It should be observed that the respondent was willing to take the oath, and he so stated in his petition. But, in response to further inquiries, he explained that he was not willing "to promise beforehand" to take up arms, "without knowing the cause for which my country may go to war" and that "he would have to believe that the war was morally justified." He declared that "his first allegiance was to the will of God"; that he was ready to give to the United States "all the allegiance he ever had given or ever could give to any country, but that he could not put allegiance to the government of any country before allegiance to the will of God." The question then is whether the terms of the oath are to be taken as necessarily implying an assurance of willingness to bear arms, so that one whose conscientious convictions or belief of supreme allegiance to the will of God will not permit him to make such an absolute promise, cannot take the oath and hence is disqualified for admission to citizenship.

The statutory provision as to the oath which is said to require this promise is this: "That he will support and defend the Constitution and laws of the United States against all enemies, foreign and domestic, and bear true faith and allegiance to the same." That these general words have not been regarded as implying a promise to bear arms notwithstanding religious or conscientious scruples, or as requiring one to promise to put allegiance to temporal power above what is sincerely believed to be one's duty of obedience to God, is apparent, I think, from a consideration of their history. . . . It goes without saying that it was not the intention of the Congress in framing the oath to impose any religious test. When we consider the history of the struggle for religious liberty, the large number of citizens of our country from the very beginning, who have been unwilling to sacrifice their religious convictions, and in particular, those who have been conscientiously opposed to war and who would not yield what they sincerely believed to be their allegiance to the will of God, I find it impossible to conclude that such persons are to be deemed disqualified for public office in this country because of the requirement of the oath which must be taken before they enter upon their duties. . . . I think that the requirement of the oath of office should be read in the light of our regard from the beginning for freedom of conscience.

. . . The long-established practice of excusing from military service those whose religious convictions oppose it confirms the view that the Congress in the terms of the oath did not intend to require a promise to give such service. The policy of granting exemptions in such cases has been followed from colonial times and is abundantly shown by the provisions of colonial and state statutes, of state constitutions, and of acts of Congress. The first constitution of New York, adopted in 1777, in providing for the state militia, while strongly emphasizing the duty of defense, added "That all such of the inhabitants of this state (being of the people called Quakers) as, from scruples of conscience may be averse to the bearing of arms, be therefrom excused by the legislature, and do pay to the state such sums of money, in lieu of their personal service, as the same may, in the judgment of the legislature, be worth." A large number of similar provisions are found in other States. The importance of giving immunity to those having conscientious scruples against bearing arms has been emphasized in debates in Congress repeatedly from the very beginning of our government, and religious scruples have been recognized in draft acts.

Much has been said of the paramount duty to the state, a duty to be recognized, it is urged, even though it conflicts with convictions of duty to God. Undoubtedly that duty to the state exists within the domain of power, for government may enforce obedience to laws regardless of scruples. When one's belief collides with the power of the state, the latter is supreme within its sphere and submission or punishment follows. But, in the forum of conscience, duty to a moral power higher than the state has always been maintained. . . . There is abundant room for enforcing the requisite authority of law as it is enacted and requires obedience, and for maintaining the conception of the supremacy of law as essential to orderly government, without demanding that either citizens or applicants for citizenship shall assume by oath an obligation to regard allegiance to God as subordinate to allegiance to civil power. . . .

Nor is there ground, in my opinion, for the exclusion of Professor Macintosh because his conscientious scruples have particular reference to wars believed to be unjust. There is nothing new in such an attitude. Among the most eminent statesmen here and abroad have been those who condemned the action of their country in entering into wars they thought to be unjustified. Agreements for the renunciation of war presuppose a preponderant public sentiment against wars of aggression. If, while recognizing the power of Congress, the mere holding of religious or conscientious scruples against all wars should not disqualify a citizen from holding office in this country, or an applicant otherwise qualified from being admitted to citizenship, there would seem to be no reason why a reservation of religious or conscientious objection to participation in wars believed to be unjust should constitute such a disqualification. . . .

32. *In re Summers, 1944.*[*]

Clyde W. Summers was a Methodist conscientious objector who was denied admission to the Illinois bar by the bar's Committee on Character and Fitness. Summers was deemed "morally unfit" because his objection to war conflicted with the oath he would have to take to support the State Constitution, which had a militia clause in it. In the Supreme Court, Summers contended that the action of Illinois denying his admission to the bar was a limitation on the free exercise of religion and a violation of the due process clause of the Fourteenth Amendment. The amicus curiae *brief submitted to the court by Professor Zachariah Chaffee and Harold Evans on behalf of the American Friends Service Committee argued Summers's cause at length, but the Supreme Court denied all contentions. By a five to four vote it held that the Supreme Court of Illinois and the bar's Committee on Character and Fitness held, within the proper limits of their jurisdiction, the right to establish qualifications for the professions practiced within that State.*

32. a. Majority Opinion.

Mr. Justice Reed for the Court.

Disqualification Under Illinois Constitution. The Justices justify their refusal to admit petitioner to practice before the courts of Illinois on the ground of petitioner's inability to take in good faith the required oath to support the Constitution of Illinois. His inability to take such an oath, the Justices submit, shows that the Committee on Character and Fitness properly refused to certify to his moral character and moral fitness to be an officer of the Court, charged with the administration of justice under the Illinois law. His good citizenship, they think, judged by the standards required for practicing law in Illinois, is not satisfactorily shown. A conscientious belief in nonviolence to the extent that the believer will not use force to prevent wrong, no matter how aggravated, and

[*] 325 U.S. 561 (1944).

so cannot swear in good faith to support the Illinois Constitution, the Justices contend, must disqualify such a believer for admission.

Petitioner appraises the denial of admission from the viewpoint of a religionist. He said in his petition:

"The so-called 'misconduct' for which petitioner could be reproached for is his taking the New Testament too seriously. Instead of merely reading or preaching the Sermon on the Mount, he tries to practice it. The only fault of the petitioner consists in his attempt to act as a good Christian in accordance with his interpretation of the Bible, and according to the dictates of his conscience. We respectfully submit that the profession of law does not shut its gates to persons who have qualified in all other respects even when they follow in the footsteps of that Great Teacher of mankind who delivered the Sermon on the Mount. We respectfully submit that under our Constitutional guarantees even good Christians who have met all the requirements for the admission to the bar may be admitted to practice law."

Thus a court created to administer the laws of Illinois as it understands them, and charged particularly with the protection of justice in the courts of Illinois through supervision of admissions to the bar, found itself faced with the dilemma of excluding an applicant whom it deemed disqualified for the responsibilities of the profession of law or of admitting the applicant because of its deeply rooted tradition in freedom of belief. The responsibility for choice as to the personnel of its bar rests with Illinois. Only a decision which violated a federal right secured by the Fourteenth Amendment would authorize our intervention. It is said that the action of the Supreme Court of Illinois is contrary to the principles of that portion of the First Amendment which guarantees the free exercise of religion. Of course, under our Constitutional system, men could not be excluded from the practice of law, or indeed from following any other calling, simply because they belong to any of our religious groups, whether Protestant, Catholic, Quaker or Jewish, assuming it conceivable that any state of the Union would draw such a religious line. We cannot say that any such purpose to discriminate motivated the action of the Illinois Supreme Court.

The sincerity of petitioner's beliefs are not questioned. He has been classified as a conscientious objector under the Selective Training and Service Act of 1940. Without detailing petitioner's testimony before the Committee or his subsequent statements in the record, his position may be compendiously stated as one of non-violence. Petitioner will not serve in the armed forces. While he recognizes a difference between the military and police forces, he would not act in the latter to coerce threatened violations. Petitioner would not use force to meet aggressions against himself or his family, no matter how aggravated or whether or not carrying a danger of bodily harm to himself or others. He is a believer in passive resistance. We need to consider only his attitude toward service in the armed forces.

Illinois has constitutional provisions which require service in the militia in time of war of men of petitioner's age group.* The return of the Justices alleges that petitioner has not made any showing that he would serve notwithstanding his conscientious objections. This allegation is undenied in the record and unchallenged by brief. We accept the allegation as to unwillingness to serve in the militia as established. While under [§5 (g)] of the Selective Training and Service Act, *supra*, conscientious objectors to participation in war in any form now are permitted to do non-war work of national importance, this is by grace of Congressional recognition of their beliefs. . . .

The United States does not admit to citizenship the alien who refuses to pledge military service. *United States* v. *Schwimmer*, 279 U. S. 644; *United States* v. *Macintosh*, 283 U. S. 605. Even the powerful dissents which emphasized the deep cleavage in this Court on the issue of admission to citizenship did not challenge the right of Congress to require military service from every able-bodied man. It is impossible for us to conclude that the insistence of Illinois that an officer who is charged with the administration of justice must take an oath to support the Constitution of Illinois and Illinois' interpretation of that oath to require a willingness to perform military service violates the principles of religious freedom which the Fourteenth Amendment secures against state action, when a like interpretation of a similar oath as to

---

* The militia of the state of Illinois shall consist of all able-bodied male persons resident in the state, between the ages of eighteen and forty-five, except such persons as now are, or hereafter may be, exempted by the laws of the United States, or of this state. (Constitution of Illinois.)

the Federal Constitution bars an alien from national citizenship.

Affirmed.

32. b. Mr. Justice Black, Dissenting.

The State of Illinois has denied the petitioner the right to practice his profession and to earn his living as a lawyer. It has denied him a license on the ground that his present religious beliefs disqualify him for membership in the legal profession. The question is, therefore, whether a state which requires a license as a prerequisite to practicing law can deny an applicant a license solely because of his deeply-rooted religious convictions. The fact that petitioner measures up to every other requirement for admission to the Bar set by the State demonstrates beyond doubt that the only reason for his rejection was his religious beliefs. . . .

The petitioner's disqualifying religious beliefs stem chiefly from a study of the New Testament and a literal acceptance of the teachings of Christ as he understands them. . . .

I cannot believe that a state statute would be consistent with our constitutional guarantee of freedom of religion if it specifically denied the right to practice law to all members of one of our great religious groups, Protestant, Catholic or Jewish. Yet the Quakers have had a long and honorable part in the growth of our nation, and an amicus curiae brief filed in their behalf informs us that under the test applied to this petitioner, not one of them if true to the tenets of their faith could qualify for the bar in Illinois. And it is obvious that the same disqualification would exist as to every conscientious objector to the use of force, even though the Congress of the United States should continue its practice of absolving them from military service. The conclusion seems to me inescapable that if Illinois can bar this petitioner from the practice of law it can bar every person from every public occupation solely because he believes in non-resistance rather than in force. For a lawyer is no more subject to call for military duty than a plumber, a highway worker, a Secretary of State, or a prison chaplain

It may be, as many people think, that Christ's Gospel of love and submission is not suited to a world in which men still fight and kill one another. But I am not ready to say that a mere profession of belief in that Gospel is a sufficient reason to keep otherwise well qualified men out of the legal profession, or to drive law-abiding lawyers of that belief out of the profession, which would be the next logical development.

Nor am I willing to say that such a belief can be penalized through the circuitous method of prescribing an oath, and then barring an applicant on the ground that his present belief might later prompt him to do or refrain from doing something that might violate that oath. Test oaths, designed to impose civil disabilities upon men for their beliefs rather than for unlawful conduct, were an abomination to the founders of this nation. This feeling was made manifest in Article VI of the Constitution which provides that "no religious test shall ever be required as a Qualification to any Office or public Trust under the United States."

The state's denial of petitioner's application to practice law resolves itself into a holding that it is lawfully required that all lawyers take an oath to support the state constitution and that petitioner's religious convictions against the use of force make it impossible for him to observe that oath. The petitioner denies this and is willing to take the oath. . . . In the *Schwimmer* and *Macintosh* cases aliens were barred from naturalization because their then religious beliefs would bar them from bearing arms to defend the country. Dissents in both cases rested in part on the premise that religious tests are incompatible with our constitutional guarantee of freedom of thought and religion. In the *Schwimmer* case dissent, Mr. Justice Holmes said that "if there is any principle of the Constitution that more imperatively calls for attachment than any other it is the principle of free thought—not free thought for those who agree with us but freedom for the thought that we hate. I think that we should adhere to that principle with regard to admission into, as well as to life within this country." In the *Macintosh* case dissent, Mr. Chief Justice Hughes said, "To conclude that the general oath of office is to be interpreted as disregarding the religious scruples of these citizens and as disqualifying them for office because they could not take the oath with such an interpretation would, I believe, be generally regarded as contrary not only to the specific intent of the Congress but as repugnant to the fundamental principle of representative government." I agree with the constitutional philosophy underlying the dissents of Mr. Justice Holmes and Mr. Chief Justice Hughes.

The Illinois Constitution itself prohibits the draft of conscientious objectors except in time of war and also excepts from militia duty persons who are "exempted by the laws of the United States." It has not drafted men into the militia since 1864, and if it ever should again, no one can say that it will not, as has the Congress of the United States, exempt men who honestly entertain the views that this petitioner does. Thus the probability that Illinois would ever call the petitioner to serve in a war has little more reality than an imaginary quantity in mathematics.

I cannot agree that a state can lawfully bar from a semi-public position a well-qualified man of good character solely because he entertains a religious belief which might prompt him at some time in the future to violate a law which has not been and may never be enacted. Under our Constitution men are punished for what they do or fail to do and not for what they think and believe. Freedom to think, to believe, and to worship, has too exalted a position in our country to be penalized on such an illusory basis. Mr. Justice Douglas, Mr. Justice Murphy, and Mr. Justice Rutledge concur.

33. *Girouard* v. *United States*, 1946.*

Girouard was a Canadian Seventh-Day Adventist who applied for citizenship. He declared himself willing to enter the Army in noncombatant service but he would not promise to bear arms. Justice Douglas, in handing down the majority opinion of the Supreme Court, declared that the precedents—Schwimmer and Macintosh—"do not state the correct rule of law," and the Court proceeded to overrule those opinions and to approve Girouard's citizenship. Three Justices dissented on the ground that Congress had not seen fit to change the language of the laws of citizenship since the Macintosh ruling, and that the Court was thereby bound by Congressional intent.

Mr. Justice Douglas delivered the opinion of the Court.

In 1943 petitioner, a native of Canada, filed his petition for naturalization in the District Court of Massachusetts. He stated in his application that he understood the principles of the government of the United States, believed in its form of government, and was willing to take the oath of allegiance which reads as follows:

> I hereby declare, on oath, that I absolutely and entirely renounce and abjure all allegiance and fidelity to any foreign prince, potentate, state, or sovereignty of whom or which I have heretofore been a subject or citizen; that I will support and defend the Constitution and laws of the United States of America against all enemies, foreign and domestic; that I will bear true faith and allegiance to the same; and that I take this obligation freely without any mental reservation or purpose of evasion: So help me God.

To the question in the application "If necessary, are you willing to take up arms in defense of this country?" he replied, "No (Non-combatant) Seventh Day Adventist." He explained that answer before the examiner by saying "it is a purely religious matter with me. I have no political or per-

* 328 U.S. 61 (1946).

sonal reasons other than that." He did not claim before his Selective Service board exemption from all military service, but only from combatant military duty. At the hearing in the District Court petitioner testified that he was a member of the Seventh Day Adventist denomination, of whom approximately 10,000 were then serving in the armed forces of the United States as non-combatants, especially in the medical corps; and that he was willing to serve in the army but would not bear arms. The District Court admitted him to citizenship. The Circuit Court of Appeals reversed, one judge dissenting. It took that action on the authority of *United States* v. *Schwimmer*; *United States* v. *Macintosh*, saying that the facts of the present case brought it squarely within the principles of those cases. The case is here on a petition for a writ of certiorari which we granted so that those authorities might be re-examined.

The Schwimmer, [and] Macintosh cases . . . stand for the same general rule—that an alien who refuses to bear arms will not be admitted to citizenship. As an original proposition, we could not agree with that rule. The fallacies underlying it were, we think demonstrated in the dissents of Mr. Justice Holmes in the Schwimmer case and of Mr. Chief Justice Hughes in the Macintosh case.

The oath required of aliens does not in terms require that they promise to bear arms. Nor has Congress expressly made any such finding a prerequisite to citizenship. . . . Refusal to bear arms is not necessarily a sign of disloyalty or a lack of attachment to our institutions. One may serve his country faithfully and devotedly, though his religious scruples make it impossible for him to shoulder a rifle. Devotion to one's country can be as real and as enduring among non-combatants as among combatants. One may adhere to what he deems to be his obligation to God and yet assume all military risks to secure victory. The effort of war is indivisible; and those whose religious scruples prevent them from killing are no less patriots than those whose special traits or handicaps result in their assignment to duties far behind the fighting front. Each is making the utmost contribution according to his capacity. The fact that his role may be limited by religious convictions rather than by physical characteristics has no necessary bearing on his attachment to his country or on his willingness to support and defend it to his utmost.

Petitioner's religious scruples would not disqualify him from becoming a member of Congress or holding other public offices. While Article VI, Clause 3 of the Constitution provides that such officials, both of the United States and the several States, "shall be bound by Oath or Affirmation, to support this Constitution," it significantly adds that "no religious Test shall ever be required as a Qualification to any Office or public Trust under the United States." . . .

There is not the slightest suggestion that Congress set a stricter standard for aliens seeking admission to citizenship than it did for officials who make and enforce the laws of the nation and administer its affairs. It is hard to believe that one need forsake his religious scruples to become a citizen but not to sit in the high councils of state.

Congress has recognized that one may adequately discharge his obligations as a citizen by rendering non-combatant as well as combatant services. This respect by Congress over the years for the conscience of those having religious scruples against bearing arms is cogent evidence of the meaning of the oath. It is recognition by Congress that even in time of war one may truly support and defend our institutions though he stops short of using weapons of war.

Reversed. *

* Justice Jackson took no part in the case. Justices Stone, Reed, and Frankfurter dissented. [Editor's note.]

Part VI

PREFACE

The Selective Service System maintained no central records of conscientious objectors who entered military service for noncombatant service in World War II. Their own estimate is that there were 25,000 conscientious objectors. Other researchers judge the number to have been closer to 50,000, a small percentage of the 13 million Americans who served in the armed forces between 1941 and 1945.

The laws that governed conscientious objectors were contained in the Selective Training and Service Act of 1940, Section 5(g):

> Nothing contained in this act shall be construed to require any person to be subject to combatant training and service in the land or naval forces of the United States who, by reason of religious training and belief, is conscientiously opposed to participation in war in any form. Any such person claiming such exemption from combatant training and service because of such conscientious objections whose claim is sustained by the local board shall, if he is inducted into the land or naval forces under this act, be assigned to noncombatant service as defined by the President, or shall, if he is found to be conscientiously opposed to participation in such noncombatant service, in lieu of such induction, be assigned to work of national importance under civilian direction.

Congress provided that "religious training and belief," rather than membership in one of the recognized peace churches, was to be sufficient basis for exemption. The wording was intended to be an expression of a more liberal interpretation of claims of conscience; yet many questions remained unanswered: Could one who professed no religion, attended no church, had no religious training claim to be a conscientious objector by reason of *belief* alone? Did the Congress intend religious training to be a necessary corollary of belief?

214

The great single innovation of the 1940 draft legislation was the provision for Civilian Public Service camps. In these camps, those objectors who could not accept noncombatant service under military authority were to perform work of "national importance" under representatives of the historic peace churches—Quaker, Mennonite, Brethren. As a matter of policy, CPS represented the desire of the government that "the judgment of individual conscience opposed to the national will should be given consideration and allowed a form of cooperation consistent with its judgments. . . ." In practice, CPS proved to be an extension of the Civilian Conservation Corps started during the depression of the 1930's. Of the first twenty-five camps set up, twelve were under the Forestry Service, eleven under the Soil Conservation Service, and two under the National Park Service. Between May, 1941, and March, 1947, 11,950 objectors worked at sixty-seven camps on such projects as soil erosion control, reforestation, and agricultural experimentation. When the shortage of labor on farms became critical, objectors were used as replacement labor. Objectors chafed under what they felt to be merely a "make-work" program, designed principally to keep them out of the public eye. Some of them volunteered and even demanded to be permitted to do more useful work in mental hospitals or social work agencies. Some conscientious objectors volunteered to be guinea pigs in medical experiments on malaria, hookworm, typhus, and the control of lice and infectious hepatitis. Diet and endurance experiments were performed on objectors who were willing to serve in special projects. In all, some 500 conscientious objectors volunteered for medical experiments and over 2,000 worked in mental hospitals (see Document 36 in this book).

The flaw in the CPS program, which had been begun with such good will, became apparent almost immediately. Although objectors contributed a total of 8,237,000 man-days of work, they received no pay. On the contrary, those in church-run camps had to support themselves or be supported by their churches or their families who, by the war's end, had raised or contributed $7,202,000. In addition, the men of the CPS qualified for none of the benefits accorded soldiers—life insurance or medical care or compensation, and their families, during their time of service, were deprived of income.

The fact that CPS men received no pay was not an oversight but a congressional—and military—policy. In testimony before congressional committees, General Lewis E. Hershey, Director of the Selective Service System, maintained that "It would be argued that conscientious objectors were free of the risks of the GI, therefore they should not be compensated." Hershey went on, "They get no pay and . . . they have to be financed. I do not want to impugn the motive of anybody, but it has been a factor in not only keeping them from going [to CPS camps], but once they get there they leave, and take 1-A-O [noncombatant service] in the army when they find out." Colonel Lewis F. Kosch, speaking before the Senate Military Affairs Committee in 1942, argued that "The very fact that a man does not get paid is one means of sorting the c.o. from the slacker." (See Document 35 in this book.)

As attorney for six objectors who later brought suit against the legality of the CPS camps, John A. Chamberlain demanded that the court consider:

> Where is the authority to compel a citizen to work without pay, and to require his family to shift for themselves? If it is answered that soldiers are so regulated, we reply that this may be a necessary part of Army discipline and is so provided by law, but [as for] C.O.'s, an act of Congress itself shows, there is no more reason for treating them as criminals than for treating all the rest of the population outside the military in the same way. If it is suggested that young men are to be discouraged from claiming to be conscientious objectors, I ask where is the authority found in the Selective Service Act for so doing?*

Thus, although CPS marked an advance in the government's policy toward c.o.'s, the feeling remained that a penalty had been exacted for the privilege of electing one particular form of alternate service. Cases challenging the constitutionality of various aspects of CPS were brought before the federal district courts, but there was no disposition on the part of the judiciary to tamper with the policy as set down by Congress.

At the war's end, there had been 15,805 violations of the Selective Service Law. Conscientious objectors accounted for 5,300 of these, and 4,300 of that number represented prosecution of Jehovah's Witnesses who had claimed exemption

---

* Sibley and Jacob, *op. cit.*, p. 441.

as ministers. The greater part of these men were paroled between 1945 and 1946, but 502 remained imprisoned (455 Jehovah's Witnesses) at the end of 1946. When President Truman issued a Proclamation of Amnesty just before Christmas, 1947, he followed the recommendations of an amnesty board that declined to advise amnesty for political objectors or pardon for Jehovah's Witnesses. Of the former group the board wrote:

> These were men who asserted no religious training or belief but founded their objections on intellectual, political, or sociological convictions resulting from the individual's reasoning and personal economic or political philosophy. We have not felt justified in recommending those who thus have set themselves up as wiser and more competent than society to determine their duty to come to the defense of the nation.*

Similarly, of those Jehovah's Witnesses still in prison, the amnesty board repeated:

> While few of these offenders had theretofore been violators of the law, we cannot condone their selective service offenses, nor recommend them for pardons. To do so would be to sanction an assertion by a citizen that he is above the law; that he makes his own law; and that he refuses to yield his opinion to that of organized society on the question of his country's need for service.**

In 1948 the provisions of the Selective Service laws were suspended, but with the outbreak of hostilities in Korea in 1951, they were restored. During the "conflict" in Korea, there were more than 50 prosecutions against c.o.'s involving such issues as the use of secret FBI reports as a basis for granting or withholding objector status.

At the end of the Second World War and the Korean War, it was clear that although the nation had moved forward in attempting to accommodate the conscientious objectors, new forms of objection had come into being, outpacing the nation. The so-called "nonreligious" objector found no safe harbor in existing laws. This man, whose objection to war might be as deep and as sincere as the Quaker's, but who based his opposition on ethical or moral or philosophical grounds,

* *Ibid.*, p. 505.
** *Ibid.*, p. 507.

found that his way led to prison. The "political" objector, who opposed war as unwise or unjust, also found that prison was waiting for him. And the "absolutist," who refused to be registered on the grounds that registration was a form of cooperation with the army, also went to jail.

A. J. Muste, one of the leading figures in America's pacifist movement, urged the absolutist to be firm in his choice of "holy disobedience." He spoke to and for those few souls who elected not to "go along" with conscription, to and for those for whom prison was the price for conviction (see Document 37 in this book).

34. Special Form for Conscientious Objectors (DSS Form 47), 1941.*

Every registrant in World War II was required to fill out a Selective Service Questionnaire (DSS Form 40). "Series X" of that form provided special coverage for conscientious objectors. The signing of series X constituted a request that a local board furnish a Special Form for Conscientious Objectors (DSS Form 47). This form became the basis for Selective Service classification.**

* United States Selective Service Special Monograph, No. 11, part 2, *Conscientious Objection* (Washington, D.C., 1950), pp. 211–18.

** Form 47 was revised in 1942. Statements A and B under Series I were clarified as follows:

A. I am, by reason of my religious training and belief, conscientiously opposed to participation in war in any form. I, therefore, claim exemption from combatant training and service. I understand that if my claim is sustained I will be inducted into the land or naval forces, but will be assigned to noncombatant service as defined by the President as (1) service in any unit which is unarmed at all times (2) service in the medical department wherever performed (3) service in any unit or installation, the primary function of which does not require the use of arms in combat. . . .

B. I am, by reason of my religious training and belief, conscientiously opposed to participation in war in any form, and I am further conscientiously opposed to participation in noncombatant service in the land or naval forces. I therefore claim exemption from combatant training and service and if my claim is sustained, I believe that in lieu of induction . . . I should . . . be assigned to work of national importance under civilian direction.

SPECIAL FORM FOR CONSCIENTIOUS OBJECTOR

Order No. --------

Name -------- -------- --------
        (First)   (Middle)   (Last)

Address --------
    (Number and street or R. F. D. route)

-------- -------- --------
(City, town, or village)   (County)   (State)

(STAMP OF LOCAL BOARD)

This form must be returned on or before --------
    (Five days after date of mailing or issue)

INSTRUCTIONS

A registrant who claims to be a conscientious objector shall offer information in substantiation of his claim on this special form, which when filed shall become a part of his Questionnaire.

The questions in Series II through V in this form are intended to obtain evidence of the genuineness of the claim made in Series I, and the answers given by the registrant shall be for the information only of the officials duly authorized under the regulations to examine them.

In the case of any registrant who claims to be a conscientious objector, the Local Board shall proceed in the ordinary course to classify him upon all other grounds of deferment, and shall consider and pass upon his claim as a conscientious objector only if, but for such claim, he would have been placed in Class I. The procedure for appeal from a decision of the Local Board on a claim for conscientious objection is provided for in the Selective Service Regulations.

Failure by the registrant to file this special form on or before the date indicated above may be regarded as a waiver by the registrant of his claim as a conscientious objector: *Provided, however,* That the Local Board, in its discretion, and for good cause shown by the registrant, may grant a reasonable extension of time for filing this special form.

D. S. S. Form 47

Series I—CLAIM FOR EXEMPTION

INSTRUCTIONS.—The registrant must sign his name to either Statement A or Statement B in this series but not to both of them. The registrant should strike out the statement in this series which he does not sign.

A. I claim the exemption provided by the Selective Training and Service Act of 1940 for conscientious objectors, because I am conscientiously opposed by reason of my religious training and belief to participation in war in any form and to participation in combatant military service or training therefor; but I am willing to participate in noncombatant service or training therefor under the direction of military authorities.

(Signature of registrant)

B. I claim the exemption provided by the Selective Training and Service Act of 1940 for conscientious objectors, because I am conscientiously opposed by reason of my religious training and belief to participation in war in any form and to participation in any service which is under the direction of military authorities.

(Signature of registrant)

Series II—RELIGIOUS TRAINING AND BELIEFS

INSTRUCTIONS.—Every question in this series must be fully answered. If more space is necessary, attach extra sheets of paper to this page.

1. Describe the nature of your belief which is the basis of your claim made in Series I above.

----

2. Explain how, when, and from what source you received the training and acquired the belief which is the basis of your claim made in Series I above.

----

3. Give the name and present address of the individual upon whom you rely most for religious guidance.

----

4. Under what circumstances, if any, do you believe in the use of force?

----

5. Describe the actions and behavior in your life which in your opinion most conspicuously demonstrate the consistency and depth of your religious convictions.

SPECIAL FORM FOR CONSCIENTIOUS OBJECTOR (continued)

6. Have you ever given public expression, written or oral, to the views herein expressed as the basis for your claim made in Series I above? If so, specify when and where.

Series III—GENERAL BACKGROUND

INSTRUCTIONS.—Every question in this series must be fully answered. If more space is necessary, attach extra sheets of paper to this page.

1. Give the name and address of each school and college which you have attended, together with the dates of your attendance; and state in each instance the type of school (public, private, church, military, commercial, etc.).

2. Give a chronological list of all occupations, positions, jobs, or types of work, other than as a student in school or college, in which you have at any time been engaged, whether for monetary compensation or not, giving the facts indicated below with regard to each position or job held, or type of work in which engaged:

3. Give all addresses and dates of residence where you have formerly lived:

4. Give the name, address, and country of birth of your parents and indicate whether they are living or not.

Series IV—PARTICIPATION IN ORGANIZATIONS

INSTRUCTIONS.—Questions 1, 2, and 3 in this series must be fully answered. If more space is necessary, attach extra sheets of paper to this page.

1. Have you ever been a member of any military organization or establishment? If so, state the name and address of same and give reasons why you became a member.

2. Are you a member of a religious sect or organization?............ If your answer to question 2 is yes, answer questions (a) through (e).

(Yes or no)

(a) State the name of the sect, and the name and location of its governing body or head if known to you:

(b) When, where, and how did you become a member of said sect or organization?

(c) State the name and location of the church, congregation, or meeting where you customarily attend:

(d) Give the name and present address of the pastor or leader of such church, congregation, or meeting:

(e) Describe carefully the creed or official statements of said religious sect or organization in relation to participation in war:

----

3. Describe your relationships with and activities in all organizations with which you are or have been affiliated, other than religious or military:

Series V—REFERENCES

Give here the names and other information indicated concerning persons who could supply information as to the sincerity of your professed convictions against participation in war:

SPECIAL FORM FOR CONSCIENTIOUS OBJECTOR (continued)

REGISTRANT'S AFFIDAVIT

INSTRUCTIONS.—The claim made on this form will not be considered unless it is supported by the following affidavit. (If the registrant cannot read, the questions and his answers thereto shall be read to him by the officer who administers the oath.)

STATE OF _____, COUNTY OF _____, *ss:*

I, _____, do solemnly swear (or affirm) that I am the registrant described in the foregoing questions and answers, that I know the contents of my said answers, and that each and every statement of fact in my answers to said questions is true, to the best of my knowledge and belief.

_____
(Registrant sign here)

_____
(Signature or mark of registrant)

Subscribed and sworn to (or affirmed) before me this _____ day of _____, 19 _____

_____
(Signature of officer administering oath)

_____
(Designation of officer)

If the registrant has received assistance from an advisor, the advisor shall sign the following statement:

I have assisted the registrant herein named in the preparation of this form.

_____
(Signature of advisor)

_____
(Address of advisor)

35. Testimony Before Congressional Subcommittees on Conscientious Objectors, 1941, 1942.*

Immediately after Pearl Harbor, Congressional subcommittees were hearing testimony regarding appropriations for the administration of the Selective Service System. The question of conscientious objectors in Civilian Public Service camps came up in the questioning. General Lewis B. Hershey's remarks reveal something of the attitude of the military mind as well as the practical problems of handling conscientious objectors within the larger framework of the Selective Service program.

A year later, in Senate testimony taken before the passage of a new manpower bill, E. Raymond Wilson spoke of the difficulties of the pacifist's position.

35. a. Testimony Before the House Subcommittee on Appropriations, December 11, 1941.

From the statement of Brigadier General Lewis B. Hershey, director of the Selective Service System:

General Hershey: We based these estimates on the assumption that the religious bodies will continue to subsist, clothe and administer the conscientious objectors in the camps. Those items have not yet become a Government charge, and we are assuming that they will not. The feeding of these individuals, the hiring of the dietitians, and the hiring of the supervisors will be furnished from money which they will give us.

Mr. John M. Houston (Kans.): Have they been doing that religiously so far?

General Hershey: Yes. You see, we have three major historical creeds. They underwrite those costs. If the boy has $35 a month, he pays it; and if he has not, his church pays it; if neither has it, the three religious groups pay it.

* National Service Board for Religious Objectors, *Congress Looks at the Conscientious Objector* (Washington, D.C., 1943), pp. 34–35, 37–49.

Mr. Joe Starnes (Ala.): Who are those three religious groups?

General Hershey: Those three religious groups are the Mennonites—about 34 types—Brethren, or Dunkards as they are many times called, and Quakers.

Mr. Joe Starnes (Ala.): How many of those conscientious objectors do we have now?

General Hershey: Somewhere around 1,500 in camps.

Mr. Starnes: Are they doing any type of work that is constructive?

General Hershey: Insofar as the Government is concerned, or doing any type of work?

Mr. Starnes: Are they doing any type of work from which the defense effort will obtain a benefit?

General Hershey: There might be a little question as to defense, in the long run. Of course, they are doing the same type of work as the C.C.C. They are working on soil conservation, reforestation, they set out trees, and we have two projects now that I think are still more pertinent. We are going to put a unit in two insane hospitals to replace men, where they are having difficulty finding male attendants for insane patients.

Mr. Starnes: General Hershey, do these conscientious objectors also object to working in a plant for the production of munitions?

General Hershey: We have some, I would say rather rare cases where we have men who are 2-A's; that is, men who are working now in plants, who might otherwise claim conscientious objection, but the great majority of them would not do so under any circumstances.

Mr. James M. Fitzpatrick (N.Y.): What is the total number?

General Hershey: You mean that we have in camps?

Mr. Fitzpatrick: Yes.

General Hershey: About 1,500. We made some plans, if you remember, when we were here about a year ago, for about 6,000, but there are several things that have helped. One is the fact that they get no pay, and that they have to be financed. I do not want to impugn the motive of anybody, but it has been a factor in not only keeping them from going, but once they get there, they leave, and take 1-A-O, in the army, when they find out.

Mr. Clifton A. Woodrum (Va.): And you let them go?

General Hershey: Yes; we not only let them go, we aid them to go into the army—any man who wants to leave our camp to enlist.

Mr. Fitzpatrick: Do they get an allowance in the camps?

General Hershey: Some camps give them $1.50 a month, some $2.50, out of the $35.

Mr. Woodrum: They take care of themselves, they are self-supporting?

Mr. Houston: Do they do any soil-conservation work?

General Hersey: Oh, yes. With very few exceptions they are good workers. Very many of them go beyond working the government time. Many of them are working fifty-some hours a week when we only require 40.

Mr. Fitzpatrick: How are they around the camp on cooking or washing dishes?

General Hershey: They hire—some such help.

Mr. Fitzpatrick (interposing): I mean in the army.

Mr. Woodrum: They will not work in the army.

Mr. Fitzpatrick: Oh, they will not work in the army?

General Hershey: No. We had a peculiar case of one man who had got inducted, trying to judge his case. He spent several weeks at Fort Sill. He will not receive any money. He will not wear a uniform, and we are trying to get his case straightened out with the Department of Justice, and he is in the peculiar position of both refusing to accept money and of refusing to wear a uniform, but yet he is nonbelligerent. That is, he went to any place that they wanted him to go, but he is simply unwilling to bear arms, that is all. He has worked free, and he will not accept money because he thinks it would compromise his position.

Mr. Woodrum: But he is not a conscientious objector?

General Hershey: Yes.

Mr. Woodrum: Oh, he is?

General Hershey: Well, that is a question, and we are having some little difficulty. That is taking some time. In the meantime, he got inducted before he made his appeal, and it just shows what some of them will do. They are a most peculiar kind of people.

Mr. Fitzpatrick: Suppose we get a man who does not belong to any of these religious orders but he is just an ordinary man, and he is a conscientious objector?

General Hershey: Well, that is where the problem comes up. Now, 70 percent of these fellows belong to the so-called historical creeds. The other 30 percent belong to about 140 different "collections" and "noncollections." The law does not give any consideration whatsoever to the conscientious objector unless his objection is founded on religious training and belief.

Mr. Houston: Have you had to take a great many of those?

General Hershey: Well, not a great many, because some of our local boards go one way and some the other, because What is religion? is a difficult thing to say. A man perhaps has read, and whether it is religion—if he comes up and says, "I am a Communist" or "I am a Socialist" or "I am a revolutionist"—that is not the way they barge in. A man perhaps has been something, in his past, and we have tried to be rather open-minded on what is "religion," and on the other hand we have tried to be rather rigid on what is "honesty," and of course we have some people helping us, because they are the ones that must pay if the man goes to a C. O. camp.

Mr. Woodrum: All right, General. Would that about cover the matter?

General Hershey: I think that seems to cover about the things we have got here.

Except for that brief report by General Hershey to the House Appropriations Subcommittee on the activities of conscientious objectors, the subject did not come up in Congress from January 8, 1941, to August 19, 1942, when Selective Service asked that C. O.'s be given some kind of accident compensation in view of the fact that they were working for nothing and were completely without legislative protection.

In August of 1942, the Afrika Korps was pounding at the defenses of Egypt. In Russia the Germans had launched the drive that carried them into the Caucasus. American Expeditionary Forces were just beginning to leave the country in numbers and the "Second Front" cry was becoming an insistent Russian plea. In the United States the steadily quickening tempo of war added women's auxiliary forces to the armed services, tightened draft deferments, prices and rations. Registration had been extended to cover the ages of 18 to 65.

And Civilian Public Service had grown to 4,000 men.

35. b. Testimony Before the Senate Committee on Education and Labor Regarding the Establishment of an Office of War Mobilization, December 1, 1942.

From the statement of E. Raymond Wilson, of the Friends War Problems Committee, with respect to the proposed manpower draft:

Senator H. H. Schwartz (Wy.), acting chairman: I would like to ask you if you can give me an estimate of the total number of people who are under the definition of conscientious objectors in this country.

Mr. Wilson: I don't know that there is any figure that would be very precise. The membership in the three historic peace churches I mentioned runs between five and six hundred thousand.

Senator Schwartz: That would be members who are already confined and those who are still in their early minorities.

Mr. Wilson: That latest figure which has been compiled, as of November 15, 1942, indicated that there are 5,124 conscientious objectors who were at that time in the sixty civilian public service camps. So, they are coming in now at the rate of five or six hundred a month.

Senator Schwartz: From your general knowledge, what proportion of those come from rural districts?

Mr. Wilson: Well, I expect close to 50 per cent. The largest single number are Mennonites and they are largely rural.

Senator Schwartz: Do any of the conscientious objectors object to doing agricultural work?

Mr. Wilson: Most of them would be willing to do agricultural work on the farm and some have been assigned to work on dairy farms in Connecticut and Wisconsin and New York.

Senator Schwartz: There is nothing, so far as you know, in that class of work, that would impinge upon their religious scruples?

Mr. Wilson: It would depend on the character of the agricultural work. For example, I was asked the other day by one of the men in the U. S. Employment Service, whether conscientious objectors would be willing to be assigned on long staple cotton farm[s] in Arizona which are producing primarily for parachutes and other military purposes and our reply was that most of them would object to that.

Senator Schwartz: Then they would probably object to producing sugar.

Mr. Wilson: There is absolutely no final line.

Senator Schwartz: Or grain from which is made alcohol for use by the army.

Mr. Wilson: If a specific assignment was to a specific crop, as long stable cotton, which is now converted 90 to 100 per cent to military uses, then a great many would object to it. On the other hand, a great many would feel that if they were doing farm work which had been done before we entered the war and was primarily designed for the support of the total population in terms of food, that that would not be a violation of their conscience.

Senator Schwartz: We do not have many agricultural products that are not of vital necessity in the successful prosecution of the war.

Mr. Wilson: That is right, and it means that there is no complete and final divorce, as I see it, from some relation to the war effort.

Senator Schwartz: When they work in hospitals, they are also working directly—I mean military hospitals and other places—working directly in the interest of the successful prosecution of the war, aren't they?

Mr. Wilson: Well, those men at the present time are assigned to mental hospitals and to general hospitals which are not connected with victims of war; the hope is, also, that they might be extended also to tuberculosis hospitals, juvenile hospitals, juvenile delinquency and other areas of great social need at the present time.

Senator Schwartz: Well, our military hospitals have a great many men who are afflicted with tuberculosis.

Mr. Wilson: Yes, and that need has been discussed, and no final decision has been reached, as I understand it, in terms of using conscientious objectors in military hospitals. Some men in the hospitals might have objections, and they have every right to be considered as well as the conscientious objectors, and so that matter has not been undertaken yet, and wouldn't be unless there would be assurance that the relationship would be mutually welcome on both sides.

Senator Schwartz: As I understand it, none of the conscientious objectors object to a successful issue of this war in so far as the United States is concerned, do they?

Mr. Wilson: Well, they would vary at that point. Conscientious objectors, of course, believe that the war method itself brings so many other issues in its train, starvation and so forth.

Senator Schwartz: Well, if we lose the war the conscientious objectors will be in a very bad state, won't they, if Hitler and his outfit control the activities of the peoples of the world?

Mr. Wilson: Yes, they would, but the conscientious objector takes the political situation wherever it is. There have been conscientious objectors in Germany, not many but a few, and in France and in Poland and in the Scandinavian countries, also in Japan.

Senator Schwartz: From what I understand, they are disappearing fast in Poland by way of the firing squad and concentration camps where they simply slowly starve to death.

Mr. Wilson: Yes. In fact, I have been told that the largest single number of conscientious objectors in Germany were members of Jehovah's Witness, a great many of them were put in concentration camps and starved to death.

So that the conscientious objectors have been willing to pay with their lives for their testimony, if necessary, feeling that they were willing to have their lives used but not willing to take life.

Senator Schwartz: I know, but after all, if totalitarianism acquires control of the civilian population of the world, there will not be any witnesses left.

Mr. Wilson: Well, human liberty has had a tremendously long and involved struggle from the days of Caesar, the early Romans, and all, there have been people who did not submit, and the history of the early Christians is an example, for the first three hundred years, totalitarianism, brutality and violence on a scale pretty nearly as bad as today and yet they did survive the catacombs and crucifixions and the burnings-in-oil, the firing squad and all the rest of it.

Perhaps one thing that totalitarianism has not been able to overcome has been the human spirit. The groups in Norway that have held out most against the Quislings have been the Norwegian churches and in Germany the Catholics and Protestants.

While men may be wrong in their religious consciences yet it seems to us that to give people an opportunity to live by their higher insights is the most precious thing in a religion and the most precious thing in a democracy.

Senator Schwartz: I am not critical of the religious opinions or convictions of anybody, but I just wonder whether it would not be a reasonable proposition for the man who has these convictions to say, "Well, it would be better to do what we could to win this war than to lose it and go through another thousand years, like we did from 400 up to 1400, where we had darkness and chaos," whether you would not be serving your conscientious principles better by saying, "Here is a short cut by which we can ultimately and more quickly establish our principle." The theory of what you understand, and what many of us understand to be the philosophy of Christ.

Mr. Wilson: The conscientious objector would take, for instance, a longer view of that. They would feel that the war came about because of a variety of questions and problems that were not solved, over the last 20 years, and, therefore, war does not arise just because of Hitler and Mussolini and the Japanese military clique, who prey upon unemployment and an alleged sense of injustice, upon attempts to secure power in the world, where power seems to be the dominating arbitrator.

And also the conscientious objector believes, from history, that military victory itself tends to be a pretty transitory thing. We were on the winning side in 1918 and the Allies had almost complete power to dictate the terms of the peace, and the major political and economic aspects of the postwar world and yet in 14 years, the struggle for peace has pretty much been lost. Chaos in Germany thrust Hitler forward, impoverishment in Italy gave Mussolini his chance, the fact that Japan nursed a sense of grievance against Russia, a feeling of insecurity against the rest of the world gave the military clique in October, 1931, an opportunity to seize power, which they have held.

So that military victory in 1918 didn't assure the peace. The C.O. is concerned about the whole range of efforts to organize the world, to get security, to work out an economic life throughout the world, that will give a better chance for peace; he is concerned about minorities in this country and abroad, concerned about steps that can be taken to transfer the world of colonies and imperialism to more of a cooperative, self-governing world and concerned about the chance we have, as the most powerful nation at the present time, to contribute by peaceful methods to the reconstruction of the world.

36. Reports of Superintendents of State Mental Hospitals on the Work of Conscientious Objectors, 1943–45.*

The work of conscientious objectors assigned to Civilian Public Service camps differed widely. Some did farm labor; some were assigned to reforestation and soil erosion projects; still others were assigned to state mental institutions when those institutions grew desperately short of staff. When the civilian work program was being terminated, superintendents were asked to give their opinions of the work of the assignees. A sampling of those comments—with their wide spectrum of differences—appears below.

The entire group of assignees reached the CPS camp unit in January 1944. We immediately assembled the group and informed them regarding the work and tried to inspire them with interest in the care of the mentally ill. Subsequently a series of 15 lectures were given to the entire group. These lectures covered such subjects as institution hygiene and sanitation; personal hygiene and sanitation for the patients; first aid; observation of patients; tact with patients and general care of the mentally ill. Several months later the group was gotten together again and given lectures regarding psychology, mental hygiene, and mental health.

The group assigned to this unit were all of the Mennonite faith. They came from the middle Southwest, largely from farming areas. We found these men to be sincere, loyal, and cooperative. They were extremely helpful and as a matter of fact I do not see how we could have operated this institution during the war without their assistance. I would like to make the following comments with regard to this CPS unit:

During the entire time that this group has been at this institution, I have never heard a complaint from the relative of a patient, or any other employee, regarding the behavior of any one of these assignees. . . .

* United States Selective Service System, Special Monograph No. 11: *Conscientious Objection* (Washington, 1950), 2 vols., pp. 216–19; 271–78.

During the entire existence of this camp we have had no instance of AWOL or malingering. . . .

When I hear so much about the difficulties which have arisen in certain other units, I am surprised that we have gotten along here with practically no difficult situations of any kind. I believe the success of this camp has been largely due to the religious training of the men and the fact that they were all of one faith.

The CPS unit at this hospital was closed out on May 30, the last man in the unit being released on that day. Looking over in retrospect the 3 years of service given by the camp, I cannot but say that it was of definite value to us, and helped carry us through a critical stage in manpower during the years of the war. However, in spite of the war now being over, we have not been able to fully replace the CPS men.

The men in our unit conformed very well to rules and regulations, and were intelligent in their approach to their tasks. Some of them were, of course, intellectually much above the type of work they were required to do; and it is unfortunate they could not have been used in a type of work more in keeping with their education and training. Some, I think, were fakirs as far as having any religious objections to army service, and in one instance at least, a man stated that he had no religion.

I think the 4-E classification is poorly conceived. In my judgment the pay of $15 a month for the work these men did was very unjust and a pitiful hardship on some men who had families.

Replying to your inquiry of May 25, I regret to have delayed answering; I have no criticism of your administration, or the CPS system. The conscientious objectors assigned to this hospital did excellent work, and materially helped us in conducting the hospital when other help was scarce. Some of the boys were neurotic and psychopathic in make-up and never should have been inducted into the service. Our group was under the supervision of the Brethren; consequently, they were properly advised and encouraged to do the right thing.

Personally, I feel that the C. O.'s are selfish and uncooperative. They resented working under rules and regulations. They were also critical of the work of others. I feel that the problem of conscientious objectors, in general, when not founded on a recognized religious basis, in time of war should result in disenfranchisement. Not even the United States, as powerful as it is, can stand when its citizens remain divided and uncooperative, when threatened with danger of extinction from the outside world.

I feel that the office of camp operations of the CPS system has done an excellent job.

The unit was opened on April 8, 1943. During its existence 69 men were assigned to the unit, and its maximum strength was 40. We have had five assistant directors. We transferred 26 men from this unit to other units and discharged 43 outright. The total number of man-days was 8,826.

In general the services of these men were good, and they were a real help to the hospitals in a very critical period. I do not know how we should have continued to operate without them. There was a time when I had less than 30 regular ward employees to take care of approximately 1,100 men. We noted a considerable letdown in the quality of the work following VJ-day. This was due in part to the resentment of the men at enforced servitude after that time and to the fact that the older and more stable employees of the unit were discharged, and were in part replaced by younger men less mature in their judgments and viewpoints. The operational difficulties of the unit I think came about through a dual control, the director taking his orders from Selective Service, and the assistant director taking his order from a church board. . . .

During World War I, I worked in an Iowa institution where we had Amish Dutch objectors. Those boys made no trouble for us whatsoever, despite the fact that their relatives did not live more than 60 miles away. I assume that we will not have many conscientious objectors left by July 1, and I assure you that we will not have any great regret at terminating this type of service. We expect we will again be short of attendants when our young people return to complete their high-school work about September 1, but I hope that we shall not be compelled to resort to conscientious objector help, at least until World War III puts in its appearance.

I have taken considerable time to summarize my opinions and experiences regarding the use of conscientious objectors in mental hospitals.

One's opinions vary when considering the value of CPS as

it relates to mental hospitals. There is no denying that when these groups of men were organized to work in the hospitals the situation was serious and theoretically their assistance should have been of inestimable value. From there on, however, the theory began to break down and there were increasing difficulties.

In my opinion, Selective Service would have accomplished more by declaring these so-called conscientious objectors unfit for military service because of mental disorders and let it go at that. It is my further opinion that they are a group of men who are anarchistic in their thinking and general plan of living, and by and large are the most selfish group of men I have ever had dealings with.

Therefore, when I attempt to make an evaluation of this portion of the Selective Service program, it is my opinion that it has been a decided disappointment and a practical failure.

It is my further opinion that the program would have been more satisfactory if it had been organized and administered under strict military discipline.

From my standpoint the dealings with the unit included a certain amount of minor aggravation, but in looking back I must conclude that this was inherent in the situation and probably could not have been avoided by some different administrative set-up. In dealing with the church people, I have quite often received the impression that they never missed an opportunity to seek their own advantages within the Selective Service regulations. The regulations themselves were of course strictly obeyed, but there were certain attitudes into which the regulations did not enter, where the church organization and some of its assignees did not seem to be quite fulfilling the noble purposes which had been proclaimed to the public in connection with the operation of CPS hospital units. . . .

Nevertheless I suppose that the above annoyances must be balanced against the value of the work performed. Among the assignees were a fair number of excellent men who caught on to their duties in a most rapid and surprising manner. The performance of the unit as a whole as regards service rendered to the hospital was good. There were never any real public relations problems although on a couple of occasions there were cranks who nearly stirred some up. None of the men got into any trouble with civil authorities. There were no administrative problems which ever reached a level which was in any way critical or jeopardized the continued operations of the unit.

During the existence of the C. P. S. unit at the Training School, the shortage of regularly employed personnel was very acute in all departments, there having been as many as fifty-seven vacancies on our staff at one time. Although C. P. S. assignees never exceeded sixteen at one time, they aided greatly in alleviating this serious condition.

Assignments of assignees were made on a basis of the greatest needs in the organization; special qualifications were, however, given consideration where possible.

We had no instance of refusal to work; all assignees were cooperative; differences in personality and abilities existed, some being more apt and possessed of greater initiative than others but by and large their services were equal to and often superior to men employed in similar tasks. Their understanding and willingness to acquire information and experience in their various assignments makes their removal through discharge keenly felt.

There was never friction exhibited between employed personnel and assignees and although some employees showed prejudice at times, no incidence of even discourtesy ever occurred which could be charged to assignees.

There have been no incidents of violence of assignees toward inmates or a breach of moral standards of either immoderate use of alcoholic beverages or of a sex nature. No quarrels between assignees have occurred nor were there any unauthorized absences.

At the time of my advent here as Manager, June 1, 1945, much of the early misunderstanding and friction had been ironed out and my relations with all have been most pleasant and satisfactory. The unit has performed a most valuable function to this hospital and, undoubtedly, has saved many veterans' lives because of the handful of civilian attendants, more serious accidents, even to homicide, could easily have taken place [sic]. This unit has been the pride and joy of the Brethren Service Committee and they have made every effort to keep the highest type of men here and have constantly, through the Personnel Committee maintained excellent discipline as well as insisting on a very high type of services being rendered.

I, personally, dislike very much to see them go, although even with the continuation of Selective Service, if it is only 18 and 19 year olds we are going to get, I believe that it should be discontinued when the older men are all gone. A mental hospital is no place for an 18 or 19 year old person.

I am pleased to report on the activities of this C. P. S. Unit. During the time this unit has been in operation, we have had a total of twenty-two men assigned to us. . . .

For the most part all . . . men did very creditable work. A few of them were outstanding in their work. The majority of the men were assigned to work as attendants. We did have one man who was outstanding as a farm worker. All of the men were of good character and we experienced no difficulty with any of them with regard to their behavior. Their relationship with the patients and employee personnel was very satisfactory. All of the unit rendered good service and were of a tremendous help to us during the critical times when it was so hard for us to get regular employees. . . .

I can only hope that the training we have been able to give these men will in part repay them for the help they have given us. . . .

In regard to the work performed, I wish to say that I do not know how on earth we would have operated without their assistance. The employment situation here had gone beyond the stage of being critical. Week in and week out we had many wards, particularly at night, without service of an attendant. I think it was miraculous that we came through without any major tragedy.

A great many of the men in the unit were most faithful and loyal to their work. They took their work seriously. They made many contributions to the humanistic side of attendant care. Their kind and sympathetic approach to the patients set a very good example to a number of the old-line attendants who felt their duty more in the sense of a guard than in the sense of a helper. A few of these men after discharge remained here in the service and are doing very good work. I do not believe I have anything more specific to add.

In answer to your recent request for a statement from us regarding our experiences with conscientious objectors as state-hospital employees, I wish to advise as follows:

The first contingent of 10 men, comprising our C. P. S.

unit reported for duty in September 1943. Our quota was gradually increased to 25 men, although the maximum in our employ at any one time did not exceed 24.

These men came to us when we were desperately short of help, particularly on our men's wards, and the majority of them were assigned to ward duty. Others were assigned to duty as farm laborers, telephone operators and cooks, and in most instances they rendered a valuable service. With but few exceptions the men were conscientious in their work and and tried to do their work well, and it was not until VE-Day and more especially VJ-Day, that there was a very noticeable dropping off in both interest and efficiency on their part.

While there was some resentment expressed at their coming by the civilian employees, I am happy to report that, beyond a few verbal skirmishes, no trouble resulted from their contacts during their entire stay with us.

On the whole, their services were considered quite satisfactory, and it must be said that without their help coming to us at a time when other help was unobtainable, the continued functioning of some of our wards and departments would have been next to impossible.

The C. P. S. Unit was of very high value to the hospital during the war. Since we had only a small group assigned to us, it was necessary to use them entirely in the direct care of mental patients with the exception of one man assigned to laboratory work. . . .

We found the group to be willing and conscientious workers who get along with the patient population. . . .

Our particular group was of miscellaneous religious faiths with superior advantages. The first 20 men to arrive at the hospital camp had an average educational background of four years of college. Naturally there was increased resentment that they should not accept the responsibilities to the Nation which were expected of normal, red-blooded Americans. . . .

The recent closing of the C. P. S. Unit at this hospital has left us with the feeling of deep obligation to these men, and their wives who joined them here, for the quiet strength and endurance of their courage to give their best to a very disrupted service in our mental hospital during World War II.

Their serious yet cheerful response to the guidance of nurse and physician teachers, their quick adjustment to an entirely new situation is an example we hope will set a standard of service in the future.

The few personnel problems presented by the very few were quickly and quietly adjusted with the help of the Mennonite Central Committee, and in our opinion the service of these men was of great value to us, and we hope to them.

We also wish to thank you for sending this unit to us, and for the cooperation we had at all times.

37. A. J. Muste, from "Of Holy Disobedience," 1952.*

A(braham) J(ohannes) Muste, minister, labor leader, pacifist, and veteran peace crusader, evolved a position of absolute conscientious objection. "Of Holy Disobedience" was published in 1952. It is a call for total noncooperation with any preparation for war. Going to prison, Muste argued, is less damaging to the soul than war.

A book which the French writer, Georges Bernanos, wrote in Brazil—to which he had exiled himself because he would not remain in France under Nazi occupation—has just been published in this country. It is entitled *Tradition of Freedom* and is a hymn to freedom, an impassioned warning against obedience and conformity, especially obedience to the modern State engaged in mechanized, total war.

In the closing pages of this work, Bernanos writes:

> I have thought for a long time now that if, some day, the increasing efficiency of the technique of destruction finally causes our species to disappear from the earth, it will not be cruelty that will be responsible for our extinction and still less, of course, the indignation that cruelty awakens and the reprisals and vengeance that it brings upon itself . . . but the docility, the lack of responsibility of the modern man, his base subservient acceptance of every common decree. The horrors which we have seen, the still greater horrors we shall presently see, are not signs that rebels, insubordinate, untameable men, are increasing in number throughout the world, but rather that there is a constant increase, a stupendously rapid increase, in the number of obedient, docile men.

It seems to me that this is a true and timely warning. It might serve as a text for a general appeal to American youth to adopt and practice the great and urgent virtues of Holy Disobedience, nonconformity, resistance toward Conscription,

* Pendle Hill Pamphlet No. 64 (Wallingford, Pa., 1952), pp. 3–34.

Regimentation and War. For the present I want to use Bernanos' words as an introduction to some observations on the discussion regarding the absolute and relative role of these "virtues" which goes on chiefly among pacifists, members of the Historic Peace Churches and other such groups. I think it will be readily apparent, however, that the principles set forth have a wider bearing and merit consideration by all who are concerned about the maintenance of freedom in our time and the abolition of war.

Most believers in democracy and all pacifists begin, of course, with an area of agreement as to the moral necessity, the validity and the possible social value of no-saying or Holy Disobedience. Pacifists and/or conscientious objectors all draw the line at engaging in military combat and most of us indeed at any kind of service in the armed forces. But immediately thereupon questions arise as to whether we should not emphasize "positive and constructive service" rather than the "negative" of refusal to fight or to register; or questions about the relative importance of "resistance" and "reconciliation," and so on. It is to this discussion that I wish to attempt a contribution. It may be that it will be most useful both to young men of draft age and to other readers if we concentrate largely on the quite concrete problem of whether the former should register, conform to other requirements of the Selective Service Act which apply to conscientious objectors and accept or submit to the alternative service required of them under the law; or whether they shall refuse to register, or if they do register or are "automatically" registered by the authorities, shall refuse to conform at the next stage; and in any event refuse to render any alternative service under conscription. We deal, in other words, with the question whether young men who are eligible for it shall accept the 1-O classification or take the more "absolutist," non-registrant position. (For present purposes, consideration of the 1-A-O position, the designation used for draftees who are willing to accept service in the armed forces provided this is non-combatant in character, may be omitted. The 1-O classification is the designation used for persons who are on grounds of religious training and belief opposed to participation in any war. Those who are given this classification are required to render alternative service, outside the armed forces and under civilian auspices, and designed to serve "the health, safety and interest of the United States.") . . .

Pacifists in general, and Christian pacifists in particular, have to ask whether in conforming with any of the provisions of a draft law and especially in rendering conscript service regarded as of "national importance" by a war-making state, they are not helping conscription to run smoothly, helping thus to force conscription on millions of youths and thus in turn promoting war, since conscription is an integral part of an armaments race. The phenomenon of increased tension between nations when they lengthen the compulsory service period for youth is a familiar one. This, of course, raises the whole question of our evaluation of the meaning and role of military conscription, to which we shall return later.

In the meantime, one or two other comments need to be made on the phase of our problem under discussion. If what is really happening is that the war-making state is inflicting an evil on people, forcing them away from their vocation, subjecting them to a measure of persecution, then it seems we ought to keep this clearly in our own minds and ought not to let the government or public assume that we think otherwise. The expressions of "gratitude" which we have sometimes heard addressed to government for "permitting" pacifists to render alternative service seem inappropriate. We cannot have it both ways: accuse the State of the grave sin of invading the realm of Christian vocation and at the same time thank it for doing us a "favor" by making the invasion less than total. The State is not doing God or Christian people a favor in recognizing conscience, though that is what most United States Congressmen think they are doing in making some provision for COs. The pacifist who in any way encourages this notion is in danger of helping to give currency to the idea that conscience is a private whim which legislators may see fit to indulge for prudential reasons, as long as those who are afflicted with this peculiarity are very few in numbers. If non-resistant pacifists get off the high ground of patiently bowing the neck to Caesar's yoke, letting Caesar inflict the scourge of civilian conscript service upon them, they are immediately on the low ground of bargaining for indulgence for a small and, in that view, not too principled or brave a minority. Standing on that lower ground they have very little bargaining *power* and the results will reflect that fact—and pretty much did during World War II. On the other hand, both in Great Britain and in the United States the sufferings which the COs endured in World War I when there was virtually no legal or social recognition of them, were, according to all competent observers, largely responsible for the fact that fairly liberal provisions for COs were made in World War II. The Army did not want to "be bothered with these fellows again."

Two Miles or None

This does not, of course, mean that if the imposition of alternative service is accepted, it should be rendered grudgingly or that feelings of hostility toward government officials with whom we deal are appropriate. Quite the contrary. If we decide to go with Caesar one mile, the Gospel enjoins us to go two! We have the choice of not going along at all or going two miles, but not a skimpy one mile.

I think it is now generally admitted that there was not a great deal of this glad, spontaneous "second miling" on the part of the conscript COs in World War II, though there was considerable talk about it among older folks. Civilian Public Service in large measure simply did not operate on the high spiritual plane that was originally hoped and is still sometimes implied or stated, but was for many making the best of a bad business, perhaps for lack of clear leading or the courage to follow another course.

It will be recalled that there were a considerable number of Civilian Public Service men who declared flatly that it was inconsistent, and indeed hypocritical, to talk of spontaneous service under conscription. "We are here," they said, "not because our desire to serve brought us here. We are here because the government as part of its war program passed a conscription law and under that law took us by the scruff of the neck and is forcing us to do this job. We have no choice but this or the army or jail. That fact is bound to color this whole experience, except perhaps for those who can shut their eyes to reality. Anyone who denies this is a hypocrite.". . .

No matter how "liberal" or "considerate" the conditions for administering alternative service may be in the estimation of government officials or the pacifist agencies, if alternative service is accepted or acquiesced in at all, it will inevitably pose grave problems from the standpoint of Christian vocation and it will not, I think, be possible to escape the contamination or corruption which "conscription" infuses into "service." . . .

The Immature Eighteen-Year-Old

We turn next to a brief consideration of the arguments for the 1-O as against the non-registrant position which center around the problem of "the immature 18-year-old youth." A number of 18-year-olds, it is pointed out, have a strong aversion to war and a leaning toward pacifism. They are, however, emotionally immature. If they have no choice but the army or jail all but a few will choose the army and are likely to be lost to the pacifist cause. They could be held and possibly even developed into a radical pacifist position, if they had a third choice, namely, civilian service. On the other hand, the youth who in the absence of such a third possibility, chooses prison rather than the army may suffer grave psychological injury. . . .

I have the impression that even a great many, perhaps the majority, of pacifist ministers will work harder to keep a young pacifist parishioner from taking the "absolutist" position and going to jail rather than into civilian service, than they would work to get the run of the mill young parishioners to think seriously about not going into the army. They seem somehow to feel that a more awful thing is happening to the young CO who goes to jail than to the 18-year-old who goes into the army. It is my impression that this same feeling is an unconscious factor in the thinking of many lay pacifists when they react strongly against the idea of COs going to prison. This puzzles me greatly. Why should they have this reaction?

Army or Jail?

To my mind—even apart from the sufficiently appalling factor of being systematically trained for wholesale killing and subjected to the risk of being killed in brutal war—there are few if any more evil and perilous situations to put young men into than the armed forces. I should feel much deeper grief over having possibly had some part in getting some youth to go into the armed forces than over having some responsibility for bringing a young man to go to prison for conscience's sake. Are the qualms people feel about youthful COs going to prison in certain instances perhaps due to the fact that taking the non-registrant position is something very unusual and regarded with social disapproval whereas becoming a soldier is extremely common and meets with the highest social approval? It may be, therefore, that there are some ministers and other older people who should examine themselves as to whether their feelings in the matter under discussion are due to the fact that they themselves might find life in the community or in the church very uncomfortable if they were suspected of having influenced a youth to take a radical anti-draft stand, whereas all men will speak well of them—or at least not too ill—if they have helped, or at least not hindered, young Christians in adjusting themselves to the idea of going into the army. Is it just possible that we older people are sometimes concerned with sparing ourselves when we think we are solely concerned about sparing teen-agers? . . .

The great mass of teen-agers are going to be put through rigorous military training with all the hardships, the toughening and the temptations which this entails. They have to be ready to undergo actual battle experience. Many of them will actually experience modern war at the front. Is what the CO undergoes in prison vastly more terrible than this? Is it as terrible? It may be said that the soldier has social approbation whereas the pacifist, especially the "absolutist" meets social disapprobation and even ostracism. This is indeed a sore trial and many cannot endure it. Frankly, I am still left with more grief and pity in my heart for the teen-age soldier than for the teen-age "absolutist" CO. I am still left with a question whether we have a right to take any time and energy away from the struggle to lift the curse of conscription from the mass of youth and put it into an effort to secure alternative conscript service for COs.

There are, as we know, teen-age "absolutists" who feel the same way and who have demonstrated that they can endure whatever they may be called upon to endure. Nor is their lot without its compensations. They, also, "have their reward."

The So-Called Non-Religious CO

Religious COs who accept the 1-O classification and older pacifists who advocate this course have also to consider the non-religious CO. Under United States Law it is the so-called religious CO who is eligible for this classification; the so-called non-religious CO, though he may by unanimous consent be equally sincere, is not. The latter has no choice except the army or jail. The fact that he is only 18 years old does not alter that. Nothing in this entire field of pacifist policy and behavior is, frankly, harder for me to understand than how religious COs and many of the leaders of the peace churches and of the Fellowship of Reconciliation, can acquiesce in this situation and accept what is regarded as an advantage, a preferred position, under it. The white CO who accepted conscript alternative service when the Negro CO was automatically forced to choose the army or prison would be in an invidious position. So would the Gentile when his Jewish comrade was thus discriminated against. But in my mind the case is far more deplorable when it is the religious and the supposedly non-religious man who are involved. The white man or the Gentile might actually believe in discrimination or not regard it too seriously when the discrimination is in his favor. But for the religious man it should surely be a central and indispensable part of his faith that discrimination, most of all where two men acting in obedience to conscience are involved, is unthinkable and that if there is discrimination, he cannot be the beneficiary of it.

At any rate, the argument that there must be alternative service because *immature* 18-year-olds must by no means be subjected to prison experience seems to me to become completely impotent in the mouths of those religious pacifists who acquiesce in the arrangement under discussion and enable it to work—unless indeed they mean to contend that the average religious CO has less stamina than the non-religious CO and that, therefore, the former should be given gentler treatment. . . .

There is one other factor which may be mentioned in this context, that we live in an age when the role of minorities is an increasingly difficult one. The pressures and the actual persecution to which they are subjected are severe. The trend is still partially obscured in the United States but if we pause to reflect that not a single bomb has as yet fallen on this country, we shall realize that this country is not an exception to the trend toward greater conformity and regimentation. As the New York *Times* editorialized some time ago in commenting on some features of the McCarran Act, if we are already resorting to such repressive measures, what will we do when a real crisis comes? In other words, while we spent a good deal of time arguing that COs should have some choice other than the army or jail, we are probably moving into a time when that will essentially be the only choice that members of minorities, including pacifists, have. It would seem then that our thought and energy should be devoted to two issues: whether and how this trend toward totalitarianism can be halted and how we may prepare and discipline ourselves to meet the tests which our fellow-pacifists in some other lands have already had to meet.

The Nature of Conscription

This, however, leads to the third and last of the issues we are trying to explore: the true nature of conscription, of modern war, and of the conscripting, war-making State—and to the attitude which pacifists consequently should take toward them.

Participation in alternative service is quite often defended on the ground that our opposition is to war rather than conscription; except in the matter of war we are as ready to serve the nation as anybody; therefore, as long as we are not drafted for combat or forced against our will into the armed services, we are ready to render whatever service of a civilian character may be imposed upon us.

Is this a sound position? Let me emphasize that it is conscription for war under the conditions of the second half of the twentieth century that we are talking about. The question as to whether sometime and under some circumstances we might accept conscription for some conceivable purpose not related to war, is not here at stake. It is academic and irrelevant. The question with which we are dealing is that of conscripting youth in and for modern war.

As pacifists we are opposed to all war. Even if recruitment were entirely on a voluntary basis, we would be opposed. It seems to me we might infer from this that we should be *a fortiori* opposed to military conscription, for here in addition to the factor of war itself, the element of coercion by government enters in, coercion which places young boys in a military regime where they are deprived of freedom of choice in virtually all essential matters. They may not have the slightest interest in the war, yet they are made to kill by order. This is surely a fundamental violation of the human spirit which must cause the pacifist to shudder.

The reply is sometimes made that pacifists are *not* being conscripted for military purposes and therefore—presumably —*they* are not faced with the issue of the nature of military conscription. I shall later contend that it is not really possible to separate conscription and war, as I think this argument does. Here I wish to suggest that even if the question is the conscription of non-pacifist youth, it is a fundamental mistake for pacifists ever to relent in their opposition to this evil, ever to devote their energies primarily to securing provisions for COs in a draft law or to lapse into a feeling that conscription has somehow become more palatable if such provisions are made by the State. It is not our own children if we are pacifist parents, our fellow-pacifist Christians if we are churchmen, about whom we should be most deeply concerned. In the first place, that is a narrow and perhaps self-centered attitude. In the second place, pacifist youths have some inner resources for meeting the issue under discussion. The terrible thing which we should never lose sight of, to which we should never reconcile our spirits, is that the great mass of 18-year-olds are drafted for war. They are given no choice. Few are at the stage of development where they are capable of making a fully rational and responsible choice. Thus the fathers immolate the sons, the older generation immolates the younger, on the altar of Moloch. What God centuries ago forbade Abraham to do even to his own son—"Lay not thy hand upon the lad, neither do thou anything unto him"—this we do by decree to the entire youth of a nation. . . .

Disobedience Becomes Imperative

Non-conformity, Holy Disobedience, becomes a virtue and indeed a necessary and indispensable measure of spiritual self-preservation, in a day when the impulse to conform, to acquiesce, to go along, is the instrument which is used to subject men to totalitarian rule and involve them in permanent war. To create the impression at least of outward unanimity, the impression that there is no "real" opposition, is something for which all dictators and military leaders strive assiduously. The more it seems that there is no opposition, the less worthwhile it seems to an ever larger number of people to cherish even the thought of opposition. Surely, in such a situation it is important not to place the pinch of incense before Caesar's image, not to make the gesture of conformity which is involved, let us say, in registering under a military conscription law. . . .

The Reconciling Resistance

. . . [It] is of crucial importance that we should understand that for the individual to pit himself in Holy Disobedience against the war-making and conscripting State, wherever it or he be located, is not an act of despair or defeatism. Rather, I think we may say that precisely this individual refusal to "go along" is now the beginning and the core of any realistic and practical movement against war and for a more peaceful and brotherly world. For it becomes daily clearer that political and military leaders pay virtually no attention to protests against current foreign policy and pleas for peace when they know perfectly well that when it comes to a showdown, all but a handful will "go along" with the war to which the policy leads. All but a handful will submit to conscription. Few of the protesters will so much as risk their jobs in the cause of "peace." The failure of the policy-makers to change their course does not, save perhaps in very rare instances, mean that they are evil men who want war. They feel, as indeed they so often declare in crucial moments, that the issues are so complicated, the forces arrayed against them so strong, that they "have no choice" but to add another score of billions to the military budget, and so on and on. Why should they think there is any reality, hope or salvation in "peace advocates" who when the moment of decision comes also act on the assumption that they "have no choice" but to conform?

Precisely in a day when the individual appears to be utterly helpless, to "have no choice," when the aim of the "system" is to convince him that he is helpless as an individual and that the only way to meet regimentation is by regimentation, there is absolutely no hope save in going back to the beginning. The human being, the child of God, must assert his humanity and his sonship again. He must exercise the choice which he no longer has as something accorded him by society, which he "naked, weaponless, armourless, without shield or spear, but only with naked hands and open eyes" must create again. He must understand that this naked human being is the one *real* thing in the face of the mechanics and the mechanized institutions of our age. He, by the grace of God, is the seed of all the human life there will be on earth in the future, though he may have to die to make that harvest possible. As *Life* magazine stated in its unexpectedly profound and stirring editorial of August 20, 1945, its first issue after the atom bombing of Hiroshima: "Our sole safeguard against the very real danger of a reversion to barbarism is the kind of morality which compels the individual conscience, be the group right or wrong. The individual conscience against the atomic bomb? Yes. There is no other way."

Part VII

PREFACE

Two questions, implicit in the matter of conscientious objection since the middle of the last century, have erupted in the 1960's. The first is the question of the so-called nonreligious, or secular objector; the second the question of the social or political objector. The secular objector argues that his opposition to war is no less real for being based upon ethical rather than on religious grounds. The political or *selective* objector, similarly, argues that his protest is valid though it is not against all wars but against one particular war. Secular and selective objection reflect new attitudes in American society, but they are not attitudes that that society as a whole is inclined to acknowledge or to indulge.

In the matter of religious objection, we must go back to the case of *United States* v. *Downer* in 1943. In a decision handed down by the Second Circuit Court of Appeals, that court found that the defendant's opposition to war, although traceable to no church membership or teaching, was nevertheless "deep-rooted, based . . . on a general humanitarian concept which is essentially religious in character. . . ." The petitioner's claim to the status of a conscientious objector was sustained.* But the same court distinguished between Downer's humanitarian objection and the political objection of one Mathias Kauten.** Judge Augustus Hand wrote:

There is a distinction between a course of reasoning resulting in a conviction that a particular war is inexpedient or disastrous and a conscientious objection to participation in any war under any circumstances. The latter, and not the former, may be the basis of exemption under the [Selective Service] Act. The former is usually a political objection, while the latter, we think, may justly be regarded as a response of the individual to an inward mentor, call

* 135 F. 2d 521 (1943).
** *United States* v. *Kauten,* 133 F. 2d 703 (1943).

254

it conscience or God, that is for many persons at the present time the equivalent of what has always been thought a religious impulse.

Thus, the Second Circuit Court was willing to interpret religion in the broadest of terms, but it rigorously denied the claims of political objectors.

The Ninth Circuit Court, in contrast, insisted upon a strict interpretation in the matter of religion. That court stated its belief that congressional intent had been plain, and that belief in a deity was essential to meet the "religious training and belief" terms of the Selective Service Act. In *United States* v. *Berman* (1946),* where the defendant was a Socialist and humanitarian who strongly opposed *all* war, the court denied the petitioner's claim to classification as a conscientious objector. "The use of the word 'religion' was not intended to be inclusive of morals or of devotion to human welfare or of policy of government."

The discrepancy between the broad interpretation of religion by the Second Circuit Court and the strict interpretation of the Ninth Circuit Court was not reviewed by the Supreme Court until 1965. The terms of the Selective Service Act, as amended in 1948, still provided that deferment for conscientious objectors was available only on the grounds of "an individual's belief in relation to a Supreme Being involving duties superior to those arising from any human relation, but [this] does not include essentially political, sociological, or philosophical views or merely a personal moral code."

In *United States* v. *Seeger,* 1965, the Supreme Court found that the defendant, since he "did not *disavow* any belief 'in a relation to a Supreme Being,' " and since he stated that "the cosmic order does, perhaps, suggest a creative intelligence," might justly come within the purview of the Selective Service Act as Congress intended it (see Document 38 in this book). The Court's decision left the language of the 1948 Act intact, and, in fact, did little to distinguish a "religious belief" from a "personal code." The legal determination of what constitutes a man's "religion" remains largely where it was before—in the hands of the lower court judges, who must decide each appeal as it is brought before them. The difficulty is not solely the Court's; it is the Congress' and the

* 156 F. 9th 377.

nation's as well, for the Court cannot go beyond the lines set down by the legislature. But neither Congress nor the voting public has shown itself disposed to clarify the status of the nonreligious conscientious objector.

The burning of draft cards was a symbolic act of protest until Congress, in August, 1965, made it a felony to "knowingly destroy and knowingly mutilate" draft cards, such acts to be punishable by a maximum fine of $10,000 or a maximum imprisonment of five years. With a sense of outrage and a florid turn of phrase, one member of the House declared, "When decent, productive people are forced to support and coddle criminals and other dregs and drones of society, chaos, degradation, and ruin are inevitable." The "dregs" he referred to were the young men who burned draft cards to protest American participation in the Vietnam war.

The first indictment under the 1965 legislation was brought against David J. Miller, a graduate of a Jesuit college and a staff member at the Catholic Worker Hospitality House (a secular organization) in New York City. Miller was convicted, given a three-year suspended sentence, and placed on two years' probation. When he deliberately violated the terms of his probation, he was sentenced, on April 6, 1967, to two-and-one-half years in a Federal prison (see Document 39 in this book).

Later in 1965, James E. Wilson and four others burned their draft cards on the steps of the Foley Square Court House in New York City. Wilson, also a member of the Catholic Worker movement, and those who joined him, were met by placards that jeered "Burn Yourselves Instead of Your Card," and "Thanks, Pinkos, Queers, Cowards, Draft Dodgers—Mao-Tse-Tung." The Federal District Judge was more restrained: Wilson was given a two-year suspended sentence and two years' probation.

It is plain that the courts have been reluctant to apply the full punishment provided under the law. Indeed, the legality of the law forbidding the burning of draft cards was itself brought under question when the first Circuit Court of Appeals in Boston, on April 10, 1967, held it to be unconstitutional. That court found that the burning of draft cards was a symbolic act, and as such was under the protection of the First Amendment and its guarantee of free speech. Judicial opinion is, thus, widely divided and the legal basis of prosecution is uncertain. When a score of youths burned their draft cards during the April 15, 1967, Spring Mobilization to End the War in Vietnam in New York City, the Federal government made no arrests.

Public opinion, however, does not practice judicial restraint. Public opinion has been virulent against such displays of disaffection. Ex-President Dwight D. Eisenhower, writing in *The Reader's Digest* in April, 1966, probably expressed the views of the great majority of Americans:

> If, in the continuing debate over the U.S. presence in Vietnam, after examining both sides, you feel that our country is wrong, you have the right to say so. You do not have the right to do this in a raucous and belligerent way that harms the cause of freedom and in the end will cost additional lives. And you do not have the right to violate the law. *In my opinion, the draft-card burners should be sent to jail—at least for the war's duration.** [Editor's italics]

When David H. Mitchell, III, refused to report for military induction, he intended his action not only as a violation of the Selective Service laws, but as a statement of his opposition to his government's foreign policy. A political objector, Mitchell contends that the United States is guilty of torture and genocide in Vietnam; that this nation has violated the statutes it helped to formulate during the Nuremberg War Crimes Trials; that we have broken provisions of the Geneva Convention, the United Nations Charter and other signed treaties (see Document 40 in this book).** Mitchell's contention is that the citizen must not obey illegal and immoral orders given by his government or by his military commanders, but each citizen must determine, for himself, whether the war his country is involved in is just.

Claiming as he does that the citizen owes primary obedience

---

* "Thoughts for Young Americans." *The Reader's Digest,* LXXXVIII (April, 1966), 90.

** In 1945, in Nuremberg, Germany, the United States, the U.S.S.R., and Great Britain brought Nazi leaders to trial for war atrocities and genocide. A year later, an eleven-nation tribunal in Tokyo held similar trials of Japanese officers. The Nuremberg Trials constituted an attempt to introduce the principle of individual responsibility for criminal acts into international law.

The Geneva Convention contains, among its other provisions, international agreements on the treatment of prisoners of war.

to international and to moral laws (assuming, of course, as he does, that these coincide), Mitchell has taken the most radical position a conscientious objector can take. He says not only, "*I* cannot fight in your war"; he says, "Your war is unjust and *you* must stop fighting it." He attempts to stop the wheels of war machinery; he hopes to thwart the government's war policy.

The courts have not been slow to perceive the social anarchy implicit in Mitchell's position. The Second District Court ruled against Mitchell and barred his lawyer's claim that evidence of alleged U.S. aggression be heard by the court. Mitchell was found guilty of draft evasion. The Supreme Court, on March 20, 1967, declined to review his case, but Mr. Justice William O. Douglas, in a dissenting opinion, declared that "there is a considerable body of opinion that our actions in Vietnam constitute the waging of an aggressive war," and stated that Mitchell should have been allowed to introduce evidence during his trial to support his claim that he might be found guilty as a war criminal if he went to Vietnam as a soldier.

Protests against the Vietnam war reverberate through our society. In the State of Georgia, Julian Bond, a Negro and a duly elected representative, was denied his seat in the Georgia legislature because of his outspoken criticism of the government's Vietnam policy, and because of his advocacy of conscientious objection as a means of social protest (see Document 41 in this book). Staughton Lynd, a professor of history at Yale University, with other private citizens, went to Vietnam in an effort to bring about a negotiated peace. Upon his return, the government revoked his passport and refused to permit him to make subsequent trips to England and to Norway where he had speaking engagements. Lynd challenged the government's action (see Document 42 in this book). The case captures many of the contradictory conditions under which conscience asserts itself in this democracy: there was, on the one hand, extraordinary freedom in that Lynd was permitted to travel to North Vietnam, a belligerent country, and that he did, in fact, meet with leaders of an "enemy" government; then, on the other hand, as if there had been rueful afterthoughts, came the restrictions upon the simplest prerogatives, the freedom to travel to the friendly nations of Western Europe.

The section ends with the case of three army privates willing to serve their tour of duty in any part of the world—but Vietnam (see Document 43 in this book). The defendants are obviously not pacifists, and they are already part of the armed forces. Their claim—and their protest—are unique to our times.

38. *United States* v. *Seeger*, 1965.*

The Seeger case actually dealt with three appellants: Daniel Andrew Seeger himself, Arno S. Jakobson, and Forest Britt Peter. The parties raised the question of the constitutionality of that portion of the Selective Service Act that defined "religious training and belief" to mean an individual's "relation to a Supreme Being."

Mr. Justice Clark for the Court:

The Facts in the Cases

No. 50: Seeger was convicted in the District Court for the Southern District of New York of having refused to submit to induction in the armed forces. He was originally classified 1-A in 1953 by his local board, but this classification was changed in 1955 to 2-S (student) and he remained in this status until 1958 when he was reclassified 1-A. He first claimed exemption as a conscientious objector in 1957 after successive annual renewals of his student classification. Although he did not adopt verbatim the printed Selective Service System form, he declared that he was conscientiously opposed to participation in war in any form by reason of his "religious" belief; that he preferred to leave the question as to his belief in a Supreme Being open, "rather than answer 'yes' or 'no' "; that his "skepticism or disbelief in the existence of God" did "not necessarily mean lack of faith in anything whatsoever"; that his was a "belief in and devotion to goodness and virtue for their own sakes, and a religious faith in a purely ethical creed." He cited such personages as Plato, Aristotle and Spinoza for support of his ethical belief in intellectual and moral integrity "without belief in God, except in the remotest sense." His belief was found to be sincere, honest, and made in good faith; and his conscientious objection to be based upon individual training and belief, both of which included research in religious and cultural fields. Seeger's

* 380 U.S. 163 (1965).

claim, however, was denied solely because it was not based upon a "belief in a relation to a Supreme Being" as required by Section 6(j) of the [Universal Military Training and Service] Act. At trial Seeger's counsel admitted that Seeger's belief was not in relation to a Supreme Being as commonly understood, but contended that he was entitled to the exemption because "under the present law Mr. Seeger's position would also include definitions of religion which have been stated more recently," and could be "accommodated" under the definition of religious training and belief in the Act. He was convicted and the Court of Appeals reversed, holding that the Supreme Being requirement of the section distinguished "between internally derived and externally compelled beliefs" and was, therefore, an "impermissible classification" under the Due Process Clause of the Fifth Amendment. . . .

Background

Chief Justice Hughes, in his opinion in *United States* v. *Macintosh,* 283 U.S. 605 (1931)* enunciated the rationale behind the long recognition of conscientious objection to participation in war accorded by Congress in our various conscription laws when he declared that "in the forum of conscience, duty to a moral power higher than the state has always been maintained." In a similar vein Harlan Fiske Stone, later Chief Justice, drew from the Nation's past when he declared that:

Both morals and sound policy require that the state should not violate the conscience of the individual. All our history gives confirmation to the view that liberty of conscience has a moral and social value which makes it worthy of preservation at the hands of the state. So deep in its significance and vital, indeed, is it to the integrity of man's moral and spiritual nature that nothing short of the self-preservation of the state should warrant its violation; and it may well be questioned whether the state which preserves its life by a settled policy of violation of the conscience of the individual will not in fact ultimately lose it by the process." Stone, "The Conscientious Objector," 21 *Col. Univ. Q.* 253, 269 (1919).

* See Part V, Document 31.

Governmental recognition of the moral dilemma posed for persons of certain religious faiths by the call to arms came early in the history of this country. Various methods of ameliorating their difficulty were adopted by the Colonies, and were later perpetuated in state statutes and constitutions. Thus by the time of the Civil War there existed a state pattern of exempting conscientious objectors on religious grounds. . . .

With the Federal Conscription Act of 1863, which enacted the commutation and substitution provisions of General Order No. 99, the Federal Government occupied the field entirely and in the 1864 Draft Act, 13 Stat. 9, it extended exemptions to those conscientious objectors who were members of religious denominations opposed to the bearing of arms and who were prohibited from doing so by the articles of faith of their denominations. Selective Service System Monograph No. 11, *Conscientious Objection*, 40-41 (1950). In that same year the Confederacy exempted certain pacifist sects from military duty.

The need for conscription did not again arise until World War I. The Draft Act of 1917 afforded exemptions to conscientious objectors who were affiliated with a "well-recognized religious sect or organization [then] organized and existing and whose existing creed or principles [forbade] its members to participate in war in any form. . . ." The Act required that all persons be inducted into the armed services, but allowed the conscientious objectors to perform noncombatant service in capacities designated by the President of the United States. Although the 1917 Act excused religious objectors only, in December, 1917, the Secretary of War instructed that "personal scruples against war" be considered as constituting "conscientious objection." Selective Service System Monograph No. 11, *Conscientious Objection*, 54-55 (1950). This Act, including its conscientious objector provisions, was upheld against constitutional attack in the Selective Draft Law cases [*Arver* v. *United States* (1918)].

In adopting the 1940 Selective Training and Service Act Congress broadened the exemption afforded in the 1917 Act by making it unnecessary to belong to a pacifist religious sect if the claimant's own opposition to war was based on "religious training and belief." Those found to be within the exemption were not inducted into the armed services but were assigned to noncombatant service under the supervision of the

Selective Service System. The Congress recognized that one might be religious without belonging to an organized church just as surely as minority members of a faith not opposed to war might through religious reading reach a conviction against participation in war. *Congress Looks at the Conscientious Objector* (National Service Board for Religious Objectors, 1943). Indeed, the consensus of the witnesses appearing before the congressional committees was that individual belief—rather than membership in a church or sect—determined the duties that God imposed upon a person in his everyday conduct; and that "there is a higher loyalty than loyalty to this country, loyalty to God." Thus, while shifting the test from membership in such a church to one's individual belief the Congress nevertheless continued its historic practice of excusing from armed service those who believed that they owed an obligation, superior to that due the state, of not participating in war in any form.

Between 1940 and 1948 two courts of appeals* held that the phrase "religious training and belief" did not include philosophical, social or political policy. Then in 1948 the Congress amended the language of the statute and declared that "religious training and belief" was to be defined as "an individual's belief in a relation to a Supreme Being involving duties superior to those arising from any human relation, but [not including] essentially political, sociological, or philosophical views or a merely personal moral code." The only significant mention of this change in the provision appears in the report of the Senate Armed Services Committee recommending adoption. It said simply this: "This section reenacts substantially the same provisions as were found in subsection 5(g) of the 1940 act. Exemption extends to anyone who, because of religious training and belief in his relation to a Supreme Being, is conscientiously opposed to combatant military service or to both combatant and non-combatant military service." (See *United States* v. *Berman.*)

Interpretation

The crux of the problem lies in the phrase "religious training and belief" which Congress has defined as "belief in a

* See *United States* v. *Kauten,* 133 F. 2d 703 (1943); *United States* v. *Berman,* 156 F. 2d 377 (1946).

relation to a Supreme Being involving duties superior to those arising from any human relation." In assigning meaning to this statutory language we may narrow the inquiry by noting briefly those scruples expressly excepted from the definition. The section excludes those persons who, disavowing religious belief, decide on the basis of essentially political, sociological or economic considerations that war is wrong and that they will have no part of it. These judgments have historically been reserved for the Government, and in matters which can be said to fall within these areas the conviction of the individual has never been permitted to override that of the state. *United States* v. *Macintosh, supra* (dissenting opinion).* The statute further excludes those whose opposition to war stems from a "merely personal moral code," a phrase to which we shall have occasion to turn later in discussing the application of Section 6(j) to these cases. We also pause to take note of what is not involved in this litigation. No party claims to be an atheist or attacks the statute on this ground. The question is not, therefore, one between theistic and atheistic beliefs. We do not deal with or intimate any decision on that situation in these cases. Nor do the parties claim the monotheistic belief that there is but one God; what they claim (with the possible exception of Seeger who bases his position here not on factual but on purely constitutional grounds) is that they adhere to theism, which is the "Belief in the existence of a god or gods; . . . Belief in superhuman powers or spiritual agencies in one or many gods," as opposed to atheism.** Our question, therefore, is the narrow one: Does the term "Supreme Being" as used in Section 6(j) mean the orthodox God or the broader concept of a power or being, or a faith, "to which all else is subordinate or upon which all else is ultimately dependent"? *Webster's New International Dictationary* (Second Edition). In considering this question we resolve it solely in relation to the language of Section 6(j) and not otherwise. . . .

Over 250 sects inhabit our land. Some believe in a purely personal God, some in a supernatural deity; others think of religion as a way of life envisioning as its ultimate goal the day when all men can live together in perfect understanding

* See Part V, Document 31, part b, in this book where that dissenting opinion appears. [Editor's note]
** See *Webster's New International Dictionary* (Second Edition); *Webster's New Collegiate Dictionary* (1949).

and peace. There are those who think of God as the depth of our being; others, such as the Buddhists, strive for a state of lasting rest through self-denial and inner purification; in Hindu philosophy, the Supreme Being is the transcendental reality which is truth, knowledge and bliss. Even those religious groups which have traditionally opposed war in every form have splintered into various denominations: from 1940 to 1947 there were four denominations using the name "Friends"; the "Church of the Brethren" was the official name of the oldest and largest church body of four denominations composed of those commonly called Brethren; and the "Mennonite Church" was the largest of 17 denominations, including the Amish and Hutterites, grouped as "Mennonite bodies" in the 1936 report on the Census of Religious Bodies. This vast panoply of beliefs reveals the magnitude of the problem which faced the Congress when it set about providing an exemption from armed service. . . .

In spite of the elusive nature of the inquiry, we are not without certain guide-lines. In amending the 1940 Act, Congress adopted almost intact the language of Chief Justice Hughes in *United States* v. *Macintosh, supra*: "The essence of religion is belief in a relation to *God* involving duties superior to those arising from any human relation." By comparing the statutory definition with those words, however, it becomes readily apparent that the Congress deliberately broadened them by substituting the phrase "Supreme Being" for the appellation "God." And in so doing it is also significant that Congress did not elaborate on the form or nature of this higher authority which it chose to designate as "Supreme Being." By so refraining it must have had in mind the admonitions of the Chief Justice when he said in the same opinion that even the word "god" had myriad meanings for men of faith:

> Putting aside dogmas with their particular conceptions of deity, freedom of conscience itself implies respect for an innate conviction of paramount duty. The battle for religious liberty has been fought and won with respect to religious beliefs and practices, which are not in conflict with good order, upon the very ground of the supremacy of conscience within its proper field.

. . . The test might be stated in these words: A sincere and meaningful belief which occupies in the life of its possessor a place parallel to that filled by the God of those admittedly qualifying for the exemption comes within the statutory definition. . . . While the applicant's words may differ, the test is simple of application. It is essentially an objective one, namely, does the claimed belief occupy the same place in the life of the objector as an orthodox belief in God holds in the life of one clearly qualified for exemption?

Moreover, it must be remembered that in resolving these exemption problems one deals with the beliefs of different individuals who will articulate them in a multitude of ways. In such an intensely personal area, of course, the claim of the registrant that his belief is an essential part of a religious faith must be given great weight. . . . The validity of what he believes cannot be questioned. Some theologians, and indeed some examiners, might be tempted to question the existence of the registrant's "Supreme Being" or the truth of his concepts. But these are inquiries foreclosed to Government. . . .

Local boards and courts in this sense are not free to reject beliefs because they consider them "incomprehensible." Their task is to decide whether the beliefs professed by a registrant are sincerely held and whether they are, in his own scheme of things, religious.

But we hasten to emphasize that while the "truth" of a belief is not open to question, there remains the significant question whether it is "truly held." This is the threshold question of sincerity which must be resolved in every case. It is, of course, a question of fact—a prime consideration to the validity of every claim for exemption as a conscientious objector. The Act provides a comprehensive scheme for assisting the Appeal Boards in making this determination, placing at their service the facilities of the Department of Justice, including the Federal Bureau of Investigation and hearing officers. . . .

Application to the Instant Cases

As we noted earlier, the statutory definition excepts those registrants whose beliefs are based on a "merely personal moral code." The records in these cases, however, show that at no time did any one of the applicants suggest that his objection was based on a "merely personal moral code." Indeed at the outset each of them claimed in his application that his objection was based on a religious belief. We have construed the statutory definition broadly and it follows that any exception to it must be interpreted narrowly. The use by Congress of the words "merely personal" seems to us to restrict the exception to a moral code which is not only personal but which is the sole basis for the registrant's belief and is in no way related to a Supreme Being. It follows, therefore, that if the claimed religious beliefs of the respective registrants in these cases meet the test that we lay down then their objections cannot be based on a "merely personal" moral code.

In Seeger, No. 50, the Court of Appeals failed to find sufficient "externally compelled beliefs." However, it did find that "it would seem impossible to say with assurance that [Seeger] is not bowing to 'external commands' in virtually the same sense as is the objector who defers to the will of a supernatural power." It found little distinction between Jakobson's devotion to a mystical force of "Godness" and Seeger's compulsion to "goodness." Of course, as we have said, the statute does not distinguish between externally and internally derived beliefs. Such a determination would, as the Court of Appeals observed, prove impossible as a practical matter, and we have found that Congress intended no such distinction.

The Court of Appeals also found that there was no question of the applicant's sincerity. He was a product of a devout Roman Catholic home; he was a close student of Quaker beliefs from which he said "much of [his] thought is derived"; he approved of their opposition to war in any form; he devoted his spare hours to the American Friends Service Committee and was assigned to hospital duty.

In summary, Seeger professed "religious belief" and "religious faith." He did not disavow any belief "in a relation to a Supreme Being"; indeed he stated that "the cosmic order does, perhaps, suggest a creative intelligence." He decried the tremendous "spiritual" price man must pay for his willingness to destroy human life. In light of his beliefs and the unquestioned sincerity with which he held them, we think the Board, had it applied the test we propose today, would have granted him the exemption. We think it clear that the beliefs which prompted his objection occupy the same place in his life as the belief in a traditional deity holds in the lives of his friends, the Quakers. . . . We therefore affirm the judgment in No. 50.

In Jakobson, No. 51, the Court of Appeals found that the registrant demonstrated that his belief as to opposition to war was related to a Supreme Being. We agree and affirm that judgment.

We reach a like conclusion in No. 29. It will be remembered that Peter acknowledged "some power manifest in nature . . . the supreme expression" that helps man in ordering his life. As to whether he would call that belief in a Supreme Being, he replied, "You could call that a belief in the Supreme Being or God. These just do not happen to be the words I use." We think that under the test we establish here the Board would grant the exemption to Peter and we therefore reverse the judgment in No. 29. It is so ordered.

Mr. Justice Douglas, concurring.

. . . The words "a Supreme Being" have no narrow technical meaning in the field of religion. Long before the birth of our Judeo-Christian civilization the idea of God had taken hold in many forms. Mention of only two—Hinduism and Buddhism—illustrates the fluidity and evanescent scope of the concept. In the Hindu *religion* the Supreme Being is conceived in the forms of several cult Deities. The chief of these, which stand for the Hindu Triad, are Brahma, Vishnu and Siva. Another Deity, and the one most widely worshipped, is Sakti, the Mother Goddess, conceived as power, both destructive and creative. Though Hindu religion encompasses the worship of many Deities, it believes in only one single God, the eternally existent One Being with his manifold attributes and manifestations. This idea is expressed in Rigveda, the earliest sacred text of the Hindus, in verse 46 of a hymn attributed to the mythical seer Dirghatamas (Rigveda, I, 164):

> "They call it Indra, Mitra, Varuna and Agni
> And also heavenly beautiful Garutman:
> The Real is One, though sages name it variously—
> They call it Agni, Yama, Matarisvan."

Indian *philosophy*, which comprises several schools of thought, has advanced different theories of the nature of the Supreme Being. According to the Upanishads, Hindu sacred texts, the Supreme Being is described as the power which creates and sustains everything, and to which the created things return upon dissolution. The word which is commonly used in the Upanishads to indicate the Supreme Being is

Brahma. Philosophically, the Supreme Being is the transcendental Reality which is Truth, Knowledge, and Bliss. It is the source of the entire universe. In this aspect Brahma is Isvara, a personal Lord and Creator of the universe, an object of worship. But, in the view of one school of thought, that of Sankara, even this is an imperfect and limited conception of Brahma which must be transcended; to think of Brahma as the Creator of the material world is necessarily to form a concept infected with illusion, or *maya*—which is what the world really is, in highest truth. Ultimately, mystically, Brahma must be understood as without attributes, as *neti neti* (not this, not that).

Buddhism—whose advent marked the reform of Hinduism—continued somewhat the same concept. As stated by Nancy Wilson Ross, "God—if I may borrow that word for a moment—the universe, and man are one indissoluble existence, one total whole. Only THIS—capital THIS—is. Anything and everything that appears to us as an individual entity or phenomenon, whether it be a planet or an atom, a mouse or a man, is but a temporary manifestation of THIS in form; every activity that takes place, whether it be birth or death, loving or eating breakfast, is but a temporary manifestation of THIS in activity. . . . Each one of us is but a cell, as it were, in the body of the Great Self, a cell that comes into being, performs its functions, and passes away, transformed into another manifestation. Though we have temporary individuality, that temporary, limited individuality is not either a true self or our true self. Our true self is the Great Self; our true body is the Body of Reality, or the Dharmakaya, to give it its technical Buddhist name."*

Does a Buddhist believe in "God" or a "Supreme Being"? That, of course, depends on how one defines "God. . . ."

When the present Act was adopted in 1948 we were a nation of Buddhists, Confucianists, and Taoists, as well as Christians. Hawaii, then a Territory, was indeed filled with Buddhists, Buddhism being "probably the major faith, if Protestantism and Roman Catholicism are deemed different faiths. . . ."

In the continental United States Buddhism is found "in real strength" in Utah, Arizona, Washington, Oregon, and California.

* *The World of Zen,* Nancy Wilson Ross, ed. (New York: Random House, 1960), p. 18. [Editor's note]

When the Congress spoke in the vague general terms of a Supreme Being I cannot, therefore, assume that it was so parochial as to use the words in the narrow sense urged on us. I would attribute tolerance and sophistication to the Congress, commensurate with the religious complexion of our communities. In sum, I agree with the Court that any person opposed to war on the basis of a sincere belief, which in his life fills the same place as a belief in God fills in the life of an orthodox religionist, is entitled to exemption under the statute. None comes to us an avowedly irreligious person or as an atheist; one, as a sincere believer in "goodness and virtue for their own sakes." His questions and doubts on theological issues, and his wonder, are no more alien to the statutory standard than are the awe-inspired questions of a devout Buddhist.

39. Draft Card Burning, 1965, 1966.

In 1965 demonstrators against the war in Vietnam began to burn their draft cards in public as evidence of their strong aversion to the government's military enterprise. Congress amended the Selective Service Act in August, 1965, and made draft card burning a federal offense. Through the summer of 1967 some sixteen persons have been prosecuted under the new law; twelve have been convicted, and four cases are pending. On October 9, 1967, the Supreme Court agreed to review the constitutionality of the issue.

39. a. House Debate on Bill to Prohibit Destruction or Mutilation of Draft Cards, 1965.*

Mr. BRAY.** Mr. Speaker, the bill that we have before us today is simple and easy to understand. H.R. 10306 is an amendment to our selective service law providing that it is illegal to knowingly mutilate or destroy a draft card. It is already illegal to alter, forge or change such a card.

The need of this legislation is clear. Beatniks and so-called "campus-cults" have been publicly burning their draft cards to demonstrate their contempt for the United States and our resistance to Communist takeovers. Such actions have been suggested and led by college professors—professors supported by taxpayers' money.

A Rutgers University professor, who prides himself on being a Marxist, publicly said that he "welcomed a Communist Vietcong victory." The board of governors refused to dismiss him.

Just yesterday such a mob attacking the United States and praising the Vietcong attempted to march on the Capitol but were prevented by the police from forcibly moving into our Chambers. They were led by a Yale University professor. They were generally a filthy, sleazy beatnik gang; but the question which they pose to America is quite serious.

These so-called "student" mobs at home and abroad make demands and threats; they hurl rocks and ink bottles at American buildings; they publicly mutilate or burn their draft cards; they even desecrate the American flag. Chanting and screaming vile epithets, these mobs of so-called "students" and Communist "stooges" attempt to create fear and destroy self-confidence in our country and its citizens and to downgrade the United States in the eyes of the world.

Such organized "student" groups in the United States have sent congratulations and money to Ho Chi Minh and have made anonymous and insulting calls to families of our servicemen killed in Vietnam.

This proposed legislation to make it illegal to knowingly

* From the *Congressional Record,* 89th Cong. 1st Sess., Vol. 111, Part 15, August 10, 1965, pp. 19871–72.
** Representative William G. Bray, Indiana. [Editor's note]

destroy or mutilate a draft card is only one step in bringing some legal control over those who would destroy American freedom. This legislation, if passed, will be of some assistance to our country if the officers and courts charged with the enforcement of the law will have the energy, courage, and guts to make use of it.

The growing disrespect for our law and institutions in America holds a real threat to our country and to our freedom. . . .

Disrespect for our American heritage and anti-American demonstrations are all a part of the cold war in some way directed by those who would destroy us. . . .

Let us have a rebirth of patriotism. Let us be proud, possessed not of an arrogant pride, but a humble pride in our greatness, in our heritage. . . .

Our Government, through fear of the public opinion at home and abroad of our enemies, is failing to adequately enforce our laws on subversion and anti-governmental attacks. . . .

When decent, productive people are forced to support and coddle criminals and other dregs and drones of society, chaos, degradation, and ruin are inevitable. . . .

If these "revolutionaries" are permitted to deface and destroy their draft cards, our entire Selective Service System is dealt a serious blow.

Mr. Speaker, I strongly urge all my fellow Members to support this legislation. . . .

The question was taken; and there were—yeas 393, nays 1, not voting 40.

39. b. Prohibition of Destruction or Mutilation of Draft Cards, an Amendment to the Universal Military Training and Service Act of 1951.

Section 462(b)(3) of Title 50, United States Code

462. Offenses and penalties

(b) Any person . . . who forges, alters, *knowingly destroys, knowingly mutilates*, or in any manner changes any such certificate or any notation duly and validly inscribed thereon . . . shall, upon conviction, be fined not to exceed $10,000 or be imprisoned for not more than five years, or both. [Editor's italics]

39. c. *United States* v. *Miller*, 1965, 1966.

On October 15, 1965, David J. Miller burned his draft card at an Army induction center in New York City. He was arrested, tried, found guilty, and sentenced to a three-year suspended term and put on two-year probation. Miller's case was heard on appeal by the Circuit Court, but that Court sustained the finding of the District Court. One of the conditions of Miller's probation was that he apply for and then carry a new draft card. When Miller refused, he was sentenced on April 6, 1967, to two-and-a-half years in a Federal prison.

Only a few days later, on April 10, 1967, the First Circuit Court of Appeals in Boston, hearing the case of another draft card burner, one David P. O'Brien, found that the law porhibiting the burning of draft cards was unconstitutional because the action in question was, as Miller had claimed, a "symbolic act," involving freedom of speech and protected by the First Amendment. Thus, two conflicting decisions by two different Federal Circuit Courts of Appeal stand. The Supreme Court, in October, 1967, has agreed to hear David O'Brien's appeal and thereby to review the constitutional issue that is involved.

1. *U.S.* v. *Miller*, District Court Decision—1965[*]
Judge Harold R. Tyler, Jr.:

Defendant Miller, who has been charged with knowingly destroying and mutilating his Notice of Draft Classification (SSS Form No. 110). . . .

1. Dismiss the indictment, or, in the alternative, to
2. Receive a bill of particulars with regard to the charge, and to
3. Discover and inspect various documents and effects, including the charred remains of his aforesaid Notice.

For reasons to be briefly hereinafter discussed, the motion to dismiss the indictment prior to trial is denied, and the motions for particulars and discovery, as will be more specifically delineated, are granted in part and otherwise denied.

Upon his motion to dismiss, Miller argues variously that:

[*] 249 F. Supp. 59 (1965).

(1) the indictment fails to charge a crime against the United States; (2) the indictment effectively denies or abridges his rights to freedom of speech, assembly and exercise of political rights, all as guaranteed to him by the First, Ninth and Tenth Amendments to the Constitution of the United States; (3) the indictment effectively denies him due process of law under the Fifth Amendment because the underlying criminal statute serves no legitimate legislative purpose; and (4) the indictment would work a deprivation of his right to be free from cruel and unusual punishment as secured to him by the Fifth and Eighth Amendments. All of these claimed deficiencies, as Miller is aware, must be found at this stage, if they are to be found at all, on the face of the indictment or its statutory underpinning.

Contention that the indictment fails to state a crime against the United States.

In order to put this contention in focus, it is necessary to indicate that defendant's basic argument consists of the following syllogism:

1. Only destruction and mutilation of a "certificate" constitutes a violation of the pertinent provision of Section 462(b).

2. A Notice of Classification is not, as a matter of fact or law, a certificate.

3. Thus, Miller's alleged destruction and mutilation of his Notice does not constitute a violation of the statute.

Simply stated, defendant's second or minor premise is erroneous. Although it may be argued that neither the provisions of Title 50 Appendix nor the regulations thereunder categorically define the Notice (SSS Form No. 110) to be a "certificate" with intention to embrace, among other Selective Service documents, the Notice in question. . . .

Contention that the indictment denies defendant his constitutional rights of free speech, assembly and exercise of political rights.

As defendant's counsel virtually conceded during oral argument of this motion, there is presently no firm factual basis for raising or passing upon the contentions under the First, Ninth and Tenth Amendments prior to trial of the indictment. Certainly, the statutory language on its face suggests no issues, let alone deprivations of rights, under the Amendments cited. The pertinent part of Section 462(b) simply makes it a crime to "knowingly destroy(s), knowingly mutilate(s) . . ." a Notice or other certificate. The indictment language is essentially that of the statute. Even defendant, then, must perceive that there is nothing on the face of either the statute or the indictment which remotely suggests any problem of free speech or free assembly or free exercise of political rights as guaranteed by the Constitution. Certainly not one of defendant's cited cases comes close to supporting his contentions in this area.

But Miller's lawyers attempt to avoid this obvious point by suggesting that the statute might affect speech or assembly upon certain hypothetical facts. Surely, counsel must know that federal courts cannot decide constitutional questions before they are squarely presented in the context of solidly determined, as opposed to hypothetical facts. . . . Moreover, it does no good at this early stage of the proceedings to suggest further, as defendant does, that mutilation or destruction of a Notice must be considered "symbolic speech" within the ambit of First Amendment safeguards. . . .

Contention that the indictment denies defendant due process of law under the Fifth Amendment.

Essentially, defendant's argument here is that the pertinent amendment to Section 462(b) serves no legitimate or rational legislative purpose. In fairness to defendant, it might be more accurate to say that under this general contention, he argues, first, that on its face the statutory language proscribing destruction and mutilation of a Notice neither enhances nor in any way significantly affects the "economic or military capabilities of the United States," and, second, on the basis of its legislative history, the new language of Section 462(b)(3) was passed by Congress without any concern for or purpose under its war powers. To illustrate, defendant points out, *inter alia*, that destruction of a Notice in itself cannot normally preclude or significantly delay service in the armed forces by the registrant, that the Selective Service System did not request such an amendment to the law and that speeches on the floor of Congress indicated beyond a doubt that, in the minds of the speaking solons at least, the new language was designed for no other purpose than to discourage critics of the government's war policies and objectives in Southeast Asia.

When called upon to decide whether or not legislation comports with necessary standards of substantive due process, the courts must "determine in each case whether circumstances vindicate the challenged regulation as a reasonable exertion of governmental authority or condemn it as arbitrary or discriminatory." . . . This is not to say, however, that courts should be governed by subjective views of the political wisdom of the legislative enactment in question; rather, the judicial branch can only be properly concerned with whether or not the statute under attack serves purposes reasonably related to legitimate powers of Congress under the Constitution—and that it so serves without discrimination or caprice.

On its face, the amended language of Section 462(b) meets the standards of substantive due process. As is widely known, for example, the regulations of the Selective Service System for at least the past twenty years have required registrants to carry their Notices of Classification upon their persons. This circumstance alone suggests that it is by no means irrational for Congress to take the additional step of making it a crime to knowingly destroy one's Notice in order to underscore the long-established duty of a registrant to maintain continuous possession of that document. . . .

Parenthetically, although I do not read defendant's briefs to explicitly make the point, it is conceivable that his serious contention here may amount to this: assuming that the due process test of a "rational basis" has been met for this particular legislation, this is not necessarily an adequate test with respect to possible abridgement of freedom of speech, assembly and the exercise of political rights. In other words, as has been discussed infra at page 62, it is theoretically possible that legislation, valid enough upon grounds of purpose and rationality, may unnecessarily impinge upon Bill of Rights protections. . . . To be sure, in the words of Mr. Justice Black in *Giboney* v. *Empire Storage Co.*, 336 U.S. 490 (1949), "It rarely has been suggested that the constitutional freedom for speech and press extends its immunity to speech or writing used as an integral part of conduct in violation of a valid criminal statute," and for this reason alone it can be well understood why the government here argues, not without persuasiveness, that upon no con-

ceivable set of circumstances can Miller ever effectively
establish infringement of his First Amendment privileges. . . .

Returning to the main theme, it would be easy to take
notice in detail of other obvious benefits to the authorities
and the public of the requirement of continuous retention by
each individual of his Notice of Classification. Enough has
been said, however, to make the obvious point that on its
face the amended language of Section 462(b) is a reasonable exercise of the powers of Congress to raise armies in
the defense of the United States. It matters not that destruction of his card will not impede the possible call-up of defendant, nor is it of any consequence that almost certainly
thousands of men in recent decades have unwittingly failed
to carry their cards at all times without ever having been
called to show or produce them. . . .

Most important here, what motivated members of Con-
grss in enacting the amended provisions of Section 462(b) is
irrelevant. This court must look only to the statutory language itself, particularly, where, as here, that language is
simple and plain on its face. Determination of the state of
mind of those legislators to whose speeches defendant specifically points and the other members of Congress voting
on this amendment is beyond the competence of this court
and in any event would be a largely irrelevant exercise. . . .
Even assuming that some Congressional members possessed
a state of mind or motives totally unrelated to proper legislative purposes, the point remains, as already indicated
above, that the simple language of Section 462(b)(3), as
amended, clearly relates to legitimate Congressional ends
under the war powers. . . .

Accordingly, the defendant's discovery motion is denied
in its entirety, without prejudice, however, to his right to
make application to the trial judge for inspection of some
or all of these same materials during the trial.

An order should be settled on notice to reflect the foregoing.

2. *U.S.* v. *Miller,* 1966*

Feinberg, Circuit Judge:
This case raises perplexing issues of whether symbolic conduct is speech embraced by the First Amendment and the

* 367 F. 2d 72.

extent of its protection thereunder. The appeal challenges the constitutionality of a federal statute prohibiting the destruction of Selective Service certificates; the ultimate question before the court is the power of Congress to enact the legislation. The constitutional issues are raised by David J. Miller, who appeals from a judgment convicting him of knowingly destroying a Selective Service System Notice of Classification. Appellant was tried without a jury before Judge Tyler in the Southern District of New York. Taking into account Miller's sincerity and background, the judge suspended execution of a sentence of three years' imprisonment and placed appellant on two years' probation. We hold the statute constitutional and affirm the conviction.

Constitutional Arguments

Since appellant does not claim here that he did not violate the statute—nor is there any room for doubt on this score—and since no procedural infirmities are raised, we turn to the constitutional arguments advanced. Appellant contends that the 1965 amendment is unconstitutional (1) on its face because its legislative history establishes that it was enacted deliberately to suppress dissent; (2) as applied to the facts of this case, because the conduct it punishes this defendant for is symbolic speech protected by the First Amendment; and (3) under the Fifth Amendment, because it serves no rational legislative purpose.

As to the first contention, going behind the terms of a statute to divine the collective legislative motive for its enactment is rarely, if ever, done by a court. . . . Ordinarily, if Congress has power to act in a field, judicial inquiry ends so long as the statute does not on its face infringe a constitutional right. The 1965 amendment appears to meet this test. Congress clearly has power under Article I, section 8 of the Constitution to "raise and support Armies," and the Universal Military Training and Service Act and the 1965 amendment thereto. . . .

On its face, the amended statute here attacked concerns administration of the draft, not regulation of ideas or the means of communicating them. . . .

To prove the "real" congressional purpose of the 1965 amendment, appellant resorts to its legislative history, a source frequently used to construe the terms of a statute. But that history is inconclusive. Even though portions—particularly remarks by two Representatives (including the sponsor of the bill in the House)—indicate a desire to suppress political dissent, the more authoritative committee reports also show a concern that destruction of draft cards "represents a potential threat to the exercise of the power to raise and support armies." It may even be conceded that the amendment was prompted by widely publicized burnings of draft cards occurring in demonstrations against this country's Vietnam policy. But neither does that control disposition of the case. . . .

The 1965 amendment clearly was intended to stop draft card burnings, but on its face the statute is narrowly drawn and does not discriminate between card-burning as protest or as something unrelated to symbolic communication. Another factor illustrates the difficulty here of adverting to motive, rather than looking primarily to the terms of the statute itself, in testing its constitutionality on its face. The duty to keep Selective Service certificates on one's person has been in existence for many years and has been held constitutional. . . .

Appellant urges the First Amendment defense even more vigorously in his alternate argument that, as applied to the facts of this case, the statute is an unconstitutional suppression of speech. Appellant reasons as follows: Symbolic speech is protected by the First Amendment; burning is a most dramatic form of communication, and there is a constitutional right to make one's speech as effective as possible, subject to the proper constitutional standard; and, finally, whether that standard be the clear and present danger test or a balancing of interests, the statute as it was applied to him is unconstitutional. . . .

Is all communicative action symbolic speech and is all symbolic speech protected by the First Amendment? The range of symbolic conduct intended to express disapproval is broad; it can extend from a thumbs-down gesture to political assassination. Would anyone seriously contend that the First Amendment protects the latter? Appellant would undoubtedly respond that peaceful symbolic acts, as contrasted to violent ones, are protected and that draft card burning is clearly the former. The distinction is significant, of course. . . . But what of other more peaceable but unconventional symbolic acts? In *People* v. *Stover, supra,* the display of offensive objects on a clothesline was a protest against high property taxes; the court held that a zoning ordinance prohibiting such conduct was constitutional. What of protests made dramatic by turning on water faucets, dumping of garbage in front of City Hall, stalling cars at an event attracting heavy traffic, burning an American flag on a street corner, or tearing up on television a court order or a document required to be kept under internal revenue regulations? Each such act may be designed to mobilize public opinion against an existing statute or government policy; yet, sincere motivation or the labeling of even nonviolent conduct as symbolic does not necessarily transform that conduct into speech protected by the First Amendment. It may be that particular considerations surrounding a specific symbolic act justify clothing it in the concept of speech. Thus, picketing, like sit-ins, may be the poor man's printing press; similarly, the technique of a "silent and reproachful presence" may be the only means of true communication in certain areas of the civil rights struggle. We mention all these acts not to decide whether they are properly characterized as speech but only to emphasize the complexity of the problem. We are not at all sure that destroying a draft card even at a public rally must be regarded as an exercise of speech, but we are willing to assume it *arguendo*, as the district court did. However, this only forms the basis for further analysis. Appellant concedes that even speech may be regulated, or in certain circumstances prohibited, provided that the proper constitutional test is met; it is here that appellant contends the 1965 amendment fails.

Appellant argues that since speech is involved, the statute prohibiting it must be evaluated under the clear and present danger test, which, in its classic statement, is:

> whether the words used are used in such circumstances and are of such a nature as to create a clear and present danger that they will bring about the substantive evils that Congress has a right to prevent. It is a question of proximity and degree. ·

. . . However, recent Supreme Court decisions have applied a balancing approach to determine the constitutionality of legislation that indirectly restricted speech. . . .

When particular conduct is regulated in the interest of public order, and the regulation results in an indirect, conditional, partial abridgment of speech, the duty of the courts is to determine which of these two conflicting interests demands the greater protection under the particular circumstances presented. . . .

Under this approach, the public interest to be protected is the proper functioning of the Selective Service System. In a world where resort to force is still the rule, rather than the exception, this is an interest of the highest order; its importance undoubtedly accounts for the many decisions rejecting First Amendment defenses to Selective Service violations. . . . Indeed, we do not understand appellant to question the need for proper operation of the draft; instead he questions whether the 1965 amendment actually serves this important end. The trial court held that it did, but appellant argues that the court gave no reasons to support its conclusion and that there are none in fact.

We conclude that forbidding destruction of Selective Service certificates serves legitimate purposes in administering the system. . . .

Against these reasons must be weighed the effect of the statute on freedom of expression. Except to prohibit destruction of certificates, the statute does not prevent political dissent or criticism in any way. It is narrowly drawn to regulate a limited form of action. Under the statute, aside from destroying certificates, appellant and others can protest against the draft, the military action in Vietnam and the statute itself in any terms they wish—and indeed did so at the rally where appellant was arrested. Appellant claims, however, that the burning of a draft card is more dramatic than mere speech and that he has a right to the most effective means of communication. But surely this generalization has its own limits. . . .

Appellant's final argument is that since the statute does not serve any rational legislative purpose the statute is an unconstitutional deprivation of individual liberty without due process of law under the Fifth Amendment. Thus, appellant points out that the 1965 amendment has been called "a silly law" in a national periodical with extensive circulation. However, it is not the province of the judiciary to praise or condemn this law; our function is to determine only the power of Congress in enacting the statute, not its wisdom. For the reasons already given at length above, we find that the statute is neither arbitrary nor without purpose, that it is reasonably related to the power of Congress to raise and support armies, and that it reinforces an obligation which has been imposed upon registrants for many years. Accordingly, the judgment of conviction is affirmed.

40. *United States* v. *Mitchell*, 1966, 1967.

In 1965, David Mitchell refused induction into the Armed Forces. He based his refusal not on pacifist convictions, but on the belief that induction would make him an accomplice, under international law *(e.g., the Nuremberg Laws, the Geneva Convention, the United Nations Charter), to crimes that the United States had committed in Vietnam and elsewhere. He was convicted of draft evasion in the District Court but the Circuit Court of Appeals reversed the decision, saying that he had been denied adequate time to secure proper counsel. His case went back to the District Court, which sentenced him to a maximum of five years in Federal prison. Both the Circuit Court of Appeals and the Supreme Court declined his petition for a new review. Supreme Court Justice William O. Douglas, however, dissented from his colleagues and found that there was validity in Mitchell's claim that he had a right to bring in evidence to prove his contention of U.S. government war crimes.*

40. a.   Court of Appeals Decision, 1966.*

Judge Harold Medina, for the Second Circuit Court of Appeals, finding that Mitchell's case had "decided First Amendment overtones," found that the lower court had denied Mitchell adequate time to find proper counsel. The case was ordered retried.

Medina, *Circuit Judge*:

Appellant David Henry Mitchell, III, appeals from a judgment of conviction, entered upon a jury verdict of guilty, arising out of a one-count indictment charging appellant with wilful failure to report for induction into the Armed Forces. . . .

Various points of law have been covered in the briefs and on oral argument but we shall confine our discussion to the decisive question, whether appellant's right to the effective assistance of counsel under the Sixth Amendment was infringed by forcing him to trial without allowing him sufficient time to obtain defense counsel of his own choice.

On May 20, 1965, appellant was indicted. He pleaded not guilty on June 14, 1965. A motion to dismiss the indictment, made on August 2, 1965, was argued on September 7, 1965, and on the same day denied. On the following day the trial judge was disposed to proceed at once to trial but certain developments to which we shall refer later led to a continuance until September 13, 1965, at which time a trial was had resulting in appellant's conviction and the imposition of a sentence to not less than 18 months and not more than 5 years imprisonment pursuant to 18 U.S.C., Section 4208 (a) (1), and the imposition of a committed fine of $5,000. Appellant has been released on bail pending the disposition of this appeal.

Of basic importance is the fact that appellant, for the 4 previous years, and up to and including September 8 and September 13, had taken the positon before the Draft Board

* *United States* v. *Mitchell*, 354 F. 2d 767 (1966).

and in the District Court that his refusal to comply with Selective Service requirements was not because he was a pacifist but because, if he submitted to the draft, the "Nuremberg Law" would render him "guilty of complicity in crimes defined by the Charter of the International Military Tribunal," specifically wars of aggression and acts of inhumanity. Apparently it was his plan of defense to attempt to prove in one way or another that the United States had been guilty of such wars of aggression and acts of inhumanity in Vietnam, Cuba, Panama, Santo Domingo and elsewhere.

Against this background the scene opens in the District Court on the morning of Wednesday, September 8. . . . Appellant informed the trial judge that he was about to dismiss Mr. Lynn and he asked for time to obtain new counsel, stating that his problem was not lack of funds but rather the difficulty of "finding a counsel who I will have confidence will represent my position in opposition." The trial judge adjourned the trial to the following Monday and said: "The condition, however, that the Court imposes upon substitution of counsel is that he be ready to proceed with the trial of the case on Monday, September 13." Appellant insisted that the time was too short. . . .

So, the question for decision by us is, under the circumstances did the trial judge abuse his discretion by granting appellant only the period between Wednesday, September 8, and Monday, September 13, to obtain the effective assistance of counsel, and thus, in effect, deprive him of such assistance? We think he did, and for that reason we reverse the judgment of conviction and remand for a new trial.

In essence, what the trial judge failed to take into consideration is that this is not "a very simple case." It has decided First Amendment overtones. [Editor's italics] It is always difficult to obtain counsel to defend an unpopular cause, especially in a time of active hostilities. Moreover, a reasonable time was required for counsel to familiarize himself with the various intricacies of the Selective Service Law and to decide upon the proper strategy to be followed at the trial in order, if possible, to obtain an acquittal, or to make a record for purposes of appeal, or to obtain as light a sentence as the circumstances might warrant. We do not say a trial judge lacks discretion to fix the ultimate date of trial in any case, including those involving constitutional overtones, the assertion of defenses that may be deemed "unpopular," and others, whether "simple" or complicated. We say only that, on this record, the time afforded appellant to secure a lawyer was not a reasonable time. . . .

Reversed and remanded.

40. b. Excerpts from Appellant's Reply Brief, 1966.*

When the case went back to the District Court, Mitchell was represented by Mark Lane, former attorney for Mrs. Marguerite Oswald, mother of President Kennedy's alleged assassin. In his brief before the District Court and later before the Court of Appeals, Lane argued that Mitchell should be permitted to present evidence in support of his allegations of U.S. treaty violations and war crimes.

Question Presented

At the trial the defendant stated that the known facts were persuasive that the very presence of American armed forces personnel in Vietnam was violative of international agreements that were binding upon the United States government and that in addition such personnel were participating in specific acts which had been clearly proscribed by international treaties to which the United States was signatory. The defendant alluded to the use of poison chemicals and poison gas, the bombing of civilian villages and the destruction of crops.

The defendant stated that he would not participate in such unlawful conduct since he was a law abiding citizen.

The defendant stated that the Selective Service system "is a major instrument in the carrying out of all these policies." He said that if he complied with the demands of government and became part of the effort to wage an illegal war in an illegal manner, he would be "violating specific laws which apply not to just the Germans, because the Germans were tried by them, but, to all men and Americans."

The Government's Response

The government brief fails to respond to the one question that had been raised by the defendant at the trial level al-

* Excerpts from the Appellant's Reply Brief, submitted to the Second Circuit Court of Appeals, as printed in *Downdraft* (September, 1966), pp. 10–14.

though the question was raised with singular clarity. The brief for the appellee asserts that it is no defense, in the present circumstances, for the defendant to raise questions of his "personal philosophical or political views." Of course, the appellee may be quite correct in that assertion but the appellee is in error in understanding that the defendant ever sought to raise such questions as personal as his own views. The appellant's defense rather rested *entirely* upon his inability to cooperate with the administration's policy in Vietnam without being guilty of violating international treaties and thus subjecting himself to the charge that he too was a war criminal.

The issue here is not the defendant's subjective reaction to war in general or even to a specific war but the application of international law and the responsibilities imposed by law upon the individual. . . .

The defendant does not contend that he did not know what he was doing; indeed, he asserts that he knew that to do otherwise would be violative of the responsibilities imposed upon him by law. While it may appear that the government has yet to fully comprehend the reason for the defendant's refusal to comply, the reason and the necessity of that action has been clear to the defendant for some time. Further, the defendant does not urge upon the Court special consideration due to "his own private ideas" but rather asks that the law of the United States, not his private idea of it but the objective majesty of the law, be applied evenly to him without regard for his private beliefs or the secret operation of his own personal conscience. . . .

The defendant believes that were he to follow the orders issued to him, he would be in violation of the law. Surely, the judiciary which is obligated to pass upon questions of law should not be urged to ignore the only question raised by the defendant because the issue that is central to his case is deemed "most sensitive" by the prosecuting authority. . . .

The defendant asks no more of this Court than a ruling in respect to the one legal question that he has consistently raised. Should he not be permitted to present evidence at the trial level regarding the nature of the American military effort in Vietnam so that the jury might exercise the right and obligation of examining the very basis for his refusal to participate in unlawful activity?

Conclusion

Appellant respectfully requests that the decision below be reversed and that the Court below be ordered to grant a new trial.

40. c. Court of Appeals Decision, 1966.*

Both the District Court and the Circuit Court of Appeals denied Mitchell's attempts to introduce evidence of United States' war crimes guilt. The District Court found Mitchell guilty of violating the provisions of the Selective Service Act, and the Court of Appeals sustained that decision.

Medina, Circuit Judge.

David Henry Mitchell, III appeals from a conviction, after a trial to Judge Clarie and a jury, of wilful failure to report for induction into the Armed Forces in violation of 50 U.S.C., Appx., Section 462.

After initially registering with Selective Service Local Board 17, appellant "disaffiliated" himself from the Selective Service and thereafter refused to cooperate with his Board in any respect. In August, 1964, appellant was classified 1A and did not appeal. Subsequently, he was ordered to report for induction on January 11, 1965. Appellant acknowledged receipt of this notice by letter but did not report as ordered.

Appellant was indicted for violation of 50 U.S.C., Appx., Section 462, tried and found guilty. This Court reversed the first conviction because the trial judge had failed to allow sufficient time for appellant to obtain counsel. *United States* v. *Mitchell,* 354 F.2d 767 (2 Cir. 1966). He was retried before Judge Clarie and a jury. The wilfulness of his failure to report for induction was all too apparent, and he was again convicted and sentenced to five years imprisonment. At trial appellant made no claim to be a conscientious objector but sought to produce evidence to show that the war in Vietnam was being conducted in violation of various treaties to which the United States is a signatory and that the Selective Service system was being operated as an adjunct of this military effort. Judge Clarie ruled out all such evidence as immaterial and this ruling is assigned as error.

The government, citing a line of cases beginning with

* *United States* v. *Mitchell,* 369 F. 2d 323 (1966).

Falbo v. *United States,* 320 U.S. 549, 64 S.Ct. 346, 88 L. Ed. 305 (1944), would preclude consideration of appellant's claims because of his failure to exhaust his administrative remedies. But, as appellant does not seek any relief which the Selective Service is empowered to grant, we will assume these cases are not in point. Rather, he seeks a declaration, in effect, that the Service must cease to function. It would be pointless in this case to require appellant to press his claims before a Board which he claims is illegal.

Similarly, as appellant asserts that the Selective Service, and not merely the conduct of the war in Vietnam, is illegal, his defenses would seem not to be premature.

[1-3] Nevertheless, appellant's allegations are not a defense to a prosecution for failure to report for induction into the Armed Forces and his evidence was properly excluded. Regardless of the proof that appellant might present to demonstrate the correlation between the Selective Service and our nation's efforts in Vietnam, as a matter of law the congressional power "to raise and support armies" and "to provide and maintain a navy" is a matter quite distinct from the use which the Executive makes of those who have been found qualified and who have been inducted into the Armed Forces. Whatever action the President may order, or the Congress sanction, cannot impair this constitutional power of the Congress.

Thus we need not consider whether the substantive issues raised by appellant can ever be appropriate for judicial determination. See *United States* v. *Hogan*s, 2 Cir., 369 F.2d 359, decided by this Court on November 28, 1966.

Affirmed.

40. d. Mr. Justice Douglas, Dissenting, 1967.*

Mitchell appealed his conviction to the Supreme Court, which declined to grant a review. Justice William O. Douglas, in a separate dissent, found that Mitchell had raised substantive questions which the Court should have agreed to hear.

Mr. Justice Douglas, Dissenting.

Petitioner did not report for induction as ordered, was indicted, convicted, and sentenced to five years imprisonment and his conviction was affirmed. 369 F. 2d 323. His defense was that the "war" in Vietnam was being conducted in violation of various treaties to which we were a signatory especially the Treaty of London of August 8, 1945, 59 Stat. 1544, which in Article 6(a) declares that "waging of a war of aggression" is a "crime against peace" imposing "individual responsibility." Article 8 provides:

> "The fact that the Defendant acted pursuant to order of his Government or of a superior shall not free him from responsibility, but may be considered in mitigation of punishment if the Tribunal determines that justice so requires."

Petitioner claimed that the "war" in Vietnam was a "war of aggression" within the meaning of the Treaty of London and that Article 8 makes him responsible for participating in it even though he is ordered to do so.**

Mr. Justice Jackson, the United States prosecutor at Nuremberg, stated: "If certain acts in violation of treaties are crimes, they are crimes whether the United States does them or whether Germany does them, and we are not prepared to lay down a rule of criminal conduct against others which we would not be willing to have invoked against us." (In-

* *Mitchell* v. *United States,* Memorandum Case No. 1012, *U.S. Supreme Court Reports,* 18 L ed 2d., April 14, 1967, pp. 132–33.

** The trial court charged the jury that the Treaty of London did not interfere "in any manner in respect to this defendant fulfilling his duty under this order."

ternational Conference on Military Trials, Dept. State Pub. No. 3880, p. 330.)

Article VI, cl. 2 of the Constitution states that "treaties" are a part of "the supreme law of the land; and the Judges in every State shall be bound thereby."

There is a considerable body of opinion that our actions in Vietnam constitute the waging of an aggressive "war."

This case presents the questions:

(1) whether the Treaty of London is a treaty within the meaning of Art. VI, cl. 2;

(2) whether the question as to the waging of an aggressive "war" is in the context of this criminal prosecution a justiciable question;

(3) whether the Vietnam episode is a "war" in the sense of the Treaty;

(4) whether petitioner has standing to raise the question;

(5) whether, if he has, it may be tendered as a defense in this criminal case or in amelioration of the punishment.

These are extremely sensitive and delicate questions. But they should, I think, be answered. Even those who think that the Nuremberg judgments were unconstitutional by our guarantee relating to *ex post facto* laws would have to take a different view of the Treaty of London that purports to lay down a standard of future conduct for all the signatories.

I intimate no opinion on the merits. But I think the petition for certiorari should be granted. We have here a recurring question in present-day Selective Service cases.

41. *Bond v. Floyd, 1966.*

On January 10, 1966, the House of Representatives of the State of Georgia refused to seat Julian Bond, a Negro and a duly-elected representative from Atlanta, because he had publicly endorsed a statement by the Student Nonviolent Coordinating Committee criticizing the government's actions in Vietnam, and because he had advised Negroes to refuse induction into the armed forces. On February 10, 1966, a three-judge Federal District Court, in a two to one decision, upheld the legislature's action. On December 5, 1966, the Supreme Court, with Chief Justice Earl Warren speaking for the Court, unanimously reversed that decision and ordered the Georgia legislature to admit Bond to his seat.

41. a. From *Summary of District Court Decision, 1966.**

Julian Bond, Dr. Martin Luther King, Jr., and Mrs. Arel Keyes, for themselves jointly and severally, and for all other similarly situated Plaintiffs v. James "Sloppy" Floyd, et al.

First Amendment does not bar Georgia House of Representatives' refusal to seat representative-elect who publicly endorsed civil rights group's support of Negroes unwilling to respond to military draft since such endorsement could reasonably be construed by House members as repugnant to oath required of each member.

The substantial issue in this case rests on the guarantee of freedom of speech under the First Amendment as that amendment has long been applicable to the states under the Due Process Clause of the Fourteenth Amendment. Some restraint is to be practiced by the courts in considering state political questions concerning particular officers as distinguished from whole systems such as are prevalent in malapportionment or racial discrimination. There is room for a balance between the separation of powers principle, a system of federalism, and individual rights protected by the Constitution.

A reasonable approach under the circumstances of this case is for the federal court to assume jurisdiction for the purpose of determining whether the representative-elect was denied due process of law, either procedural or substantive. The transcript of the hearing held on the challenge to the representative-elect demonstrates no absence of procedural due process.

As to substantive due process, there must be a rational evidentiary basis for the ruling that denied the representative-elect his seat. The denial must not have been arbitrary.

The statement he endorsed is at war with the national policy of this country. But it does not stop there. It is a call to action based on race; a call alien to the concept of the

* In *United States Law Week*, XXXIV (February 22, 1966), 2442–43. For complete decision see *Bond* v. *Floyd*, 251 F. Supp. 333 (1966).

pluralistic society that makes this nation. It aligns the civil rights organization with "colored people in such other countries as the Dominican Republic, the Congo, South America, Rhodesia. . . ." It refers to the group's involvement in the black peoples' struggle for liberation and self-determination. The statement alleges that Negroes, referring to American servicemen, are called on to stifle the liberation of Vietnam.

The call to action, which is what this court finds to be a rational basis for the decision not to seat the representative-elect, is that language stating that the civil rights organization supports those men in this country who are unwilling to respond to the military draft.

The representative-elect was careful to affirm this statement. He went further, and he was more than a private citizen; he was an officer and employee of the civil rights group and was about to become a member of the House of Representatives of Georgia. He stated that he admired the courage of anyone who burned his draft card and that, as a second class citizen, he did not think that he had to support the war in Vietnam.

Whether he should have been seated was a question presented to the House of Representatives of Georgia under our system. Whether the wisest course was followed is not for this court to say. The judgment of the court is not to be substituted for that of the House. This court's function is to determine whether the representative-elect has been denied some fundamental federal right to which he was otherwise entitled. His statements as they bore on the functioning of the Selective Service System could reasonably be said to be inconsistent with and repugnant to the oath that he was required to take. This suffices as a rational basis for the action of the House. —Per Curiam.

Justice Tuttle, Dissenting.

The representative-elect was not challenged on the ground that he was not, as specifically required by the Georgia Constitution, 21 years of age, or that he had not been a citizen of the state for the requisite two years and a resident of the county from which he was elected. Nor was he challenged on the ground that he has been convicted of treason against the state, embezzlement of public funds, misfeasance in office, bribery, or larceny or any crime punishable by the laws of this state. He was not charged with having received any interest, profit, or perquisites arising from the use or loan of public funds. He offered to take the prescribed oath of office.

Rather, he was found disqualified on account of conduct not enumerated in the Georgia Constitution as a basis for disqualification. This was beyond the power of the House of Representatives. It runs counter to the express provisions of the Georgia Constitution, giving to the people the right to elect their representatives, and limiting the legislature in its right to reject such elected members to those grounds that are expressly stated in Georgia's basic document.

41.   b.   Supreme Court Decision, 1966.*

The Supreme Court heard the case on direct appeal and unanimously reversed the action of the Georgia legislature and the decision of the District Court.

Mr. Chief Justice Warren delivered the opinion of the Court.

The question presented in this case is whether the Georgia House of Representatives may constitutionally exclude appellant Bond, a duly elected Representative, from membership because of his statements, and statements to which he subscribed, criticizing the policy of the Federal Government in Vietnam and the operation of the Selective Service laws. An understanding of the circumstances of the litigation requires a complete presentation of the events and statements which led to this appeal.

Bond, a Negro, was elected on June 15, 1965, as the Representative to the Georgia House of Representatives from the 136th House District. Of the District's 6,500 voters, approximately 6,000 are Negroes. Bond defeated his opponent, Malcolm Dean, Dean of Men at Atlanta University, also a Negro, by a vote of 2,320 to 487.

On January 6, 1966, the Student Nonviolent Coordinating Committee, a civil rights organization of which Bond was then the Communications Director, issued the following statement on American policy in Vietnam and its relation to the work of civil rights organizations in this country:

The Student Nonviolent Coordinating Committee has a right and a responsibility to dissent with United States foreign policy on an issue when it sees fit. The Student Nonviolent Coordinating Committee now states its opposition to United States' involvement in Vietnam on these grounds:

We believe the United States government has been deceptive in its claims of concern for freedom of the Vietnamese people, just as the government has been deceptive in claiming concern for the freedom of colored people in

* *Bond* v. *Floyd,* 385 U.S. 116 (1966).

such other countries as the Dominican Republic, the Congo, South Africa, Rhodesia and in the United States itself.

We, the Student Nonviolent Coordinating Committee, have been involved in the black people's struggle for liberation and self-determination in this country for the past five years. Our work, particularly in the South, has taught us that the United States government has never guaranteed the freedom of oppressed citizens, and is not yet truly determined to end the rule of terror and oppression within its own borders.

We ourselves have often been victims of violence and confinement executed by United States government officials. We recall the numerous persons who have been murdered in the South because of their efforts to secure their civil and human rights, and whose murderers have been allowed to escape penalty for their crimes.

The murder of Samuel Young in Tuskegee, Ala., is no different than the murder of peasants in Vietnam, for both Young and the Vietnamese sought, and are seeking, to secure the rights guaranteed them by law. In each case, the United States government bears a great part of the responsibility for these deaths.

Samuel Young was murdered because United States law is not being enforced. Vietnamese are murdered because the United States is pursuing an aggressive policy in violation of international law. The United States is no respecter of persons or law when such persons or laws run counter to its needs and desires.

We recall the indifference, suspicion and outright hostility with which our reports of violence have been met in the past by government officials.

We know that for the most part, elections in this country, in the North as well as the South, are not free. We have seen that the 1965 Voting Rights Act and the 1964 Civil Rights Act have not yet been implemented with full federal power and sincerity.

We question, then, the ability and even the desire of the United States government to guarantee free elections abroad. We maintain that our country's cry of "preserve freedom in the world" is a hypocritical mask behind which it squashes liberation movements which are not bound, and refuse to be bound, by the expediences of United States cold war policies.

We are in sympathy with, and support, the men in
this country who are unwilling to respond to a military
draft which would compel them to contribute their lives
to United States aggression in Vietnam in the name of
the "freedom" we find so false in this country.

We recoil with horror at the inconsistency of a supposedly "free" society where responsibility to freedom is
equated with the responsibility to lend oneself to military
aggression. We take note of the fact that 16 per cent of the
draftees from this country are Negroes called on to stifle the
liberation of Vietnam, to preserve a "democracy" which
does not exist for them at home.

We ask, where is the draft for the freedom fight in the
United States?

We therefore encourage those Americans who prefer to
use their energy in building democratic forms within this
country. We believe that work in the civil rights movement and with other human relations organizations is a
valid alternative to the draft. We urge all Americans to
seek this alternative, knowing full well that it may cost
them lives—as painfully as in Vietnam.

On the same day that this statement was issued, Bond
was interviewed by telephone by a reporter from a local radio
station, and, although Bond had not participated in drafting
the statement, he endorsed the statement in these words:

Why, I endorse it, first, because I like to think of myself as a pacifist and one who opposes that war and any
other war and eager and anxious to encourage people not
to participate in it for any reason that they choose; and
secondly, I agree with this statement because of the reason set forth in it—because I think it is sorta hypocritical
for us to maintain that we are fighting for liberty in
other places and we are not guaranteeing liberty to citizens inside the continental United States. . . .

Well, I think that the fact that the United States Government fights a war in Vietnam, I don't think that I as
a second class citizen of the United States have a requirement to support that war. I think my responsibility is to
oppose things that I think are wrong if they are in Vietnam or New York, or Chicago, or Atlanta, or wherever.

When the interviewer suggested that our involvement in
Vietnam was because "if we do not stop Communism there

that it is just a question of where will we stop it next," Bond replied:

> Oh, no, I'm not taking a stand against stopping World Communism, and I'm not taking a stand in favor of the Viet Cong. What I'm saying that is, first, that I don't believe in that war. That particular war. I'm against all war. I'm against that war in particular, and I don't think people ought to participate in it. Because I'm against war, I'm against the draft. I think that other countries in the World get along without a draft—England is one—and I don't see why we couldn't, too.
>
> . . . I'm not about to justify that war, because it's stopping International Communism, or whatever—you know, I just happen to have a basic disagreement with wars for whatever reason they are fought— . . . [F]ought to stop International Communism, to promote International Communism, or for whatever reason. I oppose the Viet Cong fighting in Vietnam as much as I oppose the United States fighting in Vietnam. I happen to live in the United States. If I lived in North Vietnam I might not have the same sort of freedom of expression, but it happens that I live here—not there.

The interviewer also asked Bond if he felt he could take the oath of office required by the Georgia Constitution, and Bond responded that he saw nothing inconsistent between his statements and the oath. Bond was also asked whether he would adhere to his statements if war were declared on North Vietnam and if his statements might become treasonous. He replied that he did not know "if I'm strong enough to place myself in a position where I'd be guilty of treason."

Before January 10, 1966, when the Georgia House of Representatives was scheduled to convene, a petition challenging Bond's right to be seated was filed by 75 House members. This petition charged that Bond's statements gave aid and comfort to the enemies of the United States and Georgia, violated the Selective Service laws, and tended to bring discredit and disrespect on the House. The petition further contended that Bond's endorsement of the SNCC statement "is totally and completely repugnant to and inconsistent with the mandatory oath prescribed by the Constitution of Georgia for a member of the House of Representatives to take before taking his seat." For the same reasons, the petition asserted that Bond could not take an oath to support the Constitution of the United States. When Bond appeared at the House on January 10 to be sworn in, the clerk refused to administer the oath to him until the issues raised in the challenge petition had been decided.

Bond filed a response to the challenge petition in which he stated his willingness to take the oath and argued that he was not unable to do so in good faith. He further argued that the challenge against his seating had been filed to deprive him of his First Amendment rights, and that the challenge was racially motivated. A special committee was appointed to report on the challenge, and a hearing was held to determine exactly what Bond had said and the intentions with which he had said it.

At this hearing, the only testimony given against Bond was that which he himself gave the committee. Both the opponents Bond had defeated in becoming the Representative of the 136th District testified to his good character and to his loyalty to the United States. A recording of the interview which Bond had given to the reporter after the SNCC statement was played, and Bond was called to the stand for cross-examination. He there admitted his statements and elaborated his views. He stated that he concurred in the SNCC statement "without reservation," and, when asked if he admired the courage of persons who burn their draft cards, responded:

> I admire people who take an action, and I admire people who feel strongly enough about their convictions to take an action like that knowing the consequences that they will face, and that was my original statement when asked that question. . . .
> I have never suggested or counseled or advocated that any one other person burn their draft card. In fact, I have mine in my pocket and will produce it if you wish. I do not advocate that people should break laws. What I simply try to say was that I admired the courage of someone who could act on his convictions knowing that he faces pretty stiff consequences.

Tapes of an interview Bond had given the press after the clerk had refused to give him the oath were also heard by the special committee. In this interview, Bond stated:

> I stand before you today charged with entering into public discussion on matters of National interest. I hesitate

to offer explanations for my actions or deeds where no charge has been levied against me other than the charge that I have chosen to speak my mind and no explanation is called for, for no member of this House, has ever, to my knowledge, been called upon to explain his public statements for public postures as a prerequisite to admission to that Body. I therefore, offer to my constituents a statement of my views. I have not counseled burning draft cards, nor have I burned mine. I have suggested that congressionally outlined alternatives to military service be extended to building democracy at home. The posture of my life for the past five years has been calculated to give Negroes the ability to participate in formulation of public policies. The fact of my election to public office does not lessen my duty or desire to express my opinions even when they differ from those held by others. As to the current controversy because of convictions that I have arrived at through examination of my conscience I have decided I personally cannot participate in war.

I stand here with intentions to take an oath—that oath they just took in there—that will dispel any doubts about my convictions or loyalty.

The special committee concluded in its report to the House that Bond's endorsement of the SNCC statement and his supplementary remarks showed that he "does not and will not" support the Constitutions of the United States and of Georgia, that he "adheres to the enemies of the State of Georgia" contrary to the State Constitution, that he gives aid and comfort to the enemies of the United States, that his statements violated the Selective Service Act, and that his statements "are reprehensible and are such as tend to bring discredit to and disrespect of the House." On the same day the House adopted the committee report without findings and without further elaborating Bond's lack of qualifications, and resolved by a vote of 184 to 12 that "Bond shall not be allowed to take the oath of office as a member of the House of Representatives and that Representative-Elect Julian Bond shall not be seated as a member of the House of Representatives."

Bond then instituted an action in the District Court for the Northern District of Georgia for injunctive relief and a declaratory judgment that the House action was unauthorized by the Georgia Constitution and violated Bond's rights under the First Amendment. A three-judge District Court was convened. All three members of the District Court held that the court had jurisdiction to decide the constitutionality of the House action because Bond had asserted substantial First Amendment rights. On the merits, however, the court was divided.

Judges Bell and Morgan, writing for the majority of the court, addressed themselves first to the question of whether the Georgia House had power under state law to disqualify Bond based on its conclusion that he could not sincerely take the oath of office. They reasoned that separation of powers principles gave the Legislature power to insist on qualifications in addition to those specified in the State Constitution. The majority pointed out that nothing in the Georgia Constitution limits the qualifications of the legislators to those expressed in the constitution.

Having concluded that the action of the Georgia House was authorized by state law, the court considered whether Bond's disqualification violated his constitutional right of freedom of speech. It reasoned that the decisions of this Court involving particular state political offices supported an attitude of restraint in which the principles of separation of powers and federalism should be balanced against the alleged deprivation of individual constitutional rights. On this basis, the majority below fashioned the test to be applied in this case as being whether the refusal to seat Bond violated procedural or what it termed substantive due process. The court held that the hearing which had been given Bond by the House satisfied procedural due process. As for what it termed the question of substantive due process, the majority concluded that there was a rational evidentiary basis for the ruling of the House. It reasoned that Bond's right to dissent as a private citizen was limited by his decision to seek membership in the Georgia House. Moreover, the majority concluded, the SNCC statement and Bond's related remarks went beyond criticism of national policy and provided a rational basis for a conclusion that the speaker could not in good faith take an oath to support the State and Federal Constitutions:

A citizen would not violate his oath by objecting to or criticizing this policy or even by calling it deceptive and false as the statement did.

But the statement does not stop with this. It is a call to action based on race; a call alien to the concept of the pluralistic society which makes this nation. It aligns the organization with ". . . colored people in such other countries as the Dominican Republic, the Congo, South Africa, Rhodesia. . . ." It refers to its "involvement in the black people's struggle for liberation and self-determination. . . ." It states that "Vietnamese are murdered because the United States is pursuing an aggressive policy in violation of international law." It alleges that Negroes, referring to American servicemen, are called on to stifle the liberation of Vietnam.

The call to action, and this is what we find to be a rational basis for the decision which denied Mr. Bond his seat, is that language which states that SNCC supports those men in this country who are unwilling to respond to a military draft.

Chief Judge Tuttle dissented. He reasoned that the question of the power of the Georgia House under the State Constitution to disqualify a Representative under these circumstances had never been decided by the state courts, and that federal courts should construe state law, if possible, so as to avoid unnecessary federal constitutional issues. Since Bond satisfied all the stated qualifications in the State Constitution, Chief Judge Tuttle concluded that his disqualification was beyond the power of the House as a matter of state constitutional law.

Bond appealed directly to this Court from the decision of the District Court. While this appeal was pending, the Governor of Georgia called a special election to fill the vacancy caused by Bond's exclusion. Bond entered this election and won overwhelmingly. The House was in recess, but the Rules Committee held a hearing in which Bond declined to recant his earlier statements. Consequently, he was again prevented from taking the oath of office, and the seat has remained vacant. Bond again sought the seat from the 136th District in the regular 1966 election, and he won the Democratic primary in September 1966, and won an overwhelming majority in the election of November 8, 1966.

The Georgia Constitution sets out a number of specific provisions dealing with the qualifications and eligibility of state legislators. These provide that Representatives shall be citizens of the United States, at least 21 years of age, citizens of Georgia for two years, and residents for one year of the counties from which elected. The Georgia Constitution further provides that no one convicted of treason against the State, or of any crime of moral turpitude, or a number of other enumerated crimes may hold any office in the State. Idiots and insane persons are barred from office, and no one holding any state or federal office is eligible for a seat in either house.

. . . .

These constitute the only stated qualifications for membership in the Georgia Legislature and the State concedes that Bond meets all of them.

. . . .

Because under state law the legislature has exclusive jurisdiction to determine whether an elected Representative meets the enumerated qualifications, it is argued that the legislature has power to look beyond the plain meaning of the oath provisions which merely require that the oaths be taken. This additional power is said to extend to determining whether a given Representative may take the oath with sincerity. The State does not claim that it should be completely free of judicial review whenever it disqualifies an elected Representative; it admits that, if a State Legislature excluded a legislator on racial or other clearly unconstitutional grounds, the federal (or state) judiciary would be justified in testing the exclusion by federal constitutional standards. But the State argues that there can be no doubt as to the constitutionality of the qualification involved in this case. . . .

We are not persuaded by the State's attempt to distinguish, for purposes of our jurisdiction, between an exclusion alleged to be on racial grounds and one alleged to violate the First Amendment. The basis for the argued distinction is that, in this case, Bond's disqualification was grounded on a constitutional standard—the requirement of taking an oath to support the Constitution. But Bond's contention is that this standard was utilized to infringe his First Amendment rights, and we cannot distinguish, for purposes of our assumption of jurisdiction, between a disqualification under an unconstitutional standard and a disqualification which, although under color of a proper standard, is alleged to violate the First Amendment.

We conclude as did the entire court below that this Court has jurisdiction to review the question of whether the action of the Georgia House of Representatives deprived Bond of federal constitutional rights, and we now move to the central question posed in the case—whether Bond's disqualification because of his statements violated the free speech provisions of the First Amendment as applied to the States through the Fourteenth Amendment.

The State argues that the exclusion does not violate the First Amendment because the State has a right, under Article VI of the United States Constitution, to insist on loyalty to the Constitution as a condition of office. A legislator of course can be required to swear to support the Constitution of the United States as a condition of holding office, but that is not the issue in this case, as the record is uncontradicted that Bond has repeatedly expressed his willingness to swear to the oaths provided for in the State and Federal Constitutions. Nor is this a case where a legislator swears to an oath *pro forma* while declaring or manifesting his disagreement with or indifference to the oath. Thus, we do not quarrel with the State's contention that the oath provisions of the United States and Georgia Constitutions do not violate the First Amendment. But this requirement does not authorize a majority of state legislators to test the sincerity with which another duly elected legislator can swear to uphold the Constitution. Such a power could be utilized to restrict the right of legislators to dissent from national or state policy or that of a majority of their colleagues under the guise of judging their loyalty to the Constitution. Certainly there can be no question but that the First Amendment protects expressions in opposition to national foreign policy in Vietnam and to the Selective Service system. The State does not contend otherwise. But it argues that Bond went beyond expressions of opposition, and counseled violations of the Selective Service laws, and that advocating violation of federal law demonstrates a lack of support for the Constitution. The State declines to argue that Bond's statements would violate any law if made by a private citizen, but it does argue that even though such a citizen might be protected by his First Amendment rights, the State may nonetheless apply a stricter standard to its legislators. We do not agree.

Bond could not have been constitutionally convicted un-

der 50 U.S.C. § 462(a), which punishes any person who
"counsels, aids, or abets another to refuse or evade registration." Bond's statements were at worst unclear on the question
of the means to be adopted to avoid the draft. While the SNCC
statements said "We are in sympathy with, and support, the
men in this country who are unwilling to respond to a military draft," this statement alone cannot be interpreted as a
call to unlawful refusal to be drafted. Moreover, Bond's
supplementary statements tend to resolve the opaqueness in
favor of legal alternatives to the draft, and there is no evidence to the contrary. On the day the statement was issued,
Bond explained that he endorsed it "because I like to think
of myself as a pacifist and one who opposes that war and
any other war and eager and anxious to encourage people not
to participate in it for any reason that they choose." In the
same interview, Bond stated categorically that he did not oppose the Vietnam policy because he favored the Communists;
that he was a loyal American citizen and supported the
Constitution of the United States. He further stated "I oppose the Viet Cong fighting in Vietnam as much as I oppose the United States fighting in Vietnam." At the hearing
before the Special Committee of the Georgia House, when
asked his position on persons who burned their draft cards,
Bond replied that he admired the courage of persons who
"feel strongly enough about their convictions to take an action like that knowing the consequences that they will face."
When pressed as to whether his admiration was based on
the violation of federal law, Bond stated:

> I have never suggested or counseled or advocated that
> any one other person burn their draft card. In fact, I have
> mine in my pocket and will produce it if you wish. I do
> not advocate that people should break laws. What I simply
> try to say was that I admired the courage of someone who
> could act on his convictions knowing that he faces pretty
> stiff consequences.

Certainly this clarification does not demonstrate any incite-
ment to violation of law. No useful purpose would be served
by discussing the many decisions of this Court which establish
that Bond could not have been convicted for these statements
consistently with the First Amendment. . . . Nor does the
fact that the District Court found the SNCC statement to
have racial overtones constitute a reason for holding it out-

side the protection of the First Amendment. In fact the State concedes that there is no issue of race in the case.

The State attempts to circumvent the protection the First Amendment would afford to these statements if made by a private citizen by arguing that a State is constitutionally justified in exacting a higher standard of *loyalty* from its legislators than from its citizens. Of course, a State may constitutionally require an oath to support the Constitution from its legislators which it does not require of its private citizens. But this difference in treatment does not support the exclusion of Bond, for while the State has an interest in requiring its legislators to swear to a belief in constitutional processes of government, surely the oath gives it no interest in limiting its legislators' capacity to discuss their views of local or national policy. The manifest function of the First Amendment in a representative government requires that legislators be given the widest latitude to express their views on issues of policy. The central commitment of the First Amendment, as summarized in the opinion of the Court in *New York Times* v. *Sullivan*, 376 U.S. 254, 270, 84 S.Ct. 710, 721, 11 L.Ed. 2d 686 (1964), is that "debate on public issues should be uninhibited, robust, and wide-open." We think the rationale of *The New York Times* case disposes of the claim that Bond's statements fell outside the range of constitutional protection. Just as erroneous statements must be protected to give freedom of expression the breathing space it needs to survive, so statements criticizing public policy and the implementation of it must be similarly protected. The State argues that *The New York Times* principle should not be extended to statements by a legislator because the policy of encouraging free debate about governmental operations only applies to the citizen-critic of his government. We find no support for this distinction in *The New York Times* case or in any other decision of this Court. The interest of the public in hearing all sides of a public issue is hardly advanced by extending more protection to citizen-critics than to legislators. Legislators have an obligation to take positions on controversial political questions so that their constitutents can be fully informed by them, and be better able to assess their qualifications for office; also so they may be represented in governmental debates by the person they have elected to represent them. We therefore hold that the disqualification of Bond from membership in the Georgia House because of his statements violated Bond's right of free expression under the First Amendment. Because of our disposition of the case on First Amendment grounds, we need not decide the other issues advanced by Bond and the *amici*.

The decision of the District Court is reversed.

Reversed.

42. *Lynd* v. *Rusk,* 1966.*

*In December, 1965, Staughton Lynd, a Professor of History at Yale University, with A. J. Muste and others, traveled to Hanoi in North Vietnam in an attempt to bring about negotiations for peace. On Lynd's return, the State Department revoked his passport. Represented by an attorney for the American Civil Liberties Union, Lynd brought suit in March, 1966, seeking restoration of his passport so that he might fulfill speaking commitments in London and Oslo. Denial of his passport, Lynd claimed, was an abridgment of his right to free speech. The State Department agreed to the issuance of a ninety-day passport (still revoking the original) and Lynd agreed, for the purposes of the single trip, not to visit unauthorized countries (North Vietnam, Communist China, Albania, North Korea, and Cuba). Lynd is contesting the State Department's authority to revoke the original passport in the United States District Court for the District of Columbia.***

Plaintiff is a citizen of the United States and resides in New Haven, Connecticut, where he is employed as an assistant professor of history at Yale University, and is a writer and lecturer.

Defendant is the Secretary of State of the United States and is the sole person vested with authority to issue passports to individuals who owe allegiance to the United States.

On December 8, 1965, defendant issued plaintiff passport No. F 1028047 valid for a period of three years to expire on December 7, 1968.

On February 2, 1966, . . . the defendant notified the plaintiff that his passport has been "tentatively withdrawn." . . .

Plaintiff has accepted invitations from the Committee on Nuclear Disarmament to attend a meeting of that organiza-

* *Staughton Lynd* v. *Dean Rusk, Civil Action 687–66, U.S. District Court for the District of Columbia, 1966.*

** Professor Lynd is currently on a one-year leave of absence from Yale University and is teaching at Chicago State College, Chicago, Illinois. [Editor's note]

tion in London, England, on April 9, 1966, and from the Norwegian Students' Association to participate in a teaching session at Oslo, Norway, on April 16–17, 1966, on the problems of the war in Vietnam.

Plaintiff seeks to leave the United States to go to England on April 7, 1966, and to return from Norway on April 18, 1966.

During his departure from the United States, plaintiff intends to travel only to the United Kingdom, to Norway, and to any countries necessarily en route. He has no plan, intent, or expectation of travelling during such period to Albania, or to the Communist-controlled portions of China, Korea, or Vietnam. . . .

Defendant has refused to authorize such passport facilities and continues to deny plaintiff the use of the passport which was previously issued to him. . . .

Defendant's action in withdrawing plaintiff's passport upon the purported authority of 8 Code of Federal Regulations 51.136 (b) and (c) denies the plaintiff of his liberty to travel, his right to engage in his profession, and his freedom to write, to speak, and to associate with other persons:

(a) without due process of law in that such regulations are not authorized by statute;

(b) without due process of law in that the language of the regulation which requires a denial of passport facilities "when it appears to the satisfaction of the Secretary of State that the person's activities abroad would . . . be prejudicial to the orderly conduct of foreign relations . . . or otherwise to be prejudicial to the interests of the United States," is vague, unreasonable, and without standard;

(c) without due process of law to the extent that it is based upon any alleged violations of travel control restrictions by the plaintiff in that it imposes a penalty and a sanction which are not authorized by statute or by regulation;

(d) without due process of law in that it imposes a prior restraint upon future activities imputed to the plaintiff; and

(e) in violation of the First Amendment in that it prohibits the plaintiff from the lawful exercise of his right to criticize the conduct of foreign relations by the Secretary of State and other officials of the United States, and of his right to associate with persons in other countries for the lawful exchange of views and information regarding the foreign policies of the United States and other nations.

Wherefore, Plaintiff prays:

(1) For an injunction restraining the defendant from enforcing 8 Code of Federal Regulations 136 (b) and (c);

(2) For an injunction restraining the defendant from withholding or revoking the passport issued to the plaintiff on December 8, 1965;

(3) For a judgment declaring that the defendant's action in refusing passport facilities to permit the plaintiff to travel to England, to Norway, and to other countries, except Albania, and the Communist-controlled areas of China, Korea, and Vietnam, is contrary to law;

(4) For a judgment declaring that 8 Code of Federal Regulations 136 (b) and (c) are contrary to the First and to the Fifth Amendments to the Constitution.

(5) For such other and further relief as may be appropriate.

———

STAUGHTON LYND
By Counsel

43. *Mora et al.* v. *McNamara,* 1967.*

Three privates, Dennis Mora, James A. Johnson, and David A. Samas** brought suit in a Federal District Court seeking to bar Secretary of Defense Robert S. McNamara and Secretary of the Army Stanley R. Resor from sending them to fight in Vietnam. The case is remarkable in that the defendants instituted suit not as civilians but as soldiers*. They did not claim to be pacifists; they did, however, register their selective opposition to what they considered an "illegal and immoral" conflict.*

The Federal Court dismissed the suit on the grounds that it lacked jurisdiction, and the defendants appealed to the Supreme Court. The Supreme Court, on November 6, 1967, denied the appeal, but as in the case of David Mitchell (see Document 40 in this book), the denial was not unanimous. Two Justices, Potter Stewart and William O. Douglas, declared that they found sufficient merits in the defendants' case to warrant the Court's attention. Justice Stewart wrote: "We cannot make these problems go away simply by refusing to hear the case of three obscure Army privates."

Mr. Justice Stewart, with whom Mr. Justice Douglas joins, dissenting.

The petitioners were drafted into the United States Army in late 1965, and six months later were ordered to a West Coast replacement station for shipment to Vietnam. They brought this suit to prevent the Secretary of Defense and the Secretary of the Army from carrying out those orders, and requested a declaratory judgment that the present United States military activity in Vietnam is "illegal." The District Court dismissed the suit, and the Court of Appeals affirmed.

There exist in this case questions of great magnitude. Some are akin to those referred to by Mr. Justice Douglas in *Mitchell* v. *United States,* 386 U.S. 972. But there are others:

* 389 U.S. 934 (1967).

** The petitioners were court-martialed and are now serving three-year sentences at Fort Leavenworth, Kansas, for disobeying orders.

(I) Is the present United States military activity in Vietnam a "war" within the meaning of Article I, Section 8, Clause 11 of the Constitution?

(II) If so, may the Executive constitutionally order the petitioners to participate in that military activity, when no war has been declared by the Congress?

(III) Of what relevance to Question II are the present treaty obligations of the United States?

(IV) Of what relevance to Question II is the joint Congressional ("Tonkin Bay") Resolution of August 10, 1964?

(a) Do present United States military operations fall within the terms of the Joint Resolution?

(b) If the Joint Resolution purports to give the Chief Executive authority to commit United States forces to armed conflict limited in scope only by his own absolute discretion, is the Resolution a constitutionally impermissible delegation of all or part of Congress' power to declare war?

These are large and deeply troubling questions. Whether the Court would ultimately reach them depends, of course, upon the resolution of serious preliminary issues of justiciability. We cannot make these problems go away simply by refusing to hear the case of three obscure Army privates. I intimate not even tentative views upon any of these matters, but I think the Court should squarely face them by granting certiorari and setting this case for oral argument.

Mr. Justice Douglas, with whom Mr. Justice Stewart concurs, dissenting.

The questions posed by Mr. Justice Stewart cover the wide range of problems which the Senate Committee on Foreign Relations recently explored,[1] in connection with the SEATO Treaty of February 19, 1955,[2] and the Tonkin Gulf Resolution.[3]

Mr. Katzenbach, representing the Administration, testified that he did not regard the Tonkin Gulf Resolution to be "a declaration of war"[4] and that while the Resolution was not

---

[1] Hearings on S. Res. No. 151, 90th Cong., 1st Sess. (1967).

[2] [1955] 6 U.S.T. 81, T.I.A.S. No. 3170.

[3] 78 Stat. 384.

[4] Hearings, on S. Res. No. 151, *supra*, no. 1, at 145.

"constitutionally necessary" it was "politically, from an international viewpoint and from a domestic viewpoint, extremely
important."[5] He added:

> The use of the phrase "to declare war" as it was used in
> the Constitution of the United States had a particular mean-
> ing in terms of the events at the time it was adopted. . . .
> [I]t was recognized by the Founding Fathers that the
> President might have to take emergency action to protect
> the security of the United States, but that if there was
> going to be another use of the armed forces of the United
> States, that was a decision which Congress should check the
> Executive on, which Congress should support. It was for
> that reason that the phrase was inserted in the Constitution.
> Now, over a long period of time. . . . there have been
> many uses of the military forces of the United States for
> a variety of purposes without a congressional declaration
> of war. But it would be fair to say that most of these were
> relatively minor uses of force. . . .
> A declaration of war would not, I think, correctly reflect
> the very limited objectives of the United States in respect
> to Vietnam. It would not correctly reflect our efforts there,
> what we are trying to do, the reasons why we are there, to
> use an outmoded phraseology, to declare war.[6]

The view that Congress was intended to play a more active
role in the initiation and conduct of war than the above statements might suggest has been espoused by Senator Fulbright
(Cong. Rec. Oct. 11, 1967, p. 14683–14690), quoting Thomas
Jefferson who said:

> We have already given in example one effectual check
> to the Dog of war by transferring the power of letting him
> loose from the Executive to the Legislative body, from
> those who are to spend to those who are to pay.[7]

[5] *Id.,* at 145.
[6] *Id.,* at 80–81.
[7] 15 Papers of Jefferson 397 (Boyd ed., Princeton 1955). In the
Federalist No. 69, at 465 (Cooke ed. 1961), Hamilton stated:

> The President is to be Commander in Chief of the army and
> navy of the United States. In this respect his authority would
> be nominally the same with that of the King of Great Britain,
> but in substance much inferior to it. It would amount to nothing
> more than the supreme command and direction of the military

These opposed views are reflected in the *Prize Cases*, 2 Black 635, a five-to-four decision rendered in 1863. Mr. Justice Grier, writing for the majority, emphasized the arguments for strong presidential powers. Justice Nelson, writing for the minority of four, read the Constitution more strictly, emphasizing that what is war in actuality may not constitute war in the constitutional sense. During all subsequent periods in our history—through the Spanish-American War, the Boxer Rebellion, two World Wars, Korea, and now Vietnam—the two points of view urged in the *Prize Cases* have continued to be voiced.

A host of problems is raised. Does the President's authority to repel invasions and quiet insurrections, his powers in foreign relations and his duty to execute faithfully the laws of the United States, including its treaties, justify what has been threatened of petitioners? What is the relevancy of the Gulf of Tonkin Resolution and the yearly appropriations in support of the Vietnam efforts?

The London Treaty, the SEATO Treaty, the Kellogg-Briand Pact, and Article 39 of Chapter VII of the UN Charter deal with various aspects of wars of "aggression."

Do any of them embrace hostilities in Vietnam, or give rights to individuals affected to complain, o˞ in other respects give rise to justiciable controversies?

There are other treaties or declarations that could be cited. Perhaps all of them are wide of the mark. There are sentences in our opinions which, detached from their context, indicate that what is happening is none of our business:

> Certainly it is not the function of the Judiciary to entertain private litigation—even by a citizen—which challenges the legality, the wisdom, or the propriety of the Commander-in-Chief in sending our armed forces abroad or to any particular region. *Johnson* v. *Eisentrager,* 339 U.S. 763, 789.

We do not, of course, sit as a committee of oversight or supervision. What resolutions the President asks and what the Congress provides are not our concern. With respect to

and naval forces, as first General and Admiral of the Confederacy; while that of the British King extends to the *declaring* of war and to the *raising* and *regulating* of fleets and armies; all which by the Constitution under consideration would appertain to the Legislature.

the Federal Government, we sit only to decide actual cases or controversies within judicial cognizance that arise as a result of what the Congress or the President or the judge does or attempts to do to a person or his property.

In *Ex parte Milligan,* 4 Wall. 1, the Court relieved a person of the death penalty imposed by a military tribunal, holding that only a civilian court had power to try him for the offense charged. Speaking of the purpose of the Founders in providing constitutional guarantees, the Court said:

> They knew . . . the nation they were founding, be its existence short or long, would be involved in war; how often or how long continued, human foresight could not tell; and that unlimited power, wherever lodged at such a time, was especially hazardous to freemen. For this, and other equally weighty reasons, they secured the inheritance they had fought to maintain, by incorporating in a written constitution the safeguards which *time* had proved were essential to preservation. Not one of these safeguards can the President, or Congress, or the Judiciary disturb, except the one concerning the writ of *habeas corpus. Id.,* 125.

The fact that the political branches are responsible for the threat to petitioners' liberty is not decisive. As Mr. Justice Holmes said in *Nixon* v. *Herndon,* 273 U.S. 536, 540:

> The objection that the subject matter of the suit is political is little more than a play upon words. Of course the petition concerns political action but it alleges and seeks to recover for private damage. That private damage may be caused by such political action and may be recovered for a suit at law hardly has been doubted for over two hundred years, since *Ashby* v. *White,* 2 Ld. Raym. 938, 3 *id.* 320, and has been recognized by this Court.

These petitioners should be told whether their case is beyond judicial cognizance. If it is not, we should then reach the merits of their claims, on which I intimate no views whatsoever.

Part VIII

PREFACE

Acts of conscientious objection in our own times have passed beyond the original grounds of protest against military service. Young people, sown like dragon's teeth by the winds of war in the 1940's, band together to do battle with what they feel to be the intolerable terms of contemporary life—germ war, cold war, the arms race, discrimination. Middle-aged men, remembering that they once went to war to "make the world safe for democracy," have felt obliged in the 1960's to oppose the course of events, the felt terrors of the times. This "quiet war" is an intense one. Determined to work some change in society, to violate laws if necessary, the new conscientious objector is more militant than his forebears. No longer is he willing to stand aside, to say, in effect, "I cannot join with you, but I will not stop you from doing as you see fit." Today, conscientious scruple is demanding that the objector attempt to turn his society from the course it has selected. With sit-ins, lie-ins, teach-ins, peace vigils, freedom marches, work stoppages, tax refusals, men of conscience attempt to change the status quo. Thoreau is heard in the land as never before: "If [injustice] is of such a nature that it requires you to be the agent of injustice to another, then, I say, break the law. Let your life be a counter friction to stop the machine."

The term *conscientious objector* is applied in the last section of this book to many different actors on the social stage, for it no longer seems possible to distinguish between the man opposed to military service and the man opposed to the military establishment; between the man who says *I will not serve in any war*, and the man who says *I will not serve in* this *war*; between the man who says *I will not be part of the army*, and the man who says *I will not give my taxes for the purchase of arms*.

The questions raised by conscientious objectors reach to the heart of the predicament of man in contemporary society: How shall the individual make his most passionate views heard in the vastness of twentieth-century diversity and largeness? To what extent is radical criticism privileged; where does treason begin? When is liberty of conscience to be defended? When does the security of the State prevail? Questions are asked; the answers are tempered in the heat of protest movements, and of daily confrontations between men.

The papers collected in this concluding section illustrate only a small range of the ferment in American society in the last decade. They do portray the tenacity and the devotion of the men and the women who have chosen the course of conscientious objection as their own way of demonstrating allegiance to America. Each man has hoped that his act will help to set the ship of State aright.

Scientists in politics

After the bombing of Hiroshima and Nagasaki, some scientists who knew most intimately the potential of thermonuclear weaponry became outspoken proponents of disarmament. Men who traditionally avoided public political commitment circulated and signed petitions in an effort to influence the government to halt nuclear tests. With the failure of such measures, Leo Szilard, one of the original members of the Manhattan Project, which developed the first atomic bomb, devoted the last years of his life to speaking out for nuclear disarmament. Szilard proposed a plan whereby interested citizens would contribute two percent of their annual income toward the creation of a Washington lobby for peace. The Council for a Livable World, founded just before Szilard's death in 1962, was the fruit of his efforts. The Council today is a registered lobby whose function is to bring information and influence to bear on congressmen when legislation bearing on world peace and disarmament is pending. The Council, in addition, contributes to the campaigns of congressional candidates whose views on peace coincide with its own.

Another articulate spokesman for disarmament, Linus Pauling, 1954 recipient of the Nobel Prize in Chemistry, proposed in his book *No More War!* a World Peace Research Organization to work within the structure of the United Nations. The suggestion is so deceptively simple it is startling to

think that it does not already exist. Both Pauling's and Szilard's proposals were conceived to work within the framework of the government. They are conservative propositions.
The radicalism of the two scientists is in their insistence
that absolute risks are involved in the continued testing and
production of atomic and hydrogen bombs. Nuclear weaponry, they argue, endangers the life of the human race on this
planet.

By some they have been called fearmongers and "weak
sisters." Their experience illustrates, as does nothing else, the
difficulties that lie in the path of those who advocate a politics of peace in the context of a world at war.

Eniwetok, April, 1958

Albert Bigelow and Earle Reynolds, not Nobel laureates,
merely citizens, made their protests against atomic war more
dramatic. When a new series of tests was scheduled for Eniwetok Atoll in the Marshall Islands in 1958, Bigelow and
three friends announced they would sail the *Golden Rule,*
a thirty-foot ketch, into the test area as an act of conscientious protest. The ketch, which had been outfitted by the
newly formed Committee for Nonviolent Action Against Nuclear Weapons, was taken over by the U.S. Coast Guard at
Honolulu. The crew was arrested and convicted of criminal
contempt for violating an Atomic Energy Commission regulation forbidding their voyage. The four were sentenced to
sixty days in a Honolulu prison. (The AEC ruling provided
for a maximum penalty of twenty years' imprisonment for
deliberate entry into any part of the test area.)

The motives of Earle Reynolds and his family were more
complex. Chance alone set them in Honolulu at the time of
the *Golden Rule* trial. Reynolds, a physical anthropologist
who was completing a round-the-world trip begun in
Hiroshima in 1954, intended to return to Hiroshima by way
of the American Trust Territories—Johnston Island and the
Marshalls (Bikini, Kwajalein, Eniwetok)—when the AEC
ruling cut across his path. Reynolds raised the legal question of whether the AEC regulation was viable or valid on
the high seas. The family believed the hydrogen tests were a
violation of the responsibility the U.S. government bore for
the safety and health of the islanders, and immoral as a

matter of public policy. Weighing the issues—and the risks—Reynolds, his wife and two children, and a Japanese national sailed the *Phoenix* into the Pacific test areas.

San Francisco to Moscow

On December 1, 1960, a rag-tag assemblage of persons in San Francisco began a 6,000 mile trek across three continents with the intention of moving people—not governments—with their message of disarmament and world peace. Under the auspices of the Committee for Nonviolent Action, the walkers believed that "anyone who could walk even a few blocks could give a visible example to the onlookers that some people think the arms race should be ended." Some of the walkers reached Moscow, and although they, more than anyone else, knew the limitations of their efforts, although they carried the blisters and the scars on their hands from holding the placards and posters, they would not have refused to march again. There have been other walkers for disarmament and for integration. They walked from Nashville to Washington, D.C., in 1962; from Quebec to Guantánamo in 1964. With Walt Whitman, they believed in the Open Road and the possibility of a life among comrades.

Taxes

When John Woolman declined to pay taxes to support the French and Indian Wars, he searched his conscience and wrote that America had been so good to the Quakers that they were "being tryed with favour and prosperity." It was so "inviteing" to devote oneself to "Merchandize and Sciences" that it was doubly hard to break the law. So much more reason, Woolman concluded, for men of conscience to be scrupulous. A small movement, begun in 1948, persistently carried out Woolman's stricture by denying to the Federal government monies with which it can buy arms. The tax refusers number less than a thousand—probably far less. Ordinary citizens, men with a variety of political allegiances, they are determined to risk imprisonment rather than lend their support, however indirectly, to war. Thoreau had written, "There are thousands who are in opinion opposed to slavery and to the [Mexican] war, who yet in effect *do* nothing to put an end to them. . . . Even voting for the right is *doing* nothing for it." The tax refusers, according to their conscience, are *doing* something about the arms race.

Civil Rights

Those Negroes and whites who have braved night riders and Ku Klux Klan terrors for the right to eat together, sit down together, learn together, vote together—have forged the civil rights movement in America. The NAACP, CORE, SNCC, the Southern Christian Leadership Conference have brought the civil rights movement to a degree of organization and militancy comparable only to the labor movement in American history.

The long fight for school integration throughout the South, the bus boycott in Montgomery, the lunch counter sit-ins, the freedom rides, the voter registration campaigns, the march on Washington—movements and men have, through the force of conscience and will, moved this country in the 1950's and 1960's toward racial integration. But in the wake of the gains won is the bloody trail of beatings, burnings, and murders. Chaney, Goodman, Schwerner are merely three of the names we know.* The names of all the others whose lives ended in similar horror are, happily for our own conscience, unknown to us. How much has been won? It is difficult and full of tears to say.

Vietnam

The Vietnam war divides Americans. Opposition to the U.S. government policy cuts across class and movements, across political allegiance and professions. It is organized and unorganized, responsible and irresponsible. Opposition comes from the floor of the U.S. Senate, where William Fulbright, Democrat of Arkansas, has been one of the most stringent critics of the Johnson administration's war policies. Opposition has come from responsible segments of the population.

---

* Andrew Goodman, James Chaney, and Michael Schwerner were civil rights workers murdered in 1964 in Mississippi.

Lawyers and college professors have felt impelled to publish their letters of protest and their petitions urging negotiation and withdrawal. The basis of America's Asian commitment is subjected to debate.

Antiwar feelings run high in the civil rights movement, where some believe the Negro should not fight for freedom abroad until he has won a fuller measure of freedom at home; and where others believe that the nonviolence that characterized a large section of the Negro civil rights movement should be extended into the political arena as well.

Opposition to the Vietnam war is strong on college campuses, where young men are precariously balanced between classroom and conscription. The draft system is under review; the present laws are openly criticized. Kingman Brewster, President of Yale University, has declared, "I personally find the present Selective Service Law and policy most objectionable." Young men who are disaffected and uneasy about their country's aims in the Vietnam enterprise carefully scrutinize the conditions of conscientious objection. And others, already drafted, arrive lately at a position of conscientious objection, and receive prison terms for their tardy discovery of private scruple.

The concluding document in this section is the statement of one Benjamin Sherman. It is, in a sense, the ultimate position of the conscientious objector in our time. Sherman is a selective objector. He does not claim to be a pure pacifist; the Christian stance is too difficult to maintain in the world today. He does not claim to be religious; there is no august church body behind him. Sherman is a citizen and a secular man. "My strength is not . . . to be completely and lovingly nonviolent. I am trying to be human." He is trying to find his own balance between private conscience and public policy.

44. Scientists for Peace.

Over the years many of the scientists most intimately connected with the production of the atomic bomb and later the hydrogen bomb became the nation's most ardent spokesmen for nuclear disarmament. The documents that follow reveal these scientists in a quasipolitical role as they petition presidents and politicians to change the course of national policy.

44.   a.   Leo Szilard, "A Petition to the President of the United States," 1945.*

Leo Szilard was born in Hungary and emigrated to England and then to the United States after Hitler came to power. At the University of Chicago, Szilard and Enrico Fermi worked out the experiments that produced the first controlled chain reactions from an atomic pile. Throughout the Second World War, Szilard worked with Fermi and others on the highly secret Manhattan Project, which led directly to the production of the atomic bomb.

When the war in Europe ended on May 8, 1945, Szilard and others hoped that their discovery would never be tested on the battlefield. The public was still unaware that an atomic bomb existed. Szilard urged President Truman not to use the bomb on Japan. Sixty-three scientists signed his petition. Nevertheless, President Truman, en route back to the United States from the Potsdam Conference, on August 6, 1945, announced to the world that sixteen hours earlier the city of Hiroshima had been wiped out, and three days later revealed the demolition of Nagasaki.

July 17, 1945

Discoveries of which the people of the United States are not aware may affect the welfare of this nation in the near future. The liberation of atomic power which has been achieved places atomic bombs in the hands of the Army. It places in your hands, as Commander-in-Chief, the fateful decision whether or not to sanction the use of such bombs in the present phase of the war against Japan.

We, the undersigned scientists, have been working in the field of atomic power. Until recently we have had no fear that the United States might be attacked by atomic bombs during this war and that her only defense might lie in a counterattack by the same means. Today, with the defeat of Germany, this danger is averted and we feel impelled to say what follows:

* In *The Atomic Age,* Morton Grodzins and Eugene Rabinowitch, eds. (New York: Basic Books, Inc., 1963), pp. 28–29.

The war has to be brought speedily to a successful conclusion and attacks by atomic bombs may very well be an effective method of warfare. We feel, however, that such attacks on Japan could not be justified, at least not unless the terms which will be imposed after the war on Japan were made public in detail and Japan were given an opportunity to surrender.

If such public announcement gave assurance to the Japanese that they could look forward to a life devoted to peaceful pursuits in their homeland and if Japan still refused to surrender, our nation might then, in certain circumstances, find itself forced to resort to the use of atomic bombs. Such a step, however, ought not to be made at any time without seriously considering the moral responsibilities which are involved.

The development of atomic power will provide the nations with new means of destruction. The atomic bombs at our disposal represent only the first step in this direction and there is almost no limit to the destructive power which will become available in the course of their future development. Thus a nation which sets the precedent of using these newly liberated forces of nature for purposes of destruction may have to bear the responsibility of opening the door to an era of devastation on an unimaginable scale.

If after this war a situation is allowed to develop in the world which permits rival powers to be in uncontrolled possession of these new means of destruction, the cities of the United States as well as the cities of other nations will be in continuous danger of sudden annihilation. All the resources of the United States, moral and material, may have to be mobilized to prevent the advent of such a world situation. Its prevention is at present the solemn responsibility of the United States—singled out by virtue of her lead in the field of atomic power.

The added material strength which this lead gives to the United States brings with it the obligation of restraint, and if we were to violate this obligation our moral position would be weakened in the eyes of the world and in our own eyes. It would then be more difficult for us to live up to our responsibility of bringing the unloosened forces of destruction under control.

In view of the foregoing, we, the undersigned, respectfully petition: first, that you exercise your power as Commander-in-Chief to rule that the United States shall not resort to the use of atomic bombs in this war unless the terms which will be imposed upon Japan have been made public in detail and Japan, knowing these terms, has refused to surrender; second, that in such an event the question whether or not to use atomic bombs be decided by you in the light of the considerations presented in this petition as well as all the other moral responsibilities which are involved.

44. b. Bertrand Russell and Albert Einstein, "An Appeal for the Abolition of War," 1955.*

In 1955, Lord Bertrand Russell, philosopher and mathematician, drafted a statement on the dangers of hydrogen wars and called on the nations of the world to abolish war. Albert Einstein cosigned the statement just before his death on April 18, 1955. Seven other scientists, five of them, like Russell and Einstein, winners of the Nobel Prize, also signed the appeal. The Russell-Einstein appeal led to the start of the Pugwash Conferences on Science and World Affairs two years later (July, 1957).** The conferences have provided the format for an East-West exchange and discussion among scientists. Ten conferences have been held.

In the tragic situation which confronts humanity, we feel that scientists should assemble in conference to appraise the perils that have arisen as a result of the development of weapons of mass destruction, and to discuss a resolution in the spirit of the appended draft.

We are speaking on this occasion, not as members of this or that nation, continent, or creed, but as human beings, members of the species man, whose continued existence is in doubt. The world is full of conflicts; and overshadowing all minor conflicts is the titanic struggle between Communism and anti-Communism.

Almost everybody who is politically conscious has strong feelings about one or more of these issues; but we want you, if you can, to set aside such feelings and consider yourselves only as members of a biological species which has had a remarkable history, and whose disappearance none of us can desire.

* *The New York Times,* July 10, 1955; Grodzins and Rabinowitch, *op. cit.,* pp. 539–41.

** Cyrus Eaton, Cleveland industrialist, offered scientists the hospitality of his home at Pugwash, Nova Scotia. The conferences, which have been held at other sites since, retained the name of their first meeting place.

We shall try to say no single word which should appeal to one group rather than to another. All, equally, are in peril, and if the peril is understood there is hope that they may collectively avert it.

We have to learn to think in a new way. We have to learn to ask ourselves, not what steps can be taken to give military victory to whatever group we prefer, for there no longer are such steps; the question we have to ask ourselves is: what steps can be taken to prevent a military contest of which the issue must be disastrous to all parties?

The general public, and even many men in position of authority, have not realized what would be involved in a war with nuclear bombs. The general public still thinks in terms of the obliteration of cities. It is understood that the new bombs are more powerful than the old, and that while one A-bomb could obliterate Hiroshima, one H-bomb could obliterate the largest cities, such as London, New York, and Moscow.

No doubt in an H-bomb war great cities would be obliterated. But this is one of the minor disasters that would have to be faced. If everybody in London, New York, and Moscow were exterminated, the world might in the course of a few centuries recover from the blow. But we now know, especially since the Bikini test, that nuclear bombs can gradually spread destruction over a very much wider area than had been supposed.

It is stated on very good authority that a bomb can now be manufactured which will be 2,500 times as powerful as that which destroyed Hiroshima.

Such a bomb, if exploded near the ground or under water, sends radioactive particles into the upper air. They sink gradually and reach the surface of the earth in the form of a deadly dust or rain. It was this dust which infected the Japanese fishermen and their catch of fish.

No one knows how widely such lethal radioactive particles must be diffused. But the best authorities are unanimous in saying that a war with H-bombs might quite possibly put an end to the human race. It is feared that if many H-bombs are used there will be universal death—sudden only for a minority, but for the majority a slow torture of disease and disintegration.

Many warnings have been uttered by eminent men of science and by authorities in military strategy. None of them will say that the worst results are certain. What they do say is that these results are possible, and no one can be sure that they will not be realized. We have not yet found that the views of experts on this question depend in any degree upon their politics or prejudices. They depend only, so far as our researches have revealed, upon the extent of the particular expert's knowledge. We have found that the men who know most are the most gloomy.

Here, then, is the problem which we present to you, stark and dreadful and inescapable: shall we put an end to the human race or shall mankind renounce war? People will not face this alternative because it is so difficult to abolish war.

The abolition of war will demand distasteful limitations of national sovereignty. But what perhaps impedes understanding of the situation more than anything else is that the term "mankind" feels vague and abstract. People scarcely realize in imagination that the danger is to themselves and their children and their grandchildren, and not only to a dimly apprehended humanity. They can scarcely bring themselves to grasp that they, individually, and those whom they love are in imminent danger of perishing agonizingly. And so they hope that perhaps war may be allowed to continue provided modern weapons are prohibited.

This hope is illusory. Whatever agreements not to use H-bombs had been reached in time of peace, they would no longer be considered binding in time of war, and both sides would set to work to manufacture H-bombs as soon as war broke out, for if one side manufactured the bombs and the other did not, the side that manufactured them would inevitably be victorious.

Although an agreement to renounce nuclear weapons as part of a general reduction of armaments would not afford an ultimate solution, it would serve certain important purposes.

First: any agreement between East and West is to the good insofar as it tends to diminish tension. Second: the abolition of thermonuclear weapons, if each side believed that the other had carried it out sincerely, would lessen the fear of a sudden attack in the style of Pearl Harbor, which at present keeps both sides in a state of nervous apprehension. We should, therefore, welcome such an agreement, though only as a first step.

Most of us are not neutral in feeling, but as human beings

we have to remember that if the issues between East and West are to be decided in any manner that can give any possible satisfaction to anybody, whether Communist or anti-Communist, whether Asian or European or American, whether white or black, then these issues must not be decided by war. We should wish this to be understood both in the East and in the West.

There lies before us, if we choose, continual progress in happiness, knowledge, and wisdom. Shall we instead choose death because we cannot forget our quarrels? We appeal as human beings to human beings: remember your humanity and forget the rest. If you can do so, the way lies open to a new paradise; if you cannot, there lies before you the risk of universal death.

We invite this congress (to be convened), and through it the scientists of the world and the general public, to subscribe to the following resolution:

> In view of the fact that in any future world war nuclear weapons will certainly be employed, and that such weapons threaten the continued existence of mankind, we urge the governments of the world to realize and to acknowledge publicly that their purposes cannot be furthered by a world war, and we urge them, consequently, to find peaceful means for the settlement of all matters of dispute between them.

44. c. The Mainau Declaration of Fifty-two Nobel Laureates, 1955.*

Scientists of widely different fields and specializations have been acutely aware of the lethal possibilities of nuclear and hydrogen warfare. Following a meeting at Mainau, Germany, a group of Nobel laureates issued this appeal to the nations of the world to abandon war.

We, the undersigned, are scientists of different countries, different creeds, different political persuasions. Outwardly, we are bound together only by the Nobel Prize, which we have been favored to receive. With pleasure we have devoted our lives to the service of science. It is, we believe, a path to a happier life for people. We see with horror that this very science is giving mankind the means to destroy itself. By total military use of weapons feasible today, the earth can be contaminated with radioactivity to such an extent that whole peoples can be annihilated. Neutrals may die thus as well as belligerents.

If war broke out among the great powers, who would guarantee that it would not develop into a deadly conflict? A nation that engages in a total war thus signals its own destruction and imperils the whole world.

We do not deny that perhaps today peace is being preserved precisely by the fear of these weapons. Nevertheless, we think it is a delusion if governments believe that they can avoid war for a long time through the fear of these weapons. Fear and tension have often engendered wars. Similarly it seems to us a delusion to believe that small conflicts could in the future always be decided by traditional weapons. In extreme danger no nation will deny itself the use of any weapon that scientific technology can produce.

All nations must come to the decision to renounce force as a final resort of policy. If they are not prepared to do this they will cease to exist.

* Quoted in Linus Pauling, *No More War!* (New York: Dodd, Mead & Co., 1958), Appendix 2, pp. 222–24.

Lord Edgar Douglas Adrian, Cambridge
Kurt Alder, Köln
Max Born, Bad Pyrmont
Walther Bothe, Heidelberg
Percy William Bridgman, Cambridge
Adolf Butenandt, Tübingen
Arthur H. Compton, Saint Louis
Henrik Dam, Copenhagen
Clinton Joseph Davisson, Charlottesville
P. A. M. Dirac, Oxford
Edward A. Doisy, Saint Louis
Gerhard Domagk, Wuppertal
Joseph Erlanger, Saint Louis
Hans K. von Euler-Chelpin, Stockholm
James Franck, Chicago
Otto Hahn, Göttingen
Werner Heisenberg, Göttingen
P. S. Hench, Rochester, Minn.
Gustav Hertz, Leipzig
Georg von Hevesy, Stockholm
C. Heymans, Ghent
Fredéric Joliot-Curie, Paris
Irène Joliot-Curie, Paris
E. C. Kendall, Princeton
Sir Hans Krebs, Oxford
Richard Kuhn, Heidelberg
Max von Laue, Berlin
Fritz Lipman, Boston
A. E. Moniz, Lisbon
Paul Hermann Müller, Basel
H. J. Muller, Bloomington
William Murphy, Boston
Wolfgang Pauli, Zurich
Linus Pauling, Pasadena
C. F. Powell, Bristol
Sir Chandrasekhara Venkata Raman, Bangalore
Th. Reichstein, Basel
Lord Bertrand Russell, Richmond
L. Ruzicka, Zurich
F. F. Sillanpää, Helsinki
Frederick Soddy, Brighton
W. M. Stanley, Berkeley
Hermann Staudinger, Freiburg

Richard Laurence Millington Synge, Bucksburn
Max Theiler, New York
A. Tiselius, Uppsala
Harold C. Urey, Chicago
G. H. Whipple, Rochester
Heinrich Wieland, Starnberg
Adolf Windaus, Göttingen
Hideki Yukawa, Kyoto
Frits Zernike, Groningen

44. d. Linus Pauling, "Scientists' Petition to the United Nations," 1958.*

Linus Pauling, Nobel laureate for chemistry in 1954, became one of this country's most ardent advocates of disarmament and cessation of nuclear testing. Pauling wrote the petition below and circulated it to scientists throughout the world.

At noon on Monday 15 January 1958 I placed in the hands of Mr. Dag Hammarskjöld, Secretary-General of the United Nations, a petition from 9235 scientists, of many countries in the world.

This petition has the title "Petition to the United Nations Urging that an International Agreement to Stop the Testing of Nuclear Bombs Be Made Now."

The petition consists of five paragraphs, as follows:

We, the scientists whose names are signed below, urge that an international agreement to stop the testing of nuclear bombs be made now.

Each nuclear bomb test spreads an added burden of radioactive elements over every part of the world. Each added amount of radiation causes damage to the health of human beings all over the world and causes damage to the pool of human germ plasm such as to lead to an increase in the number of seriously defective children that will be born in future generations.

So long as these weapons are in the hands of only three powers an agreement for their control is feasible. If testing continues, and the possession of these weapons spreads to additional governments, the danger of outbreak of a cataclysmic nuclear war through the reckless action of some irresponsible national leader will be greatly increased.

An international agreement to stop the testing of nuclear bombs now could serve as a first step toward a more general disarmament and the ultimate effective aboli-

* Pauling, *op. cit.*, pp. 160–66.

339

tion of nuclear weapons, averting the possibility of a nuclear war that would be a catastrophe to all humanity.

We have in common with our fellow men a deep concern for the welfare of all human beings. As scientists we have knowledge of the dangers involved and therefore a special responsibility to make those dangers known. We deem it imperative that immediate action be taken to effect an international agreement to stop the testing of all nuclear weapons.

Nobel Laureates Among Signers

Nobel Laureates in Physics

Max Born
  Germany
P. A. M. Dirac
  Great Britain
W. Heisenberg
  Germany
Tang-Dao Lee
  (Resident in U.S.A.)
  China
E. T. S. Walton
  Ireland
C. F. Powell
  Great Britain
C. V. Raman
  India
C. N. Yang
  (Resident in U.S.A.)
  China
Hideki Yukawa
  Japan

Nobel Laureates in Chemistry

K. Alder
  Germany
A. Butenandt
  Germany
Otto Hahn
  Germany

Leopold Ruzicka
  Switzerland
N. N. Semenov
  U.S.S.R.
R. L. M. Synge
  Great Britain
Fredéric Joliot-Curie
  France
Richard Kuhn
  Germany
Linus Pauling
  U.S.A.
A. W. K. Tiselius
  Sweden
Harold Urey
  U.S.A.
Adolf Windaus
  Germany

Nobel Laureate in Literature

Bertrand Russell
  Great Britain

Nobel Laureates in Peace

Lord Boyd Orr
  Great Britain
Albert Schweitzer
  France

Nobel Laureates in Physiology and Medicine

Jules Bordet
  Belgium
Henry Dale
  Great Britain
Gerhard Domagk
  Germany
Joseph Erlanger
  U.S.A.
Hans Krebs
  Great Britain

Otto Loewi
  U.S.A.
Hermann Muller
  U.S.A.
W. P. Murphy
  U.S.A.
A. Szent-Györgyi
  (Resident in U.S.A.)
  Hungary
Max Theiler
  U.S.A.
Hugo Theorell
  Sweden
T. Reichstein
  Switzerland
G. H. Whipple
  U.S.A.

45. Linus Pauling, from "A Proposal: Research for Peace," 1958.*

Linus Pauling received the Nobel Prize for Chemistry in 1954. His work on the molecular structure of hemoglobin and on the hereditary transmission of abnormalities led directly to his study of the dangers of radioactivity and indirectly to his writings on the need for disarmament and peace. In the light of the proposal made in the excerpt that follows, it is of interest to know that Institutes for the study of peace now exist in university centers in the United States and in Western Europe.**

How is peace in the world to be achieved? How, are the great world problems to be solved, without resort to war, war that would now lead to catastrophe, to world suicide?

I propose that the great world problems be solved in the way that other problems are solved—by working hard to find their solution—by carrying on *research for peace*.

Research consists in striving in every possible way to discover what the facts are, to learn more and more about the nature of the world, and to use all information that can be obtained in the effort to find the solution to difficult problems.

As the world has become more and more complex in recent centuries and decades there has developed a greater and greater reliance upon specialists to carry on research and to make discoveries. . . .

Research for War

During recent decades greater and greater use has been made of research and of the services of scientists and other

* Pauling, *op. cit.*, pp. 195–209.
** Some of these Institutes are the following: The Center for the Study of the Causes of War and Conditions for Peace, Utah State University, Logan, Utah; The Center of Conflict Resolution, University of Michigan, Ann Arbor, Michigan; The Center for Peace Research, Creighton University, Omaha, Nebraska; The Center for Democratic Institutions, Santa Barbara, California.

scholars in the conduct of war and the preparation for war.

The Second World War was fought almost entirely with weapons and by methods developed by scientists.

Armaments of the great nations of the world are now much different from those upon which they relied during the Second World War. The changes—the development of nuclear weapons, of jet planes, of guided missiles, of ballistic missiles, of improved radar and other methods of detection—have resulted from scientific research, both fundamental and applied.

Even the tactical and strategic techniques are now developed through research. During the Second World War the admirals and generals came to rely more and more upon advice from scientists and other specialists constituting their operations analysis groups. These groups of mathematicians, physicists, chemists, and other specialists are able to develop a far deeper understanding of modern warfare than the admirals and generals, to analyze the problems involved, and to give advice as to how war should be conducted that is far better than the conclusions that the admirals and generals themselves could reach.

These specialists devote years to the attack on the problem of how best to wage war. They make use of giant electronic computers to assist them in their attack. It may well be that some of these able men have found some imaginative and unexpected solutions to some of the military problems.

Great sums of money, hundreds of millions of dollars per year, are now being spent on research for war, and many thousands of scientists and other specialists are involved in this work. . . .

Research for Peace

The time has now come for the greatest of all problems facing the world, the problem of peace, to be attacked in an effective way.

I propose that there be set up a great research organization, the World Peace Research Organization, within the structure of the United Nations.

The duty of the World Peace Research Organization would be to attack the problem of preserving the peace, to carry out research on preserving peace in the world, to carry out research on peace. This would mean, of course, carrying out research on how to solve great world problems, problems of the kind that have in the past led to war. It would also involve attacking the problem of how to prevent the outbreak of a nuclear war by design or by accident.

The World Peace Research Organization, if it existed today, could make a thorough analysis of the problems involved in an international agreement to stop all testing of nuclear weapons. It could, after making its study, propose a system that, in the opinion of the Organization, would have the greatest safety, the smallest chance of violation by any nation, would be of the maximum benefit to all of the nations and all of the people of the world. Such a proposal would without doubt be given serious consideration by the nations of the world.

The World Peace Research Organization should be a large one. It should include many scientists, representing all fields of science, and many other specialists—economists, geographers, specialists in all fields of knowledge.

In order that these important problems might be attacked with the aid of the advice and help of some of the most able men in the world, satisfactory conditions for work would have to be provided for these men. This means that the facilities and environment would have to be similar to those in the great universities, and the outstanding authorities in various fields would have to be allowed to prosecute their studies in a fundamental and thorough way. They would, however, be at hand to help with special projects, attacks on special problems, when needed.

The multiplicity of the fields of human knowledge pertinent to the problem of peace and the complexity of the problem itself are such that the Organization should have thousands of specialists on its staff. Within two years after its inception the Organization might have a staff of about 2000 specialists, and within 10 years its staff might have increased to 10,000 specialists, plus the other staff members necessary for it to function effectively.

The specialists on the staff of the Organization should have freedom to attack the problem of peace in the world comparable to that with which professors in a university are free to attack the problems in which they are interested. They should be provided with assistants, laboratories, and other facilities of such a nature as to permit them to work most effectively. . . .

We cannot expect that the great problems in the modern world can be solved in an easy way by government officials who have many duties and who cannot devote to the problems the long and careful thought that they require for their solution. These problems need to be attacked in the way that other problems are attacked in the modern world—by research, carried out by people who think about the problems year after year.

There are great possibilities of progress in this way. If thousands of outstandingly able investigators are attacking the world problems by imaginative and original methods, working on these problems year after year, many of these problems should be solved.

It is possible that some great discoveries may be made, discoveries that would so change the world as to make the danger of outbreak of a nuclear war far less than it is at present.

The cost of supporting the World Peace Research Organization within the United Nations on the scale described, with at first 2000 specialists and many auxiliary members of the staff, increasing to 10,000 specialists in ten years, would be of the order of magnitude of 25 million dollars per year at the beginning and 100 million dollars per year ultimately.

This cost is very small in comparison with the sums expended for military purposes. The military budget of the United States at the present time is about $40,000,000,000 and that of Russia and other countries is comparable, so that we may estimate the total cost to the world of the military machines at the present time as about 100,000 million dollars per year. The cost of the proposed World Peace Research Organization within the United Nations would be only about one-tenth of one percent of this sum.

The damage that would be done to the world by a nuclear war is inestimable. What, in dollars, would be the loss to the United States if half of our people were killed? What, in dollars, would be the property damage to the United States if New York, Chicago, Philadelphia, Los Angeles, and scores of other cities were destroyed? We might say that the property damage would amount to several million million dollars. If there were a chance of one in one hundred thousand of preventing this damage, it would be well worth while to do so. It would be well worth while to pay the corresponding sum, 100 million dollars, to prevent the loss. The World Peace Research Organization would be a cheap insurance policy.

There is no doubt in my mind that the World Peace Research Organization would be able to make suggestions about international problems that would be accepted by by the nations of the world and that would lead to a significant decrease in the armaments budget. The military budget of the United States might well be decreased, as a result of these suggestions, from 40 billion dollars to 36 billion dollars per year, and then to 32 billion dollars per year, and then to 28 billion dollars per year, and so on, with an accompanying increase in national safety, rather than a decrease.

I have no doubt that the World Peace Research Organization would pay for itself in a short while. . . .

President Eisenhower in his address on 17 April 1958 pointed out that great things might be done with the sums of money now being spent on armaments. He mentioned that if the U.S. had spent only $50,000,000,000 on defense during the five years 1953 to 1958 rather than the $200,000,-000,000 that was spent, we could have constructed the entire nationwide interstate system of highways that has been planned, built every worthwhile hydroelectric power project in America, built all the hospitals needed for the next ten years and all the schools needed for the next ten years, and have been able also to reduce the national debt by $50,000,000,000.

The World Peace Research Organization should be a research organization, which makes analyses of world problems, makes discoveries, and makes proposals. It should not be a policy-making organization.

One of the greatest of the problems facing the world, closely connected with the problem of war or peace, is the population problem. In eight years the United States has increased in population by over 12 percent, from 151 million in 1950 to an estimated 175 million in 1958. The population of the whole world is increasing at nearly the same rate. Much of the increase has been due to medical progress, in decreasing the infant and childhood mortality and lengthening the life span.

As the population pressure becomes greater in some countries in the world, the danger of the outbreak of war becomes greater. The population problem is one that should be attacked by the World Peace Research Organization.

Every great nation should also have its own peace research organization. Careful analyses would have to be made by the nations of the proposals made by the World Peace Research Organization. These analyses could be made only by similar groups of specialists. In the United States, for example, a Peace Research Organization might be set up under the Science Advisor to the President. Another possibility is that it be incorporated within the Department of Peace, in case that a Secretary for Peace is added to the Cabinet. In either case, the Peace Research Organization of the United States should not be an operating organization or a policy-making organization, but a research organization.

At the present time Dr. James R. Killian is serving as Science Advisor to the President. He has appointed a staff of scientists as his advisors. They, however, are consultants, not full-time workers. Such an organization, the Science Advisor to the President and his group of part-time scientific consultants, represents a puny effort indeed for an attack on the great world problems, in which science plays such an important part. . . .

The World of the Future

We live now in a period of rapid change—a period of revolution, of nuclear revolution. Everything in the world has been changed as a result of scientific discoveries. I think that the greatest change of all is that in the ways of waging war— the change from old-fashioned molecular explosives, the one-ton TNT bomb, to the great nuclear weapon, the super-bomb that is twenty times as powerful.

This change, from molecular explosives to superbombs, has caused war to rule itself out.

Even the politicians and diplomats are changing, although they are slow to show it. They still behave at times as though war were the method to solve international disputes, but it is clear that the leaders of the great nations know that a nuclear war cannot be allowed to wreak its destruction on the world.

The time has now come for war to be abandoned, for diplomacy to move out of the nineteenth century into the real world of the twentieth century, a world in which war and the threat of war no longer have a rightful place as the instrument of national policy. We must move towards a world governed by justice, by international law, and not by force.

We must all, including the diplomats and national leaders, change our point of view. We must recognize that extreme nationalism is a thing of the past. The idea that it is just as important to do harm to other nations as to do good for your own nation must be given up. We must all begin to work for the world as a whole, for humanity.

Science is the search for the truth—it is not a game in which one tries to beat his opponent, to do harm to others. We need to have the spirit of science in international affairs, to make the conduct of international affairs the effort to find the right solution, the just solution of international problems, not the effort by each nation to get the better of other nations, to do harm to them when it is possible.

I believe in morality, in justice, in humanitarianism. We must recognize now that the power to destroy the world by the use of nuclear weapons is a power that cannot be used —we cannot accept the idea of such monstrous immorality.

The time has now come for morality to take its proper place in the conduct of world affairs; the time has now come for the nations of the world to submit to the just regulation of their conduct by international law.

46. Albert S. Bigelow, from *The Voyage of the Golden Rule*, 1959.*

Albert S. Bigelow was captain of a destroyer escort in World War II. After the war, Bigelow opened his home to two "Hiroshima Maidens," young girls who had been disfigured by atomic explosion and brought to this country for medical care. In 1957, when the United States announced the start of a series of atomic tests at Eniwetok Atoll in the Pacific, Bigelow, aged 51, and his crew announced they would sail the ketch the Golden Rule *into the test area as a deliberate act of conscientious protest.*

In 1963, Bigelow joined the Delhi–Peking Friendship March, sponsored by the World Peace Brigade.

The development of the *Golden Rule* idea—early protest in
  Nevada—the logic of the venture seizes me in its grip

The idea was a natural.

A white sail, a tiny speck in the vast blue Pacific, moving westward . . . persistently, slowly, day after day, week after week, on and into the bomb explosion area . . . this was "the play wherein to catch the conscience of the King." Mankind was unconsulted, powerless in the face of these tests. Revolted and horrified by the danger and implication of these explosions, we had no voice. But though we had no tongue, here was a most miraculous organ. The tiny white sail as it worked slowly westward would blow the horrid deed in every eye. The act would speak louder than words.

The idea first appeared in the spring of 1957. The British had scheduled a series of tests at Christmas Island, 1,000 miles south of Hawaii. Many of us were meeting, getting together, feeling intuitively that this was a time for action.

Harold Steele, a British Quaker, did act. He tried to organize a ship and crew to sail into the Christmas Island area. He and his wife only got as far as Tokyo. They were not able to organize a ship and crew. But Harold Steele was a powerful inspiration to all of us.

* (New York: Doubleday, 1959), pp. 23–25, 42–47, 270–73.

The British had scheduled the only tests in the Pacific during 1957. We were too late to organize a sailing from the United States. Furthermore, there was a question of propriety in protesting the nuclear explosions of the British when our government, the United States, was by far the worst offender. Our government did have a series of tests, an extensive series, scheduled for Nevada. It became clear that we should have to go to Nevada. Therefore, early in June 1957, we organized an *ad hoc* committee, Non-Violent Action Against Nuclear Weapons (A First Step to Disarmament).

An extraordinary urge had brought us together. Most were pacifists who had been working for many years to halt the arms race and turn its destructive degradation into constructive aspiration. We were all Americans with a deep love of freedom and our country. There were about thirty of us on the committee. Half of us were Jewish, Catholic, or Protestant, about half of us were Quakers, a few non-religious.

We knew something about the theory but very little about the practice of nonviolence when we went to Nevada. On the morning of August 6, 1957, the twelfth anniversary of the bombing of Hiroshima, about thirty-five of us assembled early in the morning in a prayer and conscience vigil outside the main gate of the Mercury project. Mercury is about seventy miles northwest of Las Vegas, Nevada, and is the entrance to the vast area of that state set aside by the Atomic Energy Commission for nuclear explosions.

Eleven of us, in twos and threes, rose from the prayer vigil at intervals, approached the main gate, talked to the forty-or-more armed men there, and crossed the line into the project as an act of protest. We were arrested, taken to a Justice of the Peace Court in Beatty, Nevada, forty miles away, and tried for "trespassing." We were given suspended sentences. Little note was taken of our action and few people have heard of it to this day. . . .

After leaving court, we returned to the prayer vigil at the Mercury gate. We continued to pray throughout the night. At dawn we experienced, from a distance of about twenty-five miles, a nuclear explosion. This was proof that our intuition, our feeling, and our senses were right. We knew that we could never rest while such forces of evil were loose in God's world. . . .

Shortly after the failure of the London [disarmament] conference [Summer, 1957] and as the United Nations was about to assemble, the United States announced, on September 15, 1957, a series of tests to take place in Eniwetok, in the Marshall Islands, in April 1958.

I knew at once that this meant me. It was a personal challenge. . . .

January 9, 1958

President Dwight D. Eisenhower
The White House
Washington, D.C.
Dear President Eisenhower:

We write to tell you of our intended action regarding the announced spring test explosions of American nuclear weapons.

Four of us, with the support of many others, plan to sail a small vessel into the designated area in the Pacific by April 1st. We intend, come what may, to remain there during the test period, in an effort to halt what we feel is the monstrous delinquency of our government in continuing actions which threaten the well-being of all men. We recognize the equal guilt of Russian authorities in this matter and plan parallel action to carry the same moral and political message to them.

You will find enclosed a statement of our reasons and the facts of our project. We are sensitive to the great responsibility you bear and assure you that there will be no deception in our effort. All action will be taken openly and trustingly in the Gandhian spirit of a non-violent attempt to effect needed change by speaking to the best in all men.

For years we have spoken and written of the suicidal military preparations of the Great Powers, but our voices have been lost in the massive effort of those responsible for preparing this country for war. We mean to speak now with the weight of our whole lives. By our effort in the Pacific we mean to say to all men, "We are here because stopping preparation for nuclear war is now the principle business of our lives; it is also the principal requirement for the continuation of human life. It is a task in which we would have our nation lead. We, by our action, would be asking our fellow citizens to accept the lesser dangers and the greater opportunity that such an approach implies."

We hope our presence in the test area will speak to that which is deepest in you and in all men: that all men are capable of love. Please consider us,

Sincerely, your friends,

FOR NON-VIOLENT ACTION AGAINST NUCLEAR WEAPONS	FOR CREW OF THE KETCH, "GOLDEN RULE"
George Willoughby, *Chairman* Lawrence Scott, *Coordinator*	Albert Bigelow William Huntington

WHY I AM SAILING INTO THE PACIFIC BOMB-TEST AREA*

My friend Bill Huntington and I are planning to sail a small vessel westward into the Pacific H-bomb test area. By April we expect to reach the nuclear testing grounds at Eniwetok. We will remain there as long as the tests of H-bombs continue. With us will be two other volunteers.

Why?

Why do I feel under compulsion, under moral orders, as it were, to do this?

The answer to such questions, at least in part, has to do with my experience as a Naval officer during World War II. The day after Pearl Harbor was attacked, I was at the Navy recruiting offices. I had had a lot of experience in navigating vessels in ocean sailing. Life in the Navy would be a glamorous change from the dull mechanism of daily civilian living. My experience assured me of success. All this adventure ahead and the prospect of becoming a hero into the bargain.

I suppose too, that I had an enormous latent desire to conform, to "go along." I was swayed by the age-old psychology of meeting force with force. It did not really occur to me to resist the drag of the institution of war, the pattern of organized violence, which had existed for so many centuries. This psychology prevailed even though I had already reflected on the fantastic wastefulness of war—the German *Bismarck* hunting the British *Hood* and sending it to the bottom of the sea, and the British Navy then hunting *Bismarck* down to its death.

I volunteered, but instead of being sent to sea, I was as-

---

* This statement, in a slightly different form, appeared in the magazine *Liberation*, February, 1958. [Editor's note]

signed to 90 Church Street in New York and worked in
"Plot" establishing the whereabouts of all combat ships in
the Atlantic. In a couple of months I escaped from this assignment and was transferred to the Naval Training Station at
Northwestern University.

I had not been at Northwestern very long when I sensed
that because of my past experience I would be made an
instructor there and still not get to sea. So I deliberately
flunked an examination in navigation and before long was
assigned to a subchaser in the Atlantic.

The Turkey Shoot

From March to October of 1943 I was in command of a
subchaser in the Solomon Islands. It was during this period
that more than one hundred Japanese planes were shot down
in one day. This was called "the turkey shoot." The insensitivity which decent men must develop in such situations is appalling. I remember that the corpse of a Japanese
airman who had been shot down was floating bolt upright
in one of the coves, a position resulting from the structure
of the Japanese life belts, which were different from our Mae
Wests. Each day as we passed the cove we saw this figure,
his face growing blacker under the terrific sun. We laughingly
called him Smiling Jack. As a matter of fact, I think I gave
him that name myself and felt rather proud of my wit.

Later in World War II, I was Captain of the destroyer
escort *Dale W. Peterson*—DE 337—and I was on her bridge
as we approached Pearl Harbor from San Diego when the
first news arrived of the explosion of an atomic bomb over
Hiroshima. Although I had no way of understanding what
an atom bomb was I was absolutely awestruck, as I suppose
all men were for a moment. Intuitively it was then that I
realized for the first time that morally war is impossible.

I think also that deep down somewhere in me, and in
all men at all times, there is a realization that the pattern
of violence meeting violence makes no sense, and that war
violates something central in the human heart—"that of God,"
as we Quakers sometimes say. For example, later, when
each of us at the trial in Nevada had told why we were
committing civil disobedience against nuclear tests, our attorney, Francis Heisler, said: "There isn't one of us in this
courtroom who doesn't wish that he had walked into the testing grounds with these people this morning." Everybody, including the police and court officers, nodded assent.

Society of Friends

However, I am ahead of my story. At the close of the war, in spite of what I had felt on the bridge of that destroyer, I did not break away from my habitual attitudes. For a time I was Housing Commissioner of Massachusetts. Like many other people who had been through the war, I was seeking some sort of unified life-philosophy or religion. I did a good deal of religious "window-shopping." I became impressed by the fact that in one way or another the saints, the wise men, those who seemed to me truly experienced, all pointed in one direction—toward nonviolence, truth, love; toward a way and a goal that could not be reconciled with war. For quite a while, to use a phrase of Alan Watts', I "sucked the finger instead of going where it pointed." But finally I realized that I did have to move in that direction, and in 1952 I resigned my commission in the Naval Reserve. It was promptly and courteously accepted. I felt a bit proud of doing it a month before I would have become eligible for a pension. Such little things we pride ourselves on!

I worshiped often with the Quakers, the Society of Friends. My wife Sylvia had already joined the Society in 1948. As late as 1955 I was still fighting off joining the Society, which seemed to me to involve a great, awesome commitment. I suppose I was like the man in Bernard Shaw's play *Androcles and the Lion* who wanted "to be a Christian—but not yet."

I was not yet ready; ready as 17-year-old Betsy Gurney had written in her journal in 1798, "I know now what the mountain is I have to climb. I am to be a Quaker."

The Hiroshima Maidens

Then came the experience of having in our home, for more than a year, two of the Hiroshima maidens who had been injured and disfigured in the bombing of August 6, 1945. Norman Cousins and other wonderful people brought them to this country for plastic surgery. There were two things about these girls that hit me very hard and forced me to see that I had no choice but to make the commitment to live, as best I could, a life of nonviolence and reconciliation. One was the fact that when they were bombed in 1945 the two girls in our home were seven and thirteen years old. What earthly thing could they have done to give some semblance of what we call justice to the ordeal inflicted upon them and hundreds like them? What possible good could come out of human action—war—which bore such fruits?

Is it not utter blasphemy to think that there is anything moral or Christian about such behavior?

The other thing that struck me was that these young women found it difficult to believe that we, who were not members of their families, could love them. But they loved us; they harbored no resentment against us or other Americans. How are you going to respond to that kind of attitude? The newly elected president of the National Council of Churches, Edwin T. Dahlberg, said in his inaugural talk that instead of "massive retaliation" the business of Christians is to practice "massive reconciliation." Well, these Hiroshima girls practiced "massive reconciliation" on us, on me, who had laughed derisively at "Smiling Jack." What response can one make to this other than to give onself utterly to destroying the evil, war, that dealt so shamefully with them and try to live in the spirit of sensitivity and reconciliation which they displayed?

I was now ready.

I Am Going Because . . .

I am going because, as Shakespeare said, "Action is eloquence." Without some such direct action, ordinary citizens lack the power any longer to be seen or heard by their government.

I am going because it is time to do something about peace, not just talk about peace.

I am going because, like all men, in my heart I know that all nuclear explosions are monstrous, evil, unworthy of human beings.

I am going because war is no longer a feudal jousting match; it is an unthinkable catastrophe for all men.

I am going because it is now the little children, and, most of all, the as yet unborn who are the front-line troops. It is my duty to stand between them and this horrible danger.

I am going because it is cowardly and degrading for me to stand by any longer, to consent, and thus to collaborate in atrocities.

I am going because I cannot say that the end justifies the means. A Quaker, William Penn, said, "A good end cannot sanctify evil means; nor must we ever do evil that good may come of it." A Communist, Milovan Djilas, says, "As soon as means which would ensure an end are shown to be evil, the end will show itself as unrealizable."

I am going because, as Gandhi said, "God sits in the man opposite me; therefore to injure him is to injure God himself."

I am going to witness to the deep inward truth we all know, "Force can subdue, but love gains."

I am going because however mistaken, unrighteous, and unrepentant governments may seem, I still believe all men are really good at heart, and that my act will speak to them.

I am going in the hope of helping change the hearts and minds of men in government. If necessary I am willing to give my life to help change a policy of fear, force, and destruction to one of trust, kindness, and help.

I am going in order to say, "Quit this waste, this arms race. Turn instead to a disarmament race. Stop competing for evil, compete for good."

I am going because I have to—if I am to call myself a human being.

When you see something horrible happening, your instinct is to do something about it. You can freeze in fearful apathy or you can even talk yourself into saying that it isn't horrible. I can't do that. I have to act. This is too horrible. We know it. Let's all act.

Summary Information on a Voyage to Eniwetok

The Department of Defense and the Atomic Energy Commission have announced they plan further test explosions of nuclear weapons next April. In the past some 50,000 square miles of the Pacific Ocean have been used for this purpose. This area is designated "dangerous to all ships, aircraft and personnel entering it" and mariners are warned to remain clear. Four Americans acting under the compulsion of conscience and reason, plan, despite warnings, to sail a small vessel into the designated area before April 1st. They intend to remain there, come what may, in an effort to halt what they believe to be the monstrous delinquency of our government in continuing actions which threaten the well being of all men. They recognize these explosions will be stopped only if this is the will of the American people. They hope by their presence and, if necessary, by their suffering to speak to the reason and conscience of their fellow Americans. A parallel project to carry the same moral and political message to the people and authorities of Russia is being organized.

WHO

Albert Smith Bigelow, 51, painter and architect, Cos Cob, Connecticut, married, with two daughters and four grandchildren. Former Lt. Commander in the Navy (commanded three combat vessels in all areas of World War II). Housing Commissioner for Massachusetts, 1947–48. A director of Unitarian Service Committee, Inc. since 1949. Now member of the Religious Society of Friends, Stamford Monthly Meeting and active in leadership of the New York office of the American Friends Service Committee. Two Hiroshima maidens lived in his home while they received plastic surgery for scars suffered from the first atomic bomb.

William R. Huntington, St. James, Long Island, New York, 50, married, with three daughters and two grandchildren. A practicing architect since 1936. World War II conscientious objector, he served as Assistant Director of the Civilian Public Service Camp at Big Flats, New York. Commissioner in Europe for the American Friends Service Committee, 1947–49, and presently member of Board of Directors of the American Friends Service Committee and chairman of the Executive Committee of its Foreign Service Section. Member of the Religious Society of Friends, Westbury Monthly Meeting. Chairman of Peace and Social Order Committee of Friends General Conference.

Two other crew members yet to be named.

Non-Violent Action Against Nuclear Weapons, a coordinating committee of leaders of several American organizations working for world peace, which sponsored the protest against test explosions in Nevada last summer, is sponsoring the project and has responsibility for raising funds needed.

HOW AND WHEN

Golden Rule, a thirty foot ketch with 500 square feet of sail, a small 24 hp auxiliary motor, and bunks for four, is now being outfitted for the journey. It will sail from San Pedro, California on or about February 10. It will touch at Hawaii and then proceed to the Marshall Islands. It will enter the designated danger area by April 1 and remain there in an effort to witness to all men that it is important that the race to extinction be stopped.

NATURE OF THE PROJECT

There will be no deception. All action will be taken openly and trustingly in the Gandhian spirit of a non-violent attempt to effect needed change by speaking to the best in all men. Participants and sponsors oppose Communist or any other totalitarianism.

WHY THIS PARTICULAR ACTION?

The time has come when action of this kind is imperative. There are some things which even democratic governments do which those who stand for the dignity and survival of man must oppose. Our leaders are following policies which will greatly intensify the arms race, not helping form an American will to lead the world away from this senseless folly. We have tried: for years we have spoken and written, protesting the folly of seeking to preserve human freedom by developing the ability to kill and hurt millions of other men, women and children. But our voices have been lost in the massive effort of those responsible for preparing this country for war.

We believe more than words are needed if the apparent willingness of Americans to accept any horror in the name of national defense is to be challenged. If the majority in our democracy consciously want these tests, their desire will prevail. We oppose them only by non-violence and self-sacrifice. We speak now with our whole lives. We can no longer acquiesce in these tests.

WHO IS PAYING FOR IT?

Concerned Americans across the country. Copies of our finance leaflet available on request. $4,000 of a $20,000 net budget are in hand. A loan has made possible the purchase of the ketch *Golden Rule*. Non-Violent Action Against Nuclear Weapons has accepted responsibility for raising the money.

THE RELIGIOUS ROOTS OF OUR ACTION

Some of us are Quakers. Most are rooted in the ethics of the Judeo-Christian tradition. We act in the belief that

—each individual, regardless of color, race, creed, nationality or moral is sacred. Any hurt to him, no matter how slight, is, ultimately, injury to the whole human race;

—as individuals, as groups, and as nations, our action is destructive if it violates the ancient concept of the oneness of man;

—punishment, retaliation and revenge cannot reform those who do evil; forgiveness and love are necessary for redemption.

We cannot support war. Nor can we support war preparation. We are convinced that the testing of nuclear weapons is blasphemy.

THE POLITICS OF OUR ACTION

There is enormous difficulty in applying these beliefs to the political world. But this is the effort men must make. We know many Americans believe the tests and our over-all preparation for war are necessary to stop the spread of Communist totalitarianism and to defend our nation. They say "There would be no problem, were it not for the Russians." We share in large part their perception of the evil of Soviet totalitarianism and the need to resist its growth. But we deny their assumption that military power is the essential, "realistic" means of dealing with this problem. We deny their assumption that the massive engine of modern war can be applied rationally, or controlled to achieve democratic ends. We believe that war strengthens totalitarianism everywhere. We believe an end to the spread of totalitarianism and the defense of our nation depends primarily on a constructive program fo peace. And we have seen that a constructive program for peace cannot be carried on simultaneously with a program for military preparedness.

We believe that all which is most valuable in our heritage would be better protected if the effort, sacrifice, resources, and intelligence devoted to preparation for war were used to develop a program of non-violent national defense, and the constructive programs American leaders talk of but do not undertake. Those interested in our reasoning and the elements of our program for peace are referred to publications like the American Friends Service Committee's studies, "Speak Truth to Power," and "Steps to Peace," and to recent speeches by General Omar Bradley and Cyrus Eaton.

But our action here focuses on the bomb tests themselves. We believe many who do not yet fully reject reliance on military power *do* see wisdom in America's stopping these tests, as the first step in a major effort to reverse the arms race. No vital risk is involved. No inspection is necessary. The Soviet Union has said it is willing to stop tests. If the Soviet Union did not respond to America's action, the Soviet Union, not the United States, would be regarded by mankind as the nation that refused to end the radiation danger and help move the world toward peace.

Many Americans know these things. But as a nation, confused by the complexity of the problem, we stand benumbed, morally desensitized by ten years of propaganda and fear. How do you reach men when all the horror is in the fact that they feel no horror? It requires, we believe, the kind of effort and sacrifice we now undertake. There are men in our national leadership who seem to understand no other language but violence. They press for continued tests in spite of the admitted risk that the end of such an arms race will be global war—that is, national suicide. Other men while recognizing the risk in stopping, see this as a lesser risk, and the only one with hope. They dare not take that risk without the support of American public opinion. There have been signs recently that the opinion is forming. Yet most who favor a risk for peace remain silent.

We hope our act will say to others: Speak Now.

WHAT PUBLICISTS CAN DO

We ask those responsible for education and for the communication of ideas and news to tell our story, to encourage serious consideration of the moral and political choices involved. We would appreciate copies of articles or letters giving reactions to our attempt.

47. Earle Reynolds, from *Forbidden Voyage,* 1961.*

Earle Reynolds and his family were completing a round-the-world voyage they had started in 1954 when their path crossed that of the crew of the Golden Rule, *and the Eniwetok atomic bomb tests. After considering the morality, the legality, and the risks involved, Reynolds and his family sailed their yacht, the* Phoenix, *into the Pacific testing area.*

In 1967, still pursuing the road of radical conscience, Reynolds sailed the Phoenix *to North Vietnam, to bring medical supplies to the North Vietnamese people.*

On board the *Phoenix*, we have a real problem. On May 2, the local papers ran a headline story that gave us shivers: *JOHNSTON ISLE H-MISSILE TESTS PLANNED.* This means a vast area around Johnston Island, just southwest of us, will be cut off, in addition to the almost 400,000 square miles north of Eniwetok, farther west. Moreover, the British have staked the area around Christmas Island, down south of us, for their own nuclear tests, which blocks off the normal route to the South Pacific. The result of all these actions is that it will be practically impossible for a sailing ship, by any reasonable route, to get to Japan from Honolulu, as long as these areas remain out of bounds.

What we need to know, at once, is: (1) When will the Johnston area be put out of bounds? (2) How big will the area be? (3) How long will this area and the Eniwetok area be out of bounds?

Our future plans depend on knowing the answers to these questions. . . .

May 10

All day yesterday at the library. Problem No. One: What is this *Golden Rule* case all about?** First item—the histori-

* (New York: David McKay, 1961), pp. 16–60, 180–81.
** Reynolds and his family arrived in Honolulu during the trial of the crew of the *Golden Rule*. [Editor's note]

cal background. Went through *The New York Times* index, and periodical index, picking out relevant items, which I read.

Second item—the legality of the AEC regulation. The regulation is *clear* enough—stay out or take the consequences (up to twenty years in prison), but of course a departmental regulation has to be based on existing law, it can't just be pulled out of a hat. But it is certain, according to what I have read, that as of last January, when Bigelow and Huntington first announced their intention of sailing into the test zone, that the AEC and the Pentagon knew of no law which could keep them out—and plainly said so. The legal experts were running around in little circles then, tearing their hair. The Navy made dark threats about pulling the boat out of the test zone, "law or no law."

However, after the *Golden Rule* was at sea, the authorities passed the regulation, based on a section of existing United States law contained in the Atomic Energy Act. This section is important enough, I think, to put down in full:

U.S. Code Title 42, Section 2201(i): Regulations Governing Restricted Data "prescribe such regulations or orders as it may deem necessary . . . (3) to govern any activity authorized pursuant to this Act, including standards and restrictions governing the design, location, and operation of facilities used in the conduct of such activity, in order to protect health and to minimize danger to life or property."

Further reading indicated that this law is part of a series of laws regulating the use of nuclear materials by outside agencies. Its purpose is to prevent misuse of these materials. The law has absolutely nothing to do, so far as I can see, with the high seas, nuclear testing, the Trust Territories, or trespass of any kind. On the contrary, there are already in the books a number of specific laws, quite adequate, I should think, to deal with any legitimate rights of the AEC.

The specific AEC regulation, purportedly based on the above law, is: U.S. AEC Title 10, Part 112, Section 112. 4: "*Prohibition.* No United States citizen or other person who is within the scope of this part shall enter, attempt to enter or conspire to enter the danger area during the continuation of the Hardtack test series, except with the express approval of the appropriate officials of the Atomic Energy Commission or the Department of Defense."

One more point: Departmental regulations, by law, require

a public hearing, and period of waiting, before becoming legally binding. The AEC seems to have waived these two requirements. The reason evidently was that there was no time to follow legal processes, since the *Golden Rule* was already on the way to the test area. On the other hand, the AEC has been testing in the Bikini area for about twelve years now.

May 14

We have had a family conference, and decided to push on to Hiroshima as soon as possible. At least, we all agree that we want to leave Honolulu. To tell the truth, the general attitude here is depressing. I think I'm as good a citizen as the next man, and I love my country as much as anyone else; but I will never agree that a man does his country a service by blinding himself to its faults. On the contrary, I am convinced that unless a citizen works actively to correct his country's faults, the mistakes which have in times past ruined other countries will also eventually cause the collapse of our own democratic structure. A war will not be necessary. . . .

HONOLULU, HAWAII
May 2, 1958

DEAR FRIENDS, ALL OVER THE WORLD:

On this date, the *Phoenix* sailed into Honolulu's Ala Wai boat harbor, officially completing a round-the-world cruise which began in Hiroshima, Japan, on October 5, 1954. . . . We know now that what began as a rather simple pleasure cruise has achieved a far more important goal. We went around the world, and discovered that meanwhile the world has gone around us. We find ourselves, as a result of our experiences, moved to dedicate our efforts, no matter how feeble, to the cause of peace and to the brotherhood of all men. . . .

When we arrived in Honolulu, the local yacht basin and the city itself were in a ferment, due to the case of the *Golden Rule*. . . . This case has interested us profoundly. Aside from the important questions it raises in the area of ethics, religion, and conscience, there are also such problems as freedom of the seas, the legality of the AEC ruling, the military necessity for the tests, the matter of world opinion, and, of course, the effect of ongoing and continued radioactive testing on world health and on the genetic inheritance of our descendants. . . .

. . . we have done our best to find out what the case of the *Golden Rule* is all about, and what its implications are. We went to the trial, we read all the accounts, we talked to many people: to the defendants themselves, to the local Quaker group (Bigelow's denomination), to one of the lawyers in the case, to the Coast Guard, to the Navy, to the local representative of AEC, to a United Nations representative, to a Marshallese student studying at the university, to ordinary citizens, and fellow yachtsmen.

Also, we spent many hours in the libraries, studying the background of AEC, the role of the United Nations Trusteeship system, the reports of atomic scientists on health hazards, and of government officials on military and political implications. We have tried to put all this information together, clearly and without prejudice.

We think we have an answer.

This is our firm and solemn conviction: The men of the *Golden Rule* are right. The Atomic Energy Commission is wrong. The future—if the world has a future—will prove these statements.

We are not speaking of technical legality or illegality. The men of the *Golden Rule* broke the law of the land in response to the dictates of their conscience. They are willingly suffering the consequences. We note their obvious sincerity, but we neither defend nor condemn their actions. Our immediate interests are the policies and activities of the Atomic Energy Commission in collaboration with our military forces, which are, in the eyes of the world, the policies and activities of the American people.

This is our belief: the present policy of AEC is leading us and the world to disaster. This last series of Pacific bomb tests should never have been begun. These tests are not fundamentally necessary to the safety of our country. We have already stock-piled enough weapons, ready for instant use, to demolish the world several times over, and so has Russia. If Russia drops 999 hydrogen bombs on us, and we simultaneously drop 1,000 bombs on them, do we win? . . .

Unless the people of the United States face up to the threat of the AEC, unless we put AEC and similar organizations back into a responsible place in our democracy, we will not long continue to have a democracy—or deserve one.

We on board the *Phoenix* are not trying to sell this point of view to anyone. We are merely presenting it for your consideration. We are trying to answer those people—and we have talked to many—who claim that Americans, paralyzed by fear of being tainted by the label of "leftist" or "crackpot," have surrendered their moral leadership in the world. . . .

As to our future plans, they have become intimately tied up with this whole testing situation. As you know, our goal is still the return to Hiroshima. We hope to arrive there before the end of this year. Here in Honolulu, we have been making the usual preparations for departure—painting, making a new mainsail, overhauling engine and radio, studying charts and pilot books, and so forth. All these activities are the normal and usual jobs in port.

But now new factors have come into the picture. For instance: A notice appeared in the newspapers recently, which said that Johnston Island—and, of course thousands of square miles of open ocean surrounding it—is to be "closed" while missiles with nuclear warheads are to be fired into the "empty" sea. Now Johnston Island is about seven hundred miles west-southwest of Honolulu, and the area lies on the usual westward sailing route to the Orient.

We have, of course, asked various local officials for clarification of this notice. No one knows anything, at least, anything they are willing to tell us. . . .

Another problem. In planning for our return to Hiroshima, we have often discussed the possibility of a leisurely cruise through the American Trust Territories. But now large portions of these areas have been "closed" to civilians. Even Guam, which is an American Territory, seems again to be under the control of the Navy, rather than the Department of the Interior. At any event, the Navy informs us that we must be screened through Washington before even the ship can enter the area, and that after entry, additional special permission must be obtained before we can get off the ship.

We are preparing the *Phoenix* for sea. It is still our in-intention to sail on to Hiroshima. We do not plan to break any of our country's laws. We have confidence in our

Phoenix. She has earned it. We trust ourselves to her strength and safety against the normal hazards of the sea.

> The *Phoenix* family: EARLE,
> BARBARA, TED, AND JESSICA
> REYNOLDS, AND NICK MIKAMI

. . . .

May 19

I spent quite a few hours during the week in the local libraries. I am now a student on the subject of freedom of the seas, international law as it applies to nuclear testing, and the Trust Territories Treaty. . . .

With regard to the freedom of the seas, a recent *Time* article (May 15) reports on the ongoing Law of the Sea Conference, now being held in Geneva. Our representative there spoke for America:

"We stand on the three-mile limit; we will continue to do so, and we will not recognize any unilateral extension beyond that limit." That's why the Coast Guard was evidently so anxious to stop the *Golden Rule* before it got beyond the three-mile limit; it knew it had no legal authority to stop the ship outside it.

A few more choice quotes which I dug up from the Department of State, 1910:

" . . . The freedom of the seas in times of peace [is] no mere slogan, but a very real fact . . . the U.S. . . . has consistently fought for the freedom of the seas."

And: "The high sea does not form part of the territory of any state. No state can have over it a right of ownership, sovereignty or jurisdiction. None can lawfully claim to dictate laws for the high seas." (But doesn't the injunction against the *Golden Rule* men claim that the United States has *special jurisdiction* over the high seas north of Eniwetok?)

And finally: " . . . No state or group of states may claim any right of sovereignty, privilege or prerogative over any portion of the high seas or place any obstacle to the free and full use of the seas." (Article 13, Laws of Maritime Jurisprudence in Times of Peace.) Interesting reading! . . . it is interesting to note what a British expert in international law (Georg Schwarzenberg, "The Legality of

Nuclear Weapons," *Library of World Affairs*) has to say about testing in the Marshall Islands:

> Whether nuclear tests carried out in a trust territory, even one which is a strategic area, comply with the letter or spirit of the relevant Articles of the United Nations Charter or a trusteeship agreement . . . may be doubted. In any case, the matter is sufficiently controversial to lend support to the suggestion made by the Indian Government in the Trusteeship Council that this would be a proper subject for an advisory opinion by the World Court.

Finally, I looked up the matter of letting the World Court rule on the legality of the Marshall Islands' case. I was definitely shocked to see that our government *refused to permit the World Court to give a decision in the matter!* It seems a decision cannot be made without the consent of the "accused." We refused to give our consent to a decision. Almost unbelievable, but true. The more I read, the more unhappily amazed I become at what my government has been doing, in my name.

May 27

. . . .

Question: When the defense of the United States clashes with the welfare of the natives of the Trust Territories, what happens? When paramount meets paramount, then what? The answer is simple. The man with the gun wins. We have the power; we did as we pleased in the Trust Territories, regardless of our treaty.

The picture is all too dismally clear. Here's the story: in discharging our obligations under Article 76 of the Trust Charter, we made a number of promises. Among other things, we swore "to protect the inhabitants against the loss of their lands and resources." Our violation of this promise is known by the whole world: we took Bikini and Eniwetok away from the natives living there, transported them against their will to other islands, which neither we nor they owned, and used their original homes as nuclear bomb testing grounds.

And again: " . . . protect the health of the inhabitants."

But our disastrous mistake of March 1, 1954, when we irradiated several hundred natives *outside* the zone, is a clear violation of this promise. The fact that it was a "mistake," that we didn't intend to do it, that we promise that we won't do it again, that we gave the people medical assistance, are all beside the point. We did it, and the people of the Marshalls are still under medical surveillance, and still deeply apprehensive. Moreover, they very much want their land back, and the compensation they were promised. As of 1956, ten years after they were removed, the United Nations Inspection Team reported that the people of the Marshalls had still not been compensated for their removal. "The Mission, in considering the displacement of population due to nuclear tests, stresses that the grievances of the Bikini Islanders are serious and that the settlement of their claims after ten years is a matter of urgency." (Linden A. Mander, "The U.N. Mission's 1956 Survey of the Pacific Trust Territory," *Pacific Affairs*, December, 1956, Vol. 29, No. 4, page 374.)

No, I believe we have very little to be proud of, in our treatment of the Marshall natives. But beyond this, I believe we have clearly violated the treaty under which we took over the former Japanese Mandated Islands. We have, therefore, no more honorably discharged our trust than did the Japanese. No arguments, no sophistry, can get around this simple fact.

I see that two different groups have entered suits against the United States, seeking to stop the testing of nuclear weapons in the Pacific. These are the so-called "fallout suits."

The first group consists of a number of world figures, including Bertrand Russell, Brock Chisholm, André Trocme, Linus Pauling, Norman Thomas, and others, including several Japanese fishermen whose livelihood was ruined by the testing. . . .*

May 27

. . . .

* The Fallout Suits (1958) represented efforts to halt atomic energy testing by means of court actions. Suits were filed in the United States and in Russia. For details see Bigelow, *op. cit.*, Appendix C, pp. 280–82. [Editor's note]

News note: Yesterday the Court of Appeals denied the motion by the crew of *Golden Rule* to set aside the injunction which prevents them from legally leaving Honolulu. In other words they're stuck here. Now what?

June 1

The men of *Golden Rule* announced today that they were going to sail on June 4, "injunction or no."

June 3

Today I sent the following cable to President Eisenhower and to Admiral Strauss, head of AEC:

> THE CREW OF THE YACHT PHOENIX, BELIEVING THAT THE ATTEMPTED PROTEST VOYAGE OF THE KETCH GOLDEN RULE IS JUSTIFIED BOTH MORALLY AND LEGALLY, RESPECTFULLY URGE THE IMMEDIATE TERMINATION OF THE PACIFIC BOMB TESTS. MOREOVER, WE URGE THAT THE RECENT RULING OF AEC, WHICH CLOSES OFF VAST AREAS OF THE HIGH SEAS, BE RESCINDED. THE PHOENIX WILL SAIL FROM HONOLULU IN THE NEAR FUTURE, CLEARING FOR THE HIGH SEAS.

Each cable cost me fourteen bucks, for which I could have bought a case of corned beef for our trip to Hiroshima, but maybe it will be worth it. . . .

June 4

. . . .

The *Golden Rule* was ready to sail at noon, and quite a large crowd had collected, mostly friendly. There were, however, two students from the University of Hawaii, with a large placard reading *PACIFISTS GO HOME*.

Promptly on schedule the *Golden Rule* began to cast off, and just as promptly the police stopped them, arrested Bigelow, and took him off to jail. In the early afternoon, he was taken before Judge Wiig and charged with conspiracy. He asked, "What conspiracy, and with whom?" but got no answer. Wiig offered to release him on his own recognizance, but Bigelow refused to promise not to attempt to sail again, and was taken back to jail.

About four in the afternoon Huntington arrived at the Honolulu airport, back from a trip to the mainland to visit his sick mother. (His place in the crew had been taken by Jim Peck, who had flown out earlier from New York.) Huntington came immediately out to the yacht harbor, and at once walked over to the *Phoenix*. At the moment I was on deck, talking to two reporters. I called out, "Hello, Bill— come aboard!" but he only waved, turned sharply, and walked back to the *Golden Rule*. From his expression and his abrupt action, I could tell that something was on his mind, but that the presence of the reporters had stopped him.

We heard shouts and the sound of an engine, and I saw the *Golden Rule* heading down the harbor. There was just time to run across, wave, and shout "good luck" before the boat had turned into the channel, under full power, with the crew crowding on sail as fast as possible. . . .

By the time the *Golden Rule* was about three miles off shore, the reporters had gotten hold of a speed boat and caught up with her, and were frantically taking pictures. The Coast Guard was caught flat-footed, because the ketch was beyond the three-mile limit and on the high seas before the Coast Guard cutter even got started in pursuit. Between five and six miles out, the *Golden Rule* was intercepted. By now, in the growing dusk, it was impossible at this distance to tell just what was happening, but by full dark the *Golden Rule* had been brought back into the harbor, under guard.

Bill Huntington is spending tonight in jail with Bert Bigelow.

. . . .

June 10

We're about ready for sea. . . .

The *Golden Rule* crew has willed us some of their charts of the Marshalls and Japan, tools, a medicine chest, and a radio, which will be a wonderful help to us. Also, they sent me a box containing four simple respirators, the type that painters with spray guns use.

They had intended to use them, of course, in the contaminated test zone. What a pitiful protection against radioactivity! As I looked at those four masks, packed neatly in their box, I felt pity for and disappointment with my fellow man. I put the masks away, and I have no intention of ever opening the box, regardless of what happens. Besides, how does one divide four masks among five people? . . .

Day before yesterday the whole family visited the Honolulu jail. All five *Golden Rule* men are now in custody, serving a sixty-day sentence.

. . . and all the time I was chatting during the visit, a nasty little voice in the back of my mind was saying, "Just what the devil do you think you're doing *here?*"

It boils down to this: It's one thing to be intellectually certain of the rightness and justice of a position; it's another thing to be emotionally prepared to face the consequences of that certainty, especially when the consequences go against deeply planted prejudices and habits. But I'll learn. Anyway, I've just survived another first: for the first time in my life I've been inside a jail. . . .

June 11, 1958. Night

We are at sea. The frantic world, at least for a time, is behind us. The breeze is light but fair, the seas moderate, and we are heading southwest under full sail. . . .

I lie in my bunk, and just overhead, the sound of Ted's movements at the tiller. It's a good world—or it could be.

June 30 (Japan time). Nineteenth day out of Honolulu

. . . .

Tonight, in the cockpit, Barbara and I had a long talk. The time has come for us to make a decision: Do we enter the test zone, or do we go around? . . .

I thought of the poem Ted had written, in the style of a Japanese *haiku:*

> How can I believe
> This soft rain that I so love
> Radioactive?

And there was a soft rain about us now, falling on us and on all the people in the world—a rain silent, invisible, undetectable by any human sense, a deadly rain, a rain of ionized atoms.

"But . . . " I said again.

"Have we any choice?"

"No," I said, "no choice."

So it's settled. I talked to Jessica and Ted. Our plans are simple: to carry on, make no physical resistance, and try to act with dignity, and I hope courage, whatever happens. I can't think beyond that. . . .

July 2 (Japan time). Twenty-first day out of Honolulu. Inside test zone

I am under arrest, with armed men aboard the *Phoenix*. We are sailing south, under protest, toward the Navy base on Kwajalein Atoll. The Navy cruiser *Collett* is our "escort." . . .

At 0820 this morning the Coast Guard cutter *Planetree* (W307) pulled up alongside, for the third time, and the master shouted: "Heave to, and prepare to be boarded."

"What is your authority?"

(The master of the *Planetree* read out some figures.)

"Am I under arrest?"

"The boarding officer will place you under arrest."

"Do you have a warrant?"

"The boarding officer will inform you of everything."

"Please understand that I consider this an illegal boarding, and I will let you come aboard under protest."

"I will so enter it in my log."

"Have you informed the Japanese Government?"

"We have no connection with the Japanese Government."

"I have a Japanese citizen on board."

"He will not be placed under arrest."

"Thank you. I will come around to port."

. . . .

July 3. En route—under arrest—to Kwajalein

At 0430 this morning, while it was still dark, Ted, on watch, called me up. He and Barbara, who had been in the cockpit with him, had just seen a gigantic flash in the western sky—obviously another bomb being tested in the current Hardtack series. We were at this moment just beyond the southern border of the proscribed zone, and hence in an area of the high seas that not even the United States claims is "out of bounds."

Ted described it as "like a gigantic flash bulb, oval in shape and at about five to fifteen degrees above the horizon." It lit up the entire sky for a moment, a dirty orange light flashing through the clouds. We are now east of Bikini, about two hundred miles.

Later I went below and turned on the radio, to a Japanese station, and very shortly afterward heard an announcement that "the United States has exploded another bomb in the Bikini test zone." Openly broadcast news in Japan, high security in the United States!

. . . .

February 20, 1961. Last Entry

Almost a year has passed since my entry of last April 26. At that time, after two turbulent years ashore in Hawaii, we were once more on the high seas, heading across the Pacific, our goal still Hiroshima, Japan.

We made it. Following a route just slightly north of the one we had taken in 1958, once again we entered the "forbidden" zone—this time without being molested, since the bomb tests had long since been concluded. In fact—except for France's three Sahara explosions—there have been no further tests of nuclear weapons since the fall of 1958. The present score (J. M. Fowler, editor, Fallout, 1960): United States, 129; U.S.S.R., 53; Great Britain, 20; France, 3. . . .

This isn't a sea story, so I'll conclude by saying that we reached Hiroshima on July 30, 1960, after a passage around the world. We pulled up to the same dock from which we had departed exactly five years, nine months, and twenty-six days ago.

We received a wonderful reception in Hiroshima. More than thirty boats sailed out of the harbor to meet us and escort us to the dock with a great display of fireworks and balloons.

Soon we settled down to family life. I gave my lectures

at the Hiroshima Women's College, and once again moved in academic circles, after almost ten years as a maverick. . . .

The last stage in the legal battle of the *Phoenix* has now been reached. On December 29, 1960, the San Francisco Court of Appeals unanimously ruled that:

> The regulation appellant [Earle Reynolds] was convicted of violating was not authorized by the statute under which it was purportedly issued and was therefore invalid. . . . The conviction therefore is without legal authority and it must be set aside and the judgment reversed.

In lay language: The regulation by the Atomic Energy Commission, prohibiting entrance into the so-called forbidden test zone, was invalid. The arrest and conviction, therefore, were illegal. This has significance, also, in the *Golden Rule* case. You will recall that the five men of the *Golden Rule* were jailed for sixty days in Honolulu, on a conviction rooted in this illegal regulation. I understand from Joseph Rauh, my attorney, that in his opinion the time limit on the Government's right to appeal to the Supreme Court has now expired. Their case is over, done, and dead.

From the whole experience we gained some positive benefits: hundreds of new friends, a satisfaction never before experienced, and the feeling that we have made at least a gesture for peace and for our country. We have also discovered a sense of dedication and purpose that we never had before.

48. Jules Rabin, from "How We Went"—San Francisco to Moscow Walk, 1961.*

On December 1, 1960, a group of young men and women gathered in San Francisco to begin a walk for peace that was to take them halfway around the world. Organized by the Committee for Nonviolent Action, the walkers hoped that, as itinerant ministers of disarmament and peace, they could reach out not to governments but to people. They offered themselves as examples of the possibilities of brotherhood. Jules Rabin, a graduate of Harvard, spent six months with the Walk as participant and cameraman.

The great adventure is over. Our Walk, which commenced in San Francisco's Union Square on December 1st, 1960, concluded in Moscow's Red Square on the afternoon of October 3rd, 1961. At 2 o'clock we filed up the short slope beside the Historical Museum. Ahead of us lay the great plaza, with the jumbled, bejeweled cake of St. Basil's Cathedral occupying the front horizon, and the tall, heavy wall of the Kremlin to our right. The Walkers were granted two hours in Red Square to conduct our final demonstration. After performing the courtesies of the press we arranged ourselves in a quiet line facing St. Basil's, and stood in silent vigil. It took some minutes for us to establish our separateness from the crowd that pressed around us, and more minutes for the activities of photographers and reporters to subside. But eventually the sense of the vigil established itself.

England has had her Aldermastons, with tens of thousands marching the few score miles to London. It is perhaps fitting that America's young and faltering peace movement should have signified her concern with a gesture of continental breadth. Ten thousand kilometers, six thousand-odd miles, the Walk carried almost through four seasons.

And the Walk in Russia, what was that really like?

Russia was climactic. To Americans of this century, Russia must always be of especial fascination, because it is

* *Liberation*, VI, No. 9 (November, 1961), 11–15.

proclaimed the forbidden land, the dangerous land . . . because Russia is the *they* of our lives. So we walked in Russia, especially during the first days, like children in a land of wonder. On our first evening in Russia, we met an overflow audience in Brest. The stage was draped in red and gold, the colors of Soviet glory. On either side of the stage were portraits of Lenin, Marx, and Engels. On the streets we had seen statues and busts of Lenin and Stalin, gleaming in silver paint, and posters, always in red, exhorting and proclaiming. That is what Russia is like on first encounter: the forbidden symbols have become vernacular elements of the civic landscape.

Russia was important to us because of this fascination, and it was important for the more serious reason that in Russia we recognized the other great voice in the dialogue of power which makes the world tremble today. Here was the central drama of the Walk, that some of us from the United States should carry to the Soviet Union the same message that we had spoken and acted on in our own country, sometimes at the price of imprisonment. We had demonstrated against military installations wherever we encountered them, in little Belgium as well as at the Pentagon, in England and both Germanys and Poland. But Russia was especially important to us because it is her power, alone, that matches the power of the United States, and uniquely provokes it. To have the ear of both these great nations, that was the heart's desire of our Walk. To demonstrate in one's own country is not too great a feat, but this opportunity to say *No* to the official *Yes* of Soviet military policy, on Soviet soil, was to us both rare and impressive.

Moscow was the terminus of our Walk, and it was a precious goal insofar as it meant the completion of our long labor, and the achievement of what we had months before set out to do. We have the impression that our Soviet hosts would have liked us to regard our entry into Moscow as an arrival at a Mecca consecrated to Peace. For as earnestly as we of the Walk expressed our concern for an immediate and total solution to the armaments race, the Soviets insisted that their concern matches ours, and outdistances it. They have endured a war which touched America only lightly; they have established professional committees for the defense of peace, and have long had laws which make it a criminal offense to foment war. A member of the Soviet Peace Com-

ACROSS THE CONTINENTS

from San Francisco to New York to Moscow

we walk

calling upon the peoples of the world to join our outcry against
  bomb tests

> nuclear weapons

> > missiles and jet bombers

> > > biological weapons

> > > > the insanely dangerous arms race, and
the total inhumanity and total destruction implicit in total war today

we walk

calling upon you, on everyone, everywhere, to join our demand
and plea that your nation and our nation and every nation

DISARM NOW — while there is still some little time!

we walk

on foot — unarmed — in hope, humility and friendliness

> **FOR NONVIOLENCE**

> > **FOR FREEDOM**

> > > **FOR SURVIVAL**

> > > > **FOR BROTHERHOOD OF NATIONS**

> > > > > **FOR WORLD PEACE**

The San Francisco to Moscow Walk for Peace is sponsored by the Committee for Nonviolent Action:

mittee, who greeted us warmly on the day following our arrival, suggested that we might have felt like the ten thousand of Xenophon as we entered the great space of the Red Square. He thought we might have wanted to cry out "Thalassa, Thalassa," as the Greeks had done when they saw the Black Sea after their long flight before the Persians, and understood that rest and the assurance of safety lay close at hand.

It is tempting to respond in an accommodating way to the kind words of a well-intentioned host. The Soviets, our last hosts along the way, wished to be generous toward us, to take us under their wing, to persuade us. I believe they would have been content to receive from us a simple accord with their call for *Mir* and *Druzhba* (peace and friendship) . . . after which we might all have dozed off in the warm, pleasant tea of that unassailable sentiment. The Russians have sloganized the term *peace* and the idea of peace—much as the West has sloganized the idea of freedom—till it seems their very own invention and property. Why would we not accept Moscow as the peacelover's Mecca, when we had heard countless times in our journey across the land the most earnest (and *believable*) protestations that the Russians desire peace above almost all else, and that they shudder to think of enduring again what they suffered between 1941 and 1945? But like harsh-minded fools we were bound to reiterate our unilateralist stand and disturb the calm of our hosts. Our position is one of refusal to assess degrees of blame in the crescendo of armaments preparations which is making the world tremble. Rather, it locates the possibility for disaster in a readiness from any quarter to respond to menace with menace, to offense with offense.

The idiocy of it. Here were two parties, ourselves and the Russians, who would turn almost boastful in declaring the depths of their concern for peace. We were the honored guests of the land, the Walkers who had done this strange thing of coming so great a distance to convey our desire and our plan for peace. Across from us stood the Russians, a people who had suffered more, in absolute numbers, than any other participants in the great war. They begged us to believe that they craved peace, that they are a peace-loving people . . . as though they feared that there are other peoples elsewhere who are perhaps peace-hating, who crave war for its own bloody sake.

We faced the Russians on numerous platforms (seventeen arranged meetings, perhaps sixty informal wayside meetings), and from either side could be found not much more than token words of regard for the full reach of the other's peace program. To the Russians we seemed like unintentional subversives. We proposed that they undertake unilateral disarmament, and that in the spirit of individual responsibility, each Soviet citizen who regarded war as intrinsically evil should on his own initiative abstain from all phases of military activity, including civilian labor in armaments industry. We made it as clear as we could that we were not a band of foxy delegates from the West who aimed to soften the Soviet's defenses for the eventual new assault by a neo-Nazi Germany—which the Soviets fear more than the hellfires of hydrogen warfare itself. We exposed the battle ribbons and battle wounds which are peculiar to pacifist activists of today: prison sentences, physical violence, and calumny, endured in our own lands in the course of our proposal of the same unilateralist position that we brought to the Soviet Union. But what stayed uppermost in their minds was the impression of a strange band from the West proposing seriously that they should disarm, immediately and irrespective of what their world neighbors might do.

To us, the Soviets seemed like the creators of their own undoing. While protesting their deep love of peace, they would reiterate with a violent passion their determination to remain militarily strong as long as the West retained any power for military assault. In the course of our several weeks in the Soviet Union, the atonality of the official—and popular—position on the questions of peace and armaments became familiar to our ears. The Soviets are determined to maintain their position of military strength—in *defense*, as they habitually allege, of the peace and of their territorial integrity—as long as their appeal for complete and general disarmament, multilaterally implemented, goes unheeded.

As persons affected by the Gandhian and Christian traditions of nonviolence, we Peace Walkers found this disharmony of the Soviet position harsh to our ears. How can one simultaneously protest that one loves peace, and avow implacable hatred and annihilation of a prospective enemy?

As persons who had endured the incredible sufferings of an unmitigated Nazi invasion and occupation, our Soviet interlocutors found our appeals for unilateral disarmament childish—we were laughed at by great audiences—and downright offensive. These audiences would shout indignantly when the full implications or our program were declared. And the fact that we were appealing in the same terms to both East and West, and that we were condemning both East and West in the same terms, seemed often not to register.

This is the depressing idiocy I speak of, that we and the Russians seem often to have talked *past* each other. Each party to our discussions would perform a careful minuet within his own sphere of logic, always in support of his own dream of a just and sound peace. But the two spheres of logic would rarely intersect, and the rival claims of programs, of resistance with armed violence and of resistance without armed violence, would be left unadjusted. And because each party regarded the other as representing a threat to his own dream of the establishment of peace, we addressed each other sometimes as antagonists, rather than as collaborators in this precious work.

To be thus at odds with our audiences was of course no new thing to us. In the West, in the United States, we had encountered identical positions, except that the implacable demon was named World Communism, instead of International Capitalism. . . .

And again, what was it really like? It is tempting to speak of a grand action in terms that suggest waving banners and all the other panoply of public occasions. (We were a public occasion—I remember dozing off on the green in a small Polish town, at the end of lunch, and waking up to find myself surrounded, like Gulliver, by a dense circle of children, all contemplating me silently.) There is a traditional language of celebration for public occasions of this scope, but it is apt to be embarrassing, inept, beside the point. I remember a strange fellow who attached himself to the Walk for several days in eastern Belgium. He wore a wide, greasy raincoat and a wide-brimmed hat pulled low on his forehead. He coursed along beside us, shouting at people as we went, "Applaud them, applaud them! Here are the Marchers for Peace come all the way from San Francisco on foot." This was one face of the Walk, and it is worth describing.

We might say: this Walk distributed so and so many hundreds of thousands of leaflets, and addressed so and so many tens of thousands of persons, East and West. We were handed bouquets of flowers in many places, and were stopped on our way, as often as half a dozen times in one day, by civic officials who wanted to convey their community's regard for us. We were somctimes like hardened theatrical troupers lending only our physical presence to these occasions: cherishing them, perhaps, because the interruption gave us a few minutes rest, besides the ten minutes we allotted ourselves after each hour's walking. We acted like hardened troupers to the cameramen who attached themselves to our Walk along the way, no longer looking around when the cine-camera buzzed, no longer startled when a photoflash bulb popped.

Mayors, burgomeisters, chairmen, we did not always heed your every word when you came out to greet us, but you will understand this if you count the number of towns we passed through, the number of formal speeches of welcome and concern that were addressed to us, sometimes after each meal of the day, sometimes before a meal, when we were aching with fatigue, cranky with hunger, wet to our chilled skins. Spring in America this year was cold and wet, and the first part of our European summer was unprecedently gray and chill. A climate for toothache.

What the March was really like. We were all of us spiritually imperfect persons; no *Bodhisattvas*, no Mahatmas. That could be to the good. Our infirmity signifies that we are of *this* existence, the same crabbed existence which exasperates the relationship between the United States and the Soviet Union. There were times in America when some of us watched the Walk with a special concern, because we asked ourselves, if not we, then who else? If we could not create among ourselves that mood of cherishing trustfulness, of expectation and concern—we pacifists, we who professed Gandhism—if we become paltry among ourselves, what could we fairly expect of the world, of men who boasted a responsible worldliness, and identified that with reality? . . .

And if I ask again, what was it really like among us, were we able among ourselves to practice the concern and confidence that one might reasonably stipulate as ingredients of the program of unilateralism and nonviolent resistance, could I give an encouraging answer? If a cosmic sport had assembled us together, to determine if we could, in microcosm, establish the harmony among ourselves that we were seeking for the squabblers in the concourse of nations, what prospects for founding a trustworthy peace does the experiment offer?

The answer is a sad one, in part. We were human, all too human; with the implications which that phrase offers of every pettiness, and of possibilities for reconciliation.

Our accomplishment is a more estimable one if we regard it on more prosaic political grounds. We did reach many people, many tens of thousands in direct encounter. And because our caravan somehow piqued the world's fancy, we reached some tens of millions through the conventional news media. No one knows how to estimate the value of this sort of impact: two and a quarter minutes on TV, a scanty, slanted article in a newspaper, which reports austerely the fact of our arrival in such and such a place, or racily, how many pairs of sneakers such and such a Walker has worn out. But some may feel the appeal of even this small notice won by the passage of our Walk. The world heard of us, the world glimpsed some of our slogans and saw us carry them into strange places. . . .

And that is what extended peace walks are made of. Fatigue, and sparse or heavy foods, strained tempers, awesome challenges, misapprehensions. There are too the gilded moments, of mutual persuasion and understanding. If I have said little about these moments, it is because the Russian experience is freshest in my mind, and there was small evidence of ideological penetration in Russia. But we did make this first *necessary* move in that direction; we have started a new path of dialogue. And perhaps people of sounder faith and more reasonable temper can carry us further on the way to reconciliation. It is necessary.

49.   James Farmer, "I Will Keep My Soul," 1961.*

*James Farmer is the former national director of the Congress
of Racial Equality (CORE), and has been one of the nation's
pioneers in the Negro Civil Rights Movement. Before assuming his position with CORE, Farmer was program director
for the National Association for the Advancement of Colored
People (NAACP) and an officer of the State, County, and
Municipal Employees Union in New York.*

On May 4 of this year [1961], I left Washington, D.C.,
with twelve other persons on a risky journey into the South.
Seven of us were Negro and six were white. Riding in two
regularly scheduled buses, one Greyhound, the other Trail-
ways, traveling beneath overcast skies, our little band—the
original Freedom Riders—was filled with expectations of
storms almost certain to come before the journey was ended.

Now, six months later, as all the world knows, the fire-
gutted shell of one bus lies in an Alabama junk yard, and
some of the people who almost died with it are still suffering
prolonged illnesses. A dozen Freedom Riders nearly gave
up their lives under the fierce hammering of fists, clubs,
and iron pipes in the hands of hysterical mobs. Many of the
victims will carry permanent scars. One of them lies in a
Detroit hospital critically ill from a cerebral hemorrhage, a
direct result of the beating he took. Others have lost their
jobs or have been expelled from school because of their participation in the rides. More than 350 men and women have
been jailed in a half dozen states for doing what the Supreme
Court of the United States had already said they had a right
to do. The Interstate Commerce Commission has now issued
an historic ruling in behalf of interstate bus integration
which may indeed mean that the suffering of the past six
months has not been in vain.

Why did we ride? What is the meaning of it all? Has the
whole thing been a stunt, a gimmick engineered by irrespond-
sible publicity seekers? Has America's prestige been dam-

* *The Progressive,* XXV, No. 11 (November, 1961), 21–22.

aged in the eyes of the world by the events that grew out of the Freedom Rides? These are questions frequently asked, and I think the answer should not be required to wait upon the verdict of history.

In 1946 the Supreme Court ruled in the Irene Morgan decision that segregation of interstate passengers in seating on buses was an unconstitutional burden upon commerce. A Freedom Ride later that year, called the "Journey of Reconciliation," cosponsored by the Congress of Racial Equality and the Fellowship of Reconciliation, demonstrated that segregated seating was still enforced on buses in the upper Southern states, and that anyone who challenged this segregation was subject to arrest and threatened violence. Through the years since that time reports have come into the office of the Congress of Racial Equality (CORE) of continuing segregation in seating on buses, especially in the deep South.

In 1960 the Supreme Court issued a ruling, in the Boynton case, banning segregation in the terminal facilities used by interstate passengers. Yet, in the months that followed reports continued to pour into our office indicating that the South was defying the Supreme Court's edict, just as some of the Southern states have defied the Court's school desegregation rulings. It was to close this gap between the interpretation and the implementation of the law that the Freedom Riders rode.

Who were the Freedom Riders? By what right did we seek to "meddle in the South's business"? Ever since the election of Rutherford B. Hayes to the Presidency in 1876, and the bargain with the South which it entailed, the Southern states have maintained that what they do with the Negro is their own business, and "outsiders" have no right to interfere. The Freedom Riders rejected this essentially states' rights doctrine of race relations. None of us, in the North or in the South, can afford the moral luxury of unconcern about injustice. Further, the states' rights doctrine is just as outmoded on the domestic scene as Nineteenth Century isolationism is on the international. Today, how can we think of outsiders keeping hands off injustice in Alabama, when outsiders all over the world can be threatened with destruction by events in a far away place like Laos? How would the dead of Korea view Mississippi's claim that only Mississippians have a right to concern themselves with injustice in that state?

So we came from all over the country, from both races and of all ages, to test compliance with the law, to exercise the right of all Americans to use all transportation facilities with the dignity of equality, to shake Americans out of their apathy on this issue and expose the real character of segregation to the pitiless scrutiny of a nation's conscience.

Outsiders? As Americans, from whatever state, all of us are Mississippians and Minnesotans, Carolinians and Californians, Alabamans and Arizonans. No American can afford to ignore the burning bus and the bloody heads of the mob's victims. Who can fail to be stirred by the new convicts for conscience, black and white, who walked with pride into Southern jails, especially in Mississippi, surrendering their own personal freedom in the struggle for a greater freedom for everyone?

Jail at best is neither a romantic nor a pleasant place, and Mississippi jails are no exception. The first twenty-seven Freedom Riders to arrive in Jackson saw the inside of two different jails and two different prisons—the Jackson City Jail, the Hinds County Jail, the Hinds County Prison Farm, and the State Penitentiary at Parchman. Jails are not a new experience for many of the Riders, but the Freedom Riders were definitely a new experience for Mississippi jails. For the first time, penal authorities in the citadel of segregation had a glimpse of the new Negro and the emancipated white. I do not think these jailers will ever be quite the same again after their experience. Nor will the other prisoners, black and white, be the same again, after having seen in the flesh men and women who do not believe segregation to be in the very nature of things, and who are willing to defy it.

Prison authorities frequently said, and really seemed to believe, that other Negro prisoners like things the way they are and have no sympathy with us, and that it was for our own protection that we were isolated from them. However, whenever the guards were not present, the Negro trustees went out of their way to show their sympathy by word and deed. "Keep up the good work," one said. "I admire you guys and what you are doing," said another. "I wish I could do the same thing, but I have to do what these people tell me to do." They smuggled newspapers in to us, delivered notes and messages between our cell block and that of the girl Freedom Riders, and passed on rumors which they had heard in the jail or in the community.

One night at the county jail, a voice called up from the cell block beneath us, where other Negro prisoners were housed. "Upstairs!", the anonymous prisoner shouted. We replied, "Downstairs!" "Upstairs!", replied the voice. "Sing your freedom song." And the Freedom Riders sang. We sang old folk songs and gospel songs to which new words had been written, telling of the Freedom Ride and its purpose. We sang new words to old labor songs, too. One stanza rang out: "They say in Hinds County no neutrals have they met. You're either for the Freedom Ride or you 'tom' for Ross Barnett." Then the downstairs prisoners, whom the jailers had said were our enemies, sang for us. The girl Freedom Riders, in another wing of the jail, joined in the Freedom Ride songs, and for the first time in history, the Hinds County jail rocked with singing of songs of freedom and brotherhood.

One evening at the county jail, after a rumor of our imminent transfer to the state penitentiary had reached us, the jailer came quietly to our Freedom Riders cell block. He called me, and we stood there with the bars between us, chatting. He did most of the talking. He told me about his family, his wife, and four or five children—the good records they had made in schools, including Ole Miss. He told me of his son's prowess in sports and of the children's marriages and his grandchildren. He told me, too, of his dislike of violence, and of his children's upbringing in that regard. The jailer stood there talking for more than an hour, in the first conversation we had had with him. This, I am sure, was his way of saying goodbye, and of telling us that he respects the Freedom Riders, and that whatever unpleasantness we might meet at the state penitentiary would be something of which he did not approve.

Mississippians, born into segregation, are human too. The Freedom Riders' aim is not only to stop the practice of segregation, but somehow to reach the common humanity of our fellowmen and bring it to the surface where they can act on it themselves. This is a basic motive behind the Freedom Rides, and nonviolence is the key to its realization.

It is not only that Southerners and other Americans have been shaken in their unjust racial practices, or out of their lethargy. Now, as a result of the Freedom Rides, the world at large, and especially the developing nations of Africa and Asia, have been offered the opportunity of viewing a new, more constructive approach to America's racial dilemma. If the world looks now it will see that many dedicated and conscientious Americans of both races, rather than sweeping the dirt of discrimination under the rug, are striving, at any cost, to remove the dirt from their house. If Africans witnessed our national shame in the necessity for the Freedom Rides, they saw our nation's hope and promise in the fact that there were so many Americans willing to risk their freedom and even their lives to erase that shame.

The world and America saw also the Freedom Rider's challenge to the traditions and fears which have immobilized so many Negroes in Dixie. In terminals in the South, and on the buses, many Negro passengers took the Freedom Riders' cue and dared to sit and ride "first class." This was another purpose of the Rides themselves: to break down the voluntary submission of Negroes to racial injustice, a submission created by generations of suppression with the rope and with fire and with economic reprisal. As I entered the white waiting room in one terminal in the South, a Negro woman passenger from the same bus caught my eye and anxiously beckoned me to follow her into the dingy but safe colored section. Moments later, when she saw me served at the lunch counter in the white section, she joined me for a cup of coffee.

In Jackson, Mississippi, forty-one Negro citizens of that community joined the Freedom Riders, ending up in their hometown jails. Now out on appeal bond, they report many threats of reprisals. But there is a new spirit among Negroes in Jackson. People are learning that in a nonviolent war like ours, as in any other war, there must be suffering. Jobs will be lost, mortgages will be foreclosed, loans will be denied, persons will be hurt, and some may die. This new spirit was expressed well by one Freedom Rider in the Mississippi state penitentiary at Parchman. The guards threatened repeatedly, as a reprisal for our insistence upon dignity, to take away our mattresses. "Come and get my mattress," he shouted, "I will keep my soul."

50. Leo Szilard, from "Are We on the Road to War?" 1962.*

In 1959, Szilard received the Atoms for Peace Award, ironically, for his part in the development of nuclear reactors. His attempt to work for the cause of peace is evidenced in the text of this speech, which he delivered at nine colleges and universities before his death in 1964. The address was printed in the Bulletin of the Atomic Scientists *on the condition that readers be invited to contribute funds to start something unique in Washington, D.C.—the Council for a Livable World, a lobby for peace.*

For a number of years now, you have had an opportunity to observe how we, as a nation, respond to the actions of the Russians, and how the Russians respond to our responses. Those of you who have watched closely the course of events in the past six months, may have been led to conclude that we are headed for an all-out war. I myself believe that we are, and that our chances of getting through the next ten years without war are slim.

I personally find myself in rebellion against the fate that history seems to have in store for us, and I suspect that some of you may be equally rebellious. The question is, what can you do?

War seems indeed to be inevitable, unless it is possible somehow to alter the pattern of behavior which America and Russia are exhibiting at present. You, as Americans, are not in a position to influence the Russian government; it follows that you would have to bring about a change in the attitude of the American government which, in turn, may bring about a similar change in the attitude of the Russian government.

It is conceivable that if a dedicated minority were to take effective political action, they could bring about the change in attitude that is needed. But such a minority can take

* The Bulletin of the Atomic Scientists, XVIII (April, 1962), 23–30.

effective action only if it is possible to formulate a set of political objectives on which it may unite.

Ever since the end of the war, the policies of the great powers have consistently followed the line of least resistance, and this line leads to an unlimited arms race. I do not believe that America can be made secure by keeping ahead in such an arms race.

There have been repeated attempts to stop the arms race by negotiating an agreement that would provide for some form of arms control. So far, all such attempts have failed, and each time they were followed by the continuation of the arms race, with renewed vigor. . . .

Many people have a black and white picture of the world; they believe that the nations fall into two classes: the peace-loving nations, and those who are not peaceloving. America, France, England, and generally speaking our allies, including Germany and Japan, are peaceloving nations. Russia and China are not peaceloving nations. Twenty years ago, the situation was somewhat different: at that time, Russia was a peaceloving nation, but Germany and Japan were not.

Many people believe that ever since the atomic bomb forced the unconditional surrender of Japan, America has unceasingly tried to rid the world of the bomb, and that Russian intransigence, alone, blocked progress in this direction.

When I listen to people who hold such views, I sometimes have the feeling that I have lived through all this before and, in a sense, I have. I was sixteen years old when the first World War broke out, and I lived at that time in Hungary. From reading the Hungarian newspapers, it would have appeared that whatever Austria and Germany did was right and whatever England, France, Russia, or America did was wrong. A good case could be made out for this general thesis, in almost every single instance. It would have been quite difficult for me to prove, in any single instance, that the newspapers were wrong, but somehow, it seemed to me unlikely that the two nations, located in the center of Europe, should be invariably right, and that all the other nations should be invariably wrong. History, I reasoned, would hardly operate in such a peculiar fashion, and gradually I was led to conclusions which were diametrically opposed to the views held by the majority of my schoolmates.

Many of my schoolmates regarded me as something of an oracle because I was able to cope with the mysteries of lower arithmetic which baffled them and one of them asked me one day quite early in the war who would lose the war. I said that I didn't know who *would* lose the war, but that I thought that I knew who *ought* to lose the war; I thought that Austria and Germany, as well as Russia, ought to lose the war. Since Austria and Germany fought on one side, and Russia on the other side, it was not quite clear how this could happen. The fact is, of course, that it did happen.

I am not telling you this in order to impress you with how bright I am. Nobody at sixty can claim to be as bright as he was at sixteen, even though in most cases it is not the intelligence that deteriorates, but the character. The point I am trying to make is that even in times of war, you can see current events in their historical perspective, provided that your passion for the truth prevails over your bias in favor of your own nation. . . .

Last September, *Life* magazine printed an article about me which said that I was in Washington trying to find out if there was a market for wisdom. Thereupon, I received a flood of letters from colleges and universities inviting me to give lectures. Most people get some pleasure out of hearing themselves talk, and so do I; yet I did not see much point in going around the country giving talks, if all I had to say was that there was no market for wisdom. Therefore, I declined all these invitations; that is, I declined them all, until Brandeis University invited me to attend a special convocation and receive an honorary doctor's degree. At that point, my vanity got the better of me, and I accepted. At Brandeis, I spoke at dinner informally to the trustees and fellows of the university, and this was my closest contact with grass roots since I moved to Washington—if, indeed, you may regard the trustees and fellows of Brandeis as grass roots.

I told them at Brandeis that I thought we were in very serious trouble; people asked me what there was that they could do about it, and I had no answer to give.

Is there, indeed, anything that these people—and for that matter I, myself—could do at this point that would make sense?

When I got back to Washington, I started to think about this, and I believe it will be best now if I simply recite to you how my thoughts developed from this point on.

The first thought that came to my mind was that in co-

operation with others, I could try to set up an organization in Washington—a sort of lobby, if you will—which
would bring to Washington, from time to time, scholars
and scientists who see current events in their historical perspective. These men would speak with the sweet voice of
reason, and our lobby could see to it that they be heard by
people inside the administration, and also by the key people
in Congress.

The next thing that occurred to me was that these distinguished scholars and scientists would be heard, but that
they might not be listened to, if they were not able to deliver votes.

Would they be listened to if they were able to deliver
votes?

The minority for which they speak might represent a few
per cent of the votes, and a few per cent of the votes alone
would not mean very much. Still, the combination of a
few per cent of the votes and the sweet voice of reason
might turn out to be an effective combination. And if the
minority for which these men speak, were sufficiently dedicated to stand ready not only to deliver votes, but also to
make very substantial campaign contributions, then this minority would be in a position to set up the most powerful
lobby that ever hit Washington.

The problem which the bomb poses to the world cannot
be solved except by abolishing war, and nothing less will do.
But first of all, we must back away from the war to which
we have come dangerously close.

Could such a dedicated minority agree not only on the
long-term political objectives which need to be pursued in
order to abolish war, but also on the immediate political objectives, the objectives which must be pursued in the next
couple of years, in order to make the present danger of war
recede to the point where attention can be focused on the
task of abolishing war?

America cannot be made secure by keeping ahead in an
atomic arms race and an agreement providing for arms control is a necessary first step toward abolishing war.

An agreement on arms control does not seem to be, however, "around the corner." It might very well be, therefore,
that *in the immediate future* America would have to take
certain unilateral steps. Some of the steps would be taken in

order to reduce the present danger of war; other steps would be taken so that if a war breaks out, which neither America nor Russia wants, it may be possible to bring hostilities to an end before there is an all-out atomic catastrophe. . . .

First of all, America should resolve and proclaim that she would not resort to any strategic bombing of cities or bases of Russia (either by means of atomic bombs or conventional explosives), except if American cities or bases are attacked with bombs, or if there is an unprovoked·attack with bombs against one of America's allies. . . .

America could and should adopt the policy that, in case of war, if she were to use atomic bombs against troops in combat, she would do so only on her own side of the pre-war boundary. . . .

It must be made clear, however, that if America adopts the policy here advocated, she thereby renounces the threat of strategic bombing as a general *deterrent*. . . .

I, personally, do not believe that America would lose much by giving up the threat of strategic bombing, because the deterrent effect of such a threat is negligible unless the threat is believable.

If America were to threaten to drop bombs on a large number of Russian cities in case of war, knowing full well that Russia would retaliate by dropping bombs on a large number of American cities, such a threat would be tantamount to a threat of murder and suicide. The threat of murder and suicide would not be a believable threat. . . .

Those responsible for the planning of strategy in the Department of Defense would concede this much.

According to persistent press reports there is, however, an increasingly influential school of thought in the Department of Defense which holds that, in case of war with Russia, America may engage in strategic bombing, aimed at the destruction of Russian rocket bases and strategic air bases. America would not bomb any of Russia's cities if she can help it, as long as Russia did not bomb any of America's cities.

This school of thought holds that, at present, Russia does not have many long-range rocket bases and strategic air bases, that the location of many of these bases is known, and that most of them are vulnerable and could be destroyed by attacking them with bombs. By building enough long-range solid-fuel rockets (Minutemen) and submarines capable of launching intermediate range solid-fuel rockets (Polaris) America may be able to keep ahead in this game for the next five years.

Those who advocate such a policy believe that if America should succeed in knocking out, say, 90 per cent of Russia's strategic atomic striking forces, then the Russians would probably speak to us as follows: "We have enough rockets left to destroy a large number of American cities, but we know that if we did this America may retaliate by destroying all of our cities. Therefore, we are going to hold our fire and we propose to negotiate peace. We concede that the power balance has now shifted in America's favor and we are now willing to yield on a number of issues on which we took an inflexible stand prior to the outbreak of hostilities." If this were to happen America would have won a victory even though it may be a victory in a limited sense of the term only.

Naturally if there is a war and America resorts to the bombing of bases in Russia, one could not expect the Russians to sit idly by and watch America picking up step by step one base after another. It follows that America would have to start the strategic bombing of Russian bases with a sudden, massive attack and to try to destroy all vulnerable Russian bases of known location, in the first attack.

There are, of course, people in the Department of Defense who have serious doubts that America would actually carry out such a first strike against bases, in case of war, yet they believe that—at the present juncture—it is a good thing to threaten to bomb Russian bases in case of war because this is a more believable threat than the threat of "murder and suicide."

I do not know just how believable this threat is, but I do know that at best we are purchasing an increased restraint on Russia's part for a year or two, and that we are purchasing it at a very high price. For whether we adopt such a strategy or merely give Russia the impression that we have adopted such a strategy, we are provoking an all-out atomic arms race and may within a very few years reach the point of no return, in this regard.

Therefore, I believe that it is imperative to oppose: (a) the adoption of plans which call for a first strike against Russian rocket and strategic air bases in case of war, and (b) the adoption of the policy of "deterring" Russia, with the threat that America would resort to such a first strike in case of war. . . .

General disarmament may, if we are lucky, eliminate war, but it would not end the rivalry between America and Russia.

It is a foregone conclusion that American efforts toward creating an orderly and livable world will be frustrated in Southeast Asia and Africa because of our failure to devise forms of democracy which would be viable in these regions of the world. The task of devising forms of democracy which would be suitable to the needs of such areas is not a task that the government can handle. Various forms of democracy may have to be devised which are tailor-made to fit the various areas. *A major private group could tackle and ought to tackle this problem.* If it is not solved, more and more underdeveloped nations may become dictatorships; some of them may have a rapid succession of dictator after dictator and, in the end, the people may have to choose between chaos and communism.

It is a foregone conclusion that America's efforts to raise the standard of living of underdeveloped nations may be frustrated in those areas where the birth rate is high, infant mortality is high, and there is little arable land left. Improvement in the standard of living will initially lead to a fall in infant mortality, and if the birth rate remains high, the population will shoot up so rapidly that economic improvements will not be able to catch up.

Our failure to develop biological methods of birth control, suitable for the needs of such areas, is responsible for this state of affairs. The development of such methods is not a task which the government can undertake. The government could not create research institutes which would attract scientists who are ingenious and resourceful enough to come up with an adequate solution. *A major private group could and should tackle this problem.*

If it should turn out that it is possible to formulate a set of political objectives on which reasonable people could generally agree, and if these objectives could count on the all-out support of a sizable and dedicated minority, then I should be impelled to go further, and I would plan to go further along the following lines:

I would ask about fifteen distinguished scientists to serve

as fellows of a council which might be called Council for Abolishing War or perhaps Council for a Livable World. The fellows (who are all scientists) would elect the board of directors, but membership on the board would not be restricted to scientists. . . .

The council would hold hearings, perhaps one every four months, and would subsequently proclaim in detail the immediate political objectives it purposes to advocate. It would communicate these objectives, perhaps in the form of a series of pamphlets, to all those who are believed to be seriously interested. Those who regularly receive the communications of the council would be regarded as members of the movement, if they are willing *actively* to support *at least one* of the several specific objectives proclaimed by the council. . . .

One of the functions of the lobby would be to help the members of the movement clarify their own minds on the political objectives they wish actively to support.

The members of the movement would be regarded as pledged to vote in the primaries as well as in the elections. As far as federal elections are concerned, they would be pledged to cast their vote, *disregarding domestic issues*, solely on the issue of war and peace.

The members of the movement would be regarded *as pledged annually to spend two per cent of their income on campaign contributions* [Editor's italics]. The members would be asked to make out a check payable to the recipient of the campaign contribution but to mail that check to the Washington office of the lobby for transmission. In this manner the lobby would be in a position to keep track of the flow of campaign contributions.

Those in high income brackets may be left free to contribute three per cent after taxes rather than two per cent before taxes.

All members of the movement would be free to wear an emblem that would identify them as members of the movement, if they wish to do so.

Those who can not spend two per cent of their income on campaign contributions may regard themselves as supporters of the movement if they spend either one per cent of their income or $100 per year, according to their preference. . . .

There are many intelligent men in Congress who have insight into what goes on; the movement could help these men to have the courage of their convictions. There are others in Congress who are not capable of such insight; the only thing to do with them is not to return them to Congress, and to replace them with better men. This may make it necessary to persuade better men to run in the primaries and to stand for election. To find such better men must be one of the main tasks of the movement, and the lobby must be prepared to help members of the movement to perform this task.

I did not come here to enlist any of you in such a movement or to launch such a movement. I came here to invite you to participate in an experiment that would show whether such a movement could be successfully launched.

First of all, I ask each of you to look into your own heart and try to discover whether you yourself would want to participate in a political movement of the kind described, provided the objectives—as formulated from time to time—appeal to you and you thought that the movement could be effective. . . .

If the result of this experiment indicates that such a movement could get off the ground, provided it were started in the right way and on a sufficiently large scale, then the Council for Abolishing War would be constituted. Presumably the council would attempt to identify 25,000 individuals who would be willing to make campaign contributions in the amount of two per cent of their income. Presumably, if the council is successful in this the fellows of the council would proceed to establish the lobby.

By the time the movement attains 150,000 members it would presumably represent about $20 million per year in campaign contributions or $80 million over a four year period.

Whether such a movement could grow further and come to represent not only a decisive amount in campaign contributions but also a significant number of votes, would then presumably depend on the future course of world events.

51. Nonpayment of War Taxes, 1966.*

A small, heterogenous group of Americans have elected refusal to pay taxes as a means of establishing their personal protest against their government's military enterprises. The reasons that motivate these men and women vary; the tax refusers share no single political commitment or philosophy. What unites them is just their refusal to pay taxes so long as the annual Federal budget is weighted so heavily by military expenditures.

Introduction

For many years people have been expressing the need for a handbook on the matter of nonpayment of taxes for war. When a person becomes interested in nonpayment, the first thing he wants to know is—How? Then he wants to know—What would happen? The answer to both questions is best found in the experience of those who have been nonpayers. Since 1941 some pacifists in the United States have been taking positions of nonpayment. Some have earned a nontaxable income. Others have confronted neighbors and government with an outright refusal to pay taxes that are legally owed, and in some cases have filed no return. . . .

When a person first asks What happens? he nearly always wants to know what happens *legally*. In this handbook we try to answer mainly by giving experiences, citing the law when the law seems clear and when it is an aid to understanding. His next question probably is what could happen occupationally, economically and socially. And what happens in these areas is sometimes more important than what happens at the hands of a tax man or a law court. This is the major reason for putting into this handbook so many "case histories" of nonpayment.

Although the movement of nonpayment is only a few

* Excerpts from the *Handbook on Nonpayment of War Taxes,* Peacemaker Movement, Cincinnati, Ohio. Prepared by the War Resisters League, 5 Beekman Street, New York, N.Y., 1966.

years old, it is not the first such movement in history. In fact, nonpayment has a long and honorable history. Early Christians refused to pay taxes to Caesar's pagan temple in Rome; Mennonites and Quakers refused to pay taxes during the French and Indian Wars, the Revolutionary War, and the Civil War; strugglers for independence in India, under Gandhi's influence, refused to pay taxes to the British Empire.

. . . .

Some Philosophical Questions

Why seek disarmament and a nonmilitary budget by unlawful means?

One has no reason to disobey a law which does not violate his principles, even though he may not like that law. But when a law cuts across the grain of his conscience, he must either violate his conscience and comply with the law, or comply with his conscience and violate the law. Many people do not like the law which forces them to pay heavily for the preparation of war. Most of them merely object to paying. Some others find that the tax law cuts sharply across the grain of their consciences, and refuse to comply as a matter of principle.

How far along the road to war should one go without resisting in more direct ways than going to the polls? When should the German people have begun their resistance to Nazi policies? Tax refusers believe that if people were to cease putting so much reliance upon the casting of strips of paper for candidates who they hope will both win and do their bidding, and if they would instead cast their whole "vote" for disarmament by refusing to buy arms, the course would be democratic and effective.

Does Tax refusal deprive the constructive functions of our support?

When a person pays taxes to the federal government he cannot choose whether his money shall go for the civil functions or for the military—all revenue goes into one pile. Thus, whatever he pays goes into both functions, with by far the larger part going to the military. On the other hand, whatever amount he owes and does not pay, he can, if he desires, turn over to agencies which work for peace. Approximately 80% of the national budget is going for past, present, and future wars. Well over 50% is expressly for war preparation. Hence, it is apparent that the major business of the federal government is war. Nonpayers of taxes feel that so long as this is so, it is useless to act as if the major business of the government is civil functions, or peaceful pursuits.

. . . .

Doesn't the government collect anyway, canceling the effect of refusal?

Unpaid taxes may be collected without court procedure. The witness is not destroyed, however, for the refuser does not take his taxes to the collector; they must be seized. But the officers of government by no means collect all unpaid taxes. Many defaults are never followed up, while others are merely looked into and let alone. In tax refusal one acts firmly to forestall war, no matter what happens eventually. However, refusal in itself might become powerful enough to change the course of history.

. . . .

Summary of Criminal Action Brought by Internal Revenue Service

Since 1948, when the nonpayment movement began, until now, 1963, only five persons have been brought before a U.S. commissioner or a district court.

. . . .

The fact that so few have been arrested shows that there has been no policy to crack down. Instead, it would seem that, for one reason or another, local officials who have brought criminal action have probably acted on their own initiative. There has been little indication that the headquarters of IRS or the Department of Justice has wanted to prosecute.

. . . .

Some Personal Experiences

Arthur Evans

"Why can't I file an income tax return today, as I have done for almost a quarter of a century?" wrote Arthur Evans, Denver M.D., to IRS on April 16, 1962.

For many years he had been filing a return, yet refusing to pay a portion of the taxes. Being his own employer, he is not subject to withholding. "I wish to let the world I love know," he continued, "that I see destruction for all of us if we do not find and act upon alternatives to war as a means of dealing with international conflict. Is not the alternative to build the institutions of peace, the institutions of law and order?"

On May 10 he had received from IRS a letter stating: "It would be appreciated if you would come to our office on May 11." On May 11 he answered: "Thank you for your invitation. Unfortunately it is not convenient for me to come in at this time to talk about 'official business.' " He also said in his letter: "When a people is taxed and their possessions are being used to perpetuate these evils, it is right to refuse to give information which will be used to extract from him his possessions for said evil purposes. To coerce an individual to be a party to any crime is in itself a further evil. When the state does so attempt to coerce me, then I in conscience must refuse to be coerced. How can any man in conscience and with a sense of honor be party to preparation for global butchery?"

IRS responded in the press that it would collect the tax from him.

Fyke Farmer

"I would be guilty as an accomplice if I contributed money to help finance the war activities of the government," said Fyke Farmer, noted Nashville lawyer in 1950 as he made a refusal on his 1949 income.

"It is the doctrine of legal disobedience which I assert," he said as he filed a suit against the U.S. government in which he asked for a refund of the $6750 he paid in escrow to the court clerk's office pending the outcome. "The object of my suit is to test whether the international law enforced at Nuremberg applies today. The question is whether we should forget about it and go all-out for the planning and preparation of war, or strive to bring into existence world courts and the necessary judicial machinery to give the law force and effect."*

Stating it another way, he said: "The Nuremberg judgment was not based on the philosophy that governments would stop war now, but that individuals would stop following the leaders who plan the wars."

"I am not in disobedience to the law," he stated. "I am obeying the law. I am claiming my immunity from the coercion of the President and the Congress of the U.S. that would render me criminal if I do not take the moral choice of refusing to support war. . . . I am a law-abiding citizen. My government has no right to force me to become a war criminal."

In 1952 he explained his thesis this way: "The taxpayer becomes an aider and abetter in the plans formulated by the military high command, if it is within his power to refuse payment and he does not so refuse. . . . The fundamental issue is whether the mad race of the governments into another war will be stopped by individuals who refuse to be led or pushed any further."

In 1954 and 1955 he won two court skirmishes when one district court judge refused twice to dismiss his suit on the ground that Fyke Farmer had a right to develop the case on the merits. The case, however, was lost when another judge (the former having died) ruled that Fyke Farmer had "no case." This judge frankly said that this judgment was made so as not to embarrass former President Truman, who would have been summoned to testify regarding the commencement of hostilities in Korea in 1950. Attempt was being made by Fyke Farmer to prove that war in Korea was unlawfully undertaken, in defiance of the Constitution.

In the spring of 1958, he lost the case in the sixth circuit court of appeals on the ground that the federal courts, in the exercise of their Constitutional power to adjudicate cases and controversies, may not pass on the criminality of the acts of the executive and legislative branches carrying out military and foreign policy.

* Compare this with Part VII, Document 40 in this book, *United States* v. *Mitchell*. In 1966, Mitchell unsuccessfully raised the same issue in his suit protesting induction into the Armed Forces. [Editor's note]

On June 9, 1958, the Supreme Court denied *certiorari*, and the case came to an end. Fyke Farmer commented on the losing of this legal struggle which lasted several years and took much time and money: "The inevitable effect of this abdication of the judicial power is to erect military and foreign policy as an authority superior to the fundamental law. Surely this will be shocking to all Americans who have cherished the idea that the Constitution, the treaties and laws, constitute the supreme law superseding governmental action in conflict therewith."

A. J. Muste

In May 1948 A. J. Muste announced that he no longer would pay income taxes. "All the arguments against tax refusal have in my own mind been laid low by the revealing and unspeakably shocking developments of recent weeks," he said. In his autobiographical articles in *Liberation*, he wrote in April 1960: "It was in connection with the problem of withholding of a staff member's income tax by a pacifist organization that my own thinking about tax refusal was forced to a decision to act." His secretary had asked that the organization pay the full salary, with none extracted for income tax.

At the time of his refusal he said, "Each citizen, each religious believer, and especially anyone who plays some part in the building of public opinion must ask what is the utmost he can do to open people's eyes to the true situation and how he can withdraw his own support from the war in every way that is open to him and regardless of the cost."

At tax deadline in 1949, he filed no return and paid no tax. As a clergyman he was entitled to a withholding-free salary at the Fellowship of Reconciliation in New York City where he was executive secretary. It was not very long before the IRS agents came to his office. It was two years, however, before they asked him to come to theirs. When they did, it was to explain his tax delinquency. After this first trip in June of 1951, he went several times. Once he was asked to sign a transcript of the conversation, but when he said he would have to read it before signing, the whole matter was dropped.

Until early 1956, IRS was rather inactive in the case. Then IRS notified A. J. Muste that it needed more time, but that the statute of limitations was about to come into effect. (In that he had filed no returns, it is not clear why the tax office thought the statute of limitations applied, unless a return had been made out by them on the basis of information from the interviews.) Asked if he would sign a paper to give IRS more time, he did so.

IRS then fixed the tax A. J. Muste owed, which he accepted as correct. IRS made an assessment, including a penalty for "fraud" (non-filing). Once there has been an assessment, the taxpayer can challenge its validity without paying, by taking the case to tax court, which is different from regular federal courts. His attorney, Harrop Freeman, felt it would be useful to have a decision that following conscience was not "fraud," and not "criminal." Chances were thought to be best in the tax court.

The tax court on March 15, 1960, found no grounds for "fraud" but found no grounds either for his exemption from tax requirements on grounds of conscientious objection to war. He decided not to appeal this decision so as to retain the favorable fraud ruling. In November 1961 he was asked again to come to the tax office. When he did, an agent told him that IRS might levy on his social security and his pension. In none of the years has he filed a return or paid any tax.

Max Sandin

Max Sandin first refused taxes in 1943. A painter living in Cleveland, he worked for himself some of the time, and was not subject to withholding. Each year he wrote to IRS, "As a conscientious objector I refuse to pay income tax, in order not to help war directly." In 1946 the government recorded a lien for $2800 against him. The same week it collected $145 on a job he had just completed. In 1959 he received notice of a lien of $2500 in back taxes. On August 29, 1961, IRS seized his social security check. He went to the U.S. Treasury and began a sit-in. "In the First World War I was sentenced to be shot for not wanting to kill," he said. Later this was commuted by President Wilson. "Now I am sentenced to starve for not wanting to buy bombs for World War III."

He was soon arrested. Taken to the D.C. General Hospital, he was given a "sanity test." At a hearing on September 11, he was declared mentally sound and released. Since that time not only have social security checks been taken, but also his pension checks from the painters' union. On September 25, 1962, he wrote to President Kennedy: "I am 73 years old and I want to live more and more. I want back my social security and my painters' union checks for which I have paid since 1937. I hope that your conscience will be your guide, because I am not asking for mercy or pardon."

52. Letters and Petitions, 1965–67.

Opposition to the war in Vietnam revealed itself not only in radical forms of protest, but also in letters and petitions of respectful disagreement. The following letters represent widely different groups in our society—professors, lawyers, writers, seminarians. Each expresses dissatisfaction with some aspect of national policy: with the conduct of the war; with harassment of antidraft demonstrators; with the government's refusal to recognize the right of selective objection. All of the following letters were sent to the President of the United States. Some of them, whole or in part, were reprinted in the news media. The texts have been obtained from the individuals who signed the documents.

52. a. Lawyers' Letter to President Lyndon B. Johnson, 1965.

December 15, 1965

President Lyndon B. Johnson
The White House
Washington, D.C.

Dear Mr. President:

As Professors of Law, we wish to express our deep concern about recent statements by officials of the Selective Service System which warn those demonstrating against administration policies that student draft deferments can be revoked for actions "against the national interest." Although Selective Service Director Lewis B. Hershey has more recently qualified this by saying that those performing "unlawful" acts will be so reclassified, there are serious doubts as to the legality of even these reclassifications.

Whatever our individual views are on Vietnam or other national issues, we are united in strongly condemning the use of the draft to stifle constitutionally protected expression of views, the inevitable consequences of such statements. We need not emphasize the special responsibilities of public officials in dealing with young people in the midst of their education. A society educating men for freedom cannot compromise its ideals by imposing penalties for the exercise of such freedom.

As to the so-called "unlawful" actions, neither the Selective Service Law nor its regulations make violations of law unconnected with the draft a ground for denying student deferment. A society which cherishes free speech and the rule of law cannot allow the lives of its citizens to be vitally affected by individual and often capricious judgments of what is "against the national interest"; nor can it permit officials to induct students into military service for allegedly "unlawful acts" when Congress has not chosen to make such acts relevant.

Mr. President, you have recently reaffirmed the traditional American dedication to freedom of speech and to the rule of law. We call upon you, and on General Hershey, to state unequivocally that the draft will not and legally cannot be used as a weapon to stifle criticism of administration policies or to impose conformity on issues which vitally affect the American people. We call upon you also to take such steps as are necessary to insure that no student is unfairly prejudiced by his participation in demonstrations, or in any exercise of his constitutional rights.

Yours very truly,

52. b. Lawyer's Committee on American Policy Toward Vietnam, 1966.

New York, N.Y., January 25, 1966.

Hon. LYNDON B. JOHNSON,
President of the United States,
Washington, D.C.

MR. PRESIDENT: Following the issuance by the Department of State in March 1965 of a memorandum captioned "Legal Basis for U.S. Actions Against North Vietnam," our committee, in consultation with leading authorities in the fields of international law and constitutional law, undertook to research the legal issues, culminating in the memorandum of law (here enclosed).*

Our committee's memorandum of law has been endorsed, among others, by Profs. Quincy Wright, of the University of Virginia; Wolfgang Friedmann, of Columbia University; Thomas I. Emerson, of Yale; Richard A. Falk, of Princeton; Norman Malcolm, of Cornell; D. F. Fleming, of Vanderbilt; David Haber, of Rutgers; Roy M. Mersky, of the University of Texas; William G. Rice, of the University of Wisconsin; Chancellor Robert M. MacIver, of the New School for Social Research; Profs. Robert C. Stevenson, of Idaho State University; Alexander W. Rudzinski, of Columbia; Darrell Randell, of the American University in Washington, D.C.; and Profs. Wallace McClure and William W. Van Alstyne, both from Duke University and the World Rule of Law Center.

For the reasons documented in our memorandum our committee has reached the regrettable but inescapable conclusion that the actions of the United States in Vietnam contravene the essential provisions of the United Nations Charter, to which we are bound by treaty; violate the Geneva accords, which we pledged to observe; are not sanctioned by the treaty creating the Southeast Asia Treaty Organization; and violate our own Constitution and the system of checks

* For the full report see *The Congressional Record,* 89th Congress, Vol. III, No. 176, pp. 24010–18.

and balances which is the heart of it, by the prosecution of the war in Vietnam without a congressional declaration of war.

The principal argument advanced in the State Department's memorandum is that our Government's action in Vietnam is justified under article 51 of the United Nations Charter sanctioning "individual or collective self-defense if an armed attack occurs against a member of the United Nations." However, South Vietnam is indisputably not a member of the United Nations and, indeed, under the Geneva accords of 1954, is merely a temporary zone. Moreover, since the Geneva accords recognized all of Vietnam as a single state, the conflict in Vietnam is "civil strife" and foreign intervention is forbidden. We do well to recall that President Lincoln, in the course of our Civil War to preserve the union of the North and the South, vigorously opposed British and French threats to intervene in behalf of the independence of the Confederacy.

In addition, the right of collective self-defense under article 51 is limited to those nations which are within a regional community which history and geography have developed into a regional collective defense system. The United States—a country separated by oceans and thousands of miles from southeast Asia and lacking historical or ethnic connections with the peoples of that area—cannot qualify as a bona fide member of a regional collective defense system for southeast Asia.

The State Department's memorandum also contends that the actions of the United States "being defensive in character and designed to resist armed aggression, are wholly consistent with the purposes and principles of the charter and specifically with article 2, paragraph 4." Yet article 2, paragraph 4, declares in clear and unambiguous language that "all members shall refrain in their international relations from the threat or use of force against the territorial integrity or political independence of any state or in any other manner inconsistent with the purposes of the United Nations."

The State Department's memorandum also attempts to justify our Government's actions in Vietnam on the ground that the "North Vietnamese have repeatedly violated the 1954 Geneva accords." But this statement ignores our Government's antecedent violations of the pledges we made. On July 21, 1954, Under Secretary of State Walter Bedell Smith in a declaration confirmed by President Eisenhower, pledged that our Government would not "disturb" the Geneva accords and would "not join in an arrangement which would hinder" the rights of peoples "to determine their own future." However, the United States departed from these pledges when, on July 16, 1955, the Diem regime announced, with American backing, that it would defy the provision calling for national elections, thus violating the central condition which had made the Geneva accords acceptable to the Vietminh. And the United States also chose to ignore the ban on the introduction of troops, military personnel, arms, and munitions into Vietnam and the prohibition against the establishment of new military bases in Vietnam territory—provisions set out in the Geneva accords. It is an historical fact that the refusal to hold the elections prescribed by the Geneva accords, coupled with the reign of terror and suppression instituted by the Diem regime, precipitated the civil war.

In the light of the foregoing, more fully detailed and documented in the enclosed memorandum, we submit, Mr. President, that the State Department has incorrectly advised you as to the legality of U.S. actions against Vietnam.

We further submit, Mr. President, that the frequent citation of the pledges given by Presidents Eisenhower and Kennedy to aid South Vietnam afford no justification for U.S. intervention in Vietnam. President Eisenhower has stated that his administration had made no commitment to South Vietnam "in terms of military support on programs whatsoever." President Kennedy insisted that the war in Vietnam was "their war" and promised only equipment and military advisers. Hence the historical facts fail to support the point advanced. Beyond this, these Presidential pledges do not even have the status of treaties, not having been ratified by the Senate. Manifestly, the obligations assumed by our Government under the United Nations Charter, with the advice and consent of the Senate, transcend any Presidential pledge undertaken vis-a-vis the South Vietnamese regime.

Our Government has often urged that our presence in South Vietnam is solely to preserve freedom for its people and to uphold the democratic process. Yet the series of regimes supported by the United States in South Vietnam have been authoritarian in character, quite without popular support and largely indifferent to the welfare of the local population. Ambassador Henry Cabot Lodge, on June 30, 1964, commenting on the consequences of massive American involvement in Vietnam, stated, "Well, that means we become a colonial power and I think it's been pretty well established that colonialism is over. I believe that if you start doing that you will get all kinds of unfortunate results: you'll stir up antiforeign feeling; there'll be a tendency to lay back and let the Americans do it and all that. I can't think that it's a good thing to do."

As we have stated, our committee has also come to the painful conclusion that our Government's action in Vietnam violates the clear provision of our Constitution which vests in Congress exclusively the power to declare war—a power not constitutionally granted to the President. The debates in the Constitutional Convention at Philadelphia make explicitly clear that warmaking was to be a purely legislative prerogative and the President was not to have the power to wage a war or "commit" our Nation to the waging of a war, although the Executive was intended to have the power to repel sudden attacks.

In pointing out that the President lacks constitutional power to make war, our committee does not imply that a declaration of war by the Congress is desirable. Rather, we mean to point out that the failure to abide and conform to the provisions of our Constitution inevitably lead to tragic situations.

In alerting the American people to the unconstitutionality of the war being waged in Vietnam, we are following the example followed by Abraham Lincoln who, in a speech made on January 12, 1848, before the House of Representatives opposing the war undertaken by President Polk, set out the reasons which impelled him to vote for a resolution which declared that "the war with Mexico was unnecessarily and unconstitutionally commenced by the President."

Our committee conducted its research because of a deep sense of responsibility as members of the bar and because of our dedication to the principle of world peace through law. It was the American lawyers who conceived and nurtured this principle, and after holding conferences on four continents (San Jose, Costa Rica; Tokyo, Japan; Lagos, Nigeria; Rome, Italy), finally convened the First World Conference on World Peace Through Law at Athens, Greece, in July 1963.

In the proclamation of Athens, the declaration of general principles for a world rule of law, among other things, declared that "all obligations under international law must be fulfilled and all rights thereunder must be exercised in good faith."

Mr. President, we submit that our Government's intervention in Vietnam falls far short of the declaration of principles at Athens, Greece, in July 1963, and is in violation of international agreements. The rule of law is the essential foundation of stability and order, both between societies and in international relations. When we violate the law ourselves, we cannot expect respect for the rule of law by others. Our present unilateral intervention is an offense, we submit, against the spirit of American institutions.

As lawyers, we feel that the national interest is best served —indeed it can only be served—by (a) a commitment that our Government will be bound by and implement the principles of the Geneva accords of 1954, and that the main provisions thereof be the basis for the establishment of an independent, unified neutral Vietnam; (b) an invocation of the provisions of the United Nations Charter to assure peace in southeast Asia; and (c) a declaration that there will be no further bombing of Vietnam, that we will agree to a cease fire, and publicly declare that the United States is willing to negotiate directly with the National Liberation Front —a point endorsed by leading Senators and Secretary General Thant and mandated by article 33 of the United Nations Charter requiring that the "parties to any dispute . . . shall first of all, seek a solution by negotiation . . . or other peaceful means of their own choice," and that all elements of the South Vietnamese people should be represented in that country's postwar government.

Respectfully yours,
ROBERT W. KENNY,
Honorary Chairman
WILLIAM L. STANDARD,
Chairman.

52. c. Committee of Chicago Professors and Writers, 1966.

May 9, 1966

President Lyndon B. Johnson
The White House
Washington, D.C.

Dear Mr. President:

We the undersigned writers of the Chicago area feel that we must express our alarm at the undeclared war in South and North Vietnam.

We are shocked by the escalation of a war which has brought horror to 30,000,000 people. We are appalled by our use of military destruction to make large areas uninhabitable. In the process of destroying military targets we have burned unarmed and innocent women and children. Our defoliation missions degrade us and our soldiers in the eyes of humanity. Our actions have been made even more outrageous by our confused denials and admissions which have obscured the true military and political situation.

While there is still time left for us to regain the leadership of free people everywhere we should give immediate consideration to the proposals of Senator William Fulbright, Senator Robert Kennedy and others for bringing an end to the conflict.

We join with the writers who recently met in New York to protest the continuation of the war and with the thousands of clergymen and educators throughout the country in urging the United States government to seek an immediate end of the war.

1. To establish a cease fire.

2. To open direct negotiations with the National Liberation Front and assure its participation in government both before and after elections to the extent that it represents the Vietnamese people.

3. To move as soon as possible to replace American troops with a United Nations or Afro-Asian police force, to assure the conditions for democratic expression and free elections.

4. To attempt the settlement of the dispute in the spirit of the Geneva accords, including the neutralization of North and South Vietnam and the removal of all foreign soldiers and foreign bases.

Yours very truly,

Nelson Algren	Jean Hagstrum	Henry Rago
Harry Barnard	Bert F. Hoselitz	Adeline Pynchon
Florence Cohen	Francis Hsu	Ernest Samuels
Jerome Cohen	Bernard Kogan	Julia Seibel
Louis Cheskin	Sidney Lens	Lefton Stavrianos
Carl Condit	Norris Lloyd	Richard G. Stern
Jack Conroy	Harry Mark Petrakis	Meyer Weinberg
Diana David	Curtis MacDougall	Arnold Jacob Wolf
Richard Ellmann	David Polish	Gordon C. Zahn

The foregoing signatures have been individually authorized on copies of this letter.

Ernest Samuels, Chairman
English Department, Northwestern University

52. d. Divinity Students' Letter to Secretary of Defense Robert S. McNamara, 1967.

April 26, 1967

Dear Mr. Secretary:

We are addressing this to you because you are Secretary of Defense, and also because we know you are a man of deep religious feeling and integrity.

We are divinity students—future ministers, priests, and rabbis—and, as you know, we have a classification in Selective Service that virtually exempts us from the Draft. We are thus enabled to evade the moral dilemma that is so troubling to many other young men who face the prospect of military service—the dilemma of whether to participate in the war in Vietnam in spite of conscience or whether to refuse to serve and risk the consequences. But we are precisely the people who should be least exempted from facing basic moral issues, and our privileged status therefore adds to our dilemma. For this reason we are more and more uncomfortable about accepting deferments not available to others, as if avoiding moral dilemmas were an acceptable way of dealing with them.

Large numbers of divinity students cannot support the war in Vietnam because they believe this war is neither in the religious tradition of just wars nor in the national interest. On the other hand, most of us believe law and order are fundamental to a free society, and for that reason many who oppose the war on moral grounds are loath to counsel others to break the law by refusing to fight in Vietnam. But if those people specially charged by society with moral responsibilities do not act on their deepest convictions, surely the whole of society is in deep trouble.

We are impressed by a proposal advanced by a minority of the Marshall Commission, the General Board of the National Council of Churches, the General Assembly of the United Presbyterian Church, the Council for Christian Social Action of the United Church of Christ, Americans for Democratic Action, and other significant groups—the proposal that the Selective Service law be amended to recognize conscientious objection to a particular war. If this proposal does not seem acceptable, can you suggest any other way to avoid a confrontation between the demands of the law and those law-abiding young Americans whose conscience will not permit them to fight in Vietnam? Without some procedure that could ease such a confrontation, we fear the grave prospect of growing numbers of young men refusing to fight in Vietnam whatever the legal consequences to themselves and the political consequences to the country. Faced by such a situation, many of us would feel obliged to decline special exemptions to face the same consequences as our peers.

We look forward to hearing from you about this deeply troubling matter.

Respectfully yours,

[1000 divinity students signed this letter]

53. Senator J. William Fulbright, from "The Higher Patriotism" and from "The Arrogance of Power," 1966.*

James William Fulbright, Democrat, United States Senator from the State of Arkansas, is widely know as the sponsor of the Fulbright Act (1946), providing for the exchange of teachers and students between the United States and other countries. Since 1959, the Senator has been Chairman of the Senate Foreign Relations Committee.

In 1966, Senator Fulbright was invited to deliver the Christian A. Herter Lectures at the Johns Hopkins School of Advanced International Studies. In the lectures, as on the floor of the Senate, Fulbright is outspoken in his criticism of the administration's policy in Vietnam and, in a wider sense, of the course of American foreign policy in the past decade. The Fulbright lectures, whatever the color of one's own political convictions, stand as an example of political courage and eloquence. Excerpts from the first and the third lectures appear below.

From "The Higher Patriotism"

To criticize one's country is to do it a service and pay it a compliment. It is ·a service because it may spur the country to do better than it is doing; it is a compliment because it evidences a belief that the country can do better than it is doing. "This," said Albert Camus in one of his "Letters to a German Friend," is "what separated us from you; we made demands. You were satisfied to serve the power of your nation and we dreamed of giving ours her truth. . . ."**

In a democracy dissent is an act of faith. Like medicine, the test of its value is not its taste but its effects, not how

---

* "The Higher Patriotism," *Congressional Record,* 89th Congress, 2d Session, CXII (April 25, 1966), 8460–64; "The Arrogance of Power," *Congressional Record,* 89th Congress, 2d Session, CXII (May 5, 1966), 10297–10308.

** Second Letter, December, 1943, *Resistance, Rebellion and Death* (New York: Random House, Inc., 1960), p. 10.

it makes people feel at the moment, but how it inspires them to act thereafter. Criticism may embarrass the country's leaders in the short run but strengthen their hand in the long run; it may destroy a consensus on policy while expressing a consensus of values. Woodrow Wilson once said that there was "such a thing as being too proud to fight"; there is also, or ought to be, such a thing as being too confident to conform, too strong to be silent in the face of apparent error. Criticism, in short, is more than a right; it is an act of patriotism, a higher form of patriotism, I believe, than the familiar rituals of national adulation.

In the three lectures which we begin tonight I am going to criticize America, I hope not unfairly, and always in the hope of rendering a service and the confidence of paying a compliment. It is not a pejorative but a tribute to say that America is worthy of criticism. If nonetheless one is charged with a lack of patriotism, I would reply with Camus, "No, I didn't love my country, if pointing out what is unjust in what we love amounts to not loving, if insisting that what we love should measure up to the finest image we have of her amounts to not loving."*

What is the finest image of America? To me it is the image of a composite, or better still a synthesis, of diverse peoples and cultures, come together in harmony but not identity, in an open, receptive, generous, and creative society. . . .

The question that I find intriguing—the question which I have chosen as the theme of these lectures although I have no answer to it—is whether a nation so extraordinarily endowed as the United States can overcome that arrogance of power which has afflicted, weakened, and in some cases destroyed great nations in the past.

The causes of the malady are a mystery but its recurrence is one of the uniformities of history: power tends to confuse itself with virtue and a great nation is peculiarly susceptible to the idea that its power is a sign of God's favor, conferring upon it a special responsibility for other nations—to make them richer and happier and wiser, to remake them, that is, in its own shining image. Power confuses itself with virtue and it also tends to take itself for omnipotence. Once imbued with the idea of a mission, a great nation easily assumes that it has the means as well as the

* First Letter; *ibid.,* p. 4.

duty to do God's work. The Lord, after all, surely would not choose you as His agent and then deny you the sword with which to work His will. German soldiers in the First World War wore belt buckles imprinted with the words: "Gott mit uns." It was approximately under this kind of infatuation—an exaggerated sense of power and an imaginary sense of mission—that the Athenians attacked Syracuse and Napoleon and then Hitler invaded Russia. In plain words, they overextended their commitments and they came to grief.

My question is whether America can overcome the fatal arrogance of power. My hope and my belief are that it can, that it has the human resources to accomplish what few if any great nations have ever accomplished before: to be confident but also tolerant and rich but also generous, to be willing to teach but also willing to learn, to be powerful but also wise. I believe that America is capable of all of these things; I also believe it is falling short of them. Gradually but unmistakably we are succumbing to the arrogance of power. In so doing we are not living up to our capacity and promise; the measure of our falling short is the measure of the patriot's duty of dissent.

The discharge of that most important duty is handicapped in America by an unworthy tendency to fear serious criticism of our government. In the abstract we celebrate freedom of opinion as a vital part of our patriotic liturgy. It is only when some Americans exercise the right that other Americans are shocked. No one of course ever criticizes the right of dissent; it is always this particular instance of it or its exercise under these particular circumstances or at this particular time that throws people into a blue funk. I am reminded of Samuel Butler's observation that "People in general are equally horrified at hearing the Christian religion doubted, and at seeing it practiced."*

Intolerance of dissent is a well noted feature of the American national character. Louis Hartz attributes it to the heritage of a society which was "born free," a society which is unnerved by deep dissent because it has experienced so little of it.** Alexis de Tocqueville took note of this tendency

* *Further Extracts from the Notebooks of Samuel Butler,* ed. A. T. Bartholomew (London: Jonathan Cape Press, 1934), p. 120.
** Louis Hartz, *The Liberal Tradition in America* (New York: Harcourt, Brace & World, 1955).

over a hundred years ago. "I know of no country," he wrote, "in which there is so little independence of mind and real freedom of discussion as in America. Profound changes have occurred since democracy in America first appeared and yet it may be asked whether recognition of the right of dissent has gained substantially in practice as well as in theory." The malady in Tocqueville's view was one of democracy itself: " . . . The smallest reproach irritates its sensibility and the slightest joke that has any foundation in truth renders it indignant; from the forms of its language up to the solid virtues of its character, everything must be made the subject of encomium. No writer, whatever be his eminence, can escape paying this tribute of adulation to his fellow citizens."*

In fact the protesters against the Vietnamese war are in good historical company. On January 12, 1848, Abraham Lincoln rose in the United States House of Representatives and made a speech about the Mexican War worthy of Senator [Wayne] Morse. Lincoln's speech was an explanation of a vote he had recently cast in support of a resolution declaring that the war had been unnecessarily and unconstitutionally begun by President Polk. "I admit," he said, "that such a vote should not be given, in mere party wantonness, and that the one given, is justly censurable, if it have no other, or better foundation. I am one of those who joined in that vote; and I did so under my best impression of the *truth* of the case."*

That is exactly what the students and professors and politicians who oppose the Vietnamese war have been doing: they have been acting on their "best impression of the truth of the case." Some of our super-patriots assume that any war the United States fights is a just war, if not indeed a holy crusade, but history does not sustain their view. No reputable historian would deny that the United States has fought some wars which were unjust, unnecessary or both— I would suggest the War of 1812, the Civil War and the Spanish-American War as examples. In an historical frame of reference it seems to me logical and proper to question the wisdom of our present military involvement in Asia. . . .

* *Democracy in America* (New York: Alfred A. Knopf, 1945), I, p. 265.
** *The Collected Works of Abraham Lincoln, 1824–1848* (New Brunswick: Rutgers University Press, 1953), I, 431.

From "The Arrogance of Power"

We are now engaged in a war to "defend freedom" in
South Vietnam. Unlike the Republic of Korea, South Vietnam has an army which is without notable success and a
weak, dictatorial government which does not command the
loyalty of the South Vietnamese people. The official war aims
of the United States Government, as I understand them, are
to defeat what is regarded as North Vietnamese aggression,
to demonstrate the futility of what the communists call
"wars of national liberation," and to create conditions under
which the South Vietnamese people will be able freely to
determine their own future. I have not the slightest doubt
of the sincerity of the President and the Vice President and
the Secretaries of State and Defense in propounding these
aims. What I do doubt—and doubt very much—is the ability of the United States to achieve these aims by the means
being used. I do not question the power of our weapons and
the efficiency of our logistics; I cannot say these things delight me as they seem to delight some of our officials, but
they are certainly impressive. What I do question is the ability of the United States, or France, or any other Western
nation, to go into a small, alien, undeveloped Asian nation
and create stability where there is chaos, the will to fight
where there is defeatism, democracy where there is no tradition of it and honest government where corruption is almost
a way of life. Our handicap is well expressed in the pungent
Chinese proverb: "In shallow waters dragons become the
sport of shrimps." . . .
The idea of being responsible for the whole world seems
to be flattering to Americans and I am afraid it is turning
our heads, just as the sense of global responsibility turned
the heads of ancient Romans and nineteenth century British. A prominent American is credited with having said recently that the United States was the "engine of mankind"
and the rest of the world was "the train."*
What romantic nonsense this is. And what dangerous nonsense in this age of nuclear weapons. The idea of an

* McGeorge Bundy is said to have said that in an interview with
Henry F. Graff, Professor of History at Columbia University, who
reported it in "How Johnson Makes Foreign Policy," *The New
York Times Magazine,* July 4, 1965, p. 17.

"American empire" might be dismissed as the arrant imagining of a British Gunga Din except for the fact that it surely strikes a responsive chord in at least a corner of the usually sensible and humane American mind. It calls to mind the slogans of the past about the shot fired at Concord being heard round the world, about "manifest destiny" and "making the world safe for democracy" and the demand for "unconditional surrender" in World War II. It calls to mind President McKinley taking counsel with the Supreme Being about his duty to the benighted Filipinos.

The "Blessings-of-Civilization Trust," as Mark Twain called it, may have been a "Daisy" in its day, uplifting for the soul and good for business besides, but its day is past. It is past because the great majority of the human race are demanding dignity and independence not the honor of a supine role in an American empire. It is past because whatever claim America may make for the universal domain of its ideas and values is countered by the communist counterclaim, armed like our own with nuclear weapons. And, most of all, it is past because it never should have begun, because we are not the "engine of mankind" but only one of its more successful and fortunate branches, endowed by our Creator with about the same capacity for good and evil, no more or less, than the rest of humanity. . . .

If America has a service to perform in the world—and I believe it has—it is in large part the service of its own example. In our excessive involvement in the affairs of other countries, we are not only living off our assets and denying our own people the proper enjoyment of their resources; we are also denying the world the example of a free society enjoying its freedom to the fullest. This is regrettable indeed for a nation that aspires to teach democracy to other nations, because, as Burke said, "Example is the school of mankind, and they will learn at no other."*

Another striking psychological phenomenon is the tendency of antagonists to dehumanize each other. . . .

Obviously, this dehumanizing tendency helps to explain the savagery of war. Man's capacity for decent behavior seems to vary directly with his perception of others as individual humans with human motives and feelings, whereas his capacity for barbarous behavior seems to increase

* Edmund Burke, "On a Regicide Peace" (1796).

with his perception of an adversary in abstract terms. This is the only explanation I can think of for the fact that the very same good and decent citizens who would never fail to feed a hungry child or comfort a sick friend or drop a coin in the church collection basket celebrate the number of Viet Cong killed in a particular week of battle and can now contemplate with equanimity, or indeed even advocate, the use of nuclear weapons against the "hordes of Chinese coolies." I feel sure that this apparent insensitivity to the incineration of thousands of millions of our fellow human beings is not the result of feelings of savage inhumanity toward foreigners; it is the result of not thinking of them as humans at all but rather as the embodiment of doctrines that we consider evil. . . .

The obvious value of liberating the imagination is that it might enable us to acquire some understanding of the view of the world held by people whose past experience and present situations are radically different from our own. It might enable us to understand, for example, what it feels like to be hungry, not hungry in the way that a middle-class American feels after a golf game or a fast tennis match, but hungry as an Asian might be hungry, with a hunger that has never been satisfied, with one's children having stunted limbs and swollen bellies, with a desire to change things that has little regard for due process of the law because the desire for change has an urgency and desperation about it that few Americans have ever experienced. Could we but liberate our imagination in this way, we might be able to see why so many people in the world are making revolutions; we might even be able to see why some of them are communists.

There are many respects in which America, if it can bring itself to act with the magnanimity and the empathy appropriate to its size and power, can be an intelligent example to the world. We have the opportunity to set an example of generous understanding in our relations with China, of practical cooperation for peace in our relations with Russia, of reliable and respectful partnership in our relations with Western Europe, of material helpfulness without moral presumption in our relations with the developing nations, of abstention from the temptations of hegemony in our relations with Latin America, and of the all-around advantages of minding one's own business in our relations with everybody. Most of all, we have the opportunity to serve as an example of democracy to the world by the way in which we run our own society; America, in the words of John Quincy Adams, should be "the well-wisher to the freedom and independence of all" but "the champion and vindicator only of her own."*

If we can bring ourselves so to act, we will have overcome the dangers of the arrogance of power. It will involve, no doubt, the loss of certain glories, but that seems a price worth paying for the probable rewards, which are the happiness of America and the peace of the world.

* July 4, 1821, Washington, D.C. Reported in *National Intelligencer,* July 11, 1821.

54. Martin Luther King, Jr., "Declaration of Independence from the War in Vietnam," 1967.*

In 1955–1956, the Rev. Martin Luther King, Jr., led Negroes in a boycott of segregated buses in Montgomery, Alabama. The boycott forced desegregation of the buses and brought King national prominence. More important, the boycott demonstrated to Negroes and to the country at large the effectiveness of passive resistance. Dr. King is President of the Southern Christian Leadership Conference. In 1964, he was awarded the Nobel Prize for Peace.

On April 4, 1967, at the Riverside Church in New York City, Martin Luther King spoke out in conscientious protest against American participation in the Vietnam war. He encouraged young men—Negro as well as white—to register as conscientious objectors. The address was an eloquent appeal, but it lost King the support of many of his own followers and threw him into company with militant civil rights leaders whose philosophies and tactics are at odds with his own. Whether the civil rights movement can pursue its own goals and also dedicate itself to bringing about an end to the war in Vietnam will be for time to answer. The Riverside address is reprinted in full below.

Over the past two years, as I have moved to break the betrayal of my own silences and to speak from the burnings of my own heart, as I have called for radical departures from the destruction of Vietnam, many persons have questioned me about the wisdom of my path. At the heart of their concerns this query has often loomed large and loud: Why are *you* speaking about the war, Dr. King? Why are *you* joining the voices of dissent? Peace and civil rights don't mix, they say. Aren't you hurting the cause of your people, they ask. And when I hear them, though I often understand

* Dr. King's address was sponsored by Clergy and Laymen Concerned about Vietnam. It was printed in a condensed form in *Ramparts,* V (May, 1967), 33–37, and is reprinted here with the permission of the author.

the source of their concern, I am nevertheless greatly saddened, for such questions mean that the inquirers have not really known me, my commitment or my calling. Indeed, their questions suggest that they do not know the world in which they live.

In the light of such tragic misunderstanding, I deem it of signal importance to try to state clearly why I believe that the path from Dexter Avenue Baptist Church—the church in Montgomery, Alabama, where I began my pastorage—leads clearly to this sanctuary tonight.

I come to this platform to make a passionate plea to my beloved nation. This speech is not addressed to Hanoi or to the National Liberation Front. It is not addressed to China or to Russia.

Nor is it an attempt to overlook the ambiguity of the total situation and the need for a collective solution to the tragedy of Vietnam. Neither is it an attempt to make North Vietnam or the National Liberation Front paragons of virtue, nor to overlook the role they can play in a successful resolution of the problem. While they both may have justifiable reasons to be suspicious of the good faith of the United States, life and history give eloquent testimony to the fact that conflicts are never resolved without trustful give and take on both sides.

Tonight, however, I wish not to speak with Hanoi and the NLF, but rather to my fellow Americans who, with me, bear the greatest responsibility in ending a conflict that has exacted a heavy price on both continents.

Since I am a preacher by trade, I suppose it is not surprising that I have seven major reasons for bringing Vietnam into the field of my moral vision. There is at the outset a very obvious and almost facile connection between the war in Vietnam and the struggle I, and others, have been waging in America. A few years ago there was a shining moment in that struggle. It seemed as if there was a real promise of hope for the poor—both black and white—through the Poverty Program. Then came the build-up in Vietnam, and I watched the program broken and eviscerated as if it were some idle political plaything of a society gone mad on war, and I knew that America would never invest the necessary funds or energies in rehabilitation of its poor so long as Vietnam continued to draw men and skills and money like some demonic, destructive suction tube. So I was increasingly compelled to see the war as an enemy of the poor and to attack it as such.

Perhaps the more tragic recognition of reality took place when it became clear to me that the war was doing far more than devastating the hopes of the poor at home. It was sending their sons and their brothers and their husbands to fight and to die in extraordinarily high proportions relative to the rest of the population. We were taking the young black men who had been crippled by our society and sending them 8000 miles away to guarantee liberties in Southeast Asia which they had not found in Southwest Georgia and East Harlem. So we have been repeatedly faced with the cruel irony of watching Negro and white boys on TV screens as they kill and die together for a nation that has been unable to seat them together in the same schools. So we watch them in brutal solidarity burning the huts of a poor village, but we realize that they would never live on the same block in Detroit. I could not be silent in the face of such cruel manipulation of the poor.

My third reason grows out of my experience in the ghettos of the North over the last three years—especially the last three summers. As I have walked among the desperate, rejected and angry young men, I have told them that Molotov cocktails and rifles would not solve their problems. I have tried to offer them my deepest compassion while maintaining my conviction that social change comes most meaningfully through non-violent action. But, they asked, what about Vietnam? They asked if our own nation wasn't using massive doses of violence to solve its problems, to bring about the changes it wanted. Their questions hit home, and I knew that I could never again raise my voice against the violence of the oppressed in the ghettos without having first spoken clearly to the greatest purveyor of violence in the world today —my own government.

For those who ask the question, "Aren't you a Civil Rights leader?" and thereby mean to exclude me from the movement for peace, I have this further answer. In 1957 when a group of us formed the Southern Christian Leadership Conference, we chose as our motto: "To save the soul of America." We were convinced that we could not limit our vision to certain rights for black people, but instead affirmed the conviction that America would never be free or saved from itself unless the descendants of its slaves were loosed from the shackles they still wear.

Now, it should be incandescently clear that no one who has any concern for the integrity and life of America today can ignore the present war. If America's soul becomes totally poisoned, part of the autopsy must read "Vietnam." It can never be saved so long as it destroys the deepest hopes of men the world over.

As if the weight of such a commitment to the life and health of America were not enough, another burden of responsibility was placed upon me in 1964; and I cannot forget that the Nobel Prize for Peace was also a commission—a commission to work harder than I had ever worked before for the "brotherhood of man." This is a calling that takes me beyond national allegiances, but even if it were not present I would yet have to live with the meaning of my commitment to the ministry of Jesus Christ. To me the relationship of this ministry to the making of peace is so obvious that I sometimes marvel at those who ask me why I am speaking against the war. Could it be that they do not know that the good news was meant for all men—for communist and capitalist, for their children and ours, for black and white, for revolutionary and conservative? Have they forgotten that my ministry is in obedience to the One who loved His enemies so fully that He died for them? What then can I say to the Viet Cong or to Castro or to Mao as a faithful minister of this One? Can I threaten them with death, or must I not share with them my life?

And as I ponder the madness of Vietnam, my mind goes constantly to the people of that peninsula. I speak now not of the soldiers of each side, not of the junta in Saigon, but simply of the people who have been living under the curse of war for almost three continuous decades. I think of them, too, because it is clear to me that there will be no meaningful solution there until some attempt is made to know them and their broken cries.

They must see Americans as strange liberators. The Vietnamese proclaimed their own independence in 1945 after a combined French and Japanese occupation and before the communist revolution in China. Even though they quoted the American Declaration of Independence in their own document of freedom, we refused to recognize them. Instead, we decided to support France in its re-conquest of her former colony.

Our government felt then that the Vietnamese people

were not "ready" for independence, and we again fell victim to the deadly Western arrogance that has poisoned the international atmosphere for so long. With that tragic decision, we rejected a revolutionary government seeking self-determination, and a government that had been established not by China (for whom the Vietnamese have no great love) but by clearly indigenous forces that included some communists. For the peasants, this new government meant real land reform, one of the most important needs in their lives.

For nine years following 1945 we denied the people of Vietnam the right of independence. For nine years we vigorously supported the French in their abortive effort to recolonize Vietnam.

Before the end of the war we were meeting 80 per cent of the French war costs. Even before the French were defeated at Dien Bien Phu, they began to despair of their reckless action, but we did not. We encouraged them with our huge financial and military supplies to continue the war even after they had lost the will to do so.

After the French were defeated it looked as if independence and land reform would come again through the Geneva agreements. But instead there came the United States, determined that Ho should not unify the temporarily divided nation, and the peasants watched again as we supported one of the most vicious modern dictators—our chosen man, Premier Diem. The peasants watched and cringed as Diem ruthlessly routed out all opposition, supported their extortionist landlords and refused even to discuss reunification with the North. The peasants watched as all this was presided over by U.S. influence and then by increasing numbers of U.S. troops who came to help quell the insurgency that Diem's methods had aroused. When Diem was overthrown they may have been happy, but the long line of military dictatorships seemed to offer no real change—especially in terms of their need for land and peace.

The only change came from America as we increased our troop commitments in support of governments which were singularly corrupt, inept and without popular support. All the while, the people read our leaflets and received regular promises of peace and democracy—and land reform. Now they languish under our bombs and consider us—not their fellow Vietnamese—the real enemy. They move sadly and apathetically as we herd them off the land of their fathers into concentration camps where minimal social needs are rarely met. They know they must move or be destroyed by our bombs. So they go.

They watch as we poison their water, as we kill a million acres of their crops. They must weep as the bulldozers destroy their precious trees. They wander into the hospitals, with at least 20 casualties from American firepower for each Viet Cong-inflicted injury. So far we may have killed a million of them—mostly children.

What do the peasants think as we ally ourselves with the landlords and as we refuse to put any action into our many words concerning land reform? What do they think as we test our latest weapons on them, just as the Germans tested out new medicine and new tortures in the concentration camps of Europe?* Where are the roots of the independent Vietnam we claim to be building?

Now there is little left to build on—save bitterness. Soon the only solid physical foundations remaining will be found at our military bases and in the concrete of the concentration camps we call "fortified hamlets." The peasants may well wonder if we plan to build our new Vietnam on such grounds as these. Could we blame them for such thoughts? We must speak for them and raise the questions they cannot raise. These too are our brothers.

Perhaps the more difficult but no less necessary task is to speak for those who have been designated as our enemies. What of the NLF—that strangely anonymous group we call VC or communists? What must they think of us in America when they realize that we permitted the repression and cruelty of Diem which helped to bring them into being as a resistance group in the South? How can they believe in our integrity when now we speak of "aggression from the North" as if there were nothing more essential to the war? How can they trust us when now we charge *them* with violence after the murderous reign of Diem, and charge *them* with violence while we pour new weapons of death into their land?

How do they judge us when our officials know that their membership is less than 25 per cent communist and yet in-

* The press and some critics have quoted this sentence out of context. I had no intention of equating the U.S. and Nazi Germany. Indeed, recognition of American democratic traditions and the absence of them in Nazi Germany, makes it all the more disturbing if even some elements of similarity of conduct appear.

sist on giving them the blanket name? What must they be thinking when they know that we are aware of their control of major sections of Vietnam and yet we appear ready to allow national elections in which this highly organized political parallel government will have no part? They ask how we can speak of free elections when the Saigon press is censored and controlled by the military junta. And they are surely right to wonder what kind of new government we plan to help form without them—the only party in real touch with the peasants. They question our political goals and they deny the reality of a peace settlement from which they will be excluded. Their questions are frighteningly relevant.

Here is the true meaning and value of compassion and nonviolence—when it helps us to see the enemy's point of view, to hear his questions, to know his assessment of ourselves. For from his view we may indeed see the basic weaknesses of our own condition, and if we are mature, we may learn and grow and profit from the wisdom of the brothers who are called the opposition.

So, too, with Hanoi. In the North, where our bombs now pummel the land, and our mines endanger the waterways, we are met by a deep but understandable mistrust. In Hanoi are the men who led the nation to independence against the Japanese and the French, the men who sought membership in the French commonwealth and were betrayed by the weakness of Paris and the willfulness of the colonial armies. It was they who led a second struggle against French domination at tremendous costs, and then were persuaded at Geneva to give up, as a temporary measure, the land they controlled between the 13th and 17th parallels. After 1954 they watched us conspire with Diem to prevent elections which would have surely brought Ho Chi Minh to power over a united Vietnam, and they realized they had been betrayed again.

When we ask why they do not leap to negotiate, these things must be remembered. Also, it must be clear that the leaders of Hanoi considered the presence of American troops in support of the Diem regime to have been the initial military breach of the Geneva Agreements concerning foreign troops, and they remind us that they did not begin to send in any large number of supplies or men until American forces had moved into the tens of thousands.

Hanoi remembers how our leaders refused to tell us the truth about the earlier North Vietnamese overtures for peace, how the President claimed that none existed when they had clearly been made. Ho Chi Minh has watched as America has spoken of peace and built up its forces, and now he has surely heard the increasing international rumors of American plans for an invasion of the North. Perhaps only his sense of humor and irony can save him when he hears the most powerful nation of the world speaking of aggression as it drops thousands of bombs on a poor, weak nation more than 8000 miles from its shores.

At this point, I should make it clear that while I have tried here to give a voice to the voiceless of Vietnam and to understand the arguments of those who are called enemy, I am as deeply concerned about our own troops there as anything else. For it occurs to me that what we are submitting them to in Vietnam is not simply the brutalizing process that goes on in any war where armies face each other and seek to destroy. We are adding cynicism to the process of death, for our troops must know after a short period there that none of the things we claim to be fighting for are really involved. Before long they must know that their government has sent them into a struggle among Vietnamese, and the more sophisticated surely realize that we are on the side of the wealthy and the secure while we create a hell for the poor.

Somehow this madness must cease. I speak as a child of God and brother to the suffering poor of Vietnam and the poor of America who are paying the double price of smashed hopes at home and death and corruption in Vietnam. I speak as a citizen of the world, for the world as it stands aghast at the path we have taken. I speak as an American to the leaders of my own nation. The great initiative in this war is ours. The initiative to stop must be ours.

This is the message of the great Buddhist leaders of Vietnam. Recently, one of them wrote these words: "Each day the war goes on the hatred increases in the hearts of the Vietnamese and in the hearts of those of humanitarian instinct. The Americans are forcing even their friends into becoming their enemies. It is curious that the Americans, who calculate so carefully on the possibilities of military victory, do not realize that in the process they are incurring deep psychological and political defeat. The image of America will never again be the image of revolution, freedom and democracy, but the image of violence and militarism."

If we continue, there will be no doubt in my mind and in the mind of the world that we have no honorable intentions in Vietnam. It will become clear that our minimal expectation is to occupy it as an American colony, and men will not refrain from thinking that our maximum hope is to goad China into a war so that we may bomb her nuclear installations.

The world now demands a maturity of America that we may not be able to achieve. It demands that we admit that we have been wrong from the beginning of our adventure in Vietnam, that we have been detrimental to the life of her people.

In order to atone for our sins and errors in Vietnam, we should take the initiative in bringing the war to a halt. I would like to suggest five concrete things that our government should do immediately to begin the long and difficult process of extricating ourselves from this nightmare:

1. End all bombing in North and South Vietnam.

2. Declare a unilateral cease-fire in the hope that such action will create the atmosphere for negotiation.

3. Take immediate steps to prevent other battlegrounds in Southeast Asia by curtailing our military build-up in Thailand and our interference in Laos.

4. Realistically accept the fact that the National Liberation Front has substantial support in South Vietnam and must thereby play a role in any meaningful negotiations and in any future Vietnam government.

5. Set a date on which we will remove all foreign troops from Vietnam in accordance with the 1954 Geneva Agreement.

Part of our ongoing commitment might well express itself in an offer to grant asylum to any Vietnamese who fears for his life under a new regime which included the NLF. Then we must make what reparations we can for the damage we have done. We must provide the medical aid that is badly needed, in this country if necessary.

Meanwhile, we in the churches and synagogues have a continuing task while we urge our government to disengage itself from a disgraceful commitment. We must be prepared to match actions with words by seeking out every creative means of protest possible.

As we counsel young men concerning military service we must clarify for them our nation's role in Vietnam and challenge them with the alternative of conscientious objection. I am pleased to say that this is the path now being chosen by more than 70 students at my own Alma Mater, Morehouse College, and I recommend it to all who find the American course in Vietnam a dishonorable and unjust one. Moreover, I would encourage all ministers of draft age to give up their ministerial exemptions and seek status as conscientious objectors. Every man of humane convictions must decide on the protest that best suits his convictions, but we must *all* protest.

There is something seductively tempting about stopping there and sending us all off on what in some circles has become a popular crusade against the war in Vietnam. I say we must enter that struggle, but I wish to go on now to say something even more disturbing. The war in Vietnam is but a symptom of a far deeper malady within the American spirit, and if we ignore this sobering reality we will find ourselves organizing clergy-and laymen-concerned committees for the next generation. We will be marching and attending rallies without end unless there is a significant and profound change in American life and policy.

In 1957 a sensitive American official overseas said that it seemed to him that our nation was on the wrong side of a world revolution. During the past ten years we have seen emerge a pattern of suppression which now has justified the presence of U.S. military "advisors" in Venezuela. The need to maintain social stability for our investments accounts for the counterrevolutionary action of American forces in Guatemala. It tells why American helicopters are being used against guerrillas in Colombia and why American napalm and green beret forces have already been active against rebels in Peru. With such activity in mind, the words of John F. Kennedy come back to haunt us. Five years ago he said, "Those who make peaceful revolution impossible will make violent revolution inevitable."

Increasingly, by choice or by accident, this is the role our nation has taken—by refusing to give up the privileges and the pleasures that come from the immense profits of overseas investment.

I am convinced that if we are to get on the right side of the world revolution, we as a nation must undergo a radical revolution of values. When machines and computers, profit and property rights are considered more important than people, the giant triplets of racism, materialism, and militarism are incapable of being conquered.

A true revolution of values will soon cause us to question the fairness and justice of many of our past and present policies. True compassion is more than flinging a coin to a beggar; it is not haphazard and superficial. It comes to see that an edifice which produces beggars needs restructuring. A true revolution of values will soon look easily on the glaring contrast of poverty and wealth. With righteous indignation, it will look across the seas and see individual capitalists of the West investing huge sums of money in Asia, Africa, and South America, only to take the profits out with no concern for the social betterment of the countries, and say: "This is not just." It will look at our alliance with the landed gentry of Latin America and say: "This is not just." The Western arrogance of feeling that it has everything to teach others and nothing to learn from them is not just. A true revolution of values will lay hands on the world order and say of war: "This way of settling differences is not just." This business of burning human beings with napalm, of filling our nation's homes with orphans and widows, of injecting poisonous drugs of hate into the veins of peoples normally humane, of sending men home from dark and bloody battlefields physically handicapped and psychologically deranged, cannot be reconciled with wisdom, justice, and love. A nation that continues year after year to spend more money on military defense than on programs of social uplift is approaching spiritual death.

America, the richest and most powerful nation in the world, can well lead the way in this revolution of values. There is nothing, except a tragic death wish, to prevent us from re-ordering our priorities, so that the pursuit of peace will take precedence over the pursuit of war. There is nothing to keep us from molding a recalcitrant status quo until we have fashioned it into a brotherhood.

This kind of positive revolution of values is our best defense against communism. War is not the answer. Communism will never be defeated by the use of atomic bombs or nuclear weapons. Let us not join those who shout war and through their misguided passions urge the United States to relinquish its participation in the United Nations. These are days which demand wise restraint and calm reasonableness. We must not call everyone a communist or an appeaser who advocates the seating of Red China in the United Nations and who recognizes that hate and hysteria are not the final answers to the problem of these turbulent days. We must not engage in a negative anti-communism, but rather in a positive thrust for democracy, realizing that our greatest defense against communism is to take offensive action in behalf of justice. We must with positive action seek to remove those conditions of poverty, insecurity and injustice which are the fertile soil in which the seed of communism grows and develops.

These are revolutionary times. All over the globe men are revolting against old systems of exploitation and oppression, and out of the wombs of a frail world, new systems of justice and equality are being born. The shirtless and barefoot people of the land are rising up as never before. "The people who sat in darkness have seen a great light." We in the West must support these revolutions. It is a sad fact that, because of comfort, complacency, a morbid fear of communism, and our proneness to adjust to injustice, the Western nations that initiated so much of the revolutionary spirit of the modern world have now become the arch anti-revolutionaries. This has driven many to feel that only Marxism has the revolutionary spirit. Therefore, communism is a judgment against our failure to make democracy real and follow through on the revolutions that we initiated. Our only hope today lies in our ability to recapture the revolutionary spirit and go out into a sometimes hostile world declaring eternal hostility to poverty, racism, and militarism.

We must move past indecision to action. We must find new ways to speak for peace in Vietnam and justice throughout the developing world—a world that borders on our doors. If we do not act we shall surely be dragged down the long, dark, and shameful corridors of time reserved for those who possess power without compassion, might without morality, and strength without sight.

Now let us begin. Now let us re-dedicate ourselves to the long and bitter—but beautiful—struggle for a new world. This is the calling of the sons of God, and our brothers wait eagerly for our response. Shall we say the odds are too great? Shall we tell them the struggle is too hard? Will our message be that the forces of American life militate against their arrival as full men, and we send our deepest regrets? Or will there be another message, of longing, of hope, of solidarity with their yearnings, of commitment to their cause, whatever the cost? The choice is ours, and though we might prefer it otherwise we *must* choose in this crucial moment of human history.

55. Benjamin Sherman, Statement of Conscientious Objection, 1966.*

The last document in this book is, fittingly, the statement of a conscientious objector, Benjamin Sherman. He is currently classified 1-A by his local draft board. He has appealed his classification and the Federal Bureau of Investigation is investigating his claim. The American Civil Liberties Union has agreed to defend him when his case comes, in time, before the courts.

Benjamin Sherman does not claim to be a pacifist nor is his conscientious objection based upon formal religious doctrine. He makes no flamboyant accusations of American war crimes; he has not burned his draft card. But Sherman is opposed to the Vietnam war, and although his statement is phrased in subdued and careful language, Sherman and other young men like him are pressing the country at large to consider a new and radical form of conscientious objection—selective objection, the conscientious objection to a particular war. They are claiming the right, as citizens and as men, to make moral distinctions between the justness of one war and another.

Basically, the reason I am claiming conscientious objector status to the war in Vietnam is that the incongruity of my actions as a civilian were in a sense worse than that of the military in Vietnam. For I was fighting the war from "a desk," afforded the safety and freedom of the United States, and not overtly subject to the constant sight of cruelty and death that an armed forces sponsored visit to Vietnam might have done. I was employed as a part-time design draftsman, involved in the design and manufacture of instruments eventually going on ordnance equipment involved in the killing in Vietnam. This employment, by the nature of my involvement in it, had made it possible for me to receive occupational deferments (2-A classification) from service in the

---

* Benjamin Sherman's Statement was obtained from the New York Civil Liberties Union.

armed forces for the approximately four years I was work-ing there. My continued employment at this company, to my knowledge, would have made additional deferments pos-sible. I left this employment because I could no longer ra-tionalize my work there with my growing disgust and anger at our government's actions in Vietnam and my own shame to be involved in helping this government in this course of action.

My period of employment at this company made it pos-sible for me to attend art school and work as a sculptor without financial burden. I was, in effect, killing in the morn-ing and seeking to create in the afternoon. The incongruity of these two acts unfortunately took too long a time to stab into the depths of my conscience. I was not endangering my life; perhaps this is what made the burial of conscience pos-sible for those years. One often builds a "shell" around the conscience to avoid the fact that man is horribly cruel to his fellow men. But I believe all but the most hardened of individuals has some cracks in this "shell." It is frightening to me, and often disheartening to see groups and govern-ments trying to stuff untruths and inhuman chauvinistic catch phrases into these hopeful cracks in an effort to com-pletely prevent any compassion for our fellow human be-ings to flow from us.

In the final analysis I could no longer avoid being affected by the news stories and discussions on Vietnam that I heard and read. I could not hide the fact from myself, that I was taking a cowardly position by accepting the protection of this occupational deferment, when I believed the war unjustifi-able, inhuman, and opposite to every ideal I wished to live for.

I am not a political sophisticate; maybe I am naive; my knowledge of the intricacy and intrigues surrounding the whole Vietnam situation is very limited indeed. But instinc-tively I cannot and will not fight against a people who, from all the information I have been able to glean, are being horribly and unjustifiably maimed and killed.

I am not a pacifist; I wish I was. I am the product of a society not geared to this type of thinking. I am not excep-tional in this case. I would like to think that it is easier and not particularly courageous to do the right thing. Our society covertly teaches us differently. Intimidation and dis-trust, whether I like it or not, have colored my reactions to situations. The pacifists, I believe, through their achievement of casting off our society's conditionings, are the hope of ever achieving some sort of peace and love between men.

I am trying to be human. My strength is not, as such, to be completely and lovingly non-violent. But I am trying to fight an unfortunate human trait of character which I know is wrong. Violence and killing, for any reason, cannot be right. I am trying to clean myself bit by bit.

I am seeking this status of conscientious objection to the war in Vietnam although I know objection to a particular war is not permitted in the C.O. statutes, because I believe our conscience is often the truest guide in achieving some sort of understanding, love, and compassion for our fellow human beings. And our conscience *must*, not the written statutes, be our guide if we are ever to achieve world peace, and, in a narrower sense, peace of mind.

The anticipation of receiving a prison sentence is very real to me. A jail sentence will prevent me from continuing to work as a sculptor; this, in essence, is like cutting out my tongue, for I believe I can speak best through my work. Every day of work is now precious to me. My wife and I both feel this way; we will not compromise our ethical and moral principles, and we both agree this is more important than the statutory consequences of these beliefs and feelings.

EPILOGUE

The documents come to an end, but there is no real conclusion to this book. Newer aspects and problems of conscientious objection are emerging. In Denver, Colorado, in April, 1967, an Air Force Captain, Dale E. Noyd, an eleven-year career officer, filed suit for classification as a conscientious objector to a particular war. He requested in his suit that he be reassigned from Vietnam duty or be permitted to resign. In Fort Jackson, South Carolina, in May, Captain Howard Brett Levy was court-martialed for refusal to teach medicine to Green Beret aidmen destined to fight in Vietnam. The court-martial heard another doctor, Captain Ivan Mauer, say that he too would refuse to give such instruction. Captain Levy's lawyer, Charles Morgan, Jr., of the American Civil Liberties Union, argued that if medical aidmen can be ordered to kill, the doctors who are instructors of such aidmen may refuse to give them instruction. The government in this case contended that no military man "may arrogate to himself the privilege of passing on the wisdom and propriety of his commanding officer." In other instances, courts-martial have been instituted against soldiers who participated in anti-Vietnam demonstrations or spoke out against the war, raising the question of whether free speech is subject to restraints upon a man's induction. We seem to be witnessing a new and unique stage in the history of conscientious objection, where objectors, for the first time, are men already in the Armed Forces of the United States.

As conscientious protests quickened, reaction also stirred. Representative Seymour Halpern, Republican of Queens, New York, urged his fellow congressmen to enact a law making the burning of the United States flag in protest demonstrations a federal offense. Representative F. Edward Hebert, Democrat of Louisiana, told the Assistant Attorney General to "forget the First Amendment" and to prosecute the militant civil rights leader Stokeley Carmichael, former president of the Student Nonviolent Coordinating Committee (SNCC), for urging Negroes to defy the draft.

As this book goes to press, the government has brought an indictment in Boston against Dr. Benjamin Spock, author and pediatrician; the Rev. William Sloane Coffin, Jr., chaplain of Yale University; and three others for conspiring to counsel, aid, and abet young men to refuse to serve in the armed forces and to violate other requirements of the Selective Service law. The indictment cites four of the five defendants as participants in a nationwide draft-resistance program that called for the disruption of the induction processes and for men of draft age to turn in their draft cards. Dr. Spock and Mr. Coffin allegedly distributed a statement carrying 2,000 signatures and entitled "A Call to Resist Illegitimate Authority," and a speech entitled "A Time to Say No."

The defendants do not deny their actions. Quite the contrary. They affirm the financial support and moral encouragement they gave to young men who wished to avoid the draft. Yet, they are not pacifists. Dr. Spock, for one, supported the United States's participation in World War II and its intervention in Korea. The defendants in the case of *The United States of America* v. *Coffin, Ferber, Goodman, Raskin, and Spock* are challenging the legality and *morality* of the current United States involvement in Vietnam. They take the age-old position that, even if the draft laws should be constitutional, and even if the nation is constitutionally correct in its Vietnam policy, there exists a higher moral law that a man may choose to follow regardless of the consequences.

The legalities of the issue are plainly with the government. Laws were deliberately broken. The moralities, however, will be debated for a long time to come. It is meaningful, too, that the two best-known defendants in this case are a pediatrician and a college chaplain, men who are particularly sensitive to the moral dilemmas of American youth.

Action and reaction—the dynamics of the democratic process go on. If any final word is to be said it must be that where dissent can flourish, where dissenting arguments are heard in open courts, where controversial laws are publicly debated, and sometimes broken, there is much to be proud of. In this New World, in a new age, conscience may yet make heroes of us all.